G000113783

Open learning
in the
mainstream

edited by
Mary Thorpe and David Grugeon

Published by Longman Information and Reference,
Longman Group Limited, 6th Floor, Westgate House, The High,
Harlow, Essex CM20 1YR, England and Associated Companies
throughout the world.

© Longman Group Limited 1994

All rights reserved. No part of this publication may be reproduced, stored in a retrieval
system, or transmitted in any form or by any means, electronic, mechanical,
photocopying, recording or otherwise, without the prior permission of the Copyright
owner or a licence permitting restricted copying issued by the Copyright Licensing
Agency Ltd., 90 Tottenham Court Road, London W1P 9HE.

A catalogue record for this book is available from The British Library

ISBN 0-582-23897-8

Typeset by The Midlands Book Typesetting Company
Printed in Great Britain by BPC Wheatons Ltd, Exeter

Contents

Contributors

John Allred chairs the Library Association's sub-committee on Adult Learning and Libraries. He has researched extensively on the role of Libraries in Open Learning and has been involved as a consultant with the development and evaluation of information and library support systems for adult learners.

Sue Bergin is a lecturer in Basic/Core Skills at West Nottinghamshire College, Mansfield, England. She has taught in adult basic education (ABE) in a variety of settings including community centres, a women's refuge, adult education centres and colleges of further education. She was Research Worker for the North West of England on the 'Open Learning in ABE' research project.

Christine Butterworth works in teacher training and professional development in the field of further and adult education, and training. She has been involved in developing systems for the accreditation of prior learning in the Open University's Centre for Youth and Adult Studies and in the School of Post Compulsory Education and Training at the University of Greenwich.

Tony Dodds has spent most of the last thirty years working to promote the role of distance education in Africa. He is Executive Director of the International Extension College at Cambridge, and has worked with generations of professionals across the developing world on joint IEC, London University Institute of Education courses.

Richard Edwards is Lecturer in Post-compulsory education in the School of Education at the Open University, UK. He previously worked in the field of educational guidance and writes on many aspects of the provision of education and training for adults. He is co-author with Robin Usher of *Postmodernism and Education*, Routledge 1995.

Matthew Godsell, a Nurse Teacher at Avon and Gloucestershire College of Health, co-ordinates the learning disabilities input into the Common Foundation Programme.

David Grugeon has been engaged in open learning for over thirty years, since he was the first fulltime officer of the National Extension College. A former Regional Director and Pro Vice Chancellor of the Open University, he was founder editor of the pedagogical journals *Teaching at a Distance* and *Open Learning*. His current commitment involves collaborative networks with further and adult education.

Andrew Haldane is Director of Staffordshire Open Learning and Chair of the British Association for Open Learning. He has had management experience in industry and has taught management subjects in Higher Education. Recently he has worked on a number of projects related to flexible provision of Further Education under the auspices of the Employment Department's Work Related FE Development Fund.

Maureen Haldane is a Senior Lecturer in Education at Manchester Metropolitan University. She has many years teaching experience in secondary schools and spent three years as an Advisory Teacher for Flexible Learning in TVEI.

Mary Hamilton is Senior Research Fellow in the Centre for the Study of Education and Training, Lancaster University. She has carried out a number of projects in the areas of Adult Basic Education, both literacy and numeracy. She is a founder member of the national network, *Research and Practice in Adult Literacy* (RaPAL) and a core member of the Lancaster Literacy Research Group.

Maureen Hanley is currently Head of Research and Development at Wirral Metropolitan College. Her main areas of interest include curriculum development and management; achievement-based resourcing; personal development; different approaches to learning.

Rosemary Hawksley is Head of External Services at Stockport College. She carried out the initial feasibility study for the College Flexible Learning development, managed the Centre from 1987–90 and now has senior management responsibility for it, along with College marketing, Business Development Services, and European Developments.

Dr Denise Hevey is the Director of the Open University's Vocational Qualifications Centre. In 1989 she was seconded to the Local Government Management Board to manage the Under-Sevens project which developed national occupational standards as the basis for NVQs in Child Care and Education. She now heads a small team with responsibility for supporting NVQs and related issues throughout the Open University.

Gill Kirkup is a Senior Lecturer in Educational Technology in the Institute of Educational Technology at the Open University UK. She has particular interests in women studying by distance education and women studying in traditionally masculine subject areas, and has published widely in these areas. She also teaches Women's Studies.

Dr Diana Laurillard is Head of the programme on Learner Use of Media, part of the Institute of Educational Technology at the Open University. She has spent twenty years in research, development and evaluation of audio-visual and computer-based materials in education and training, covering a wide range of subject areas. She has published *Rethinking University Teaching: A Framework for the Effective Use of Educational Technology* (Routledge 1993), and an edited book *Interactive Media: Working Methods and Practical Applications* (Ellis Horwood, 1987).

Roger Lewis has worked for leading UK open learning organisations, including the Open University, in a number of capacities including materials production, tutor support and management. Through the National Extension College and Open College, he has also acted as a consultant to public and private sector organisations wishing to introduce new methods of learning. In his current role Roger is responsible for stimulating the introduction and maintenance of new methods of learning within a new university. In doing this he emphasises the importance of a clearly articulated university strategy, fully consulting all those affected.

Robin Mason is Head of the Centre for Information Technology in Education at the Open University, UK. Her research involves the use of telecommunications in distance education, and these are increasingly applied in trans-national contexts. She has written extensively on the educational applications of teleconferencing: computer conferencing and multi-media conferencing.

Margaret Miers, who has long experience of working with the Open University, is a Senior Lecturer at the University of the West of England. She co-ordinates the Sociology Theme Team, Avon and Gloucestershire College of Health.

Professor Ian McNay heads a research and development centre on higher education management at Anglia Polytechnic University. His commitment to open management and open learning has been demonstrated for groups from 16–90+ in academic and administrative posts in four countries in Europe, including eleven years in the British Open University, and staff and institutional development work with participants from over thirty five countries round the world.

Ron Munroe was Vice Principal of Stockport College at the time that flexible learning was being developed and implemented and gave it senior management support throughout this time. He is now Principal of West Cheshire College.

Andy Northedge has been with the OU for many years; as a researcher in tuition and counselling, as an educational adviser to course teams, and as a course author. In recent years he has set up the OU Access Unit and developed the first OU modular Access course, *Living in a Changing Society*. He is author of the widely used text *The Good Study Guide*.

Barrie Oxtoby has had a full career in manufacturing industry, embracing shipbuilding/marine engineering, machine tools, power generation and automotive engineering. He joined what was British Leyland in 1977 and is Rover today. He specialises in the design and application of learning processes to bring about change in the business, through people. He was a member of the concept, launch and operation teams of the Rover Learning Business in 1990.

Nigel Paine is Chief Executive of the Scottish Council of Educational Technology (SCET). He is a member of the Training and Development Lead Body and a member of the Teaching and Learning Advisory Group of the Scottish Higher Education Funding Council. He has written widely on Open and Flexible Learning and edited the National Extension College's 25th Anniversary book *Open Learning in Transition*, 1988.

Vivienne Rivis was formerly head of the National Educational Guidance Initiative (1988–1993). From 1982–1988 she was Co-ordinator of the Bradford Education Advice Service for Adults. She is now Assistant Director, The Higher Educational Quality Council, with responsibility for the quality enhancement of guidance and learner support and co-ordination of quality audits in UK Higher Education institutions.

Greville Rumble is Director, South East Region at the Open University UK. His prime interests are in the management, planning, costing and economics of distance education. He has consulted and published widely in these areas.

Steve Ryan is currently Head of the Centre for Educational Technology and Development, at De Montfort University, Leicester. He has been involved in a number of collaborative open and distance learning projects both in the UK and Europe. He is particularly interested in the application of the new technology to open and distance learning.

Lee Taylor is former Director, Equal Opportunities at the Open University, and now Project Officer for Investors in People at the OU. She was founding chair of the UK Equal Opportunities Higher Education Network, and is involved in national policy development in this area. She is particularly interested in EO as a strategic change issue, and in international comparative work in this area. She has written and lectured widely in the field of EO.

Mary Thorpe is Director of the Institute of Educational Technology at the Open University. She has been engaged in teaching research and development at the Open University for twenty years. Her publications include *Evaluating Open and Distance Learning* (Longman, 1993) and the edited reader *Culture and Processes of Adult Learning* (Routledge, 1993).

Kevin Wilson has worked for the UK Open University since 1971 and is currently Staff Tutor in the Arts Faculty based in the East Midlands Region. He has contributed widely to courses on both British and European history and culture and is presently Chair of the Open University's *What is Europe?* course team. He has chaired the EADTU Humanities Programme Committee from its inception and in this capacity has written various papers on course collaboration and joint course activity.

Peter Wilson is the Co-ordinator of the Leicestershire Open College Network and is currently Chair of the National Open College Network. He was previously involved in setting up the South Yorkshire Open College Federation, and has been closely involved in developing the technical specification of the FEU's National Credit Framework.

Alan Woodley is a Senior Research Fellow in the Open University's Institute of Educational Technology. He has had over twenty years' experience carrying out research into the characteristics of OU students, their progress and subsequent outcomes. He is particularly interested in issues of access and equal opportunities and is currently working on the evaluation of the OU's 'Living in a Changing Society' access modules.

Lord Young of Dartington is world famous as a man of ideas who gets people to adopt and implement those ideas. Having drafted the Labour Party Manifesto for the great reforming Labour Government in 1945, he retrained as a sociologist, founding the Institute of Community Studies and seeding the Consumers' Association, the Advisory Centre for Education, the National and International Extension Colleges and much, much more. When the first Open University TV programmes went on air in 1971, doubling BBC educational output, he coined the memorable phrase: 'the obsolescence of childhood education'.

Introduction

What constitutes 'open and distance learning' in the nineties? To what extent are the varieties of provision which claim the title, actually open, and to whom are they open? Do we see for example, any flags of convenience, where open learning is the title, but closed learning is the practice? What has been the impact of open and distance learning where it has been used extensively? These are some of the questions which the contributors to this volume have addressed in the fields in which they have expertise. 'Open learning', 'flexible learning' and 'resource-based learning' have become catch phrases that have moved from the margins of provision to the mainstream, in strategies for post school education and training. This is a collection therefore which is intended both for readers who want to know what has been happening in a particular area, as well as for those who know the field and want to see more evaluative accounts of what has been going on.

An exploration of the varieties of practice that might count as open learning involves tracing some of the most far reaching changes in the provision of education and training, whether given the 'open' label or not. If it is possible to speak of a movement, in a field driven by opportunism as well as idealism, then it is possible to say that the open learning movement has contributed both in terms of ideology and of specific forms of provision to virtually every sector of education and training for adults. How have open and distance approaches developed to meet the challenge? How have they interacted with the cultures and attitudes of both providers and learners, in the contexts in which they have been used? 'What opportunities and what potential dangers do the new technologies offer?' 'Is open learning now incontrovertibly "in the mainstream"'? (Smith and Kelly, 1987).

One of the effects of expansion however, is that the diversity of provision which, even during the eighties, could be included under the so called 'umbrella term' of open learning (Thorpe and Grugeon, 1987), is now so wide as to make generalisation hazardous, if not impossible. It is wise in these circumstances, to remember the distinction which Rumble has emphasised, between 'open' as an adjective qualifying a particular type of learning, and 'open-learning' as a sort of compound noun for a particular type of provision, distinct from others (Rumble, 1993). He argues for openness as a quality which may exist to a greater or lesser extent in any form of provision, traditional or innovative.

However, as Rumble admits, practitioners are free to use the term as they wish, and the frequency with which they have done so has contributed a plethora of variations of provision to fit the circumstances or the nature of the accreditation involved. For some there have also been political reasons for a clear separation between open and distance learning (Rumble, 1993), and for these reasons also it is important to distinguish between concepts of openness, and the provision so labelled. One of the aims of this book is to provide the reader with an opportunity to question such provision and to see to what extent it is open in the sense of the various dimensions which Lewis has outlined — dimensions of time, place, pace, enrolment, accreditation and so on (Lewis, 1993). The apparent success of the field makes it more not less important to remember the aspirations and goals which were embodied in its origins, in practice which was at the margins of existing mainstream provision, and challenging many of its norms. As Ross Paul has argued, we can identify in these aspirations an 'ideal-type', embodying values such as egalitarianism, and social responsibility in relation to those previously under-represented in higher education (Paul, 1993). As he says, 'From this perspective, almost no formalised provision of education will reach the ideal on all the continua suggested, for the extreme would not be an institution at all but some form of what Ivan Illich envisioned in his *Deschooling Society* (1971)' (Paul, 1993).

Although it is possible thus to clarify terminology and to suggest open learning is best seen as ideal-type rather than achieved reality, in practice it is difficult to avoid some degree of imprecision. It has been useful for example to assume that open learning is a generic form of provision with many species or varieties of type. Distance education for example, creates openness in the sense of physical accessibility, because attendance at an institution is not required in order to study successfully. Distance educators indeed may feel that theirs is a field with rather better defined boundaries than open learning, and with an established body of theory (Keegan, 1993). Physical separation between the acts of teaching and the acts of learning (Moore, 1993) is still a core criterion for a definition of the field of study. But there is no shortage of disputes even here, over the nature of concepts such as distance, interaction and educational technology (Evans and Nation, 1993 Keegan, 1993).

However, the identity and success of the distance education field for at least two decades has assured the continuing currency of the term even in countries such as the United Kingdom where 'open learning' is more likely to be used by practitioners in mainstream provision. In other countries, distance education may be the more popular or familiar term, and in any event, there is a widespread assumption that it does refer to provision in which self instruction dominates, with little if any face-to-face teaching on campus. This form of provision has generated an important literature on which a number of the chapters here draw in particular, and which is especially relevant to the issue of the expansion of electronic and communications media.

Distance education has indeed already been 'periodised' in the work of Garrison and Bates who see three 'waves' or generations of provision created by the features of the technologies which dominate at each stage. The development of open learning as a whole will also be affected by the changes fuelled by these new technologies of computer networks, satellite and fibre optic transmission. Open learning however has also been associated with innovatory programmes in existing institutions rather than the establishment of 'special' forms of teaching and learning in single mode organisations such as the various 'Open Universities' established now in many countries. The developments in open learning as a result, have been a two-way story of mutual change and influence, between a particular variant of open learning, and the institution in which it develops.

When the present editors brought together *Open Learning For Adults* in 1987, it was possible to identify a limited range of types of provision — workshops, campus based flexible learning and distance learning being the main ones. While these types of provision are still alive and well, we are also seeing a rapid transformation of all forms of provision into a more market-oriented and consumer-oriented, in some cases a more student-oriented, service, drawing upon many of the practices pioneered by the open learning movement, if not necessarily drawing on all of the ideals embodied in the ideal-type.

This expansion of open learning is one of two main themes in this collection. The first theme addresses the issues generated by this 'two-way story' created by the opening up of provision for learning opportunities in every sector of formal education and training. All of these sectors have been changed, to some or to a great extent, by the concept of openness in learning and its application to the issues of what constitutes accessibility and effective learning opportunities for a particular constituency of learners and clients. There has been a realisation that opening up provision requires more than the add-on workshop or self-study pack for part-time learners.

The goal of opening up the provision of education and training, in the sense both of its physical accessibility and of its learning effectiveness for non-traditional learners, has become a claimed priority in all sectors and has generated changes to virtually every aspect of what is taught as well as to how. Open learning centres and workshops still have a role to play, but it is now possible to achieve a much wider range of qualifications, and to study across the breadth of the curriculum using open learning approaches. As several of the chapters in this collection demonstrate, in some contexts the distinction between open learning and conventional learning has virtually disappeared, in a radical re-think of what it means to create the most open and therefore the most effective learning opportunities, whether in the context of a college or a profit-oriented organisation in the private sector.

The second theme in this collection, concerns the expansion of technologies of electronic media and telecommunications. Education and training are the latest area within which traditional forms of production and consumption (if for the moment we can use the metaphor of knowledge being 'produced and consumed') are being transformed by the application of electronics and communications technologies. Just as technologies of physical production processing have transformed virtually every industry, so now technologies for information storage, transfer, retrieval and display, are transforming institutions for education and training. The effects on learning, occupational roles and employment in these institutions may well be as far reaching as they have been in industry and services.

These expansions of computer-based, multimedia, interactive technologies for teaching and learning are often tagged with the label of 'open' or 'distance' learning. Although the technologists who generate new products and new ways of doing things are often not the same people and may not share the same goals as those who have promoted open and distance learning approaches (Duning, 1993), they are inextricably linked in an expansion which is difficult to track because of the speed with which it is revolutionising institutions and roles, as well as the possibilities for learners.

Technology is being used to transform both conventional and distance or off-campus study, through its potential to deliver learning resources to any location served by the telephone or by cable, and to allow the user to manipulate or interact with what has been delivered. To what extent such provision is open in every sense of the word, is a matter for evaluation. At this stage however, open learning/distance learning (the two are often used interchangeably by both practitioners and media reportage) and technological innovation are yoked together in popular perception and in the media. Hardly a day passes without news of some further expansion, whether in the form of access for new groups of learners or of radical change to the structure of existing forms of teaching and learning.

One such article in April 1994 included news of major education and training establishments with plans to deliver courses through computer-based and interactive technologies. Video Arts, producer of well known training videos featuring the actor John Cleese among others, had (it was reported) linked up with Philips, the electronics firm, to produce interactive CD-i versions of its existing videos (*Independent on Sunday*, 24.4.94). The report included news about the UK National Extension College, home-based access as well as work-based access to training and updating, and the success of a firm (Futuremedia) producing interactive multimedia training for around one thousand companies and predicting massive expansion to individual consumers. The article included the now familiar mix of positions in such reporting:

- The expansion of communications technology into education and training is expanding open and distance learning. ('The revolution in multimedia technology has given added impetus to the already expanding world of open learning.')
- ODL means lower costs ('The costs of open learning are, on average, 60 per cent of those of conventional training methods.')
- Providers of education and training are forming commercial alliances with the private sector for the development of ODL provision.
- Economic imperatives require all of us to become ODL users ('As people accept that the job-for-life is becoming a rather quaint and outmoded concept, the need to learn new skills and acquire fresh qualifications is taken as read if you want to stay employed.')
- Access to new interactive technologies is increasingly financially possible for individual consumers as well as for organisations, and this creates new market possibilities for both providers and hardware manufacturers, nationally and internationally.
- Interactive technologies mean more people learn more. ('People studying this way retain more. They are experiencing the information: they get to have a go through interactive exercises. Rather than being passive recipients in the learning process, they are active participants. It is not surprising that they have better recall.')

- Governments see the expansion of ODL as a way of achieving their targets for a skilled workforce.

This mix of positions and promotion is aptly summed up in the conclusion to the article:

> An increasing number of pundits, educationalists and computer professionals agree that learning interactively makes sense. The Government's push to encourage people to improve their education and training through National Vocational Qualifications is well suited to open learning, allowing those who sign up and log-on to study at their own pace. As hardware prices fall, wide availability in an interactive format would give huge impetus to this study mode. Smart companies are wising up. As software sellers know, home computers and TV screens offer huge potential for education and training. How long before plugging a CD-i into the TV for an interactive multimedia study session — or a CD-ROM drive into a personal computer — becomes as commonplace as nipping out to get the latest movie release on video? Or at least as signing up for a correspondence course. (*Independent on Sunday*, 24.4.94)

Reports such as these can be found in any industrialised country and they help set the agenda for anyone writing about the field of open and distance learning in the nineties. What began as a challenge to traditional forms of provision around goals of learner centredness and equality of access, has now become part of the rapid global commercial expansion of electronic and communication technologies. There has for some time now been a concern about the lack of clarity, about the political expediency even, in use of the terminology in the field, whether 'distance', 'open', 'flexible' or 'resource-based' learning is at issue. Disputes over terminology such as the series carried by the journal *Open Learning* during 1990, are not a purely 'academic' exercise. They are one aspect of a very necessary analysis of the expansion of a field of practice, which is changing as it expands. What began as a creative response by educators to the possibilities opened up by widespread ownership of radio and television receivers, is now propelled by economic imperatives as these shape governments, providers of education and training and producers of the commercial products of the technologies themselves. That which was practiced in the margins in other words, is not necessarily identical with that which is being practiced in the mainstream. Unlike the reporter in the *Independent's* article on the issue, we may not all want to equate the expansion of technology into all forms of education as the expansion of open learning *per se*.

If ODL itself is undergoing yet another of its chameleon like changes, so also are the institutions which implement it. The change of greatest importance here is the expansion within the post-compulsory sector, funded to an increasing extent by the users (including here both learners and sponsors) themselves and by collaboration with the private sector. Governments everywhere urge the need for mass provision of further and higher education, and seek successively to reduce the unit costs of such provision. Institutions of higher education teach more students with the same number of full-time staff and seek to bridge the gap by using communications media of one kind or another, and by employing part-time staff. Their management style has shifted from a collegial to a corporate approach in many areas of operation, and the idea of a university as a geographically present community of scholars and students has probably had its time.

Open and distance learning has come of age, and faces the challenges of maturity, which must certainly include a critical analysis of what it is and what its effects have been or appear likely to be. The slow growth of postgraduate qualifications in the field during the eighties is likely to expand rapidly. Harry et al. see this as 'a coming of age for the field of study (which) may lead to the abandonment of over-ambitious claims for this form of education which, on examination, may prove to be only hopes which do not correspond to the concrete realities of the types of courses on offer from the institutions. This should lead to a needed maturity with the faults and failings of distance education, as well as its successes and glamour, revealed.' (Harry et al., 1993). This is one of several publications in a series aimed precisely at the postgraduate student market, with collections incorporating noted theoretical positions about the nature of distance education, and some limited reflections on its practice. If open and distance learning are to feed into postgraduate studies it is vital that such theoretical and conceptual analysis occurs.

However, in a field which has been driven not primarily out of theoretically driven research but out of social action and practical response to economic conditions, there is a parallel need of equal importance to document and to reflect upon the mushrooming variety of provision which is taking place, and upon the changes to the whole structure of education and training which they have helped bring about. The contributors to this collection are well placed to outline and to reflect on these changes, whether to a particular sector or to modes of teaching and learning.

The book is organised in four parts. Part I focuses on the ways in which structures of provision have been and are being changed through the expansion of open and distance learning.

Rumble considers the dilemmas this has created in the university sector, where different institutional models of provision of open and distance learning have been in place for decades but now face new challenges of competition and government reductions in funding. He addresses the issue of what is the most appropriate institutional form within which to provide for both on- and off-campus study — single or mixed mode institutions. He rather suggests that the days of the specialised institution are over — surely (he argues), the logic of combining both campus based and distance approaches will favour the mixed mode institution? It may be that the vagaries of government funding and policy making favour this argument in one context but not in another. Logic and university finance are not necessarily close bed fellows.

Rumble also provides us with a challenging critique of the ideology of distance and open learning, requiring us to consider whether at least part of the drive to develop heories (certainly in the field of distance education), has been the need to legitimise a practice given sometimes a derisory press by conventional institutions in the past. If so, distance educators in this sense are in good company; theory building may often follow successful practice. And in the form of institutions such as the National Extension College or the many open universities the world over, this is practice which has been adequately, sometimes notably successful, in the business of enrolling and accrediting student learning.

Lewis continues the focus on higher education and argues that a narrow definition of openness, as access via removal of the barriers of time and place, has kept many initiatives at the margins of provision. Openness in its fullest sense, in terms of the curriculum and its assessment, is needed to enable universities to respond to the challenges they face and to make radical changes to the whole of their teaching. If, as he says, institutional managers currently lack successful HE models and experience to draw on, they would find constructive thinking and practice in the further education sector from which to draw inspiration. Wilson argues the case for open systems in educational provision, through the development of credit accumulation and transfer. From the learner's perspective, systems which do not allow a diverse range of learned outcomes to be accredited, or which do not enable the accumulation and transfer of credit, are effectively closed to some of the most important of their needs. This implies change to some of the most deeply embedded assumptions and practices in the system, and Wilson's overview of the Credit Accumulation and Transfer approach might profitably be read alongside the related chapters from Paine, Hanley, Hawksley and Munroe.

Paine's chapter shows how, in the Scottish context, decisive and radical intervention in the further education sector (a sector rather similar to the community college provision of North America) has driven change in the university sector. Equally important, is the opportunity his chapter affords to emphasise that openness for the biggest sector of learning post-16 is based as much on modularisation and computer-based systems of administration for enrolment and timetabling, as it is on the provision of course packages and distance tutoring.

Bergin and Hamilton's chapter moves to the adult education sector, with a discussion of the findings of research into the provision of open learning centres for adult literacy and numeracy — the Basic Skills Open Learning Centres set up between 1988 and 1992. The introduction of these centres alongside the existing adult literacy provision throws into sharp relief the issue of what counts as 'open', for here we have the opportunity to contrast the practice of an existing service that always aimed at learner-centred provision, meeting the diverse needs of all users of the service, with an explicitly titled 'open' provision, based on the model of self-instruction via learning materials with limited face to face tuition. Their findings suggest that while this strategy may have made a local contribution, it has not served the needs of all legitimate users of an adult basic education service, and raises policy issues about the most productive use of resource for a national service which is open in terms of both access, equality and learning effectiveness.

Allred's analysis of the role of the public library service asserts a positive theme of 'service not delivery', drawing distinctions between a support role for libraries, and an independent role as an open resource for learners, recognised as part of their mainstream operation. Although open learning in libraries may, as he claims, be 'a refocusing of services already provided', he demonstrates how that requires library staff to change their perceptions of role and to change the resources that are stored as well as their delivery to learners. The Haldanes too emphasise the changing roles of staff responsible for learning and training programmes, with a remarkable convergence of approaches between industry and education.

McNay's chapter provides a challenging conclusion to Part I and a bridge to the chapters in Part II, particularly those which focus on his three key issues of modular course structures, delivery via learning packages, and the articulation of course outcomes, in terms of competence. The challenge comes from the question posed as to whether the original and desirable goals of these innovative approaches have been, and are being undermined by the forms they have taken as they become mainstream policy and universal practice. Has the move from margins to mainstream transformed, obliterated even, the virtues which the originators of such open learning reforms intended? The specification of learning outcomes is vital to open learning for example, but this is now being developed in the UK by the introduction of a national system of vocational competence as the basis for accreditation. Does this actually close down learning options rather than open them up, by tying accreditation to current job specifications and funding learning only in so far as it underpins such accreditation? Clearly there are different positions on these and the other issues raised, but the challenge and the evidence presented, underline how important it is to monitor the expansion of so called 'open' approaches, and to maintain a critical review of their effects.

Part II moves from the issues of systems and structural change, to those of course delivery and assessment. Some chapters here provide case studies of provision which exemplify and develop the issues identified in Part I. Hanley and Hawksley and Munroe for example provide a useful comparison of two colleges each with a rather different approach to a college-wide strategy for open learning. Ryan summarises some recent collaborative projects seeking to draw on the combined strengths of higher education institutions whilst still retaining the flexibility of each department to tailor courses to their own needs. Here we begin to get inside the attempts to create open options for full-time, campus-based students as well as for the part-time adult learner, by the collaborative production of materials through project initiatives and networking. A key message, for post secondary institutions, is that lecturers need time 'to be involved in the selection, adaptation and integration of materials into their teaching programme'.

The next two chapters in Part II introduce new initiatives in accrediting learning, especially learning which occurs outside institutions for education and training, and considers the challenges these create for distance modes of open learning in particular. As open learning consolidates its position as part of the mainstream, it will not be able to ignore other movements for change such as the competence based National Vocational Qualifications, and the accreditation of prior learning. The proponents of both these approaches might claim that they open up learning; NVQs make possible the accreditation of workplace skills, and APL the accreditation of any learning which can be evidenced and related to a recognised institution's awarding system. Such approaches promise a recognition of what the learner brings into their contact with a formal institution, and the basis for progression on to further learning and accreditation. In the case of APL, the process itself can be liberating for those who work through a process of reflection and validation of the learned outcomes their experience has generated. Butterworth and Edwards reflect on the practical implications of supporting students through such a process, and identify particular problems for an institution such as the UK Open University. The challenge of operating at a distance and creating systems which can work nationally, makes responsiveness to the individual student extremely difficult, and tips the balance in favour of the articulate and already knowledgeable applicant. An institution teaching primarily face to face finds it easier to resolve issues which so often arise from the unique circumstances of each student, and for which general guidelines are of limited usefulness. Butterworth and Edwards also emphasise that APL is not a cheap option, either for institution or student, and often depends on sophisticated tutorial support to enable applicants to complete the process successfully. Once again, any notions of this form of openness in learning as either quick, easy or inexpensive need to be treated with scepticism.

Although Vocational Qualifications present a very different case from APL, there is a rather similar challenge to the large scale versions of distance education, which Denise Hevey outlines. The virtues of systems of provision available nationally have a negative side in built-in inflexibilities, particularly over assessment where the competence-based approach can require costly and labour intensive procedures if it is to be done well and to realise the assessment on demand goals of NCVQ. Where some would rule out distance education however, Denise Hevey offers an impressive list of contributions which it can make, and readers will benefit from other relevant chapters, McNay and Paine for example, in balancing the many issues which arise in using distance education to deliver vocational qualifications using this (currently controversial) form of competence-based and criterion-referenced testing.

Barrie Oxtoby's chapter which follows, offers an account of learning in the workplace which incorporates accreditation but goes well beyond it in a process of embedding learning within the continual change required to achieve and maintain Rover's corporate goal of delivering 'extraordinary customer satisfaction'. The role of learning in this process has developed out of the open learning centres first set up in 1982 during the 'Open Tech' initiative led by the UK Government's Manpower Services Commission and partially funded by that body. These centres were devolved to the local plants of the company, the better to integrate them into the business and their role has expanded to include much more than their original computer-based delivery of learning. In this case, the company sees itself as having moved on from 'open learning' in order to create an organisation in which learning is the 'primary driver' and the means by which an ever faster process of change is brought about. With the recent sale of Rover to the German car manufacturing company BMW, it is too soon to know what effects there will be on the company's acclaimed success as a learning organisation. However, where the initiation and support of learning has been embedded within a company at all levels, as is described, it seems likely that it will be changed by shifts in the leadership and strategic goals of the company as a whole. What developments are possible beyond 'the learning organisation', and whether they open up learning in new ways, remains to be seen.

Gill Kirkup and Lee Taylor complete Part II with a chapter focused on institutional and curriculum accessibility in relation to women, and in the context of distance education. They contrast radical feminist and institutional equal opportunities practice, arguing that some at least of the goals of both can be incorporated in interventionist policies for organisational change. They draw on evidence of women's participation in distance education as students, and on the history of two equal opportunities initiatives introduced during the early nineties at the UK Open University. Guidelines on language and imagery were produced during 1993, so that authors of teaching material, administrators and other interested staff might consider the impact of the language they use on how people experience their age, disability, ethnicity or their gender. The Guidelines also suggested the use of non-sexist language, and this element in particular provoked very strong reactions both inside and outside the university. Other projects oriented to encouraging women's access to OU courses have received only very positive reactions, yet the move to change ways of speaking clearly presented a threat for some who objected to it. In an institution where the written word is still the single most important teaching and learning medium, the degree to which language is perceived to welcome or to exclude, to be open or closed, has a large effect on the perceived openness of the institution. The impressions created by the language used in higher education particularly, are experienced as excluding by many students who enter via access routes (Rosen, 1993). The authors argue that women's place in distance education is more than a numbers game, and illustrates both the importance and the difficulty of changing relationships where power is exercised, particularly perhaps in those relationships where power is exercised most subtly and (for some) imperceptibly. This is an area where the legitimacy of intervention has been challenged, and change in conventional ways of acting and of expression have been resisted. The struggle clearly continues.

In Part III we focus in more detail on the learning process and how it might best be supported and developed, taking into account the diversity of kinds of learning as well as the diversity of learners who may now use some form of open learning. Vivienne Rivis demonstrates not only that guidance is a necessary condition for openness in learning, but that the two fields of practice have grown alongside each other and in some ways, in collaboration with and in support of each other. Her account of how both became a vehicle during the eighties for the introduction of market principles into education and training, offers a constructive and insightful critique of the development of open learning and guidance in tandem. She argues convincingly that the student-centred ideologies of both guidance and open learning can be manipulated and are vulnerable to policies which appear to develop them, but in reality create the form without the content.

Several authors have outlined the way in which innovative practice in education aimed at creating an open experience for learners, though not under the title of 'open' or 'distance' learning, has come to present a particular challenge to self-proclaimed open learning. One such field of practice for example has been the access movement, a broad church of adult oriented provision seeking ways of building on the experience and strengths of learners to create opportunities for personal growth and accreditation, with progression on to further qualifications for those interested in that. Access courses aimed at taking students not formally qualified for university study, to a point where they can work alongside other university degree students on a conventional programme, has been one of the success stories of the 1980s. As Andy Northedge says in his chapter, it was not at all clear what a distance education version of open learning had to offer to a 'localised, person-sensitive, confidence building form of education', and thus, 'the Open University, which had been the access university in the seventies, found itself little more than an onlooker as the access movement burgeoned a decade later.'

The Open University's success in the 1990s, in providing materials and a structure for teaching and learning at access course level, requires the kind of explanation which Northedge provides, in his account of the learner empowerment enabled by materials which create a conceptual structure for study, and a bridge between the language and ideas of students and those of the disciplines within which they plan to study. Northedge's account of study as primarily a social process of initiation into and practice within a discourse, is used both to illuminate the vulnerabilities and (relative) powerlessness experienced by the beginning student, and to highlight the job that teaching (both materials and face-to-face interaction) has to do: 'From this perspective, studenthood is an "apprenticeship", during which the student is initiated into the practices, values, and ways of thinking of the discourse and a selection of its key ideas and current debates.'

The course which has been developed has also led to imaginative collaborations between different providers whose resources have thus been strengthened and extended to provide a new opportunity for learners, and at a modest cost, albeit one which cannot compare with many existing access courses based in colleges and offered free to students. The advantages of excellent materials however, may offset this lack of subsidy for the distance mode, which is more flexible and time effective for many users.

Correspondence teaching has been the bed rock of some systems of distance education, and completely absent from others. Matthew Godsell and Margaret Miers use a dialogue format for their exploration of the values which are embedded in the practice of tutor commenting, and the messages, both hidden and overt, communicated to students about what kind of learning they should be engaged in. The authors burrow deeply inside the process of marking and its moderation, in order to pursue the challenge that open learning risks offering the form of openness without its content — 'You are worried that we are spending too much time checking knowledge retention rather than promoting learning or even thinking, and that if we make more use of open learning we're giving them (the students) more responsibility for managing their learning when all that we are doing is pushing them along pre-set paths towards a prescriptive educational product.' Readers must judge for themselves whether and how the dialogue gets resolved, and in the course of doing so, be challenged to confront some of the most recalcitrant of problems facing the committed open tutor. However, the improved understanding of teaching staff in post-secondary education, with regard to individual tutorial support by the written word, is a major contribution that open learning has brought to more traditional 'face-to-face' education. It may prove even more crucial as student 'faces' in groups become more blurred with expansion of student numbers. If Open Learning has a more central role to play in teaching and learning than before, it is partly because the very separation of different elements has enabled unusual concentration to occur — in print, audio-visual, written tutorial etc. It is also because certain issues have been highlighted — student progress, needs of disabled students, quality of openly available teaching materials. Alan Woodley reflects on the complex phenomenon of drop out, and indicates various methods of analysis and action. While there are sometimes exceptional identifiable factors 'it is more usually a multi-causal problem that requires multiple, partial solutions'.

Diana Laurillard in her chapter, brings together an explicit account of the component processes of academic learning and reviews the potential of various communications technologies to enable a version of each process to take place. Since new technologies are often introduced under the label of 'open' or 'distance' learning, our field carries a particular responsibility to give educational goals priority over the mechanics of implementing the hardware and software of such technologies. A useful catch phrase was coined at the 1994 Canadian Association for Distance Education Conference to sum up our scepticism about the current emphasis on a technological fix: 'technology's the answer, but what's the question?' Diana Laurillard's review of what each of the media can 'carry' in the way of presentation, interaction, adaptation and reflection by a learner, would be a good place to start to construct some of the questions about teaching and learning for which technology might be an answer.

Technology also provides a good bridge between Part III and Part IV, because we are at the beginning of a process of globalisation in education and training, led by the expansion of technology, just as we have seen the production and consumption of goods and services break through many of the restraints of national boundaries and geography to create a global economy. For more than a decade now, distance education has enabled some universities to teach students living virtually anywhere, providing they can meet the requirements of assessment arrangements. The establishment of the Open Learning Agency of Australia in 1992 offers another interesting case. A consortium of three universities led by Monash University, acts as broker between any university offering its courses, and the student/user wishing to study such courses. These 'students' do not register with the university whose course they study, though they may chose to do so if they wish to complete their studies on campus, or to validate their claim to have accumulated sufficient credits for a qualification such as a degree. The OLAA is open to any Australian citizens, whether resident in Australia or not, and its potential to enrol students/users from other countries is clear, although it may have no wish so to do.

The OLAA is but one version of many examples of collaboration between universities and between universities and industry, which makes clear that distance teaching has contributed to pressures for change which will transform traditional institutions such as universities, as well as the experience of the students of the future. Distance teaching has in effect been a Trojan Horse for the armies

of technology. It has demonstrated that it is possible to teach to
the same standards as conventional universities, in institutions
resourced and staffed so to do. Courses developed by the UK Open
University for example, always have an external assessor and an
external examiner who carry academic status within their subject
expertise, and oversee the standards both of materials and of the
assessed work of students and staff. Opposition to the expansion
of distance education, on the grounds of educational principle,
has been swept aside by such evidence of academic rigour as
this has provided, within the context of the standards created by
a particular institution.

In Part IV, Robin Mason outlines the different kinds of
arrangements under which students in one country may be able
to study courses developed by an institution in another country.
As she says, the difficulties of institutional collaboration, especially
between different cultures and ways of doing things, are considerable. Kevin Wilson's chapter which follows, provides a case study
of such difficulties as well as the rewards from the first collaborative
course produced by five European distance universities, as members of the European Association of Distance Teaching Universities. The EADTU programme committees for European Law
and Business Administration may not choose for their European
courses, the model of full collaboration which the course 'What
is Europe?' followed. However there is a positive symbolism
about choosing to work jointly throughout the course production
process, for a course which addresses the issues of history, ideology
and nationhood bound up in the idea of what it means to be
'European'.

Tony Dodds' chapter makes sure that any risk of 'Euro-
centrism' is short lived — at least in terms of our concerns here with
the international role of open learning. In the context of Africa, it
is the history and potential of distance education rather than any
other version of open learning, because the problems of physical
access, staffing and educational resource generally create obvious
problems for more campus based alternatives. Tony Dodds' focus
on countries which are underdeveloped and materially poor (though
with the exciting new possibilities created by a democratically
elected government in South Africa) raises the issue of the links
between individual aspirations in learning, and the development
of communities and countries. This is a theme to which Michael
Young returns in his Afterword, which ends our collection.

Michael Young is one of the leading educational reformers
in Britain, whose work has had international effects through the
establishment of the UK Open University, and through the work
of the National Extension College and the International Extension

College in all of which he was a moving force. His invitation to speak at Churchill College, Cambridge University in April 1994, in honour of the twenty-fifth anniversary of the Open University, provided the occasion for a happy economy of effort — the preparation of a chapter for this book became the basis of the speech delivered at Churchill College. The ease of style and the inspiration of this chapter were warmly received at the time, and we are delighted to provide the vehicle whereby that speech can have some permanence and wider currency.

The chapter can speak for itself, but two themes seem appropriate to emphasise in concluding this introduction. First, is the theme of the effects of distance education, in particular the way in which they work with the forces of commerce and commercialisation, dissolving the close links within communities and creating ever more opportunities for people to live, work and play individually. The values of student-centred learning have played into this context in ways which may not have been foreseen by those with well intentioned motives for the reduction of institutional authority in education. Perhaps Michael Young would include himself among this group, and no one among us can foresee all the uses to which our best intentions may contribute. In any event, he draws our attention now to the theme of individualisation and its effects, with persuasive force and characteristic humour.

He also argues for research into open learning, and this provides the concluding point in our introduction. Technology has advanced to the stage where the important question is not 'can we do?' but 'should we do?', and in answering such a question we would do well to provide ourselves with evidence of the effects of what is already in place under the label of open learning. Although the dominant players in our field are likely to be the private sector companies who research and develop new technologies, together with donor governments, it is not the case that educators and trainers have no choices — and no responsibilities to create the best conditions for those who will be learning. If we do not maintain a critical evaluation of the developments in our field and of their educational effects, no-one else will, and the value of what we can contribute to its future development will be reduced. Cost effectiveness, commercial values even, are not new considerations for practitioners of open learning. Economic and commercial pressures however are much more intense than ever before, and we will need the support of research in pushing for systems or features in new developments, which we think will be in the best interests of learners and of maintaining educational values. The value of research here is not just an academic issue or a

desirable extra, but central to maintaining our knowledge base and
authority to create systems for education and training which are
effective learning opportunities for those who might legitimately
seek to use them.

References

Bates, A. (1993) 'Technology for distance education: A ten year perspective'
in Harry, K., John, M. and Keegan, D. (eds.) *Distance Education: New
Perspectives*, London, Routledge.

Duning, B. (1993) 'The coming of the new distance educators in the United
States: the telecommunications generation takes off' in Harry et al., op. cit.

Evans, T. and Nation, D. (eds.) (1993) *Reforming Open and Distance Education*,
London, Kogan Page.

Garrison, D. R. (1993) 'Multifunction microcomputer enhanced audio conferencing:
moving into the third generation of distance education' in Harry et al.,
op. cit.

Harry, K., John, M. and Keegan, D. (eds.) (1993) *Distance Education: New
Perspectives*, London, Routledge.

Keegan, D. (ed.) (1993) *The Principles of Distance Education*, London, Routledge.

Kelly, M. and Smith, P. (eds.) (1987) *Distance Education and the Mainstream*,
Beckenham, Croom Helm.

Lewis, R. (1993) 'What is open learning?' in Tait, A. (ed.) *Key Issues in Open
Learning, A Reader. An Anthology from the journal* Open Learning *1986–1992*,
Harlow, Longman.

Moore, M. G. (1993) 'Theory of transactional distance' in Keegan (ed.) op. cit.
pp. 22–38.

Paul, R. H. (1993) 'Open universities — the test of all models' in Harry, K.,
John, M. and Keegan, D. (eds.) op. cit. pp. 114–125.

Rosen, V. (1993) 'Black students in Higher Education' in Thorpe, M., Edwards,
R. and Hanson, A. (eds.) *Culture and Processes of Adult Learning*, London,
Routledge.

Thorpe, M. and Grugeon, D. (eds.) (1987) *Open Learning for Adults*. Harlow,
Longman.

Rumble, G. (1993) 'Open Learning, distance education and the misuse of
language' in Tait, A. (ed.) *Key Issues in Open Learning*, Harlow, Longman.

Part I
Structures and institutional change

1 Mixed modes of teaching and learning: structures, resources, and developments

Greville Rumble

This chapter looks at the merging of distance and traditional forms of education. Two terms are commonly used in the literature — *dual mode* and *mixed mode*. I wish to make a distinction between:

(a) Institutions (or departments within institutions) which offer two distinct kinds of courses, one using traditional classroom-based methods and the other distance methods. Such courses are taken by groups of students which the institution regards as distinct from each other, the one on-campus, the other off-campus, external, or distant. Students enrolled in one of these modes may or may not be allowed to crossover to take courses in the other mode. I shall refer to this kind of provision as *dual mode*.

(b) Courses which are presented in a way that enables a student to decide whether they wish to study the course on-campus or off-campus and at a distance. The former involves attendance at tutorials, seminars, classes, and lectures, as well as independent study from books and other resources. Opportunities to interact directly, face to face, with the teachers exist to a greater or lesser extent. The latter involves first and foremost independent study using materials, with little opportunity to meet teachers face to face, though contact with teachers through the mail, e-mail, telephone, audio-conferences and video-conferences may be possible. Students who enrol on a course use the appropriate mix of media and methods that suit their need. I shall refer to this kind of provision as *mixed mode*.

I shall suggest that the development of mixed-mode teaching is desirable. Before I do so, however, I wish to examine some of the reasons why the two methods involved (face-to-face or contiguous teaching, and distance teaching) have been regarded as distinct.

The technological basis for separatism

Twenty years ago the distinction between distance and face-to-face education was rather easier to make than it is now. Distance education used 'mediated' forms of teaching and communication (that is, forms of teaching and communication which require the use of media of one kind or another) while traditional forms of education involved direct face-to-face contact with the teacher. Typically, distance educators used print, audio-cassettes, video-cassettes, radio, and television to carry the educational content to the learner, while traditional educationalists used a combination of face-to-face teaching and guided independent study (normally print-based). Distance education suffered in the comparison because there were relatively few ways in which a student could interact in a two-way conversation with the teacher: there might be occasional face-to-face seminars or tutorials, but they were few and far between and attendance at them was often not a practical proposition for those following a distance course. Some systems used telephone contact (one-to-one or one-to-several), radio-phones, and two-way radio, but their use was not widespread. All used written letters (and sometime taped audio-messages), but this lacked the immediacy of 'normal' interaction in the tutorial, class, seminar or lecture. To counter some of the implied weaknesses, distance educators began to simulate conversations in their texts — giving rise to Holmberg's now famous concept of a simulated 'guided didactic conversation' which he first articulated in 1960 (Holmberg, 1960).

Recent technological advances, notably electronic mail, computer conferencing, audio-conferencing, and video-conferencing, have provided distance educators with the means of interacting with their students in both real time and asynchronously, and have to some extent broken through the two-way communications barrier which faced earlier generations of distance educators, though the real breakthrough will only come when these technologies are embedded in the home and in all work places.

At the same time, traditional educators have been facing problems — notably those resulting from the expansion of student numbers without comparable increases in staff numbers. As a result the numbers attending tutorials, seminars, and lectures has grown — so much so that latecomers to lectures may have to sit in adjoining rooms to receive the lecture through closed-circuit television or rely instead on reprographed lecture notes distributed by their lecturers. The pressure of numbers has made it more difficult to talk to, and discuss things with, students. At the extreme, lectures are broadcast on open air television to many thousands of students in many different locations, as in the Chinese Radio and Television University system. Ultimately, one reaches the situation in which even the students on-campus study in the main through media, thus finally eroding any real distinction between the off-campus distant and the on-campus student.

The philosophical basis for separatism

The literature on flexible and distance learning commonly distinguishes between institutions which teach by traditional means, those which teach by distance means, and those which use both approaches. This distinction mirrors the literature on the definition of distance education, which has sought to distinguish between the two forms of education. Keegan (1990, p. 6), one of the seminal thinkers in this field, has argued that 'distance education is a coherent and distinct field of educational endeavour'. Not surprisingly, therefore, his definition of distance education emphasises among other things:

1. 'The separation of teacher and learner which distinguishes it from face-to-face lecturing', though he does admit the 'possibility [within distance education] of occasional meetings for both didactic and socialisation purposes', and
2. 'The use of technical media, usually print, to unite teacher and learner and carry the educational content', though he rigorously excludes 'from the concept of distance education . . . all uses of educational technology in classrooms, lecture theatres, or laboratories of conventional institutions . . . where the technology is a supplement to and not a substitute for the teacher' (Keegan, 1990, pp. 38, 26).

Theoretically, of course, there are forms of education which are 'pure' distance education, and others which are 'pure' traditional, face-to-face teaching. However, even Keegan's definition admits to some fuzziness about the terms. In practice, as we shall see, the distinction hardly stands up at all. Within the constraints that limit them, educationalists are quite simply choosing from the range of teaching strategies available to them to design programmes and courses to meet educational, pedagogic, and client needs.

Nevertheless, the supposed differences between distance and traditional forms of face-to-face education led to the early emergence of typologies of educational institutions which stressed the differences between institutions which (1) teach only by traditional means, (2) teach only by distance means, and (3) use both approaches. The first two categories came to be called single-mode institutions while the third category came to be referred to variously as mixed-mode or dual-mode institutions. In practice, the image of two wholly separate methods of education was so powerful that it was generally assumed that institutions using both methods taught some courses which were presented wholly by distance means to one group of students, and others which were presented wholly on campus to another, separate, group of students. I refer to this approach as dual mode.

It is instructive to reflect on why the distinction between distance and traditional forms of education was ever made as hard and fast as it was. The first reason was the deep insecurity felt by many distance educators about the status and validity of their craft. Correspondence education developed relatively late (around about the 1830s and 1840s). It provided an alternative to the dominant educational paradigm of face-to-face teaching, whether in the form of individual tuition or group-based classroom teaching. Early correspondence schools involved no personal face-to-face contact between the teacher and the pupil. Students' motivation to succeed had to be high. In its absence, they dropped out. The drop-out rate was generally high. Unscrupulous entrepreneurs saw that they could profit from such a business if they could persuade people to enrol and pay their tuition fees up front: those who had the motivation to succeed became advertisements for success; those who dropped out ceased to cost the school any money. Early drop-outs thus increased profits. Although there were some very good correspondence schools, by the middle of the present century correspondence education had a poor image, based on shady practice and poor results.

Technological innovation, the increasing recognition that the rising demand for education could not be met by expanding traditional educational institutions, the recognition that people had life long educational needs which could be better served by more flexible and open education systems, the evident success of some distance teaching institutions, and the growing volume of research into distance education, helped change the image of distance education during the 1970s and 1980s. The new-found confidence of those working in the field was echoed in Keegan's call for 'a firmly based theory of distance education . . . which can provide the touchstone against which decisions — political, financial, educational, social — can be taken with confidence' (Keegan, 1990, p. 5). However, such a concern implies a degree of separatism from traditional forms of education. It suited some distance educators to endorse separatism.

The structural basis for separatism

There is little doubt that most countries have a pool of frustrated or latent demand for entry to education. This comes from adults who lacked the opportunity to study when they were young, or who now need to gain new knowledge and skills, but lack a way of doing so; and from those young persons who were qualified for entry to a higher level of education, but for whom there are no places available in the traditional schools, colleges and universities. This demand spans all educational levels: primary education or its equivalent for adults; secondary education for older children, young adults, and adults; and tertiary level education for young adults and adults.

At primary and secondary levels, one response was to establish new institutions designed to make use of mass communications to support monitors guiding children in the classroom. A number of ETV (Educational Television) schools were set up around the world (e.g. Mexico, Ivory Coast, American Samoa, El Salvador, Brazil), with enthusiastic support from funding agencies. However, some organisations were set up specifically to provide distance education versions of the school curriculum (e.g. Centre National de Télé-enseignement, France; National Extension College, UK; Calvert School, Maryland, USA).

At the tertiary level a few universities (notably in the United States, Australia, and Canada) had, ever since the late nineteenth or early twentieth centuries, accepted the role of teaching remote, off-campus or external students. Countries where this was accepted practice tended not to set up single-mode distance teaching universities, but rather to expand the provision of external studies by the traditional universities. Elsewhere, it was clear that the traditional universities were unlikely to adopt teaching methods which would meet the needs of adult learners. In both the UK and the Netherlands, for example, they were uninterested in the needs of adult learners. The decision to establish a single-mode distance teaching university in these countries was, therefore, an entirely rational response to the traditional universities' lack of interest in the adult market. It was a different kind of decision to that taken in a number of other countries (Venezuela, Thailand, India, Philippines, etc.) where distance teaching universities were set up because it was clear that the traditional universities could not accommodate the demand from young people, and distance provision seemed a cost efficient way of meeting it.

The separatism inherent in the establishment of single mode distance teaching universities was quickly justified by those involved. First, it was said that the administrative structures of campus-based universities was unsuited to the development and management of distance teaching programmes (Peters, 1973, p. 310; Perry, 1976, p. 55; Daniel and Smith, 1979, p. 64). The very different cost structure of distance and traditional education made it difficult to argue the case for a budget for distance education in the same forum as that used for traditional education (Snowden and Daniel, 1980, p. 76; Swinerton and Hogan, 1981, p. 1). Secondly, it was argued that the needs of part-time, adult students would be better served if the institution taught wholly at a distance. The marginalisation of distance education students in dual-mode institutions is often cited as a reason for retaining separatism — and indeed, evidence from some dual-mode systems at the University of Zambia, in the Indian Correspondence Directorates, and from the United States, suggests that this is so (Siaciwena, 1988, p. 201; Singh, 1979, p. 87; Hall, 1991, p. 31).

From this, it is not too great a step to argue that distance teaching institutions should remain separate, single mode institutions. This argument reminds one of Peters and Waterman's adage, 'stick to the knitting' (Peters and Waterman, 1982, p. 292). They argued that 'the typical diversification strategy dilutes the guiding qualitative theme' (p. 293). Those who see distance education as distinct from traditional forms of education will endorse the arguments for separatism. They may also add that embracing a mixed mode role will (a) dilute the expertise in the technology and processes of materials development and the delivery of support services to students which distance education institutions undoubtedly often have, and (b) may well undermine their overall economies of scale by introducing the higher unit costs of face-to-face teaching into their provision.

The argument for separatism needs to be put in context. The distance teaching universities in particular invested a considerable amount of effort in research into distance education, and to establishing the credibility of what they were doing. Much of this work was and is valuable. But in the process many of them cut themselves off from the wider educational world. Arguments designed to prove that distance education was a separate discipline (see Rumble, 1988) reflected the search for status and acceptance, and strengthened the separatist tendency in the field. Because the universities were seen as the centres for research and thinking in distance education, this separatism affected others in the field. In time, those involved began to believe their own propaganda, and cease to consider some of the other directions that could be taken.

Given this, it is perhaps not surprising that many of the distance education programmes in traditional universities were set up as separate administrative and teaching units (e.g. Indian Correspondence Studies Directorates). Since they were seen as marginal to the main mission of the institution, and probably as a drain on resources, it is not surprising that they had low status. It is also not surprising that developments in the integrated use of distance and face-to-face methods largely arose outside of the formal education system, in the open learning movement.

The conspicuous exception to this tendency was Australia, where an integrated or mixed mode approach to external studies (by distance means) emerged within the universities. Developed within the University of New England as the 'New England integrated mode', it required academic staff to teach both on- and off-campus students. Even so, New England separated out the administration of distance students from their on-campus colleagues, the former being done by a separate administrative and evaluative unit. However, at Deakin University, which at first had a similar structure to New England, the separate administrative unit was done away with in 1982, thus integrating distance students into the mainstream teaching and administrative structures. Australian commentators came to dub this shift in perception 'convergence' (cf. the title of Smith and Kelly's 1984 book). More recently, Jevons and Guiton (1992, p. 257) have spoken of 'interlocking study modes' based on the principles that the same curriculum is taught on- and off-campus, and that the same range of courses is offered in each mode. Students can then choose which mode to study in.

Mixed mode institutions seem to offer a number of advantages. First, they have a much wider range of teaching strategies open to them. Secondly, they can, at least potentially, provide their distance students with a much wider range of courses. Most distance teaching institutions (whether single or dual mode) actually provide a rather limited range of course options, because of the high cost of investment in developing and producing course materials and the danger that, if they present too many courses, they will have too few students registered on each course to keep unit costs within reasonable bounds. In contrast, mixed mode institutions can video-tape lectures and produce lecture notes and student guides for relatively little additional cost, thus providing off-campus students with a mediated version of an on-campus course. The quality of such offerings may not match that of the purpose-designed distance courses produced by the better single mode distance teaching institutions, but they are often fit for their purpose. Thirdly, at least in those mixed mode institutions which have adopted an integrated approach, there is a genuine attempt to ensure parity of academic standards and concern for student well-being, thus overcoming one of the main objections to the mixed mode approach.

Developments in traditional institutions: towards a mixed-mode approach

Governments the world over are seeking to lower the unit costs of education. At times, this is accompanied by pressure to increase the number of places available. In such cases, total expenditure on education may rise even though the unit cost falls. At other times, cuts are accompanied by falling rolls. However, even here, the pressure is on to reduce unit costs. As unit costs fall, so traditional institutions have to seek more efficient ways of teaching students.

Distance educators have never had a monopoly on media. Educational technology of one form or another has been used in education for years, as an adjunct to face-to-face teaching. Hawkridge (1983) provided a snap-shot of its widespread use in education at the beginning of the 1980s. Technology has also been used by a wide variety of providers of open learning and flexible training. Precisely what 'open learning' is, is a matter of debate (see Rumble, 1989), but to the extent that it has been used to describe a form of technology-based training 'providing choice at the level of the individual learner' (Temple, 1991, p. 172), it has shown itself to be a cost-effective way of training staff and improving their effectiveness, and of embedding learning within organisations. At the European level, the importance of what the European Commission calls 'flexible and distance learning' for meeting the forecast shortage in skills, and the role of technology in its provision, is a major concern in the Commission (Van Den Brande, 1993).

The potential value of technology-based approaches to education and training is therefore acknowledged. By the mid-1980s Lockwood and Davies (1985, pp. 190–8), discussing ways in which the efficiency of UK universities could be improved, identified increasing class sizes, and adopting programmed-independent study, programmed learning, the use of learning packages, and distance learning. More recently a Working Party of the Committee of Scottish University Principals (CSUP) has reported. Pointing to the new emphasis on quality and performance in teaching, the perception that higher education should serve the needs of the economy more effectively, the demand that it develop and sustain closer links with industry, and the pressing need to increase efficiency and provide economies in the processes of teaching and learning (CSUP, 1992: 1–2), the report draws attention to the advantages of and potential for using technology-based teaching and learning and distance learning (pp. 13–17). While traditional methods will continue to be used, resource-based learning and self-instructional materials, at times packaged into courses suitable for distance learning, will help [traditional] institutions provide a more open system and achieve the necessary economies of scale to cope with expansion (p. 22). In particular distance and computer-based learning methods will enable them to develop 'asynchronous location-independent teaching' (p. 35). The creation of distance learning courses by consortia, and the adoption of existing distance education courses from another institution, can both complement campus teaching and enable additional courses to be offered (p. 37).

The University College of Southern Queensland approached the same outcome from a rather different direction. The College has adopted a mixed mode approach which integrates 'conventional face-to-face teaching and distance education techniques' (Taylor and White, 1991: Executive summary). As Taylor and White explain:

> the concept of mixed-mode seems to have arisen when students studying full-time in the on-campus mode found it useful to undertake a number of units of study via the distance education mode to cater for timetable clashes and/or personal preference. The success of the distance education mode . . . led to initiatives which resulted in an integration of the aforementioned modes of study. Thus instructional materials originally prepared for use in the distance education mode have been adapted to supplement and modify conventional on-campus teaching (p. 1).

The College had already developed and was offering distance courses (i.e. was a dual mode institution). This enabled it to take the decision to provide the packages to on-campus students and, at the same time, reduce by about 50 per cent the amount of face-to-face teaching content (pp. 7, 13). Not surprisingly Taylor and White indicate some resistance to the changes, given a survey that indicated that the teaching staff had a distinct preference for conventional on-campus teaching (p. 16). On the other hand, the students favoured the mixed mode approach (p. 24).

It seems clear that traditional institutions have an incentive to adopt technology-based and distance learning methods to teach on-campus students, expand their provision off-campus, and cope with general expansion both on- and off-campus. Dual mode institutions which already produce distance learning materials have an incentive to use them on-campus as well. The danger is, of course, that both dual and mixed mode systems merely 'added on' distance learning — which is why some systems fail to achieve a quality product. I would suggest, however, that mixed mode institutions are most likely to succeed, provided they adopt a strategic, holistic approach towards open learning, choosing teaching strategies to meet the needs of their students, and enabling students to move between the various modes at will.

Resources

The early literature on the economics of distance education stressed the cost-efficiency of distance education relative to traditional, classroom-based face-to-face education. In fact, as subsequent studies have shown, distance education is not necessarily cheaper than traditional education. It all depends on how the systems are designed, and how many students there are being taught. As Rumble (1992, p. 36) points out, relatively few studies compared the cost of distance education with the increasing number of part-time day and evening courses, and correspondence and distance education versions of courses, to be found in 'traditional' universities. A study by Muta and Sakamoto (1989), however, showed that the revenue costs of the Japanese University of the Air, while lower than the costs of traditional provision, were higher than the costs of both evening and correspondence programmes at private Japanese universities. Distance provision within a dual or mixed-mode context can be very cost-efficient relative to single-mode distance education. The significance of these figures is not that this will necessarily be the case everywhere, but that in looking at the economic advantages of distance education, one needs to compare the costs of single-mode distance teaching institutions with other alternatives to traditional education, including dual- and mixed-mode solutions.

Taylor and White (1991) reported on the costs of mixed-mode provision at the University College of Southern Queensland, in comparison with that of its off-campus distance and on-campus traditional face-to-face programmes. The relative costs of the different modes are influenced by 'the basic philosophy of the University College . . . that approximately equal budget allocations should be made to the teaching of all students, notwithstanding whether they are taught in an on- or off-campus mode' (p. 27), so that the teaching cost per learner of three modes is comparable (on-campus, Australian $700, distance mode off-campus $693, and mixed mode on-campus $803 — the latter assuming no cost recovery from students for the materials provided them) (Taylor and White, p. 33; Rumble, 1992, p. 37). However, the amount of face-to-face teaching in the off-campus (23.8 hours) and on-campus mixed-mode (28.2 hours) remains quite high in comparison with distance programmes in other institutions, and could probably be reduced by half to save perhaps 15 per cent of the total cost of each of these two modes. It seems clear that mixed mode provision need be no more expensive than traditional face-to-face provision, particularly if the costs of developing and producing the materials are also being off-set by their use in off-campus distance programmes.

White (1992, p. 60) has rightly pointed out that 'distance teaching, like campus-based teaching, can be as cheap or as expensive as is wished'. He also points out that campus based institutions 'will discover that if they elect to teach in the distance mode as well as face to face they will first have to overcome the hurdle of producing quality multimedia instructional materials . . . if their efforts are to be taken seriously . . . to compete will be so costly and time consuming on their part as to require a significant redistribution of resources.' (p. 59). He rightly suggests that the distance teaching universities have an existing lead in the quality of their products and, I would add, in relevant expertise, and that campus-based universities entering the field 'will have to divert a lot of resources to set up the necessary distance teaching infrastructure or they will market a product of inferior quality' (p. 60). While this is true if their purpose is to compete at a technological level, by trying to emulate the quality and breadth of materials of distance teaching institutions, many part-time students will settle for poorer quality materials coupled with a reasonably high level of face-to-face teaching. This may well be what the students want — many UK Open University students ask for increased levels of tuition (Thorpe, 1988, p. 66) — but it will, of course, tend to restrict the geographical reach of the programme. Nevertheless, provider-led estimations of quality are not the final determinant of sales. Ultimately what matters is the customer's perception.

Strategies for the future

Campus-based institutions are beginning to widen their markets by teaching off-campus. It follows that institutions teaching at a distance, whether single- or existing dual mode, are facing increased competition. Most campus-based institutions have a wide range of courses which they can turn into distance-taught versions relatively cheaply. The quality may not be very good, but in the competition for students this may not matter much. In terms of recruiting students, the institution's 'brand name' may well be more important than the quality of its distance teaching products relative to other, better, distance providers. Such competition is serious for distance teaching institutions. While many of them appear monopolistic, their problem is one of 'relative superiority' (Ohmae, 1983, p. 50). Relative superiority arises where one institution or a group of them have a dominant market share (as traditional institutions have in respect of on-campus teaching). Such institutions can afford to enter a new market (distance education), offering the incentive of low prices to would be students. They can do this because their distance education offering is often small in scale. One or two such providers are unlikely to have much impact on a monopoly supplier, but as the number of providers increases, and as they grow bigger, so they can eat into the latter's monopoly position. The latter's ability to compete is made difficult by the fact that they are not normally competing against the mixed mode institutions' primary markets (on-campus studies), but in their secondary markets (off-campus studies). They can therefore be undercut by dual mode institutions using marginal costing as a basis for pricing (p. 52). While there are various strategic options open to distance education institutions to counter this threat (see Rumble, 1992, pp. 41–3), apart from competing on quality one of the more fruitful counters would be to gain the advantages of dual mode institutions by taking over or setting up their own campus-based operations, and then by offering real customer choice in the form of mixed mode provision.

Pascale (1991, p. 11), commenting on Peters and Waterman's book, made the point that 'nothing fails like success . . . great strengths are inevitably the root of weakness. . . . The golden adage "Stick to your knitting" becomes an epitaph. This is because our fixation on "what is" obscures that other aggravating necessity of worrying about "what isn't" and "what might be"'. Of the forty three excellent companies which Peters and Waterman identified in 1982 as having demonstrated at least twenty years of superiority over their competitors, financially and as industry leaders in innovation and adaptability, two-thirds had slipped from the pinnacle only five years later (Pascale, 1991, p. 16).

The distance teaching universities have been a remarkable success. But if one defines the business one is in as 'education' rather than 'distance education' or 'traditional education', then a rather different perspective emerges, in which one uses the methods of both modes to meet the needs of their learners. There is little doubt that the world of education is changing. The methods perfected by distance educators are now being used in other settings — in flexible and open learning, and within the campus, to help cope with expansion, and as a means of meeting the needs of more and more varied customer bases. The synergy arising from a mixed mode approach seems obvious. As the differences between face-to-face and distance education providers becomes less obvious, it becomes more attractive to contemplate the merger of the modes, to their mutual benefit. The age of the single mode institution (and indeed of the dual mode one) may well be coming to an end.

References

Committee of Scottish University Principals (1992) *Teaching and Learning in an Expanding Higher Education System*, Edinburgh: CSUP.

Daniel, J. S. and Smith, W. A. S. (1979) 'Opening open universities: the Canadian experience'. *Canadian Journal of Higher Education*, 9 (2) pp. 63–74.

Hall, J. W. (1991) *Access Through Innovation. New Colleges for New Students*, New York: American Council for Education and Macmillan Publishing Co.

Hawkridge, G. (1983) *New Information Technology in Education*, London: Croom Helm.

Holmberg, B. (1960) 'On the methods of teaching by correspondence', in Lunds universitets årsskrift, N.F. Avd., 1 Bd. 54 Nr 2, Lund: Gleerup.

Jevons, F. and Guiton, P. (1992) 'Distance education and internal studies: Interlocking study modes', in Ortner, G., Graff, K. and Wilmersdoerfer, H. (eds.) (1992) *Distance Education as Two-way Communication. Essays in Honour of Börje Holmberg*. Frankfurt am Main: Peter Lang.

Keegan, D. (1990) Foundations of distance education, 2nd edn., London, Routledge.

Lockwood, G. and Davies, J. (1985) *Universities: The Management Challenge*, London: SRHE and NFER-Nelson.

Muta, H. and Sakamoto, T. (1989) 'The economics of the University of the Air of Japan revisited'. *Higher Education*, 18 (5) pp. 585–611.

Ohmae, K. (1983) *The Mind of the Strategist. Business Planning for Competitive Advantage*, Harmondsworth: Penguin Books.

Pascale, R. (1991) *Managing on the Edge. How Successful Companies Use Conflict to Stay Ahead*, London: Penguin.

Perry, W. (1976) *Open University. A Personal Account by the First Vice-Chancellor*, Milton Keynes: Open University Press.

Peters, O. (1973) *Die didaktische Struktur des Fernunterrichtsm Untersuchungen zu einer industrializierten Form des Lehrens und Lernens*, Weinheim: Beltz.

Peters, T. J. and Waterman, R. H. (1982) *In Search of Excellence. Lessons from America's Best-run Companies*, New York: Harper and Row.

Rumble, G. (1988) 'Animadversions upon the concept of distance education as a discipline', *Journal of Distance Education*, 3 (1) pp. 39–56.

Rumble, G. (1989) '"Open learning", "distance learning", and the misuse of language'. *Open Learning*, 4 (2) pp. 28–36.

Rumble, G. (1992) 'The competitive vulnerability of distance teaching universities'. *Open Learning*, 7 (2) pp. 31–45.

Siaciwena, R. M. C. (1988) 'The external degree programme at the University of Zambia'. *Prospects*, 18 (2) pp. 199–206.

Singh, B. (1979) 'Distance education in developing countries — with special reference to India', in Hakemulder, J. R. (ed.) (1981) *Distance Education for Development*. Bonn: German Foundation for International Development.

Smith, P. and Kelly, M. (1984) *Distance Education and the Mainstream: Convergence in Education*, London: Croom Helm.

Snowden, B. L. and Daniel, J. S. (1980) 'The economics and management of small post-secondary distance education systems'. *Distance Education*, 1 (1) pp. 68–91.

Swinerton, E. N. and Hogan, T. P. (1981) 'A tested budget model for a non-traditional degree program'. Madison, Wisconsin: University of Wisconsin. Mimeo.

Taylor, J. C. and White, V. (1991) *The Evaluation of the Cost Effectiveness of Multi-Media Mixed-mode Teaching and Learning*, Canberra: Australian Government Publishing Service.

Temple, H. (1991) *Open Learning in Industry*, London: Longman.

Thorpe, M. (1988) *Evaluating Open and Distance Learning*, London: Longman.

Van Den Brande, L. (1993) *Flexible and Distance Learning*, Chichester: John Wiley.

White, V. (1992) 'Responses to Greville Rumble's article "The competitive vulnerability of distance teaching universities"'. *Open Learning*, 7 (3) pp. 59–60.

2 Embedding open learning in higher education

Roger Lewis

Abstract

Openness in learning has two aspects: first, access; secondly, openness once the student is within the learning programme. Both are important: if they are brought together, all students, on- and off-campus, can be provided for. Higher Education (HE) has until recently used open learning only to increase access. It now shows signs of turning to the second aspect, as a means of responding to current challenges. The chapter explores how far HE has progressed, and the issues that still need tackling if the benefits of open learning are to be fully realised.[1]

HE: the challenges

HE currently faces a range of challenges in its external environment. It is expected:

— to widen access
— to handle increased student numbers recruited in the late 80s/early 90s[2]
— to create an environment for the increasingly diverse student body
— to maintain quality
— to ensure students develop transferable skills, including capacities needed for effectiveness in employment.

And to achieve all this within a reduction of per capita funding.

These pressures combine to call into question current ways of organising the teaching and learning environment.

Open learning in HE to date

Until recently, open learning has been perceived by HE as only marginally useful. The 'conventional' universities[3] have followed the Open University in defining 'open learning' largely in terms of access. Thus open learning is seen as relevant only to certain segments of the population, those unable to attend 'conventional' provision because they are mature, or in work or disadvantaged. This perception has usually led to the delivery of an existing curriculum by 'new' means — learning packages supported by telephone and postal contact, occasional face-to-face classes and (in some recent cases) computer conferencing. These methods are 'new' in that they are not generally used within the institutions' mainstream delivery. The resulting schemes, largely distance learning in nature, are designed and run by enthusiastic staff in small stand-alone units, some of which were set up by government funding in the mid 1980s, with the express intention that they should be self-sufficient.

A wider definition

But to its proponents, open learning has always meant more than opening up existing curricula to new student groups. It has also involved opening up the curriculum once learners have gained access. Not only can time, place and pace be opened, but also method, content, assessment and other aspects of the curriculum and its delivery. Not only to new student groups, but also to mainstream students. And all this with the aim of developing more confident, competent learners, able to achieve their objectives with increasing freedom and independence (Lewis and Spencer, 1986).

In Further Education (FE) attempts were made systematically in the 1980s to realise this broader vision. Workshops such as that at Bradford (Sands, 1984) showed the possibility of converting all delivery within a curriculum area to a flexible or open basis. The Further Education Unit published a number of resources advising on how openness might be 'embedded' across departmental boundaries (Further Education Unit, 1983, 1984 and 1987).

The broader definition makes it much easier to see how open learning can be used to widen the choices of *existing* students (full or part time) on *existing* courses, thereby helping HE to respond to the challenges outlined at the start of this chapter.

Contribution of open learning to the challenges

Outside the Open University, open learning has been used at the edges of HE. Yet we know from other sectors, such as industrial training, that — if properly implemented — it can be used to achieve strategic objectives. The challenges to education and training providers are set out in column one of Table 2.1; they correspond to the HE challenges listed earlier. Notes on the potential contribution of open learning are in column two. Two points should be emphasised. First, the word 'contribution': open learning is not a panacea. Secondly, the phrase 'if properly implemented': open learning will make its contribution only if it is used appropriately and is adequately resourced.

In HE progress has to date been made mainly in the first area: the widening of access. There are now signs, however, of a growing awareness of the potential of open learning as a response to the other priorities. Some of these signs are set out below.

Some new universities have mission statements stressing the role of open learning (or associated strategies, such as 'student-centred

Table 2.1 The potential contribution of open learning

Challenge	OL's potential contribution
Widen access	OL offers portable learning resources, extending the reach of conventional provision
Large numbers	OL has evolved systems and structures to handle large numbers of dispersed learners
Respond to students from a variety of backgrounds	OL focuses on individuals' circumstances and creates flexibility e.g. on where, when and how they learn
Quality	The provision of a public package enables programme content to be inspected
Transferable skills	OL schemes develop independence and self-organisation
Deliver learning cost effectively	Growing evidence exists of the cost effectiveness of OL as a delivery method (Coopers and Lybrand/Open University 1990).[4]

learning' or 'resource-based learning') in responding to the external challenges in the environment. The University of Humberside strategic plan (1992–3), for example, highlights a commitment to become 'a mass higher education university committed to teaching and learning'. To achieve this it plans, amongst other objectives, to build more flexible delivery structures and to introduce new learning strategies. There is thus an explicit link between mission and institutional arrangements for teaching and learning. Humberside aims to switch 'the balance of student activity . . . from formal teaching towards a more supported student-centered approach'. Thames Valley University has a similar mission: to 'move systematically towards resource-based teaching and learning'.

Recent years have seen an increase in learning material production in HE. Several universities have set up open learning materials production units. Sunderland, for example, is now selling materials in mathematics, chemistry and learning skills.

The Open Learning Foundation (OLF) was established in the late 1980s by around twenty of the then polytechnics. The main thrust of the OLF was, and remains, the collaborative development and production of learning materials, for use in member institutions. As well as the materials themselves, a great deal of writing, editorial and project management expertise has been built up in member universities across England and Wales. The OLF is now extending its role into implementation, consultancy and research.

Interest is also apparent in acquiring open learning materials from other sources — most obviously the UK Open University, but also universities in other countries with their own materials, with whom UK institutions are increasingly in contact.

For sound practical reasons, most OLF materials are in the form of print. Experimentation in the application of newer media to learning has also taken place, facilitated by the Computers in Teaching Initiative (CTI) and the Teaching and Learning Technology Programme (TLTP). A useful summary of commissioned projects can be found in the MacFarlane Report (CSUP, 1992). The intention of both programmes is to achieve economy of scale: materials, developed by HE consortia, will first be embedded in member institutions and then made available widely throughout the HE system.

What has yet to be done?

Thus there are definite signs that HE is taking open learning and related developments seriously. Research commissioned by the

OLF in 1993 concluded that the argument for open learning, at least within its member institutions, has been won: the issue is how to turn policy into action. Changes in teaching and learning on any significant scale have far-reaching implications for:

— buildings and space
— equipment (e.g. workstations, desktop publishing facilities)
— learning materials (e.g. open learning resources, software)
— systems (e.g. IT networks)
— structures (e.g. for proposing and validating courses)
— staff roles and responsibilities.

All this requires the reallocation of existing resources — time, space, imagination, funding — to create a new learning environment.

Yet institutional managers currently lack successful HE models and experience to draw on. They are venturing into unknown territory. The rest of this chapter looks at just some of the key areas that need to be addressed: curriculum development, learning materials, learning locations, extended use of new technology, staffing, the students themselves, and a programme of underpinning research.

Curriculum development

Changes are already underway to develop a curriculum structure responsive to learner choice. These include:

— short, pick-and-mix 'modules' or 'units'
— explicit learning outcomes and assessment methods, to enable learners to inspect the curriculum in advance
— systems that enable students to follow individualised routes and programmes

Learning materials

Specially-designed learning materials are often necessary if learners are to be given choices over how they learn. Such materials are indeed the most obvious sign of the use of open learning. Current production activity has been summarised earlier. The *existence* of materials is, however, very different from their *use*. Of all education and training sectors, HE is the least willing to use 'other peoples' materials'. Traditions of academic freedom, and the independence of the individual lecturer in his or her own classroom, run counter to sharing materials — even when these have been generated by colleagues.

According to the MacFarlane Report the learning environment of the future will be richly supplied with supportive learning materials in a wide variety of media, originated by many producers and used flexibly by students: at home, at work, from a distance and in large campus-based resource centres. These materials will enable students with differing learning styles and preferences to choose their own methods of learning. With more flexible delivery methods, the current pressure on resources — characterised by situations when everyone needs to use the same resource at the same time — will be lessened.

To realise this vision, MacFarlane argues that materials will have to be shared nationally, to achieve the twin benefits of quality and cost-effectiveness. Much attention will have to be paid to achieve this, as the auguries from OLF and TLTP experience do not seem to be immediately encouraging.[5]

Learning locations

For conventional universities, learning has been exclusively campus-based. We are now seeing a major change. The places in which learning has to be supported are growing increasingly diverse, including not only the immediate campus, but also:

— other sites of the same institution (which may be widely separated)
— the campuses of associated UK institutions (such as franchised colleges)
— the campuses of European and international partners
— the workplace (via partnerships with employers)
— the home.

Greville Rumble's chapter elsewhere in this book explores the implications of this.

Extended use of new technology

Information technology will increasingly underpin the learning environment. It will be used:

— to produce learning resources
— to enable students to access resources and information
— to provide assessment and feedback, both formally for large numbers of students and informally for individuals wishing to test themselves
— to sustain communication between geographically-distant students and tutors, as in computer-mediated conferencing

— to manage the learning process, maintaining records of learner progress and routes through the curriculum
— ultimately, to enable students to manage their own learning directly.

Staffing

It is a commonplace these days that its staff are an organisation's most important asset. They are usually also its most expensive resource. Both statements are true of HE.

If open learning is to succeed, the staff involved must fully support it. In the end, the individual 'supporter' mediating between package, system and learner, makes or breaks the learning method. Yet there is plenty of anecdotal evidence to suggest that academic staff in conventional universities are at best suspicious of open learning and at worst downright hostile. The reluctance to use 'other people's materials' was mentioned earlier. Additionally, staff question the motives behind the introduction of new learning methods: cost-cutting? the thin end of the redundancy wedge? impoverishment of the student's experience? The situation is additionally complicated by the creation of new roles and posts such as teaching assistant, learning advisor and learning centre administrator.

Open learning requires that areas traditionally under the custodianship of academics be made explicit, so that students are in a position to exercise choice for themselves. These include the content of the curriculum, and how it is learned and assessed: the 'mysteries' of HE. This both challenges and changes the role of the HE lecturer.

Thus a major change of attitude is likely to be necessary in most institutions — part of a wider cultural change. The benefits of changed learning methods need to be communicated. These include:

— more specialised and professional roles for some academics
— teamworking with other colleagues
— a reawakening of enthusiasm for teaching, through trying out new methods
— the opportunity to relate to students as individuals.

It will not be enough for managers to *require* staff to follow their lead. As Clark points out, one aspect of academic freedom is collective resistance to demands perceived as coercive: 'many centrally-announced reforms leave no lasting deposit because internal constituencies are not effectively summoned to support them. When a system is bottom-heavy, groups at the grass-roots are key participants in implementing policies and reforms' (Clark, 1983).

People management in HE traditionally has a low profile. The Fender Report stresses the need for human resource managers to act as '"architects" of a new system' rather than '"clerks of works" operating in a more or less purely administrative mode' (CVCP, 1993). This will require a more proactive and analytical approach to performance management. At the moment 'staff development' is often seen as a cure-all, yet many problems arise from sources other than the capability of individuals — such as unclear job descriptions, and lack of feedback on performance. The Employment Department's Investors in People initiative offers institutions a ready-made framework for reviewing their whole human relations strategy. Several of the new universities plan to achieve Investor in People status.

The students

We need to remember that the biggest under-used resource in the system is the student. Activating this resource is vital, both for educational reasons and to achieve cost-effectiveness.

Experience even in well-run and established open learning schemes such as the Open University, suggests that students are often resistant to the idea of learning by 'new' methods. They seem instinctively to prefer to be 'taught' — even though they may not enjoy the process! The situation is more complicated when open learning is introduced into on-campus learning, with 18-year-old clients, in an environment known to be constrained by resources.

The MacFarlane Report lists support students may need if they are to exercise greater responsibility for their own learning. This includes an initial diagnostic process and structured induction to 'new' methods such as peer learning, self-assessment and the uses of technology. The role model their tutors set is also critical — hence the emphasis on this earlier in the chapter.

Students should also have a say in the design and operation of the learning environment. Institutions need to be proactive in encouraging students to give their views, and in setting up systems to collect user feedback.

Underpinning research

MacFarlane points out that much underpinning research is needed, to find out more about key issues in the new learning environment. High on the agenda is the development of new 'cost models for different kinds of teaching support, and a student-support cost model which takes into account the costs of the different types of support environment through which a student progresses' (CSUP, 1992).

Conclusion

The above agenda is demanding. To some, it may seem futuristic. But each component is in place, at least embryonically, somewhere — though scattered across institutions rather than all present in any one university. For the changes are already happening, though often by stealth, piecemeal, unplanned and unacknowledged. The challenge is to integrate each detail into a coherent new system to support learning. This is inevitably a medium to long-term commitment.

The concept of shifts along a continuum may help. MacFarlane uses the term 'shift' to emphasise progression along a spectrum of teaching/learning support, ranging from simply imparting information at one end to 'comprehensively managing the complete learning support process at the other end' (CSUP, 1992). A more detailed breakdown of the parameters on which choice may be progressively given can be found in *What is Open Learning?* (Lewis and Spencer, 1986).

This is how the process could work on one dimension: changes in the use of learning materials by academic staff.

Lecturer uses own handouts
↓
Team of lecturers compiles a 'reader' to support lecture provision
↓
Team of lecturers selects a text book to complement the reader, produces a study guide and reduces lecture provision
↓
Lecturers adapt and use open learning materials produced by the OLF, within a new pattern of delivery.

Finally, although this chapter has discussed change at the institutional level, we must not forget that each individual teacher can go through a similar process within their own area of responsibility.

References

Clark, B. R. (1983) *The Higher Education System*, University of California Press, Berkeley. Quoted in Becher, T., *Freedom and Accountability* in 'Professional Curricula' a chapter in Becher, T. (ed) (1994) *Governments and Professional*

Education, Society for Research into Higher Education (SRHE) and Open University Press.

Committee of Scottish University Principals (CSUP) (1992) *Teaching and Learning in an Expanding Higher Education System*, Edinburgh, CSUP. This is known as The MacFarlane Report, after its chairman, Alistair MacFarlane.

Committee of Vice-Chancellors and Principals (CVCP) (1993) *Promoting People: A Strategic Framework for the Management and Development of Staff in UK Universities*, London, CVCP, January. This is known as The Fender Report, after its Chairman, Brian Fender.

Coopers and Lybrand/Open University (1990) *A Report into the Relative Costs of Open Learning*, Milton Keynes, Open University.

Further Education Unit (1983) *Flexible Learning Opportunities*, London, Further Education Unit. Birch, D. W. and Latcham, J. (1984) *Flexible Learning in Action*, London, Further Education Unit. Lewis, R. and Pates, A. (1987) *Learning Workshops*, London, Further Education Unit.

Humberside, University of (1993) Strategic Plan, Vice Chancellors Office, September.

Lewis, R. and Spencer, D. (1986) *What is Open Learning?*, Open Learning Guide 4, London, National Council for Educational Technology.

Open Learning Foundation (OLF) (1993) Unpublished consultancy report.

Sands, T. (1984) 'The Bradford mathematics workshop' in Lewis, R. (ed) *Open Learning in Action*, London, National Council for Educational Technology, pp. 138–153.

Thames Valley University, oral communication with Director.

Notes

1. I should like to thank the following for their help with an earlier version of this chapter: Robert Adams, Richard Baker, Neil Bolton, Derek Crothall, Richard Freeman, Bob Hunter, Ian McNay, Margaret Noble, Lyn Shipway, Doug Spencer, Malcolm Tight and Lorna Unwin.

2. Full-time student numbers, and total student numbers both grew by the same proportion between 1981 and 1991: 52 per cent. Source: Department for Education, Statistical Bulletin 17/93, June 1993.

3. The Open University and 'open' universities in other countries were created specifically to design and deliver 'open' programmes. The term 'conventional universities' refers to all other universities — whether these are 'old' or 'new'.

4. Coopers and Lybrand/Open University is a survey of fifty companies' use of open learning, with special attention to questions of cost effectiveness. Savings of 30–50 per cent in delivery time (with similar cost savings) were common. The MacFarlane Report (CSUP, 1992) quotes similar findings, but points out that more research is needed in HE. Generally, significant numbers are needed to justify the initial investment; ironically, as pointed out earlier, open learning has often been used for small numbers in HE.

5. There are several reasons for this: the length of time taken by development, problems with equipment and software compatibility, reluctance of staff to use material they have not themselves developed. *Beyond Lectures*, The Report of the Information Systems Committee Courseware Development Working Party, UFC Information Systems Committee, July 1992 stresses the additional need for integration into the curriculum: 'the potential . . . benefits cannot be achieved unless an appropriate organisational infrastructure is in place'.

3 Credit accumulation and transfer: towards an open system

Peter Wilson

Introduction

This chapter attempts to locate the recent development of proposals for a comprehensive framework for credit accumulation and transfer (CAT) within a broader consideration of how CAT can lead to the development of more open systems of qualifications and curriculum organisation in post-school education and training.

The chapter refers explicitly to the work of the Further Education Unit (FEU) in developing the specifications for a national credit framework. It goes on to imagine how a CAT system might operate within this framework, and how this system embodies principles of 'openness' that could be more widely applied across the post-school sector in the future. Indeed, although the paper focuses on post-16 education and training, the principles explored are not age-related and may equally be applicable to the school sector.

The chapter refers in some detail to the work of Open College Networks (OCNs). This is because OCNs offer the most widespread working examples currently available of accreditation bodies working within the specifications of the national credit framework. It should be noted that many other possible futures can be imagined for the development of a CAT system. However, the principles of OCN accreditation offer fertile ground for further investigation and development if a future CAT system is to be as

flexible and accessible as it will need to be in order to be called a
genuinely Open System.

An open system

The specifications of the credit framework are intended to support
an Open System of CAT. It is worth spending a few moments
here to elaborate on this concept of an Open System, since it is
central to the purpose of the CAT system which is envisaged by
those involved in the development of the credit framework.

Theories of Open Systems derive from within the general
domain of Systems Theory developed in the 1950s and 1960s
(Pugh, 1990). More recently, Open Systems theory has been
applied in the context of organisational management to produce
systems models that address the emerging context within which
commercial organisations seek to develop their responsiveness to
the rapidly changing demands of technologically advanced markets
for their goods and services (Peters, 1987).

The basic conceptual underpinning of an Open System is
that it should be based on the minimum number of critical
specifications that will enable it to function with integrity. The
corollary of this concept is that such a system will, therefore, be
open to the maximum number of potential users.

Open Systems are, therefore, designed to permit the highest
level of flexibility and the widest possible access that is consistent
with the effective operation of this system. The rationale for
commercial organisations developing this level of flexibility and
accessibility is that, in order to maximise market penetration,
the organisation has to be able to respond quickly to the variety
of different demands that clients or customers make on the
organisations.

Open systems in the context of post-16 education and training

We can recognise in the above commercial rationale for an Open
System some of the elements of the post-16 curriculum (flexibility,
accessibility, responsiveness) that are present within many of the
major curriculum and qualifications reform initiatives of recent
years.

It may be worth identifying some of the specific features of this
post-16 landscape in order to establish more clearly the relevance

of the concept of an Open System to some key developments in the sector:

> The key feature of the FE system is its diversity.
> (Stubbs, 1993)

> We want local people to make local decisions about local issues.
> (Dawes, 1990)

> We want to knock down barriers. We want more choice. We want wider opportunities.
> (Major, 1991)

> We want colleges to take greater responsibility for their own provision, in order to respond to the wide variety of needs in the communities they serve.
> (Patten, 1992)

To summarise, the greater the diversity of need or demand in the post-16 sector, the more appropriate Open Systems theory becomes in constructing an organisational model of the post-16 curriculum which will enable users of the system to respond to these demands. This paper proceeds on the assumption that the environment within which post-16 institutions will operate in the foreseeable future will become more, rather than less, diverse. Indeed, we may suppose that one of the reasons why the credit framework proposals have produced such a positive and enthusiastic response among colleges and other post-16 institutions is that this need for a system which responds to diversity is well understood by those in the field (FEU, 1992, 1993).

An open system of CAT

If we examine some of the key features of the credit framework within this context of diversity, we can begin to see how this vision of a future Open System of CAT will support greater flexibility and wider accessibility within the post-16 sector:

A. Comprehensiveness

One of the key specifications of the credit framework is that it is potentially able to encompass all achievements in learning. In other words no distinctions are made within the credit framework between particular types of achievement. If a user of the CAT system is able to conform with, or apply the specifications of, the credit framework — i.e. to represent learning achievements in coherent sets of outcomes, clustered in units to which a credit value can be ascribed and the achievements of learners can be verified for the award of credit — then those achievements can be brought within the scope of the credit framework.

Units within the credit framework are, therefore, very flexible. They are not classified as 'vocational', 'academic', 'recreational', 'optional', 'core', 'applied', 'theoretical' or in any other way that may restrict their flexibility. This feature also means that the credit framework permits the maximum level of accessibility, since its critical specifications are not classified so as to exclude any potential user.

B.   Access to the system

Like other Open Systems, the CAT system to be supported by the credit framework, is also potentially open to all users. Just as the specifications eschew any kind of classification of achievement, so they also make no distinctions between the types of users of the framework. An Open System of CAT will be technically disinterested in who develops units, what kind of institution seeks to use the system or what kind of learner seeks to earn credit within it.

Again, we can see how the vision of an Open System of CAT can serve the needs of a wide range of institutions, curriculum offers and learners within the post-16 sector. Provided a user is able to demonstrate that the credit framework specifications are being applied with integrity, and that learner achievements are open to verification, the CAT system places no restrictions upon who may, or may not, use the credit framework specifications as a device for organising the post-16 curriculum and measuring the achievements of learners within it.

C.   Requisite variety

We have already identified the feature of the 'minimum specifications' of the credit framework as a critical feature of an Open System of CAT. We also need to focus here on a further feature of Open Systems theory — that of 'requisite variety'. This feature states simply that, in a diverse environment, organisations must have a level of flexibility that enables them to respond to diversity without compromising the effectiveness of the organisation itself. Too little flexibility will mean the system is unable to respond to demand; too much will threaten the ability of the organisation to function. This is the principle of 'requisite variety' (Beer, 1974).

One of the fears expressed about Open Systems developments (not just in post-16 education and training) is that they err too far on the side of flexibility and threaten to compromise the integrity of the system. So, for example, it could be argued that the openness and flexibility of the credit framework specifications might lead to the disintegration of qualifications or learning programmes into an anarchy of incoherent and unconnected units of little benefit to either providers or learners.

Indeed we may draw here on some of the lessons from theories of chaos and complexity which illustrate consistently, in a variety of contexts, the tendency of any system to develop from within itself rules of combination, organisation and internal control that will construct order and coherence to the extent that users of the system demand it. The evidence from other applications of Open Systems theory suggests this will not happen (Peters, 1987).

D. Interaction with other systems

We should also note of course that a CAT system will exist alongside other kinds of system outside the credit framework that will tend to impose their own rules of coherence that will impact upon an Open System of CAT. Indeed, we should see the creation and maintenance of this ability of other systems to interact with the CAT system as a necessary specification of the credit framework itself.

In this context the stability of the credit framework will enable rules of credit accumulation, credit transfer, recognition and progression within the CAT system to be developed that may all be influenced by, for example:

 (i) the identification of national standards represented through particular outcomes
 (ii) the organisation of unit-based qualifications
 (iii) the requirements of professional bodies for particular kinds of achievement to be demonstrated
 (iv) the nature of requirements for progression within the post-16 sector
 (v) the sequencing of materials and texts based on the credit framework specifications
 (vi) the premium placed on particular kinds of achievements by funding agencies.

In this context an Open System of CAT can be characterised as an essentially 'weak force' which, because it seeks to be comprehensive in scope, is necessarily open to the different influences of other systems with which it may come into contact. Because the specifications of the credit framework are being developed explicitly to take account of these other systems, we should not worry too much about the potential of the credit framework proposals to bring about the disintegration of the post-16 curriculum as we know it! Perhaps we should end this section with a quotation from an early exponent of chaos theory:

> Any minor world that breaks apart falls together again
> (Fagen and Becker, 1974)

A different kind of system

As the above examples illustrate, the proposals for an Open System of CAT constitute a different kind of development in the post-16 sector. We should note here that the credit framework is not:

    a new qualification
    a new curriculum model
    a new funding mechanism
    a new agency for development.

In short the credit framework is intended to underpin a process of change and development in post-16 education and training that is qualitatively different from those to which institutions and practitioners in the post-16 sector have become accustomed over the past few years. This process of developing an Open System of CAT is:

  (i)   organic rather than mechanistic
 (ii)   dependent on subscription rather than prescription
(iii)   bottom up rather than top down
 (iv)   long term rather than short term
  (v)   localised rather than centralised.

Again, we should emphasise the appropriacy of this form of development to both the concept of an Open System, and to the particular features of the post-16 curriculum which such a system is intended to support. The development of the baseline specifications of the credit framework illustrates this process and is already beginning to create an organisational sub-culture among those individuals and institutions involved in credit framework developments which will support an Open System of CAT (Wilson, 1993a).

Key features of the credit framework

A. The unit

A unit within the credit framework is defined as:

a coherent and explicit set of outcomes (FEU, 1992).

This apparently simple definition, which draws explicitly on the characteristics of the NVQ framework, meets the requirement of 'minimum critical specification' necessary to the functioning of an Open CAT System. The definition of the unit displays the following characteristics:

(i) it is detached from any reference to delivery or curriculum organisation
(ii) it has no 'size' referents, whether based on time or number of outcomes
(iii) it has no particular shape.

These specifications mean that the Unit can be used as the comprehensive 'atom' of a CAT system (with learning outcomes as its 'particles'). It is the basic building block of the system, though we should use 'building block' in its genetic rather than its mechanical sense in order to capture the real nature of the Unit.

If the above seems to define the unit in such a way as to make it too esoteric a concept to be useful in a CAT system, this is partly true. However, we must remember that the credit framework specifications relate not just to the Unit but also to credit and level. It is the *combination* of these critical specifications which provides the stability to the framework — the subtraction of any one will render the framework incapable of supporting a CAT system.

B. The credit

Of all the features of the credit framework, it is the credit itself which is perhaps the most 'slippery' of concepts. In *A Basis for Credit?*:

a credit is awarded for those outcomes which a learner,
on average, might reasonably be expected to achieve in a
notional 30 hours of learning.

The 'notional time' basis of the credit has been the source of some criticism and a great deal of misunderstanding. (Interestingly though, it is proving unproblematic in practice). Some of these criticisms have been addressed elsewhere (Wilson, 1993). Nevertheless, three key features of the credit are worth emphasising here:

  (i) 'notional time' is not used as approximation of 'real time', but as an easily-shared device for ascribing value to learner achievements that is both flexible and comprehensive
 (ii) the definition of the credit contains within itself a combination of both notional time and learner achievement
(iii) the credit provides a device for valuing the outcomes of learning which is derived from a shared understanding of the process of learning.

If we bring these characteristics together we can see that, far from tying learner achievement in to a 'time-serving' model of learning, it is the credit which enables this achievement to be freed from the constraints of time. In other words the credit functions as a kind of 'universal joint' between systems of organising and delivering the post-16 curriculum and systems of valuing learner achievement.

The insertion of 'the credit' into the relationship between these two kinds of system permits a rational but indirect relationship to be developed between them. We must remember that 'notional time' is not applied *directly* to the value of units within the credit framework. 'Notional time' is used to develop the specifications of the credit; the credit is used to give value to a unit. Because the credit contains within itself both time and outcome-based referents it is able to function as a connecting device between time-based and outcome-based systems without requiring that the critical features of one system are imported into the other.

If this seems an unnecessarily complex view of the credit, perhaps its critical features are best expressed more practically:

> The insertion of the concept of credit into the system
> of post-16 education and training enables measures
> of achievement to be developed that are free from the
> constraints of particular processes of learning, and processes
> of learning to be developed that are free from the constraints
> of particular kinds of achievement.

Thus we can see how the specification of the credit serves the needs of an Open System of CAT to be flexible, accessible and comprehensive in scope.

C. Level

It has taken some time to develop a set of descriptors for at least the lower levels of the credit framework (Wilson, 1993). In themselves these level descriptors represent a deliberate fusing of both theoretical and practical concepts of level in education and training. They are intended to be functional devices, rather than precise definitions. We can identify four key functions of these level descriptors:

 (i) to provide stability to the credit framework by giving it horizontal axes
 (ii) to offer users of the framework a model of progression within which to provide learning opportunities
 (iii) to permit rules of recognition and combination to be developed that enhance access and progression for learners
 (iv) to permit the flexible operation of an Open System of credit accumulation and transfer.

A great deal of the recent discussion about levels in post-16 education and training has focused on the concept of equivalence. In other words, level has been used to identify (in theory at least) qualifications and learning programmes that are supposed to have equivalent value (e.g. 'An Advanced GNVQ equals two "A" Levels'). We should note that the determination of equivalence between qualifications and learning programmes is not a function of levels within the credit framework, though the framework itself does offer a rational means of comparison between qualifications.

Within the credit framework, in order to meet the functional needs outlined above, levels have one critical characteristic: **levels are applied to units.**

This specification means that learning programmes and qualifications may be made up of units at different levels. This simple device means that, although the credit framework will assist those who seek to compare different post-16 awards with each other, the functions of a CAT system are capable of being supported without reference to the level of a particular qualification. This straightforward specification not only stimulates far greater flexibility in the design of qualifications and learning programmes, it also dissolves problems of 'equivalence' by permitting far more flexible rules of combination and progression to be developed which can function effectively without requiring that one particular award is precisely equal to another.

Of course a CAT system is very interested indeed in the concept of equivalence. Indeed the whole system of credit transfer will depend upon it. We should remind ourselves, however, that it is the credit value of units within the credit framework that will support this concept of equivalence in a CAT system, not the level of a particular qualification.

These three specifications of unit, credit and level are developed
further in other papers (Wilson, 1993). Nevertheless, by underlining some of the key features of the credit framework in this way,
I hope that the primary purpose of the framework — to support
an Open System of credit accumulation and transfer — begins to
be apparent. It is the logic of this future CAT system that must
determine the nature of the credit framework that is to support it.
How might this transition from credit framework to CAT system
be managed?

From credit value to credit

In practice of course, this neat conceptual distinction between
framework and system becomes blurred. As more institutions
become involved in credit-based developments, it becomes clear
that the 'baseline technology' of the credit framework is capable
of supporting a wide range of innovations. So for example,
achievements are organised into Units; unitisation stimulates
more flexible approaches to delivery; the credit framework is
used to allocate resources to support these flexible approaches.

In all these developments, the credit is used as an instrument
to ascribe a measure of value to the curriculum. The critical leap
to a CAT system has yet to be made. This critical leap is embodied
in the act of giving value not just to the curriculum, but directly
to the achievements of learners. In other words a CAT system has
as its central purpose the awarding of credit to learners. We may
summarise this distinction by referring to the application of the
specifications of the credit framework to the curriculum as 'the
ascribing of credit value' and the operational purpose of a CAT
system as 'the awarding of credit to learners'.

So the critical leap from credit framework to CAT system
arises at the point of establishing a mechanism for awarding credit
to learners. As the development of a credit framework continues
the necessity to develop such a mechanism becomes critical. How
might this credit-awarding process be developed in a way that is
consistent with the principles of an Open System?

The open college network model

Those involved in development of an Open System of CAT
based on the specifications of the credit framework outlined by
the FEU are fortunate in being able to draw on functioning
models of credit-awarding bodies in the post-16 sector offered

by Open College Networks (OCNs). These provide some useful examples of answers to the question of how applicable might the experiences of OCNs be to the comprehensive intention of an Open CAT system to enable all learners to receive credit for their achievements in learning?

Learning from the periphery

In *Understanding Organisations* Charles Handy (1985) characterises the effective learning organisation as one which is able to learn most from what he refers to as 'the periphery' of the organisation. In other words, the most important lessons for any organisation to learn are those which are received and reported by those people who represent the organisation in its contact with others. Information from the margins of the organisation about how its goods and/or services are received by its clients or customers is information critical to the ongoing development and well being of the organisation itself.

If we regard the system of post-16 education and training as an organisation, then the experience of OCNs in operating at the margins of the organisation can feed important information into the heart of the system which can have an important influence on the future development of the organisation itself. Indeed, the historical commitment of OCNs to the same principles of accessibility, flexibility and quality now embraced (in principle) by post-16 education and training itself, makes their experiences of particular value to the whole sector. How far do these experiences meet the needs of an Open System of CAT?

Key features of OCNs

This is not the place to describe fully the OCN approach to awarding credit (see Mager, 1991). The purpose of this following section is to highlight some of the organisational characteristics of OCNs and to show how these characteristics might support the development of an Open System of CAT.

(i) Networking

In an Open System, no unnecessary restrictions are placed on the access of users to the system. OCNs embody this principle in their own structures. No type of provider is excluded from membership of an OCN. No particular type of achievement lies outside the scope of OCN accreditation (though some exists at a different level). The principles and practices of accreditation have been developed in order to provide the maximum possible access to the system of awarding credit.

(ii) Variety

Open Systems thrive on variety. It is the accessibility of an Open System which provides its essential motor of change and development. Providing users adhere to the minimum critical specifications that permit the system to function, no restrictions are made on how the user makes use of these specifications. The cross-sectoral membership of OCNs and their explicit intention to offer their services to learners who are themselves 'at the periphery' of more formal qualifications systems creates an ongoing impetus of new demands on the procedures for awarding credit that is necessary to the continued development of an Open System.

(iii) Local comprehensiveness

OCNs are explicitly local organisations. Within this local context, however, they work across the more traditional boundaries that separate national awarding bodies. This comprehensive scope not only engenders the variety essential to an Open System, it also ensures that OCNs are more directly responsive to changes in the demands of their users (both providers and learners) than larger bodies with a 'national' perspective.

Existing approaches to the organisation of post-16 awards have tended to reflect this centralised, vertical division between the responsibilities of different awarding bodies. As some of the principles of Open Systems theory penetrate the organisational culture of post-16 education and training in the UK, the devolved, 'horizontal' and local structures of OCNs are beginning to become located closer to the mainstream of organisational development as the post-16 sector prepares itself for life in a different kind of environment.

(iv) Benchmarking

Because OCNs are local organisations, they naturally develop different approaches to the actual procedures of accreditation. Each new OCN that becomes a member of the national network brings to NOCN an accreditation model that, while meeting NOCN's minimum critical specifications, builds explicitly on the good practice generated through existing members of the Network. The process of becoming first an associate member of NOCN, then proceeding to full membership with the active support of NOCN itself ensures that each new OCN becomes operational with a set of procedures for awarding credit that embodies best practice from every other OCN (NOCN, 1991). Once again, the variety of OCN's local organisations and the specific process of drawing them into NOCN's own minimum critical specifications for awarding credit create a mechanism for benchmarking quality that makes maximum use of the flexibility of an Open System.

(v) Continuous improvement

This approach to the development of OCN accreditation within NOCN mirrors the principles which OCNs themselves apply to the accreditation of learner achievements in their locality. OCNs do not work to a nationally-determined set of standards about what these achievements should be. Instead, OCNs operate an accreditation system which is explicitly intended to stimulate flexibility, accessibility and diversity in the offer of learning opportunities within a framework of credits and levels. The accreditation of these opportunities engages providers in ongoing relationship with an OCN that leads to the continuous improvement of the provider's offer to learners within accredited programmes. This principal of continuous improvement is itself derived from the organisational culture of Open Systems theory applied to the quality assurance processes of many leading-edge commercial and industrial organisations (Deming, 1993).

(vi) Holographic development

In his writings on Learning to Learn within organisations, Morgan, (1986) uses the metaphor of a hologram to describe the model through which effective learning organisations process information. A holographic organisation, is one which a single part encompasses all the critical features of the whole. Instead of a model in which functions and tasks are grouped in different parts of the organisation, each part is capable of fulfilling all the functions and tasks necessary to offer the essential services which the organisation exists to provide (see Usherwood, 1993, for an extension of this metaphor).

This organisational model is particularly suited to survival and development in an Open System. It is a model which stimulates rapid learning both within and between different parts of the organisation; creates multiple opportunities for intra-organisational benchmarking; and provides an effective mechanism for continuous improvement. If we identify the National Open College Network as such an organisation, we can conceptualise each member of NOCN as a hologram, capable of offering all the essential services of accreditation necessary to a functioning CAT system. So a national body seeking accreditation for a learning programme within the credit framework can approach NOCN through any one of its member organisations and receive the same service that is available through any other member.

This is not only a very flexible approach to organisational development, it is also an extremely cost-effective way of providing a service. Within an Open System of CAT, the ability to approach the system through twenty-three or more points (the number of current members and associates of NOCN) provides a measure of accessibility to accreditation that is entirely consistent with the intentions of the CAT system that will operate within the credit framework.

Field-testing the credit framework proposals

In identifying these critical features of Open College Networks, I should emphasise that I am not suggesting that OCNs are necessarily the sole organisational model relevant to the functioning of a future CAT system. Indeed, I am not claiming that OCNs are at this juncture capable of fulfilling all the requirements of such a system. Nevertheless, just as the credit framework has drawn on OCN experiences for both the specifications of the framework and for the processes of awarding credit, so it may yet draw from the operational models of OCNs themselves in creating a specific organisational culture within which an Open System of credit accumulation and transfer might function.

Indeed, it is this ability of the post-16 sector to draw upon the practical experiences of OCNs, and to use their structures to field-test credit-based developments that is enabling a national credit framework to establish itself on the solid ground of practitioner experience. If we now identify the post-16 education and training sector as our 'learning organisation', we can see the advantages to the mainstream of the sector of being able to learn from the experiences of those who have previously operated at its periphery. Lest this use of the term be misunderstood, I am not suggesting that Open College Networks are inconsequential bodies, rather that they have developed organisational forms that embody the principles of flexibility, accessibility and responsiveness more explicitly than other parts of the sector.

Conclusion

I have tried to capture in this paper something that goes beyond a mere descriptive account of the proposals for a national credit framework, and instead tried to locate this development within a wider debate about the organisational forms of the post-16 curriculum and bodies that operate to support it. My contention is that, as we move towards the year 2000 and begin to speculate on the climate in which the post-16 sector will be operating in the twenty-first century, the development of a national credit framework provides an essential underpinning for the organisational culture that will be needed to sustain the continuing wellbeing and growth of the sector.

Of course this is only one possible future. It remains to be seen whether the establishing of a national credit framework and a functional system of credit accumulation and transfer are as close to fruition as they appear to be at the time of writing. Nevertheless, without such a framework and such a system, the post-16 sector of the future will surely remain trapped within organisational forms that will inevitably limit its future flexibility and accessibility.

References

Beer, S. (1974) *Designing Freedom*, London, Wiley.

Dawes, R. (1990) Introduction to the original TEC Prospectus, Department of Employment.

Deming, W. E. (1993) *The New Economics*, Boston, Massachusetts Institute of Technology.

Fagen, D. and Becker, W. (1974) *Any Major Dude*, The American Broadcasting Music Inc.

FEU. *A Basis for Credit?* (1992) and *A Basis for Credit?* (1993) London, Further Education Unit.

Handy, C. (1985) *Understanding Organisations*, London, Penguin.

Mager, C. (ed) (1991) *The Open College Network Handbook*, Leicester, UDACE.

Major, J. (1991) Introduction to the FE White Paper. Department for Education.

Morgan, G. (1986) *Images of Organisation*. London, Sage.

NOCN (1991) *Quality Assurance: National Arrangements*, London, National Open College Network.

Patten, J. (1992) Speech to the Inaugural Conference of the Association for Colleges.

Peters, T. (1987) *Thriving on Chaos*, London, Pan.

Pugh, D. S. (ed) (1990) *Organisational Theory: Selected Readings*, London, Penguin.

Stubbs, W. (1993) Introduction to *Funding Learning*, Further Education Funding Council.

Usherwood, T. (1993) *The Primary Care Organisation: Team or Hologram?* University of Sheffield Medical School.

Wilson, P. (1993a) *Developing the Technical Specifications for a National Credit Framework in Discussing Credit*, London, FEU.

Wilson, P. (1993b) *Beyond a Basis for Credit?* London, FEU.

4 Action plan and after: open learning in the mainstream throughout Scotland

Nigel Paine

To be thus is nothing, but to be safely thus. Macbeth, Act III (Scene (i)).

Introduction

This chapter will attempt to sketch out a number of developments in Scotland related to the opening up of the post-school curriculum and the unique integration that has occurred over the past ten years between mainstream reform and innovative pressure on the margins of the education system by pioneers and the committed few.

The idea that we are suddenly in the midst of a revolution in post-16 education which will make the curriculum more appropriate, broader based, more flexible and open to many more people, rings slightly hollow in Scotland where steady commitment and planned development for over ten years has yielded quite stunning results. The purpose of this chapter is to track the various strands of development and show how they demonstrate that the philosophies underpinning open learning are near the centre of educational philosophy and practice. The story of Scottish school and post-school development is one of evolution, not revolution, and because of this, most innovations occur quietly. This is not reflected in the rest of the UK where pressure to change quickly has caused a considerable amount of public debate.

Two or three small examples will illustrate the problem. In an article published on 24 October 1993 in the *Sunday Times* (Smithers, 1993b), the author attempted to explain current developments in pos⁺ 16 education which showed that the vocational path (mirroring GCSEs and 'A' Levels in England and Standard Grade and Highers in Scotland) will transform the qualification base of the country and create a genuinely appropriate and broad-based education system that will attempt, by the year 2000, to give 50 per cent of 18-year-olds a '2 "A" Level' or equivalent qualification. These new vocational qualifications are known as GNVQs in England, Wales and Northern Ireland and GSVQs in Scotland. A report published by OFSTED, the Inspectorate organisation in England and Wales (Office for Standards in Education, 1993), criticised the delivery of Level II GNVQs in schools, while praising the quality of Level III GNVQs. The implication in both articles is that vocational courses are new, different and fraught with problems concerning standards and quality.

The equivalent programmes in Scotland draw upon six or seven years experience in modular, competence-based provision. They assemble and focus what exists now and the issues concerning their delivery are less contentious and certainly less debated. They reflect continuity rather than change and are couched in a now familiar language of modules, units and vocational qualifications.

The anomalous position concerning Scotland's role in vocational training within the UK is further reinforced by a recent report commissioned by Channel 4 Television which criticised the entire underpinning of competence-based vocational qualifications (Smithers, 1993a). Every reference is to the London based National Council for Vocational Qualifications and problems with their qualifications. The whole episode passed by unremarked in Scotland where SCOTVEC — the NCVQ equivalent organisation offering identical qualifications — was subject to no such barrage of bad publicity. At this point, we ought to go back a few years and sketch out the development.

The action plan

The Action Plan was published in 1983 by the Scottish Education Department (SED, 1983). It envisaged the abolition of all the then current non-advanced further education courses and the replacement of a largely obsolete curriculum with around 1,500 40-hour competence-based modules which could be combined to form Scottish Higher National Diplomas or other significant vocational qualifications.

This remarkable shift in focus for further education was completed in eighteen months. Currently there are over 3,200 modules being delivered to virtually every person over the age of 16 whether as part of mainstream education or as a complement to more academic curriculum and there are over 1.2 million student modules studied each year.

The Action Plan became the National Certificate when it was taken on board by the merged Scottish Technical Education Council and Scottish Business Education Council — SCOTVEC, the Scottish Vocational Education Council — and virtually from day one schools began to use modules to infill the curriculum for senior pupils and to offer a more vocational route to those not keen on, or unable to take, an academic path. Many school pupils, therefore, take 'Highers' in S5 and S6 with a range of vocation modules to 'fill out' the timetable and increase the curriculum breadth.

Having established the National Certificate, SCOTVEC moved on to its advanced courses and they have now been 'unitised' and made competence-based. This means that the entire SCOTVEC output is modular and extremely flexible. This also infers that some of the new universities in Scotland are now teaching competence-based and conventional courses side by side in Higher Education and that students are moving from Higher National Certificates into degree courses on a fairly regular basis. The Higher National Certificate/Diploma is, therefore, de facto an entry point into higher education opportunities and a bridge from an essentially vocational route to academic route. Part of the acknowledged success of the SWAP (Scottish Wider Access Programme) was due to the already available, fully articulated, curriculum which formed the rungs of the ladder of progression (Scottish Office Education Department, 1993b). SWAP attempted to open up Higher Education opportunities to adults by providing tailor made 'access' courses coupled with guaranteed Higher Education course places. These, of course, comprised specially chosen National Certificate modules and/or Higher National Units.

All of this is not without problems. A huge lecturing workforce had to be converted to a programme of competence-based assessment and around that a network of external assessors and verifiers had to be trained and quality standards implemented. A recent HMI report (Scottish Office Education Department, 1991) soundly endorses the overall philosophy and shows that the early difficulties have largely been overcome and that the modular programme is part of the mainstream within both schools, Further Education and the newer universities. Indeed the influence of the unitised programme in advanced Further Education has led Napier University to modularise its entire degree offering. The modules are not competency-based and are of varying lengths, but it offers tremendous savings in efficiency across programmes where common modules can be studied by a wide range of students and also enormous flexibility and choice from their growing numbers of undergraduates.

It is possible, therefore, for a young person or a mature student to enter the post-16 education system and progress through to a degree learning in a way that is almost unrecognisable from that of his or her peers ten years previously. If we couple that with SCOT CATS (the Credit Accumulation and Transfer Scheme), then that path can include swapping courses or even institutions on the route to Higher Education qualifications.

Open to flexible learning

Across the same time span significant developments have been made in the development of both the philosophy and an approach to open learning and the actual provision on the ground. Back in 1981, when early open learning initiatives began in Scotland, notably the Open Learning Research Programme based in SCET, there were approximately forty-five courses available by open and distance learning and some of those had very tight attendance and residential restrictions imposed upon them. Many of them were administered by a body known as The Scottish Co-ordinating Committee for Distance Learning Schemes in Vocational Further Education (SCCDLSVFE). One of the functions of this Committee was to turn away any potential student who could enrol as a 'normal' student. This was very much a second preference route for a handful of people if you could wade through the bureaucracy and stick out the programme of unsophisticated materials and limited tutorial backup. Nevertheless, it had its successes and a number of people owe their business qualification today to that programme.

Currently, there are too many opportunities to print in a directory. SCET's *Open Learning Directory* ceased publication in 1989 (Scottish Council for Educational Technology, 1989) when the numbers of programmes went into the thousands and its purpose to direct, mostly adult learners, to an appropriate centre was redundant as most centres offered most programmes or could point the learner to a centre that could help.

Around this shift a philosophical change took place which is illustrated in Table 4.1.

In a recent report produced for the Scottish Office (Scottish Council for Educational Technology, 1993) the term flexible learning was embraced rather than open and/or distance learning. The common definition in the report, based on wide discussions with a range of providers throughout Scotland, was that a number of key concepts underpinned our understanding of flexible learning. These were:

- Widening *access* by removing barriers to overcome geographical isolation work or family commitments
- giving learners more *control* over their own learning, e.g. over what they learn, how they learn and the pace at which they learn
- helping them to take more *responsibility* for their own learning and helping them to learn how to learn
- Providing appropriate *support* for individuals according to their needs.

These principles were explicit in the ethos of the original Action Plan report.

Many colleges in Scotland now have some form of flexible learning unit. This is usually a resource base where students can work on materials (often media-based materials) to cover basic skills and remediation or where they can self refer for broadening the learning experience.

Anniesland Further Education College located on the western extremity of Glasgow now operates three flexible learning units within the college covering Communications, Numbers and IT skills and is establishing a fourth unit in a housing scheme — Drumchapel — located four or five miles from the college as part of an urban regeneration programme.

Table 4.1

Old	New
From a focus on geographical distance	-> Focus on a whole range of barriers that exclude people from educational opportunities.
From centrally organised distance schemes	-> Locally-based provision
From entirely paper-based materials	-> Mixed media
A focus on access	-> A focus on process
From specialist	-> Mainstream
From safety net	-> Ladder of opportunity
College provider centred	-> Learner/community centred

At the recent college graduation ceremony, students, mostly mature adults, from Drumchapel featured prominently in the ceremony for a whole range of HND/HNC and other awards. Many of those were taught either in Drumchapel itself, at the college or in a combination of locations, some using flexible learning materials in addition.

The further education sector in particular, is increasingly seeing itself as mixed mode, in other words it will put together learning programmes to suit the needs of those individuals or organisations identified as forming part of its customer base. Each lecturer will be expected to be able to deliver competence-based and knowledge-based curriculum on the one hand and conventional teaching or open and flexible learning support on the other. It would be an exaggeration to say that this is ubiquitous but it is true to say that each of the forty-two Further Education colleges has some kind of emphasis on more flexible provision and in some colleges this is now a sizeable proportion of total full time equivalent student numbers.

The wider access movement

From the mid 1980s Scotland launched a Wider Access Programme which is still known by the acronym SWAP. The first SWAP graduates are now coming through into the job market. SCET, as an employer in the west end of Glasgow, has interviewed an increasing number of mature adults recently graduated from one of Glasgow's universities and looking for their first job with graduate status.

It is largely agreed that the SWAP programmes have been very successful in taking a small, but significant, number of adults through a programme of courses at non-advanced, advanced and ultimately degree level. There have been numerous partnerships between Further and Higher Education guaranteeing places at the next stage of development providing the learner is successful at the previous stage. There are, however, one or two problems with SWAP which still have to be resolved:

(i)   The learner not completing the SWAP programme is not necessarily a failure. A learner can decide that he/she has reached an appropriate point and leave the programme as a satisfied and successful customer. This is not often reflected in the statistics.

(ii) The learner begins with very flexible provision and as he/she works his/her way into the Higher Education system, the provision becomes less and less flexible. This puts increasing demands on the learner in addition to the higher level of study and can cause unnecessary constriction.

(iii) There is very little financial incentive or financial support for an adult to move into full-time study. Part-time opportunities for degrees are still limited apart from the broad provision of the Open University in Scotland.

Participation rates

The Open University in Scotland has the highest participation rate per head of population in the UK (Open University in Scotland, 1993). Participation rates in Higher Education have always been higher in Scotland than in the rest of the UK by between five and seven percentage points. In other words, the target figures for England and Wales are what is currently achieved in Scotland. It is also true that the changes in SCOTVEC provision have substantially increased student numbers over the period 1985–6 through to 1990–1, the last figures released by the Scottish Office Statistical Service.

The participation in vocational Further Education in Scotland (excluding Higher Education) moved from 177,466 enrolments in 1985–6 to 228,956 in session 1990–91 (The Scottish Office, 1993). This represents an increase of nearly one-third at a time when the number of 16–18 year olds in Scotland was steadily dropping. In terms of the age group of students, the figures for under 16, 16–18 and 19–24-year-olds has remained roughly constant at the 1985–6 level, whereas the numbers aged 25+ has risen by over half during that same period. The largest numbers of students are studying for National Certificate qualifications as would be expected (this is some 47.8 per cent of the total). The participation rate is remarkably even throughout Scotland, although Fife and Tayside have a significantly higher participation rate touching almost 40 per cent of 16–18 year olds in both authorities. The Orkney Islands has the lowest participation rate ranging from 25 per cent down to 15 per cent depending on the year. It must be recognised, however, that the numbers in island communities are very small and therefore significant swings will occur year on year.

The comparative figures for full-time Higher Education courses in Scotland indicate that the total number of graduates and diplomates successfully completing full time Higher Education courses in Scotland has risen from 20,600 in 1983–4 to 26,200 in 1990–1, a rise mirroring that of vocational Further Education of 27 per cent. Not all graduates and diplomates from Scottish universities are domiciled in Scotland, but nevertheless the picture shows a decline in the Scottish population of 18–24-year-olds from just over 620,000 in 1984 down to just over 560,000 in 1991, with a corresponding rise in graduates from 20,600 to 26,200. The growth pattern is mirrored in both the older and the newer universities.

Technology

The widespread use of technology has made the developments illustrated above possible. The use of technology should not be narrowly focused on the delivery of learning materials. In effect, this has been a fairly minor contribution to the development; far more significant has been:

 (i) Large computer systems to manage the increased complexity caused by modular provision and competence-based assessment.
 (ii) Complex administrative systems that are able to track and timetable more flexible provision and cope with multiple entry and access points from educational institutions.
(iii) The widespread use of computers to develop, design and print learning resources. This has minimised the cost of production and kept the need to stock large amounts of materials to a minimum.
(iv) The use of communications technologies such as voice and/or video-conferencing, E-mail, computer conferencing, fax machine, etc., to help learners keep in touch with each other, with their support staff and with the institution itself.

Tony Bates (1991), defined the challenge of new technology as 'the third generation distance education'. He suggested that multimedia learning and the widespread use of new technologies would transform the way in which learning was delivered and more importantly, the learning process itself. He points out that thus far, most distance education organisations have really played at the margins of technological innovation rather than taking it into the main stream.

This concept of the three generations mirrors the way in which the commercial and industrial world has absorbed technology. A recent paper by ICL (1990) indicated that there were three stages in the use of technology. Stage one was the use of stand-alone machines, essentially improving individual productivity. The second stage was local networks of machines and wider networks where groups of employees could communicate, share information, etc., across the narrow confines of one organisation or the wider confines of multi-sited organisations. Both of these developments could be incorporated within existing working practices, but for the third stage, the whole work practice and work design could be transformed by technology. It was only then that the full productivity of technology could be realised. This is similar to the use of technology for learning. Its true potential will transform both the development, delivery and process of learning itself. How has Scotland done with regard to this?

The answer is, really, not very well, but no worse than anyone else. The flexible learning units I mentioned are largely technology driven, but they are all based upon stand-alone machines. At the very most they share a printer. There is very little use of multimedia in education, although a number of interactive videos and one full motion, full screen CD-I disc has been produced for staff development in schools and further education (Scottish Interactive Technology Centre, 1992).

Some of the most exciting developments, however, are located in the north of Scotland where a combination of enhanced EC funding and an excellent telecommunications structure has led to some innovative uses of remote tuition whereby the tutor can take control of a remote student's (or students') computer(s) and interact directly with the learner using voice communication in parallel with on-screen communication. This has been particularly effective in teaching business skills, including the use of spread sheets, where part of the learning process is familiarity with the functionality of hardware or software. Scotland leads Europe in the use of these technologies and a recent conference organised by the Association for Community Enterprise in the Highlands and Islands (ACE-HI) had visitors from all over the EC to hear of developments in Scotland and they have a number of good partnership agreements with colleges in France, Spain and Portugal (ACE-HI, 1993). Indeed, a group of southern French adults are studying for an English teaching qualification in their local GRETA (FE college) and will be awarded a SCOTVEC TEFC qualification. Teaching is done locally and assessment and moderation are carried out through a number of technological links with France from Inverness College.

Conclusions

In an article written by Lucille Pacey of the Open Learning agency in British Columbia, Canada (Pacey, 1992), she said that:

Using the business vernacular, it is time for us to focus our energies and to identify and communicate our competitive edge in terms of level of service, types of service and exemplary quality of service. References and economic reports and economic reform policies continue to tie healthy, prosperous economies to a well-trained, educated and participating workforce. The potential contribution that open learning can bring to that economic agenda is massive, but technologies will need to become a naturally integrated part of our practice. The information age will empower individuals to choose their participation in a way that suits their needs and they will not wait for distance educators to continue their debate about the use of technologies and fostering the learning process.

There is no evidence that the contribution which open and flexible learning developments in Scotland have made to economic and social development across all areas and cross-sectors of the economy is tangible and measurable.

The Minister of Education in Scotland, Lord James Douglas Hamilton, at a lecture on the future of adult education in Scotland (Scottish Office Education Department, 1993a), suggested that 'All of the education institutions and organisations must constantly review the service they deliver to ensure that they are responding to the highest possible percentage of the population.' The nature of that review should not only include the mode of delivery, but also define, if learners' needs change, the exact vehicle for communicating learning to the learner.

The EC has recognised the importance of this. Under Article 128 of the Maastricht Treaty, education comes under the aegis of the Community for the first time and a Green Paper on the European dimension of education was produced in September 1993 to acknowledge this and look at the ways forward (Commission of the European Communities, 1993). Paragraph 37 says 'Open and distance learning presents a whole range of possibilities for giving the younger generation the ability to adapt to changes in the workplace or even to retraining, facilitating the transfer of knowledge.' Then in Paragraph 39 'However, it must be stressed that the use of new technology is not limited to open and/or distance learning.

'Indeed, multimedia systems are called to play an increasingly important role in the transmission of knowledge in increasing the range of places where learning happens.

'Community action on the use of new technology in education should, therefore, be particularly concerned with such developments,

Table 4.2

Now	Tomorrow
Sporadic use of technology	Integrated use of technology
Information from technology	Information from the global information networks
Flexibility in institutions	Customer centred at the core
A range of appropriate qualifications	A coherent record of achievement throughout working life
College-based by and large	College, home, workplace competency-based without distinction
Some people learning	Everybody learning

especially those involving the joint development of teaching material.'

The Green Paper is a prelude to Community activity and Community funding through the fourth framework programme and illustrates the way in which the Community's policies are developing.

Scotland is aligned fully with this broader philosophy and can make a contribution to the wider European debate if called upon to do so. The changes of the last ten years have created more coherence where fragmentation existed previously, more opportunities and have allowed the end consumer of education to take a driving seat in defining structure and practices available in the present.

It is inconceivable that the clock will be turned backwards, but at the same time, where we are now is really only the springboard for where we want to be tomorrow. We can identify that in Table 4.2:

The prognostication is good. The problems significant, but not insurmountable. There is no alternative if we wish to maintain or increase the quality of life offered to young people and adults.

References

ACE-HI (1993) *Transnational Distance-Learning: The Highland Euroform Conference.* Nairn, 30 June–1 July 1993.

Bates A. W. (1991) 'Third generation distance education: the challenge of new technology'. *Research in Distance Education,* 3(2) pp. 10–15.

Commission of the European Communities (1993) *Green Paper on the European Dimension of Education, COM (93)457.* Luxembourg, Office for Official Publications of the European Communities.

ICL (1990) *The Use of Technology in Industry: An ICL Report.* London, ICL.

Office for Standards in Education (1992) *GNVQs in Schools: The Introduction of General National Vocational Qualifications 1992,* London, OFSTED.

Open University in Scotland, 60 Melville Street, Edinburgh EH3 7HF. Tel: 031 225 2889. Figures available from this address.

Pacey, L. (1992) 'Strategic planning and open learning: turkey tails and frogs' in Scriven, B. et al. (eds) *Distance Education for the Twenty-First Century. Selected Papers from the 16th World Conference of the International Council for Distance Education.* Thailand, ICDE and Queensland University of Technology, pp. 436–46.

Scottish Council for Educational Technology (1993) *Flexible Learning.* Unpublished report produced by SCET for the Scottish Office Education Department.

Scottish Council for Educational Technology (1989) *Open Learning in Scotland 1989/90,* Glasgow, SCET.

SCET produced an Open Learning directory in 1980 and then every year until 1989. The number of courses listed went from 45 to over 2,500 during that period.

Scottish Education Department (1983) *16–18s in Scotland: An Action Plan,* Edinburgh, SED.

Scottish Interactive Technology Centre (1992) *Skills for Appraisal Interviewing.* Compact Disc — Interactive. Edinburgh, SOED.

The Scottish Office (1993) 'Students registered in vocational further education in Scotland 1990–91'. *Statistical Bulletin Education Series,* Edn/F7/1993/9, July.

Scottish Office Education Department (1993a) *Adult Education in Scotland: Planning for the Future.* A Speech by Lord James Douglas Hamilton, Minister of Education. Edinburgh, SOED.

Scottish Office Education Department (1993b) *Scottish Wider Access Programme: A Preparation for Higher Education: A Report by HM Inspectors of Schools.* Edinburgh, SOED.

Scottish Office Education Department (1991) *Six Years On. Teaching, Learning and Assessment in National Certificate Programmes in Scottish Further Education Colleges: A Report by HM Inspectors of Schools.* Edinburgh, HMSO.

Smithers, A. (1993a) *All Our Futures: Britain's Education Revolution. A Dispatches Report on Education.* London, Channel 4 Television.

Smithers, A. (1993b) 'Vocational education leads revolution in the classroom'. *The Sunday Times,* Issue 8827, 24 October.

5 Who's at the centre? The experience of open learning in adult basic education

Sue Bergin and Mary Hamilton

Open Learning Centres aimed to complement rather than compete with existing basic skills provision by giving a wider choice of learning opportunities for new and existing students. (ALBSU, 1991)

Introduction

Adult Basic Education has developed in the U.K. since the mid-1970s when it was first officially recognised that there were large numbers of adults who were not confident in many situations in using their skills in reading, writing, communicating and basic maths. There was a large popular response to the literacy campaign mounted by the BBC on television and radio and, with volunteer help, tuition was set up in local education authorities throughout the country (Jones and Charnley, 1978).

However, it was not until 1988 that The Adult Literacy and Basic Skills Unit (ALBSU)[1] set up the first of a series of Basic Skills Open Learning Centres across England and Wales. Altogether, almost £7 million was made available for setting up a series of eighty-three Open Learning Centres between 1988 and 1992 (ALBSU, 1993a, p. 5). These were essentially resource centres, well equipped with microcomputers and offering opportunities for supported self-study.

Although Adult Basic Education (ABE) has always aimed to be a flexible, open-access service, making use of many styles of learning and teaching, this was the first time the term 'open learning' had been used to describe and promote a particular model of good practice.

This high profile innovation happened alongside a series of other important developments which together are changing the shape and direction of basic education in England and Wales towards a more vocationally oriented, formal and standardised service.

This chapter sets out to explore how far ALBSU's aim for these centres to 'complement rather than compete with existing basic skills provision' reflects what has been happening in practice. In it we argue that setting up the Basic Skills Open Learning Centres often added to existing provision, but also opened up tensions within the whole ABE provision in a given locality. This was because of the context in which the centres were introduced and because of the particular model of open learning they embodied. We raise important questions about the extent to which Open Learning Centres serve the needs of all ABE students or have reinforced the shift to a narrower and less open ABE service.

The development of Adult Basic Education

In 1973 over half of the local education authorities made no provision for adult literacy at all. Within a few years all made some provision and most had recognised the need for provision of a wider range of basic education for adults and taken some steps to fulfil that need. The role of the voluntary sector in campaigning for provision, in alerting public opinion and in galvanising decision makers into action was a crucial one (ALBSU, 1985, p. 2).

From the early 1970s, the settings for ABE provision have varied across the country with sessions going on wherever there was a need for the provision and space for it to happen, for example, in church halls, in schools, in libraries, in local community centres, in people's homes, and in colleges. ABE was classed as part of adult education in most local education authorities. It has relied heavily on volunteer tutors and has shared the same resourcing and timetabling patterns as other part-time courses for adults.

Most basic skills work had been centred around individual teaching or small group work. Few students were able to get more than 1–2 hours of teaching a week and many

programmes closed down during the lengthy adult and
further education breaks in the summer and at Christmas.
(ALBSU, 1993a, p. 7; see also Mace, 1979, p. 70).

The ABE service had not been resourced so as to achieve a
high-profile, well-funded and well-equipped base for basic skills
work in England and Wales before the arrival of the Basic Skills
Open Learning Centres in 1988. In addition, the Open Learning
Centres, as specific, dedicated venues for basic education as
compared to the variety of temporary and often loaned venues
within the established provision, were able to offer longer opening
hours and a permanent collection of resources which staff and
students could access without having to carry resources from one
location to another.

The existing provision, whilst often necessarily having limited
access times, in many other ways offered open access for prospective students (see Sanders, 1988). There was a conscious
philosophy that basic education should not replicate the closed
and forced education of the school years with people who were
returning to education as adults to improve their basic skills.
Central to this approach was the notion of student-centred or self-
directed learning — enabling students to make informed choices
and decisions about their own learning — which is also a key idea
in 'open learning' (see Paine, 1988, introduction pp. ix, 90). In the
established provision, there was often a commitment, interpreted
differently in different programmes, to literacy, numeracy and
communication skills as activities for empowering people in their
lives and communities: 'We strongly believe that education exists
for the learners and should serve *their* purposes, not those of the
tutor or the organising body . . . to enable people within that
community to organise their own learning to meet their own needs
— both as individuals and as groups . . . The most important
thing to remember is that learning . . . is about sharing knowledge
and decisions' (ALBSU and the National Federation of Voluntary
Literacy Schemes, 1983, p. 2)

Over the years, a great deal of innovative practice was
developed and shared which put this philosophy into action:
'. . . a participatory approach has been the "bedrock" of adult
literacy tuition . . . students not as passive receivers but as active
participants in their own learning' (ALBSU, 1985, p. 9). For
overviews of this work, see Hamilton, 1989; Mace, 1992; Charnley
and Withnall, 1989. Reports of particular projects can also be
found in, for instance, the Inner London Education Authority
Afro-Caribbean Language and Literacy Project, 1990; Bonnerjea,
1988; issues of the Research and Practice in Adult Literacy

(RaPAL) Bulletin and publications from the Lee Community Education Centre; Moss, 1984.

The open learning in Adult Basic Education Research Project

In 1991, Lancaster University and Goldsmiths College, University of London, obtained funding from the Universities Funding Council to work with students and staff in order to explore the impact of open learning in ABE.

The information presented here comes from two main sources within the project (entitled 'Open Learning in ABE'): first, from a questionnaire sent to all the original Basic Skills Open Learning Centres funded by ALBSU and to a matching sample of established ABE providers across England and Wales and secondly from in-depth interviews and observation with students and staff in three case-study sites in the North West of England. Quotes from these people are personalised, but real names are not necessarily used, unless this is what individuals wanted.[2]

Complementarity and competition

In the national questionnaire, we asked staff working in both Open Learning Centres *and* in the established basic education provision to indicate which of the following dimensions of complementarity and competition they had experienced in their locality with the setting up of the Open Learning Centres (see Table 5.1).

Table 5.1 Complementarity and competition in ABE provision

Which of the following has happened in your local area?		
Responses from:	*Established ABE*	*OLCs*
	N=52 %	N=66 %
shared expertise	96	94
joint training activities	83	82
materials development	69	61
lack of understanding	46	42
resentment of different resourcing levels	31	59
feelings of fear or threat	25	52

(*note*: the percentages do not total 100% as all places gave more than one response.)

From these responses, it seems that *both* the established adult basic education provision and the newer Open Learning Centres have experienced high levels of *both* complementarity and competition with the spread of open learning in the field of adult basic education in England and Wales.

The dimensions most cited as having occurred in any given area are those of complementarity: 96 per cent of established basic education providers and 94 per cent of Open Learning Centres reported having shared expertise between staff in the different provisions. Eighty-three per cent of established providers and 82 per cent of Open Learning Centres reported having had joint training activities and 69 per cent of established providers and 61 per cent of Open Learning Centres reported having developed materials together. So, on these dimensions at least, there is agreement that complementarity and even collaboration have taken place between the different provisions. This reflects the fact that systems for complementarity and co-operation were often already in place and operational through existing local and national training programmes for ABE staff.

Alongside this complementarity, there are significant dimensions of competition between the Open Learning Centres and the established provision. Open Learning Centres reported that they had sensed more resentment at different resourcing levels between the two providers (59 per cent) than the established provision claimed had happened (31 per cent). This variation may suggest that established centres did not want to appear resentful of increased funding for provision in a field to which they are committed.

However, it is understandable that with the advent of the new, well-resourced centres, feelings of resentment and competition would flare up within the service. One Open Learning Centre commented that in their locality the established provision was 'delighted that we have it, but understandably demoralised at their own lack of resources'. No doubt this was quite a common response throughout England and Wales, for, in many places, while the money seemed to be pouring in to fund and resource the new Open Learning Centres, the established provision struggled to survive; as one established provider commented: 'Resourcing the ABE provision has been very limited this year and there has been no increase of budget other than an inflation-linked sum, which in effect has proved to be a minor cut. No separate resource budget has been made available for ABE this year.'

Again, there was a big difference claimed about feelings of fear or threat at the establishment of the Open Learning Centres, with 52 per cent of Open Learning Centres and only 25 per cent of established providers saying this had happened in their locality. Both providers seemed to think that such feelings had been felt most 'initially', but had 'now decreased' or 'now dispersed'. It seems that the memories of such feelings are stronger and have lingered longer for the Open Learning Centres than for the established providers who tend to mention feelings of fear or threat far less in their responses.

The tensions that arose between providers do not appear to have been addressed by ALBSU, either in their strategy for establishing the Open learning Centres, or in their reports on the success of the centres. But it seems important to acknowledge that this has been a part of the experience of innovation and change under conditions of scarce resources.

Another of the main aims behind the establishment of the Basic Skills Open Learning Centres was to give '. . .a wider choice of learning opportunities for new and existing students' (ALBSU, 1991, p. 4). We now want to move on to consider this in some depth as the focus of this chapter.

Does open learning offer a wider choice of learning opportunities for new and existing students?

Certainly, on one level, it seems that any *expansion* of provision, whatever it's form, will result in a wider choice of learning opportunities for new and existing students. However, given the funding difficulties and uncertainties discussed earlier, it is *not* clear that expansion across the *whole* of the basic educational provision in England and Wales was what was going on over the period when the Open Learning Centres were established. Clear patterns of expansion and contraction within ABE are difficult to track and monitor nationally.

In our questionnaire, we explored this issue with staff in both Open Learning Centres and in the established provision. When we asked 'What effects has the establishment of an Open Learning Centre had on provision in your area?' we received the responses shown in Table 5.2.

The responses presented in Table 5.2 indicate that both Open Learning Centres and the established ABE providers felt that the setting up of an Open Learning Centre within their locality had a number of important effects, particularly in terms of increased choice and opportunity, raising the profile or enhancing the 'image' of ABE locally, of generating more opportunities for

Table 5.2: Effects of the establishment of an Open Learning Centre on provision in the area.

	Established ABE	*OLCs*
	N=46 %	N=65 %
increased choice, widened opportunities, more flexible opening, broadened provision for students	57	60
broadened opportunities/experience/expertise of staff	30	22
more and better resources and facilities	35	31
improved progression routes	7	12
encouraged self-directed learning	7	6
raised the profile/enhanced the image of ABE locally, become a central referral point, been a catalyst for change, a challenge for ABE style	30	46
brought provision into the area or become the provision locally	7	5
little or no effect locally	9	3

(*note*: percentages do not add up to 100% as all respondents gave more than one reply to the question)

staff to develop their experience and expertise and of creating more and better resources and facilities in ABE. Only 9 per cent of established providers and 3 per cent of Open Learning Centres felt the effects had been negligible or non-existent within their area.

For both providers, it seems that while many had experienced funding difficulties and staffing cuts which had affected their provision as described earlier, alongside this they also felt that the setting up of an Open Learning Centre had broadened the range and choice of learning opportunities available locally for students: 60 per cent of Open Learning Centres and 57 per cent of established ABE providers felt this had happened in their localities.

However, this was also the response that had the most additional comments, written in by staff to *explain and elaborate* what was meant by their reply. These additional comments tell us much more and suggest that beneath the apparent widening of learning opportunities lie concerns, among some providers, that open learning opportunities are only open to certain kinds of people and particular kinds of need.

Of the responses which focused on widening of choice and opportunities within ABE, 35 per cent of established providers and 21 per cent of Open Learning Centres specifically mentioned particular student groups who had benefited from this widening of provision. There was agreement that these students were somehow 'new' to ABE. This corresponds with ALBSU's statement that the Open Learning Centres aimed to widen the choice of learning opportunities for new students and the figures in their final report that of the 39,212 users of centres between 1990–92, 57 per cent were new to basic skills (ALBSU, 1993a, p. 6).

The question arises as to *who* these new students are and what has happened to the existing students in ABE. From the questionnaire responses there emerges a picture of *who* these 'new-to-ABE' students in Open Learning Centres are. Tables 5.3 and 5.4 summarise this picture.

These comments, whilst supporting the general notion that Open Learning Centres have widened choice and opportunity within ABE, also make clear that these opportunities have often been available for *new groups of students* who did not previously take part in ABE. They are 'especially those in the middle category — a bit more advanced than beginners . . .' The Open Learning

Table 5.3: Open Learning Centres say open Learning Centres have . . .

OPEN LEARNING CENTRES SAY
OPEN LEARNING CENTRES HAVE . . .

'widened the boundaries of traditional ABE.'

'brought more people into education, especially those in the middle category — a bit more advanced than beginners, but not confident enough to do college courses.'

'attracted some students who did not previously take part in ABE.'
'attracted "non-traditional" students.'
'tended to "cream-off" the post-basic students.'

Table 5.4: Established providers say Open Learning Centres have . . .

ESTABLISHED PROVIDERS SAY
OPEN LEARNING CENTRES HAVE . . .

'attracted different students.'

'plugged a gap . . . for more independent learners.'

been 'used mainly for students "in the fast track" who want to study intensively and can work independently.'

created a 'widening of opportunity for many students, but does not meet the needs of those most lacking in confidence.'

created 'to some extent a form of streaming.'

Centres have 'tended to "cream-off" the post basic students', attracted people who are already fairly independent and confident learners, and in doing this may be moving towards 'a form of streaming' in basic skills provision. A questionnaire cannot, with its limitations, tell us much more about what has been happening with the student groups in ABE. To explore the issues raised by these comments further, we will focus on the qualitative data from the three case-study sites within the North West of England.

Previous experiences of learning in adult education

Amongst the student user groups in the North West case-study sites there were signs of such 'creaming and screening' going on in the Open Learning Centres. For instance, if one takes prior learning in adult education as an indicator of students who can be said to be of 'middle range' in terms of 'ability' and confidence, then some form of selection seems to be operating.

Of the twenty-eight students interviewed in the two Basic Skills Open Learning Centres in the case-study sites in the North West, sixteen had experience of prior learning in *adult education*. Such experiences covered a wide range and included, for example, 'O' Levels and GCSEs in maths and English, open college courses, evening classes in flower arranging, art, woodwork, Spanish, DIY, shoe repairing, dressmaking, and advanced tailoring. They included a variety of other assessed courses in areas such as nursery nursing, vehicle engineering, medical and general secretarial/typing courses, electrical engineering and catering. This breadth of prior learning experience in adult education was not found amongst students we interviewed in the established provision. The majority of students in the established provision had experience of prior learning in basic education but not in the wider adult education sphere.

We do not want to suggest that people with such experiences of prior learning in adult education should be excluded wholesale from basic education because they somehow 'don't fit' with the usual definition of need in basic skills, although one student in an Open Learning Centre was quite clear who Basic Skills Open Learning Centres should be for: '. . . there's thousands of people who have learning difficulties — it's for them; the others shouldn't be entitled — they're denying other people who've got learning difficulties a place.' (Terence, Interview 27.4.92).

What we *are* suggesting is that while many of these people are 'new' or 'non-traditional' students to basic education, they are not new to adult education. They are more experienced learners, attracted by Open Learning Centres, who are not usually present in such large numbers in the established basic education provision in England and Wales. Whilst ALBSU acknowledges that 57 per cent of student-users of Open Learning Centres were new to basic skills, they do not expand on this to explain *who* these people are and what makes them 'new' to basic education. We want to raise the issue of who gets access to open learning in A.B.E. and explore the practitioner claims that Open Learning Centres are attracting people from the 'middle range' of 'ability' and that some form of 'streaming' is operating.

Specific learning goals

Another dimension of the selection of students for open learning is that of specific goals. Whilst every student in basic education is encouraged by tutors to establish clear goals for their learning (via the use of systems such as the initial interview and assessment and by formulating a learning programme with review sessions to monitor progress), the nature and apparent clarity of these goals varies between students.

For example, there appear to be differences between students who have vocationally-specific goals such as to pass a Nursing Test, to get a GCSE Maths, to pass a Pitmans typing test and so on and other students who seem to have more directly person-specific goals such as being spurred on to learning how to 'spell better' as their children grow up or wanting to be able to write a letter to a friend, or to be able to 'do maths' with confidence.

We do not want to suggest a hierarchy of goals, but do want to point up some differences in the nature of the goals which students in the case study sites identified for themselves in their learning.

Those students who had goals which were vocationally-specific also often seemed to be those students who had a clear idea of where they had to go in terms of the resources/materials available in the Open Learning Centres: staff seemed to find it easier to map out with these students the routes they should take through the materials in order to work towards and hopefully achieve their goals. A possible distinguishing aspect of the nature of these vocationally-oriented goals as compared to other specific goals such as those mentioned above is that they tended to be *limited and short-term*. This meant that both students and tutors could be clear about what they were working towards and how to go about this: often the stages/steps seemed clear, particularly in comparison with the apparently *wider and long-term* specific goals held by other students. With these students the learning journey and activities often seemed more tutor-led/directed through suggestions of what to work on next and the journey sometimes seemed depressingly never-ending. Students in this position were frequently unable to develop a sense of direction and independence in their learning. Their needs were somehow less tangible and this meant a great deal of reliance on tutors to suggest what they could work on next.

It seems that the difference in the nature of the specific goals held by students had a dramatic effect on the role taken by the tutors in supporting students and encouraging them to take control of their learning. The more limited and short-term the specific goal, the clearer both students and tutors were in knowing the routes through the resources and the sequencing of activities towards the goal. This shared clarity helped students to be more independent and self-directing in their learning.

Independence and self-direction in learning

As we noted above, the notion of independence and self-direction in learning is one which is often associated with open learning, and is an association which was made time and time again by ABE staff in their responses to our national questionnaire and in the case study sites.

Self-directed learning is notoriously difficult to define (see Caffarella and O'Donnell, 1989; Brookfield, 1985; Boud, 1988; Davenport, 1993) and staff used a variety of terms to express their own views of it. When asked who 'does well' in a Basic Skills Open Learning Centre, many staff in the case-study sites responded along the lines of: 'Well, they're people who are highly motivated and can work independently on a task, once it's explained . . . I think it's people who can concentrate . . . and work on a task without needing constant encouragement and support. Yeah, I think it's motivation really.' (an Open Learning Centre co-ordinator, Interview, 17.6.92)

Independence and self-direction in learning were often linked up with other difficult-to-define concepts like 'motivation', 'commitment' and 'responsibility', for example:

> . . .What it needs to come in here, and these are words
> I've used so many times, are motivation and commitment.
> You've got to be motivated and committed to come in here
> because you're working by yourself, with tutor support, with

the resources that we supply you with . . . Provided they're
committed and motivated and providing they're happy to
work by themselves and they recognise the fact that they
haven't got their own personal tutor two and a half hours
of the session that they're in — unlike one or two of our
students think they have — I think they're alright (an Open
Learning Centre tutor, Interview, 28.5.92).

and:

. . . open learning can be very threatening and it can be
much more demanding on the student because they have
to take on perhaps more responsibility for learning . . . (a
college-based open learning coordinator, Interview, 9.6.92).

Many staff felt that with some students they were unable to
offer the tutor support required to encourage students to develop
self-direction or independence in their learning. This was often
the case because the Basic Skills Open Learning Centres tended
to use volunteer tutors less than the established ABE providers:
'What we've found that we can't or don't adequately address are
the needs of low-level literacy students because open learning is
more print-dependent than a class-group, so self-access and self-
direction . . . for basic literacy students doesn't seem appropriate,
they're better in a class with volunteer support' (an Open Learning
Centre tutor, Interview, 10.6.92).

Staff : student ratios in Open Learning Centres have a crucial
effect on the amount of support available for students in their
learning. Inadequate support ratios were frequently cited as the
justification for being unable to cater for the needs of some groups
of students, for example: 'As a sort of guide, yes, we don't take
non-readers, we can't support non-readers because we haven't got
the staff : student ratio to do that, so I mean we just wouldn't
have anybody who was a complete non-reader' (an Open Learning
Centre co-ordinator, Interview, 17.6.92).

Staff : student ratios in Open Learning Centres were also seen
by staff as crucial in the process of encouraging the development
of self-directed learning with students and where the support ratios
were inadequate this process was severely damaged: '. . . we're just
in the position now where we just have not got this one-to-one time
with people telling them all about open learning and self-directed
learning and I suppose a lot of people are thrown in at the deep
end really . . . they don't have the amount of time given to adjust'
(an Open Learning Centre tutor, Interview, 10.6.92).

As Hartree (1984) points out, the assumption that adults are
naturally self-directed learners is not borne out by reality and can
be damaging to student progress within open learning if time

and resources are not available to encourage the development of self-direction with learners.

Many of the students we interviewed in the case-study sites were aware of the association between open learning and independence and self-direction. They were also keenly aware of the difficulties of getting tutor support and of the need to be fairly self-directed in their own learning style/approach from the beginning. People frequently made comments like: '. . . I've got into it quite quickly — I've got used to working by myself. I can motivate myself, I don't need anybody standing over me saying "get this done" and "get that done". You have to be able to understand things, I mean some people can't work like that, they need someone to show them. I mean, there are staff here, but they're not always around, you've got to be able to work things out for yourself' (Susan, an Open Learning Centre student. Interview 11.5.92).

It appears that Open Learning Centres have experienced a conflict between the requirement of student self-direction and independence in learning and the available levels of tutor support which can only be resolved by attracting students who have already clearly defined goals, with high levels of motivation and an ability to work on their own.

The picture of students who seem to be attracted to Basic Skills Open Learning Centres and who seem to be able to work well in such a learning environment begins to look something like the students in Figure 5.1.

Of course, this picture raises the immediate question of what happens to the potential learners who do *not* fit this picture? In the next section, we pursue this by looking at those who are referred elsewhere.

Access and referral

Some Open Learning Centres have explicit entry criteria. Others, whilst not operating a 'criteria for entry' system, are quite clear about who they can cater for and who they cannot, for instance: '. . . when people come in, I'm usually the first person they speak to . . . they speak to me about what they want to do, and I suppose I judge from that if we're the right centre . . . and I always think I've made the right decision, that if they can't read or write, I don't feel it's fair wasting their time and making an appointment for [the co-ordinator] to see them' (Open Learning Centre Administrator, Interview, 17.6.92).

Referrals indicate clearly those students an Open Learning

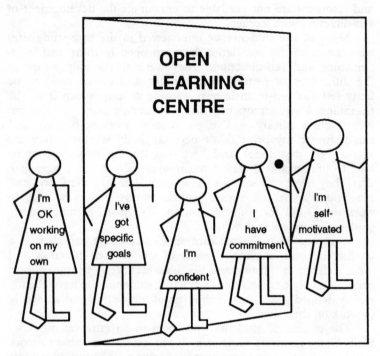

Figure 5.1 Students attracted to Open Learning Centres

Centre feels able to cater for and those people it does not. From Figure 5.2 it can be seen that Open Learning Centres are referring groups of students elsewhere who, traditionally, might have expected to have been part of a basic education service.

Twenty-eight per cent of Open Learning Centres say they refer people who are beginner readers, 64 per cent refer people who have learning difficulties and 53 per cent refer people who are speakers of other languages (ESOL students).

Many Open Learning Centres referred students on to other providers locally. The most cited referrals from Open Learning Centres were made to the established ABE provision, the English for Speakers of Other Languages (ESOL) provision, the local Further Education college, and, for students with learning difficulties, to 'life-skills' or 'self-advocacy' groups.

Referrals of such students are made by Open Learning Centres who say: 'we have not got the facilities'; 'we do not have the staff or work-packs, etc. to deal with them'; 'independent learning materials are not available for ESOL students'; 'we are not a

Figure 5.2 Open learning centre referrals to other provision (N=63) (Percentages do not add up to 100% as all centres gave more than one response. Data from National Questionnaire)

special needs centre'; 'open learning is too poorly staffed to provide real support, especially for those with reading difficulty'.

Referral, in itself, is not necessarily a negative thing. Both Open Learning Centres and established providers regularly refer students on to provision which is seen as better suited to meet their needs. It cannot be expected that any one provider could effectively meet the needs of all potential students. But, with so many centres referring, the concern arises as to whether or not these other providers, to whom referrals are being made, have the resources and staff necessary to cater for the needs of the students whom Open Learning Centres and established providers of basic education say they have not.

Another concern is *why* has open learning, which is seen as a *new* approach to widening access in ABE, come to be defined in practice as suitable only for *some* students — for those who can work independently, who do not lack confidence, who are more advanced than 'beginners' and so on (see Figure 5.1) — and why has open learning been unable to develop in ways which meet the needs of the many students in ABE who do not fit these criteria?

It seems that increasingly the definitions of ABE and Basic Skills needs are being streamlined and refined in ways that result in people being 'defined away' from a provision which is becoming increasingly segregated and no longer operates as a whole and open educational service for adults.

The answer may lie not in any inherent limitation of 'open learning', but in the way it is resourced and structured and currently functions within the wider arena of ABE. This is reflected in responses from ABE staff in our project and in ALBSU's current definition of basic skills which states that: 'Basic skills does not include necessarily wider provision for adults and young people with special needs, English as a Foreign Language (EFL) or general access and return to study courses . . .' (ALBSU, 1993b, p. 7). Particular groups of students are being marginalised by this definition — not only from Open Learning Centres, but from the wider ABE provision as a whole. For ESOL students (who *are* included in this definition of basic skills work) gaining access to open learning provision is still very difficult since, as we have seen, they are frequently referred elsewhere.

Concluding comments

From the research data discussed here, it seems that Basic Skills Open Learning Centres may not be as 'open' as the name implies, at least not for *some* students.

The Centres have been successful in recruiting students. They have been particularly successful in attracting people who are *new* to basic education. These new students are often people who are confident, experienced learners, who have established clear learning goals for themselves and who are already fairly self-directed, motivated and committed to their learning, even if it means 'doing it on their own', with little tutor support. In this way, the Basic Skills Open Learning Centres seem to have been most successful for students who are 'post-basic' and 'can work independently'. Within the range of people attracted to ABE, these are the students who can progress most rapidly and who have the least complex needs for support.

The big question is what has happened to the learning opportunities available for ABE students who do not fall into these categories and why have the Basic Skills Open Learning

Centres developed in ways which mean particular types of students find them unable or unwilling to meet their needs as adult learners in basic education?

There seems to be a general redefinition of basic skills work happening which results in particular groups of people being excluded from the long-standing philosophy of open access which was held by basic education providers. The new Open Learning Centres have not countered this trend but, if anything, have compounded it and have added another split to a provision which is beginning to look increasingly segregated and less like a comprehensive and open educational service for adults.

ALBSU funding for the Basic Skills Open Learning Centres ceased in 1992. While most centres have been integrated into colleges or community education, many have suffered losses of staffing and resources and a few have lost their original premises. Provision is changing yet again and is facing great difficulties in trying to maintain a quality and accessible service. ALBSU statistics for 1992–3 show that while the overall number of students in ABE has fallen slightly and numbers of paid staff have been reduced by 10 per cent, waiting lists for tuition are at their highest levels since monitoring began in the 1970s (see ALBSU 1993c).

Crucial change has been brought about through the government White Paper *Education and Training in the 21st Century*, published in 1991 and the Further and Higher Education Act which came into effect in April 1993. Funding of basic education is now predominantly managed not by local education authorities but by the further education sector via the Further Education Funding Council (FEFC). Many providers are uncertain about the future of basic education. As one of the respondents in our 1993 follow-up questionnaire put it; we '. . . feel we have been thrown up into the air but we do not know yet where or whether we will land'.

How accessible the basic educational provision of the future will be remains to be seen. Funding both from further education colleges and from external agencies like local Training and Enterprise Councils (TECs) is increasingly outcome-related. Funding is increasingly tied to performance. Performance is measured in highly quantifiable terms through outcomes such as recruitment, retention and increases in student numbers, completion of courses and achievement of certificates.

We are continuing to track the impact of these changes. One of the early effects has been the exclusion of 'students with very basic educational needs and those lacking in confidence who need long-term support rather than instant success' and has led to provision catering increasingly for 'mainstream' college students. There has been a real 'pressure to move provision towards students likely to show satisfactory outcomes and accreditation'. In some areas this switch in funding and focus for basic educational work has meant that '. . . valuable work in the community has been dropped because it does not fit the FEFC criteria . . .'[3]

The basic education service in England and Wales is undergoing one of the biggest and potentially most profound changes it has had to deal with. We have argued that it is essential to assess the contribution of the Open Learning Centres within this wider context. The current trends in policy and practice seem to be combining to create a more narrowly defined ABE student and curriculum. Streamlining a service can have positive effects, but the danger is that many of the people who need it most will be marginalised and unable to gain access to essential basic education opportunities in the future.

References

ALBSU and The National Federation of Voluntary Literacy Schemes (1983) *Action and Words: sharing literacy skills in community groups.*

ALBSU (1985) *Adult Literacy: the first decade.*

ALBSU (1991) *Open Learning Centres in England and Wales.* Interim Report.

ALBSU (1992) *Basic Skills in Further Education Colleges.*

ALBSU (1993a) *Open Learning Centres.* Final Report.

ALBSU (1993b) *Challenges and Choices: basic skills provision after the Act.*

ALBSU (1993c) *Annual Report.*

Bonnerjea, L. and Freud, B. 1988 *Workbase — a basic skills and education pack for manual workers*, London, ALBSU.

Boud, D. (ed) (1988) *Developing Student Autonomy in Learning*, London, Kogan Page.

Brookfield, S. (ed) (1985) *'Self-directed learning: From theory to practice'. New Directions for Continuing Education*, 25, San Francisco, Jossey-Bass.

Caffarella, Rosemary, S. and O'Donnell, Judith, M. (1989) *Self-Directed Learning.* Adults: Psychological and Educational Perspectives 1, Department of Adult Education, University of Nottingham, England.

Charnley, A. and Withnall, A. (1989) *Developments in Adult Basic Education: Special Development Projects 1978–1985*, ALBSU.

Davenport, J. (1993) 'Is there any way out of the andragogy morass?' in Thorpe, M., Edwards, E. and Hanson, S. (eds) *Culture and Processes of Adult Learning*, London, Routledge.

Hamilton, M. (1989) *'The development of adult basic education in Britain'* in Entwistle, N. (ed) *The Handbook of Educational Ideas and Practices*, London, Croom Helm.

Hartree, A. (1984) '"Malcolm Knowles" theory of androgogy: a critique'. *International Journal of Lifelong Education*, 3, pp. 203–10.

ILEA (1990) Afro-Caribbean Language and Literacy Project in Further and Higher Education *Language and Power* Inner London Education Authority.

Jones, H. and Charnley, A. (1978) *Adult Literacy: A Study of Its Impact.* National Institute of Adult Education, Leicester.

Lee Community Education Centre (1985–88) *Papers in the Problems of Representation Series*, Lee Centre.

Mace, J. (1979) *Working with Words: literacy beyond school*, London, Writers and Readers Publishing Co-operative.

Mace, J. (1992) *Talking about Literacy*, London, Routledge.

National Council for Vocational Qualifications (1993) *GNVQ Information Note*.

Moss, W. (1984) *Breaking the Barriers: Eight case studies of Women Returning to Learn in North London* Access to Learning for Adults (ALFA) London.

Paine, N. (ed) (1988) *Open Learning in Transition*, London, Kogan Page.

RaPAL (Research and Practice in Adult Literacy) Bulletin is published three times a year. Details from Sally Murphy, Bolton Royd Centre, Manningham Lane, Bradford, BD8 7BB.

Sanders, J. (1988) Open To Question: Opportunities in adult basic education. RaPAL Bulletin No. 7 Autumn.

Notes

1. ALBSU is the national agency for adult literacy, numeracy and related skills in England and Wales. It is a non-teaching agency which offers consultancy services, staff development and training. It also funds Local Development Projects and publishes learning materials for basic education work.

2. Copies of the final report of this research project, of Thematic Issue papers, of a student 'Ways of learning' resource pack and book of student writings are all available from The Centre for the Study of Education and Training, University of Lancaster, LA1 4YL. Tel: 0524–592679.

3. All the anonymous quotes in this paragraph are responses to our follow-up questionnaire which was sent out in 1993 to the same providers as the original questionnaire in 1992.

6 Library-based open learning

John Allred

> 'The aim of public libraries to provide unlimited knowledge is
> in total harmony with the aim of non-traditional education: to
> provide unlimited opportunity. The possibility for joining the two
> should not be permitted to pass by.' (Carnegie Commission,
> 1973)

Library-based open learning — a deliberate service in its own right

Library-based open learning is defined here as the deliberate
provision by a library service of professional assistance and a
range of facilities to be used by a person in order to learn on
their own terms for their own purposes, at their own pace at a
time and place convenient to them. This is not to say that the
library will act in isolation to other providers of open learning, but
to explain that this chapter addresses the role of the library in its
own right in open learning not, as it so often is, in a purely support
role to its parent organisation (college or school) or to some other
educational programme (basic literacy). This can be summed up
for the library as 'Service, not delivery'.

Library services in schools and colleges and in public libraries
have become more important as a learning resource partly due to
the impact of the new information technologies on educational
practice. Educational policies have also reinforced this profile by
emphasising the individual learner as a 'customer', with course
work tailored to the learner's or trainee's own needs in industry or
for self-development, and with the opportunity for individualised
courses to be built up from a range of modules. Such flexibility has

put considerable demands on school, college and public libraries to assist in providing the student with their individual learning resources. School library services in authorities providing adequate resources for stock and professional staff show a high degree of supported individualised learning.

Education traditionally has been institutionally based and offered to students in groups on terms laid down by the provider in the form of conditional entry, regular attendance with prescribed methods of instruction and with assessments against objectives not set by the student. Libraries, academic public and special, though still institutions, can support open learning by not having to be party to so many of the constraints of traditional education. Yet they still provide a structure and organise resources that can direct and sustain learning in ways that improve the chances of achieving the outcomes desired by the learner. Open learning packs have set a new standard in structured learning. The best are attractive, fun to use, and educationally sound. This has been true also of the best books for learning provided by libraries.

A library is all about structure, selecting, collecting, organising, indexing, conserving and updating information in its many different forms. It also provides the facilities and staff to make the best use of that information. These resources can assist learners who are:

- seeking information as part of the process of identifying and clarifying a need for learning and learning goals
- seeking information on the range and suitability and accessibility of learning methods and resources
- requiring referral to other resources and support and to assessment and accreditation
- identifying and locating books, other documents and audio-visual materials, using on-line information, needed to support the learning and skills aimed at acquiring the skills of abstracting and applying information to a task be it writing an essay or building a wall.

Librarians become involved with learners formally under such programmes as 'instruction in library use' or by informally responding to a learning enquiry about bricklaying which appears as the over-simplified question 'what kind of cement should I use . . .?'

The development of open learning in libraries

Libraries, places in which knowledge is collected and organised so as to enable this knowledge to be passed on and built upon, are as old as, or even older than, institutional education. They have an interesting and honourable place in opening up learning.

The ancient libraries of Babylon and Alexandria, were great teaching centres. The spirit of the Renaissance in Europe was open to self-directed scholars from other little known, but unique collections such as that at Lincoln in the 12th century (Thompson, 1967, p. 284). The medieval universities of Europe were attractive to students because of their book collections as much as for anything else. The coffee houses of the 18th century in London had circulating libraries and the self-help academies and institutes of the eighteenth and nineteenth centuries often had a library at their centre (Armytage, 1965, p. 51). The public library movement in the nineteenth century received political support for its educational value at a time when *laissez-faire* government policies prevented any significant direct investment into educational, institutions (Great Britain, Parliament, 1849).

These examples do not present the library as the main component in education, nor as a substitute for it. They do, however, demonstrate the symbiotic nature of the library and education, with the library at the open end of the system. This symbiosis is not without its tensions.

Libraries in academic institutions, school, college and university libraries, are ambiguous. As an open learning resource they bring together in one place the totality of the documented knowledge required by the faculty and students. The learner can travel wherever and however they wish in a good library, whatever boundaries the official curriculum may wish to fix. Nevertheless the library is often physically distant from the learner, is large and difficult to use, time consuming and clearly institutional.

An open learning pack, that is, a structured learning plan comprising all, or most, of the learning resources in a variety of media necessary to achieve the learning goals, together with assessments to measure the achievement of these goals, is but the latest example of a process in which teachers, often with librarians, have encapsulated their educational programmes. Reading lists, programmed texts, assignments and workbooks are the more traditional encapsulations and they are to be found in libraries, laboratories, workshops and drop-in learning centres. A collective name for these places is Learning Resource Centres. In America in the 60s and 70s the name of 'Library College' was used for educational institutions that had library use as their central learning method.

Some of the tension is revealed in the history of the Open University and, more recently, the Open College, when early expectations of heavy library use by Open University students were not realised. The structure and the resources supplied by the Open University were so professional, and so comprehensive, that there was little time and probably no need for the student to use a library as well. This changed with the development of project-based courses.

The impact of the Open College on library services was almost non-existent for the same reason. The Open College learning packs aimed to provide the learner with a complete set of resources apart from the tutorial and workshop facilities. These facilities were provided by the local college centres. The Open College admitted that they would see any need to use a library as, in part, a failure to provide a comprehensive set of materials (letter from David Grugeon to The Library Association). Quite clearly the role of the library here was seen as that of 'common carrier', a simple delivery mechanism for learning resources not immediately to the learner's hand. The example certainly does raise the question of how self-contained education or training should be. The term open learning also may be ambiguous.

Open learning in public libraries in the USA

The scope for public libraries to become partners in their own right alongside those institutions supporting adult learning was demonstrated most forcefully in a major project in the United States during the 1970s. In 1971 the Carnegie Foundation funded the Commission on Non-traditional Study sponsored by the College Entrance Examination Board (CEEB). This two-year study discovered a very wide range of programmes available for individualised study that defied definition (Carnegie Commission, 1973). These programmes were only useful to those who knew of their existence and the Commission saw public libraries as the ready-made centres for information, materials, assistance, and advice. They were centres which were already providing this sort of service to the community.

In 1973 a national programme was launched by the new national Office of Library Independent Study and Guidance Projects set up by the CEEB. Eleven public libraries participated in a highly structured programme under the directorship of Jose Toro involving comprehensive staff training and standardised monitoring. The Adult Independent Learner Project has been well documented (Birge, 1981, pp. 118–135; Mavor, Toro and De Prospo, 1976; Dale, 1979) and the lessons have been studied by educators and librarians.

After 1975, when the funded project came to an end, some of

the public libraries failed to maintain their specialised services to
adult learners. On the other hand a large number of other special
projects and activities supporting adult learners appeared, and
continue to appear, in public libraries in America. Denver public
library had its 'On your own' programme and Chicago their 'Study
unlimited'.

The climate changed between 1970 and 1990 in the USA.
The Adult Independent Learner Project had adopted the PPE
(Program Planning and Evaluation) model and had trained large
numbers of library staff in setting service objectives and evaluation
at a time when justification of expenditure could no longer rest
on the abstract value of the public library as a 'good thing'. The
US Public Library Data Service defines the effectiveness of the
service to users in terms of eight roles, one of which is that of
'independent learner support centre'. In 1988 43 per cent of the
libraries selected that role as their first or second priority goal.
Interpretations of the figures can allow for other roles that other
libraries may adopt. This is a sophisticated and realistic approach
to public library management that avoids penalising libraries and
staff that become more involved with users demanded by such a
role as that of open learning.

Open learning in public libraries in the United Kingdom

The American experience underlined the weakness of managing
adult learning support in public libraries as an add-on service.
It was costly, had few takers, and ran into competition with the
colleges. The fact that a highly structured project, with resources
devoted to staff training and evaluation, largely disappeared
illustrates the reluctance of the library profession to alter, and
the difficulties of finding time from the heavy burden of library
housekeeping to attend to the needs of individual users.

In the UK, instead of defining adult learning separately
and providing a special service, we tried to extend the existing
services by providing support for open learning at a time when
the traditional library services were already being developed to
serve adult learners in many other ways. The warm reception
and recognition given to the visitors from the American Adult
Independent Learner project when they visited several sites in
the UK in 1978 was a mark of the growing confidence of
public librarians that their role could move from the passive,
common carrier, to the more active roles, backup, self-help to

direct service identified in British Library research (Allred and Hay, 1979, p. 22). Some examples of these services were revealed in research conducted by the Council for Educational Technology in 1984 (Smith, 1987).

The move away from the role of back-up to other organisations to the more direct role of a self-help service for learners began when libraries drew the attention of individual learners to the resources offered by the library. These resources are considerable, ranging from local history kits to language tapes, from community information packs to on-line information services but, in the main, users are not identified as learners. Leicestershire County Libraries, after studying its community, produced around twenty displays of stock in 1985 which were circulated around libraries in the county together with short but detailed leaflets describing learning resources for different topics such as baby care, psychology, local history and gardening. These displays contained up to four copies of each item and stayed at each library for three months. In some cases they were linked to local classes.

The leaflets were not annotated reading lists but were a learning resource. They were based upon the open learning concept and included information about useful periodicals, local societies and other contacts described in ways that could help a person to develop their interests and skills. In addition a general brochure called *Learn how to learn with your library* was published describing how the learner could get the best out of the library services available. The project ran for five years and was successful at arousing interest especially from people who admitted they would not be likely to attend an adult education class. Even so, some of the library staff still found it difficult to grasp the use of books as learning resources and treated the exercise in the manner of a traditional book display (Smith, 1987, pp. 130–134).

The public library can be induced to extend local educational resources for adults, or to compensate for their reduction, by mediating information about other services available, a valuable part of opening learning. This function is recognised now as part of educational guidance (UDACE, 1986, p. 8). In 1985 this was an innovation in many places. Network Scotland, an independent agency with its roots ten years earlier in the Adult Literacy Campaign's Telephone Referral Service, provided an information and guidance service to Scotland via a national telephone service handling around 5,000 enquiries a year. Involvement with public libraries followed a suggestion for 'local information points' from the MSC project *Scottish Referral Services Network* 1983. The experience was a valuable one in the way it highlighted the opportunities and difficulties.

The opportunities were taken to supplement the library's traditional stock of reference works on careers, education and community development with up-to-date and specialised leaflets on health education, social benefits and tenancy problems for example and with referral to Network Scotland itself. Library staff were trained in short group sessions but here the difficulties appeared. Alarm about the implications of offering advice instead of just access to documents was reinforced by the same lack of awareness of open learning and was fed by a breakdown in personal links between staff at Network and the libraries. It was an opportunity lost for public libraries to identify themselves with the information and its use, though co-operation later with TAP (Training Access Points) information services, and the outcomes of experiments with the provision of open learning packs described below, has done a great deal to involve library staff with learning information and with the adult learners who make use of it.

A key function of open learning is to enable the potential learner to move into the available learning networks and to become aware and informed of the options open to them. Since the early work of ACACE (the Advisory Council of Adult Continuing Education) on links to learning (ACACE, 1979), and the research by Linda Butler into the part played by public libraries (Butler, 1988) public librarians have appreciated the extent to which their services, information and networks, can be of assistance. A survey in 1990 (Barnes and Allred, 1991) found that nearly 40 per cent of public library authorities were involved in educational guidance networks and all kept files of information about educational opportunities. The down side was that library staff's part in the networks was usually as an inactive committee member, and the information collected by the library was comprehensive in local educational authority provision only and invariably not indexed in any way. A qualitative ranking put 20 per cent of libraries as offering a good or very good guidance support and a further 34 per cent as average.

By 1990 it only needed a catalyst to fuse these different elements, self-help resources, educational guidance, referral networks, into a truly open learning service for adults in public libraries. The catalyst appeared in the form of an initiative from the Employment Department.

As the recession in the late 1980s deepened local authorities had to deploy all their resources to limit the economic and social effects on their communities. In Clwyd County local communities were, in effect, given their libraries as a community learning resource (Smith, 1987, p. 83). The response was enthusiastic and by 1988 the County Library service had attracted Manpower

Services Commission funding for the provision of open learning packs in selected libraries as a further way to meet the clearly expressed demand for alternative learning resources for the community. The initiative in Clwyd was effective enough for a larger pilot project in which ten public libraries were to stock open learning packs, and in which staff were to be trained in open learning delivery to the appropriate standards in the Employment Department's manual (Employment Department, 1990). This project was aimed at unsponsored individual learners. Through the good offices of the National Open Learning Association (now the British Association for Open Learning) close contacts were promoted between a public library and its nearest Open Learning Centre for the selection and delivery of open learning packs and for training. The project was monitored by The Library Association and the results were encouraging (Allred and Heeks, 1992).

The research provided evidence that the target groups of people could be persuaded to become open learners, and that borrowing open learning packs from the public library was an extremely cost-effective way of increasing the take-up of open learning generally. Dutch Open University research shows that home use of learning materials is more intensive than use in a study centre (*OLS News*, 1993).

Half of the users in the pilot project were in the age range 25–39, an unusually large proportion for public library users. One-fifth claimed to have only a basic education. One-third were unwaged and most of these were female. Nearly three-quarters of all users had no previous experience of learning on their own with this type of material and this was the decisive factor in funding a full national programme.

Library staff were universally praised for their helpfulness and three libraries notable for their competent staff had a higher percentage of people following up on their learning. Overall 70 per cent followed up on the learning experience in some way with further learning. Completing the work programme in the pack made no difference to the likelihood of a learner following up the learning in some way afterwards. A third said that they had learned a lot and only 15 per cent said that they had lost interest or use for the learning that they had undertaken.

There was a wide variety of reasons for learning with the open learning packs and many people surprised themselves with the outcomes. Three-quarters of the users said that the material was what they wanted, though half did not complete the course laid out in the packs. One-third of the people said they had enrolled, or were about to enrol, on a taught course related to the topic of the pack borrowed. Even where a pack had been returned uncompleted by a learner, who said it was not what was wanted, the result was a decision to find a more intensive way to study the subject. This, together with the other learners who wanted tutorial assistance but could not make contact with colleges over Christmas, shows that personal support is required for many people. Even calls from library staff 'to see how you are getting on' were welcome and not considered to be intrusive. The issue of tutorial and other personal support is discussed at the end of this chapter.

The UK *Open for Learning* project 1992

The results of the pilot project provided ample support for a national programme in England. A White Paper referred to government plans to widen access to open learning, with funds again being provided through the Employment Department, using public libraries as front-line providers (Great Britain, 1992, para. 3.27). There are similar developments in Scotland and Wales. Every library authority in England is able to apply to join the project and to receive direct financial support for the provision of open learning packs and equipment to try these out in the library. The goal of the programme is to attract into open learning adults who are not aware of, or who are not willing or able to take up, open learning by other means. The project is ambitious and apparently unique in Europe. 23 per cent of public libraries in the UK now (1992) stock open learning packs (half of them at only one service point) and nearly 21,000 loans were recorded in 1991–92 (Allred, 1992).

The sums of money for each library are not large though the total project expenditure exceeds £1.1 million. The contract with each library requires staff to be trained and the adherence to the Code of Practice (Employment Department, 1990). There is national publicity and support from the British Association for Open Learning who are contracted to manage the project (Willetts, 1991). Monitoring is being carried out by the Library Association. The project is important because it sets out to provide a specialised service conforming to national standards. The money given to each library is sufficient to encourage a decision in favour of providing the service but not enough to jeopardise the continuation of the service on mainstream funding. The experience of the pilot project was that all libraries continued with an open learning service after the cessation of external funding. It has proved to be a natural extension of the public library service.

The libraries are expected to have especially close links with their local TECs (Training and Enterprise Councils). These Councils in England and Wales are companies set up by the Employment Department using public and private funds. Their function is to respond to local needs for the development of a more skilled workforce. The TECs administer many initiatives that harmonise with the *Open for Learning* project, for example Open Learning Credits, and the Skillchoice and Gateways to Learning guidance programmes. In some cases the TEC has supplemented the national resources with additional funds and support for local libraries. One TEC is using the public libraries for its recognised open learning delivery points.

Issues

Academic libraries' role in open learning is problematical as long as the library delivers the materials needed by the teaching faculties. If the role is reversed and the teaching faculty becomes just one further, though major, resource for a learner then the library teams up with the guidance services, so well developed in many schools, further education and higher education institutions, to provide impartial information about opportunities, learning materials and access to wider learning networks. During the learning the student can return to the library for support, exploring and using further information without losing control of the situation.

Public libraries are really now open for learning. In many places staff have been trained to recognise a learner and to adapt the standard library loan procedures and to make equipment available to suit the individual. A growing equality of partnership between the library and neighbouring educational institutions provides for the easy exchange of information, educational guidance and personal support in the best interests of the learner. The best service can add up to a comprehensive, unbiased information and support system for learners of all kinds providing direct access to a wide range of learning materials and associated hardware with staff on hand to assist in their use, and with referral to all the other ways of learning in what can be a very cost-effective service (Bamber, 1993; Library Association, 1989).

There are limitations and problems. The lack of integrated tutorial support may, or may not be, a problem depending upon the circumstances. Apart from the difficulty of accrediting the learning the research has not shown it to be a major issue. Learners who did want this form of support seemed to move easily on to a more formal taught course. Others saw a positive advantage in being able to try out their learning in private.

Open learning is not distance teaching. It implies an opportunity for the learner to self-develop, to make their own interpretations and conclusions in response to the integral feedback in the learning materials (Hodgson, Mann and Snell, 1987). This means that library 'delivery' is not necessarily failing if tutorial support is not taken up. If the materials, facilities and other information in the library is effective the learner can achieve much whilst still remaining in charge. For example, one learner having difficulty with an accounting pack was shown an instructional book on the same subject which proved exactly what was wanted.

Open learners invariably do have difficulty in maintaining their enthusiasm for the task and in keeping to a timetable. One public library, Sunderland, with Wearmouth TEC, has recognised the function for library staff of mentor and carried out formal training. Other libraries, for example Clwyd County, have been moving in this direction. The task of mentor is to assist the learner to draw up a learning contract with targets and a timetable for themselves, to point to appropriate and accessible learning resources (which may include a tutor), and to review progress with the learner and to encourage them. An evaluation of the experiment in Sunderland showed that the members of the public had difficulty in recognising that librarians were providing this service, but they readily accepted the support when explained to them. They thought it a service for which librarians were well suited, and there were a number of instances where the librarian assisted in ways that were, for them, quite straightforward (for example, extending the time for a loan of a pack, or finding out about relevant organisations in the town). The librarians found considerable satisfaction in the relationships and there was no doubt that learners were encouraged by these more systematic contacts with library staff.

The library staff in Sunderland were trained on the job by short courses, open learning, and by short staff placements in the TEC's Open Learning Centre. The training of library staff for work with open learners is now much in demand and a number of initiatives are appearing. Some Clwyd county library staff are now working for accreditation as assessors in open learning delivery. The Library Association is exploring the range of skills and the types of training that could be exploited by staff involved in the work of guidance and open learning delivery. Though demanding a change in attitudes to service the additional workload does not appear to be an intolerable addition to the hard pressed library staff. In fact the numbers are a very small proportion of all public library users and stock. Essentially open learning in public libraries is a refocussing of services already provided.

The range of materials for open learning in the UK particularly is increasing considerably now. An estimate gives around 10,000 open learning packs that are commercially available on almost every subject. It can be a major problem to identify, purchase and prepare these for use in a library. Some of the copyright conditions are uncertain. The British Association for Open Learning and the Library Association are improving the situation by encouraging better understanding by authors and publishers of open learning packs of the ways in which librarians can extend the market still further by introducing new users to open learning. There is a move to standardise the way in which open learning packs are recorded in catalogues and bibliographies along similar lines to standard bibliographical descriptions for books, but incorporating the special features of open learning packs that are linked to organisations providing tutorial support and to accreditation (ADSET, 1993).

To sum up. There is a new climate in learning brought about by political and economic change, together with new technologies for the production of learning resources, that has enabled libraries, especially public libraries, to rediscover their roots as 'the people's university'. Their many service points constitute a readily available open door to the diffident and to the motivated learner alike. Though clearly not able to meet every learning need the library is also a natural place to receive information and redirection, when this is needed, to other resources in the maze of support for adult learning.

References

ACACE (1979) *Links to learning: a report on educational information, advisory and counselling services for adults*, Leicester, The Advisory Council for Adult Continuing Education.

ADSET (1993) *Using learning information. A guide to handling information in education and training*, 2nd edn. 4 vols, Kettering, The Association for Database Services.

Allred, J. (1992) *Open for Learning: Open and Flexible Learning in Public Libraries, the Baseline Survey*, London, The Library Association.

Allred, J. and Hay, W. (1979) *A Preliminary Study of the Involvement of Public Libraries with Adult Learners*, Leeds, The School of Librarianship, Leeds Polytechnic.

Allred, J. and Heeks, P. (1992) *Open Learning in Public Libraries: Evaluation of an Employment Department Training Agency Initiative*, Rev. edn. London, The Library Association for the Employment Department.

Armytage, W. H. G. (1965) *Four Hundred Years of English Education*, Cambridge University Press.

Bamber, A. (1993) *Look Up — and Learn. Library Association Adult Independent Learning Guidelines for Libraries and Learning Resource Centres*, London, Library Association Publishing.

Barnes, C. and Allred, J. (1991) *Educational Guidance for Adults and Public Libraries*, Leicester, the National Institute of Adult Continuing Education.

Birge, L. E. (1981) *Serving Adult Learners: a Public Library Tradition*, Chicago, American Library Association.

Butler, L. (1988) *The Role of Public Libraries in the Provision of Educational Guidance for Adults*, London, The British Library Research and Development Department. (Library and information research report 22).

Carnegie Commission on Non-Traditional Study (1973) *Diversity by Design*, San Francisco, Josey-Bass.

Dale, S. (1979) The adult independent learning project: work with adult self-directed learners in public libraries' in *Journal of Librarianship*, 11(2), pp. 83–106.

Employment Department (1990) *Ensuring Quality in Open Learning*, Rev. edn. Sheffield, The Employment Department.

Great Britain. Parliament. The House of Commons (1849) *Report from the Select Committee on Public Libraries*, London, Parliament, the House of Commons.

Great Britain. Parliament. The House of Commons (1992) *People, Jobs and Opportunity*, London, HMSO. (Cm 1810.)

Hodgson, V. E., Mann, S. J. and Snell, R. (1987) *Beyond Distance Teaching — Towards Open Learning*, Oxford, Oxford University Press.

Library Association (1989) *Open Learning, a Policy Statement*, London, The Library Association.

Mavor, A. S., Toro, J. O. and De Prospo, E. R. (1976) *Final Report Part I: the Role of the Public Libraries in Adult Independent Learning*, New York, College Entrance Examination Board.

OLS News (1993) 'Results of a research by the Dutch Open University' in *Open Learning Systems News*, **45**, p. 3.

Smith, V. (1987) *Public Libraries and Adult Independent Learners: a Report*, London, Council for Educational Technology. (Working paper 27.)

Thompson, J. W. (1967) *The Medieval Library*, New York, London, Hafner Publishing Company.

UDACE (1986) *The Challenge of Change: Developing Educational Guidance for Adults*, Leicester, The National Institute for Adult Continuing Education for the Unit for the Development of Adult Continuing Education.

Willetts, D. (1991) *Open Learning in Public Libraries: a Practical Guide to Implementing Open Learning*, Baldock, The British Association for Open Learning for the Employment Department.

7 Managing flexible learning

Andrew Haldane and Maureen Haldane

Introduction

This chapter suggests a convergence between the two cultures of education and industry as a consequence of changes arising from the creation of an information society and the consequent need to respond by creating a learning society.

A growing acceptance of new management styles and structures and a growing interest in the concept of the 'learning organisations' is seen as matched by changes in teaching/learning styles and methods as educationalists respond to the challenge of 'life-long learning'. Managers of flexible, self-reliant workers will need to deploy process skills comparable to those deployed by managers of flexible, self-reliant learners. Flexible Learning may then become the means of cementing a new relationship between education and industry based on a shared goal of helping learners to achieve unprecedented levels of expertise and the personal qualities necessary to deploy that expertise in a rapidly changing world of work.

The chapter also seeks to illustrate such convergence by reference to the pilot year of a post-experience programme at Manchester Metropolitan University to develop teachers in the role of facilitator/manager of Flexible Learning. This project sought to examine the extent to which Management Charter Initiatives (MCI) management standards, either in actual wording or in substance, could serve as descriptor of the role of a teacher as a manager/facilitator thereby demonstrating a comparability of competence between what may have been regarded as different cultures.

In recent years we have become accustomed to a series of

initiatives such as Education/Industry partnerships, curriculum changes, the encouragement of more employer governors and the influence of TECs and LECs each intended to make education manage itself in a more businesslike fashion and/or to become more responsive to the needs of industry. It is not our intention to argue the merits or demerits of such measures but merely to observe that they appear to be predicated as a means of bringing together two different organisation cultures and mindsets.

If we accept that at present there is at least some cultural mismatch at the education/industry interface it may be that intervention is not the only force for convergence. Education and industry are both in the throes of responding to major societal changes arising from a new industrial revolution driven by information technology which may result in more commonality of goals and values.

The projected impact of new technology and suggested responses were described in two complementary reports (*Skills Shortages in Europe* and *Schools and Industry*) to the European Commission Task Force Education, Human Resources and Youth by IRDAC (Industrial Research and Development Advisory Committee, 1990).

Although IRDAC makes references to the influence of new technologies on organisation structures and working relationships it is the expansion of training and education opportunities needed to cope with the new industrial world order which is its particular focus. IRDAC compares the ageing demographic profile of Western Europe with the much younger populations in emergent industrial competitor nations. It cites South Korea's aspiration to have 80 per cent of its 18-year-olds eligible for University admission by the year 2000 as a powerful illustration of the depth and breadth of the skills base needed. Countries who wish to become or remain advanced nations will need to reconsider their ideas as to the limits of individual potential and how it can be realised as the rate of technological advance accelerates:

> IRDAC above all is convinced that education and training issues related to industrial competence and competitiveness have an overriding importance in relation to the future well-being of Europe and its citizens . . . .

ERT (The European Round Table of Industrialists) has also expressed similar views (ERT, 1992) identifying lifelong learning as 'a key concept to our success for tomorrow'.

IRDAC concludes that a quantum leap in the skills base of Western Europe comparable to that targeted by Pacific Rim countries cannot be achieved simply by raising the aspirations and attainment of the next generation but will require dramatic increases in adult continuing education and training — in effect for most people learning will become a lifelong experience. This will necessitate a concerted response by all stakeholders: individuals, employers and society as a whole. However, as continuous learning becomes more widely recognised as the engine driving faster, continuous, incremental change at the workplace, and therefore the key to business success, employers will find employee development much closer to the heart of their corporate planning process. They are increasingly likely to see themselves as 'Learning Organisations', (see for example Mills and Friesen, 1992; Beard, 1993) whose strategy and structure provide an environment where innovation can flourish through the growth of the organisation's knowledge and skills base.

If the expertise of the organisation as an entity is to evolve, then individuals within it must be alert to all opportunities to extend their knowledge and skills in a variety of ways:

- through continuing education and training
- through learning on the job
- by accessing a range of information systems and analysing data
- through their own research and the research of others
- by sharing expertise among colleagues
- by sharing with appropriate external collaborators
- by recruitment.

The learning organisation and total quality management

However Learning Organisations, functioning within a Learning Society, will need to stimulate learning that is quantitatively and qualitatively different in order to respond to changing working practices.

Total Quality Management (TQM) is one of the influences which is helping to shape new management styles. Tribus (1992) has described a Total Quality Management ethos as seeking to create 'autonomous team players.' In analysing the leadership skills required for successful quality management Johnson (1993) sees employee awareness, motivation and commitment as the keys to success. Leadership is thereby expressed more through empowerment of individuals rather than through the exercise of power. Further evidence of a more people-centred approach to management may be deduced from the fact that 'people satisfaction' is one of the five criteria by which companies entering for the European Foundation for Quality Management's (EFQM) Quality Award are judged. Thus the concept of the learning organisation is closely linked to the TQM concept with its emphasis on continuous improvement and the motivation and development of people.

Indeed the two may be intertwined via something of a 'chicken and egg' relationship. Langford (1992) suggests that the pursuit of quality is itself a learning process from which a learning organisation will ultimately emerge while Maul and Gillard (1993) believe that managers need first to create learning organisations in order to achieve total quality management.

The hierarchical authoritarian organisation structures associated with the fast receding mass production of manufactures deploying comparatively low technology are being replaced by organisation structures with far fewer levels of authority.

Although comparatively recent research has suggested that changes to organisation structure may lag behind the development of innovative business plans (Burdett, 1992; Cascio, 1993) there is also evidence that the reduction in levels of management hierarchy is both a response to financial strictures, and, more positively, to the development of responsive flexible organisations, which can thrive in a climate of change (e.g. Lundberg, 1991; ERT, 1991).

IRDAC sees new technology and IT as 'affecting' the internal structure and management of all enterprises and the relationships between them. This restructuring would be expressed by a tendency in more successful firms toward horizontal integration 'as opposed to the traditional pattern of vertical hierarchical control'.

Reducing the number of layers of management has implications for the levels of responsibility and authority which individuals are required to exercise (see also Baaken, Gould and Kim, 1992) further reinforcing the trend toward people at all levels becoming required to take both more personal responsibility and more shared responsibility within teams rather than merely receive and execute orders.

IRDAC also saw the relationship between new technology and work organisation as resulting in greater diversity and also mutual dependence. IRDAC is, however, quite explicit about the learning methods necessary to realise such a vision:

> . . .delivery mechanisms based on new technology and innovative teaching and learning approaches. Traditional face to face formats and lectures have a lot of intrinsic value but are not the appropriate solution for the quantum leap which is needed in continuing training.

To function effectively Learning Organisations need a workforce which possesses an existing relevant competence but whose members possess or develop the skills of 'learning to learn'. They also require well developed skills in applying their learning creatively if the organisation to which they belong is to evolve and prosper through innovation.

Whilst managers can create an organisational environment in which learning may flourish, individuals will also be required to take more responsibility for their own learning.

Indeed the personal qualities people need to deploy as life-long learners are very similar to those which they deploy as empowered workers (Johnson, 1993) or autonomous team players (Tribus, 1992) i.e. initiative, self-reliance, originality, problem solving skills and analytical skills.

Meyer-Dohm (1993) in contrasting the past mass production paradigm with the present lean production paradigm at Volkswagen also identifies parallels between working methods and skills/knowledge development in these two different manufacturing cultures.

He sees in a mass production culture, knowledge supplanted by operating instructions, encapsulated in a technical solution from which the operator is isolated and left with 'no more latitude than the built in means of control will permit'.

In the lean production environment Meyer-Dohm suggests that the knowledge that matters is innovative knowledge rather than repetitive knowledge. He suggests that in order to make an impact on people innovative knowledge must be experienced at first hand. This observation adds support to the suggestion that different learning methods are appropriate to new industrial environments.

The new learning culture is seen as requiring problem orientated thinking, team work and communication skills so that ideas for continuous improvement can 'burst the bounds of hierarchy'.

In examining the changes in management culture which are leading to a much greater emphasis on unlocking individual skills we have already made reference to a growing need to develop personal qualities and skills which are not task specific.

Broader occupational competence

The CBI report *Towards a skills revolution* expressed this in the following terms:

As employers increasingly require the skill necessary for adaptability and innovation in employment, education and training need to be broadly based, concerned not just with technical understanding of the job but competence in the broader work context. Broader occupational competence should be concerned with adaptability, management of roles, responsibility for standards, creativity and flexibility to changing demand.

The report goes on to highlight the implications of the above proposition with this statement:

Task competence is not enough to meet this need, although some employers concentrating on their short-term needs may believe it is. Competence must, as it should when properly defined, go beyond the merely procedural.

The CBI's report also called upon the UK government to set world class 'targets for education and training'. A subsequent government discussion paper *The Strategy for Skills and Enterprise* (1992) set out National Education and Training Targets. Seven of the eight targets are expressed in measurable terms, such as numbers attaining particular NVQ levels; it is perhaps significant that one of the four foundation learning targets is expressed in qualitative terms:

Education and Training provision to develop self-reliance, flexibility and breadth (National Training Task Force) (NTTF), 1992)

If this more generic capability, seen as reflecting personal qualities increasingly desirable in the world of work, is also perceived as a foundation learning target, it implies that such capability is not entirely inherent and can be cultivated. It also implies that the process through which learning occurs and not simply content may be of growing importance. Handy (1992) explored this issue using a taxonomy developed by Katz (1955) who suggested three categories of skill necessary to run an organisation successfully: technical skills, human skills and conceptual skills.

Whilst Katz acknowledged that all three types of skill were necessary to run an organisation, yesterday's technology created a pressure to minimise the deployment of human and conceptual skills and to emphasise technical skills — automation creating automatons. It would appear that tomorrow's technologies offer the opportunity to delegate technical skills to machines while precipitating a pace of change which requires human and conceptual skills to flourish. That is not to say that the ever expanding horizons of technical knowledge can be ignored — it is only possible to delegate successfully expertise one possesses —

however, technology provides both a fast track for utilising current technical knowledge and a fast track for acquiring more.

Katz had suggested that technical skills could be taught and human skills learnt but that conceptual skills were inherent. However Handy asserted that conceptual skills too could be developed. He subsequently commended the development of conceptual skills beyond, as well as within, the confines of directly work-related learning in the following manner:

> The new professionals and managers will badly need the capacity to step outside their narrow all-consuming world of business and draw upon the widest possible range of imagery to cope with the challenges of change and uncertainty.

Handy not only recommended a novel a week to top-up executives' 'reservoirs of ideas, insights and imagery' but also suggested fostering partnerships with Universities to develop their understanding of European history and philosophy, political theory and English literature. He also reflects the CBI view of the need for educational breadth expressing concern that time invested in developing technical competences in engineering and accountancy may leave too little time for developing human and conceptual skills. In similar vein Meyer-Dohm (1993) envisages 'the dominance of engineering sciences and related disciplines at the workplace replaced by ever closer co-operation with humanities in the field of work organisation'.

Handy's alternative proposition that conceptual skills may also be capable of nurture is consistent with that of Flavell (1985). Flavell described the higher-order cognitive processes as metacognition and suggested that in common with other cognitive skills metacognition could be enhanced through learning.

Tomkinson and Kilner (1991) cited Flavell in their analysis of the active nature of learning which formed a part of their critical evaluation, in terms of current educational theory and other relevant sources, of the Flexible Learning Framework (Employment Department, 1991) developed within TVEI (Technical and Vocational Education Initiative). The way in which the term Flexible Learning came to be used within TVEI has some relevance to the proposition developed in this chapter and is therefore worthy of some discussion.

Flexible Learning: autonomy and co-operation

The Flexible Learning Management Cycle (Figure 7.1) describes a process very similar to an Objective/Task/Review model of

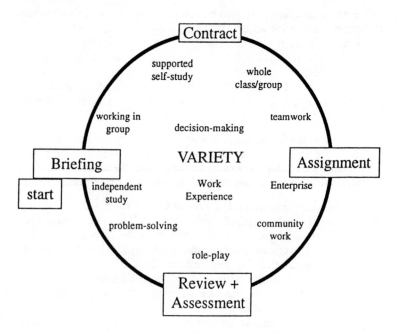

Figure 7.1   The flexible learning management cycle

management in an organisation geared to continuous improvement and continuous incremental change. It is a reminder that autonomy, self-reliance and initiative are unlikely to flourish in a totally unstructured environment. It provides a simple structure which allows greater scope for the development of conceptual and human skills as opposed to a more formal structure which may stifle the development of metacognitive cognitive processes. Lean production whether in education or industry must be efficient as well as worker-friendly.

The rationale for the TVEI model lay in the value of students taking more responsibility for their own learning. The model drew on a variety of teaching/learning strategies involving both autonomous and co-operative learning. It was seen as a means of harnessing the advantages of discovery learning but within a managed learning situation, intended to ensure that breadth and depth of curriculum coverage were not diluted in the process.

The target age range for TVEI (14–19 years) embraced not just the schools sector but also included those 16 to 19-year-olds who choose to enter Colleges of Further Education. This sector has also made significant use of Distance Learning. Support for developmental activity related to all aspects of Flexible, responsive provision of FE has also been available via the Work-Related FE Development Fund. In FE colleges the use of specially prepared Flexible Learning materials with students who attend College on a full or part-time basis is becoming more widespread (Dixon and Haldane, 1994). Such materials are designed to provide adequate coverage of underpinning knowledge while stimulating an active learning style. Tutors still play a key role as managers/facilitators of learning with a greater emphasis on one-to-one and small-group tuition.

Distance Learning materials designed for maximum flexibility in time and place of use are of necessity comprehensive and self-contained. While well-structured tutor/mentor support is recommended such resources can sometimes be successfully used by entirely independent learners. Learners who may previously have been over-reliant on their teachers as a single source of knowledge provision, could become more self-reliant as learners by using a comprehensive self-study pack but they would not necessarily enhance their alertness to all potential sources of information nor realise the applicability of the contents of that pack in a variety of different practical situations. Many exponents of Flexible Learning, particularly in the schools sector, consciously sought to avoid the assumption that such an approach was dependent on comprehensive, carefully structured learning materials. Caution as to young, full-time students becoming over-reliant on learning resources and thereby benefitting less from the active learning inherent in more autonomous teaching learning strategies, is understandable. It is however an issue which can be addressed both through the design of the resources themselves and through imaginative tutor support.

The realities of life-long learning mean that comprehensive learning resources will become much more widely used in continuing education. However, if metacognitive skills are to be fostered, more creative tutoring and mentoring and extra activities involving more diverse practical tasks may be needed. More emphasis on the pedagogical aspects of technology-based training will be required, not only to avoid the creation of what are, in effect, entertaining drill and practice routes to the development of a 'narrow task-based competence' (CBI, 1989), but also to explore the extent to which multimedia may be able to help enhance metacompetence.

Multimedia courseware potentially offers new ways to capture the imagination and interest of learners. Software tools may also in future help facilitate action planning and assessment. The opportunity to access and navigate multimedia information databases either on compact disc or remotely will also provide unparalleled opportunities for learning by discovery. The model set out in Figure 7.2 still envisages an important role for the interpersonal dimension in learning. For some distance learners this may mean the virtual presence of their tutor or a group of fellow students as videophone/videoconferencing technology advances.

For situations (including full-time study) where groups of learners have more ready access to tutor support, Flexible Learning has provided a means and a framework for shifting the emphasis away from teaching and the teacher and towards learning and the learner, through a variety of learning experiences. In this way it provided an additional means of fulfilling the wider goal of educators to maximise the whole potential of learners — technical skills, human skills and conceptual skills.

Whereas in the recent past pressures toward vocational relevance in the curriculum may have been perceived by educators as pushing them toward delivering a narrow task competence, the reverse is now true. The active, more autonomous, learning

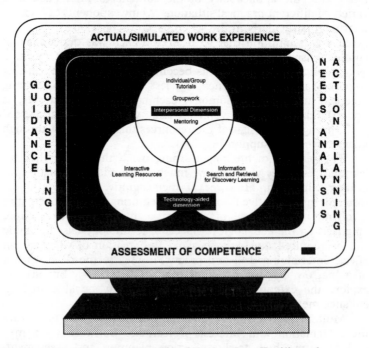

Figure 7.2   Clover Leaf Model of Technology Facilitated Learning in the Flexible College

processes being deployed within schools and colleges reflect the more autonomous workplace culture of which lifelong active learning is a part.

Both industry and education are coming to recognise the value of initiating and deploying high order human conceptual skills as well as high order technical skills.

Education and industry: teacher and manager

In these circumstances a key indicator of cultural convergence between education and industry may be the evolution of the teacher as a manager of learning, adopting a management style comparable to the manager of the future rather than the manager of the past.

This chapter will subsequently illustrate such an approach to the development of teachers as managers of Flexible Learning (i.e. as managers of the processes of learning rather than educational management in its wider sense). Prior to outlining a model of the professional development of teachers based on a convergence of management culture and educational culture it is appropriate to explore the rationale for this approach more fully.

Any exploration of possible convergence of cultures between Business and Education would need to address a quite fundamental difference in objectives. Business enterprise is based on the pursuit of long-term profit maximisation. It may be true that education has become absorbed with financial issues as the pursuit of a better educated, more qualified population places ever greater pressure on the resources available, however its primary goal remains more concerned with expanding the horizons of human potential than with expanding financial returns.

The conflicting pressures on education were summed up quite succinctly in the publicity for a conference in San Diego early in 1993. The conference theme was how teachers and administrators who are committed to lifelong learning might find ways to enhance the quality of their services while remaining fiscally responsible.

Whilst education providers, whose focus is people development, may find themselves financially squeezed, organisations whose focus is financial enrichment may find that technological advance increases the extent to which a healthy bottom line is dependent on maximising human potential.

Meyer-Dohm (1993) looking forward to current and future strategy for the automotive industry speaks of 'capital investments in tangible assets supplemented by investment in human capital'.

Studies such as that of Malerba (1993) see learning by firms or knowledge capital as engines of growth and consider learning processes to be the basis for trajectories of technical change. The government's choice of title for the 'Investors in People' programme is in itself intended to project a similar message and we have in the UK a national target that 50 per cent of large/medium organisations should achieve such status by 1996 (NTTF, 1991).

If, in Western Europe and elsewhere, education and industry are moving toward a new and common vision of a learning society their different perspectives are likely to be to some extent retained. We would appear to be moving toward a situation where there are some 'learning organisations' for whom learning is, increasingly, the means to an end and others for whom it is an end in itself — perhaps converging not toward total consonance but toward a mirror image each reflecting the other's good practice (see Figure 7.3).

While cultivating new and closer relationships with employers, educators will still have to place the learners' needs at the centre of their concerns. Lifelong learners' personal agendas may overlap significantly those of their employers but they will need to cope with a world where many will need to change careers several times (IRDAC, 1990), perhaps making significant changes in career direction. They may also have hopes and aspirations which their present employment would be unlikely to fulfil. Otala (1993) identified two components of lifelong learning — operational capability and strategic capability. Those employers who wish to

TECHNOLOGICAL
AND SOCIETAL
CHANGE

INDUSTRY					EDUCATION	
Primary Goal	Maximise profits				Maximise Individual Potential	*Primary Goal*
Means of Attainment	People Development within Learning Organisations	Expertise Exchange			Cost Effectiveness	*Means of Attainment*
	Manufacturing & Information Technology				Learning Technology	

Figure 7.3

prosper in a continuously changing advanced industrial society will increasingly need to take an interest in the strategic capability of their workforces. However, individual lifelong learners should also be encouraged to adopt a personal strategic agenda consistent with their own hopes, ambitions, aptitudes and interests.

IRDAC also addresses the cost of the additional learning that is needed and reflects that employers, society, and from time to time the individual will pay their share. This sharing of responsibilities has been examined in more detail by Otala (1993) who developed a model for sharing responsibility between different stakeholders based on the extent to which different models of lifelong learning provision may have different foci.

Otala was mapping a sea-change in levels of continuing education and training provision which can only be afforded by society if learners exhibit higher levels of autonomy, inquisitiveness and enthusiasm for acquiring learning from diverse sources. If the vision of a Learning Society espoused by Ball (1991) is to be realised there will need to be an emphasis on intellectual development at least equal to the trend in recent years for Western societies to become much more conscious of physical health, diet and exercise.

This new Learning Society cannot, however, be the preserve of an intellectual elite, as learning targets of competitor nations remind us. Mouton and Blake (1984) perceived education systems of the recent past as obstacle courses designed to select an elite rather than maximise the potential of all participants. Very high wastage rates in education were consistent with a mass production culture. Hierarchical, bureaucratic management structures which did not give full scope for creative talent, only required, by tomorrow's standards, very small numbers of highly qualified people. The process of natural selection in nature has never required all, or even most, of the fittest to survive, merely that they should have a higher statistical probability of survival than less fit compatriots. Past, ill-founded assumptions that the cream will always float to the top need to be challenged. The UK Open University over twenty-five years stands as eloquent testimony to how frequently qualifications gained in initial education understate individual capability. How many people could name from among their immediate circle of family, friends and acquaintances examples of significant educational underachievement? Such wastage of capability is no longer acceptable whether the nurturing of individual talent is viewed as a human right or as a unit of economic performance.

Ball (1991) has suggested that for many people, one of the major obstacles to success is the constraining of attainment within timeframes linked to public examinations usually taken at particular ages. New qualification structures offer a potential solution if initial education is able to adjust better to individual patterns of learning which may be more complex than current options such as streaming imply.

The Flexible Learning Framework (Tomlinson and Kilner, 1991) when applied to initial education, is intended to provide a means of making provision more responsive to individual need, enhancing student outcomes by:

> Being able to deal with students as individuals with benefits stemming from this such as optimising learning opportunities for all, increasing learner motivation through relevance increasing the rate of learning and raising achievement.

If we are to capture the inquisitiveness and zest for learning which most infants exhibit, and sustain it throughout life, then learning methods which give individuals a greater sense of personal ownership are required. In an analogy to the Total Quality Management Principle of 'delighting the customer' Davies (1993) asserts that the love of learning can be rekindled at any age. He sets out the challenge to seek delighted learners expressed in the following terms:

> Whether in kindergarten, primary or secondary school, College, University, Company or at home, the challenge of any concept, fact, truth, story, materials or learning encounter, has to be to charm, entice, ease, humour and enrapture the learner.

Delighting the customer represents an even greater challenge when the customer is a learner rather than the purchaser of a product or service. 'Learning' is the outcome of education or training. The learner is, therefore, the person who produces the product as well as being the customer. The teacher as an enabler, facilitator or manager of learning experiences must generate sufficient delight to stimulate informal learning at work or in the community as one of life's pleasures, rather than as a compulsory duty culminating in an actual or metaphorical consigning of schoolbooks to the dustbin.

A key objective of the TVEI Flexible Learning initiative was to deploy teaching/learning strategies which develop the habit of learning through personal enquiry. The Flexible Learning Framework (Employment Department, 1991) suggests processes and methods for effective initial education which, with minor adaptations to the wording, could describe processes and methods within a learning organisation and indeed within a lifelong learning society (see Figure 7.4). In addition, the method of work organisation within a Flexible Learning group, reflects that within the lean production or 'flat pyramid' organisation, it involves individuals working autonomously and co-operatively as a part of teams while being given clear leadership and where appropriate, direct input from the teacher/manager.

Knowles (1992) compared the values of traditional learning and the values of lifelong learning which he saw as relevant to the industrial age and the information/learning society respectively.

Common Factors include:

- high levels of individual/team autonomy
- work in teams/small groups
- active/experiential learning with constructive feedback
- review for continuous improvement as a two-way process
- developing ownership of the task
- involvement in the planning and use of resources

In addition the use of a variety of learning methods and learning experiences, the gaining of topicality and breadth, the involvement of all group members in a variety of tasks (e.g. presenting outcomes of group work) could be seen as analogous to job rotation, job enlargement and job enrichment in industry. The parallels between changes in working methods and management styles in industry and the comparable changes in learning methods and learning management styles are set out in Figure 7.5. This sets Knowles' analysis of key characteristics of traditional and lifelong learning values alongside equivalent characteristics of the New Industrial age as compared with those of the recent past. This comparison is seen as consistent with Meyer-Dohm's (1993) description of modern working methods designed to minimise monotony and replace constant repetition of a narrowly defined task by cycles of work involving a range of activities.

In future those who acquired their initial knowledge base through passive learning experiences will be less well equipped than those who, from their earliest educational experience, were enabled to be more proactive. Those who are encouraged to develop initiative and self-reliance in their quest for learning may perhaps be more likely to exhibit such characteristics in other aspects of their daily life.

The cultural convergence between education and industry suggested in this chapter is not only a function of the lifelong learner/worker experience but also that of the teacher/manager.

If, as has been suggested earlier, the managerial dimension of

Managing Student/ Teacher Partnerships

Aims of the Teacher:
To enable Students to
discuss and understand the objectives of the programme of study
identify short-term and longer-term targets which are relevant both to the achievement of the programme objectives and their own development needs
negotiate learning activities which contain relevant targets
identify and gain access to appropriate support
review and assess target attainments

Outcomes for the Students:
Students are able to
negotiate own learning targets
construct and agree an individual action plan with specific tasks, outcomes and timescales
reflect on progress
gain constructive feedback on progress
review and negotiate record of what has been achieved
identify further learning needs
set further learning targets and agree action
make further progress on their individual action planning

Managing Student Use of Resources

Aims of the Teacher:
To enable Students to
access sources of learning without going through the teacher
gain topicality and breadth through using a variety of resources
plan how to use resources and with what purpose
develop core skills, eg self and information management competencies, literacy, numeracy, communications and inter-personal skills
develop competence in using sources of learning, eg a resource centre, a library, a town hall, a local firm

Outcomes for the Students:
Students are able to
identify, plan access to and use relevant resources
manage information and other outcomes of use
select, analyse, present and report
use databases including electronic
use IT for above and other purposes
develop 'ownership' of learning and of competencies which accrue from direct interaction with resources

Managing Student Learning Pathways

Aims of the Teacher:
To enable Students to
reach high levels of achievement in relation to their capabilities
suit learning tasks and activities to their needs
proceed at their optimum pace
be involved in planning and organising their learning
have a Record of Achievement which is progressively updated as a result of formative assessment and self-appraisal

Outcomes for the Students:
Students are able to
work in teams, small groups or as individuals in carrying out their action plans
access appropriate support, eg careers officer, database, at relevant times in order to carry out their plan
manage the achievement of learning targets; collect, present and record outcomes thus developing a portfolio of work
have their achievements accredited when they decide they are ready

Figure 7.4   Flexible learning framework

Traditional learning emphasis:	Lifelong learning values:	The Industrial Age	The New Industrial Age
Memorisation and repetition	Excitement and love of learning	Repetitive tasks	Concern for people satisfaction
Linear and concrete intellectual development	Total human capacity in ethical, intellectual and physical development	Linear Production methods static rigid processes	Emphasis on people development
Static and rigid processes	Thinking, creativity and personal esteem	Departmentalised Organisations	Thinking, creativity and intuition
Conformity	Diversity and personal esteem	Managers giving orders	Diversity and personal esteem
Individual/competitive efforts	Co-operative/collaborative efforts	Narrow training in task competence	Co-operative/collaborative effort
Content learning Teachers as information providers	Process learning of quality content Teachers as learning facilitators	Job uniformity	Commitment to total quality managers as facilitators — Broad training beyond task competence
Departmentalised learning cultural uniformity	Interdisciplinary learning cultural differences and commonalities	Isolated working environments	Job variation/Job enrichment
Isolated teaching environments	Collaborative teaching environments	Technology as an isolated tool	Collaborative working environments
Technology as an isolated tool	Technology as an integral tool		Technology as an integral tool
Restricted use of educ. facilities	Flexible use of education		Flexible use of training
Parental involvement	Extensive parental involvement		Involvement of all stakeholders
Autonomy of the community	Community partnerships		Community partnerships
The Industrial Age	An information/learning society		

Figure 7.5 A comparison between traditional learning and lifelong learning

the teacher's role, particularly when accentuated by the adoption of flexible learning, reflects the new management culture emerging in industry, this has implications for staff development methods in education.

Developing the management of learning

Although we have been focusing mostly on the teacher's role as manager of learning processes rather than on their contribution to the management of an educational institution, it was in the latter context that the authors first encountered management training methods used by industry to develop human and conceptual skills of managers.

Cheshire LEA had developed the Cheshire Education Management System (CEMS) for developing senior and middle managers in schools and colleges in the late 1980s. The model was derived from the Coverdale Management programmes (Babbington-Smith and Sharp, 1990) originally developed to help industry manage change.

Although some individual managers in schools may personally adopt rather formal management styles the management structure and, in many schools, the management process was perceived as similar to that of a business organised to manage change. For example the allocation of certain specific responsibilities to assistant teachers, with additional allowances in recompense, provided the basis for a highly devolved management structure. This devolution typically extends to mainscale teachers as a consequence both of pressure of work and the traditional sense of vocation within the profession. Some Further Education Colleges, being typically rather larger organisations, had, in the past, adopted a more hierarchical structure but by the late eighties organisation structure changes, more consistent with need for greater responsiveness, were well established.

The education service, therefore, potentially represented fertile territory for evolving management styles comparable to those being adopted by industry as it prepares for the 21st century.

The CEMS model sought to develop a combination of autonomous and collaborative working competence, together with methods of work organisation, which allowed such an ethos to flourish.

In addition to the process skills developed by the CEMS programme a 'systematic approach' (Taylor, 1992) to work organisation was inculcated. This model had also been successfully trialled in a teaching situation (Savory, 1990). Experience of small scale trials of Flexible Learning within TVEI was producing feedback to the effect that the Flexible Learning Management Cycle described a time-efficient set of alternative teaching/learning strategies which allowed process skills to be developed without detriment to coverage of content.

However, a minority of staff were expressing concerns about actual/possible additional pressures of preparation time, plus occasional planning/organisational problems.

The 'systematical approach' planning model and the Coverdale/ CEMS approach to developing autonomous/collaborative working skills influenced the approach to delivery of staff development for Flexible Learning and appeared well received.

Based on this experience the possibility that other con-temporary approaches to developing management competence in industry might be applicable to the management of learning was investigated, with particular reference to situations where the managerial dimension of the teacher's role had been accentuated by the adoption of Flexible Learning. In particular the possibility that the management standards developed through the Manage-ment Charter Initiative (MCI) might serve as a description of the process of managing learning was investigated.

In most instances the language used in the standards was generic and a limited disguise, reframing financial references by using words such as 'resources' allowed the standards to be shown to teachers without their origin being obvious. They were almost unanimously accepted as accurate descriptors of a teacher's job, but this very limited contextualisation shed limited light on how alternative teaching/learning strategies might affect the managerial dimension of the teacher's role.

Subsequently post-experience staff development in the Man-agement of Flexible Learning was offered as a Certificate of Professional Studies in Education of Manchester Metropolitan University. The pilot programme, supported by South and East Cheshire TEC and Employment Department embraced the TDLB Assessor and Verifier awards in addition to further examination of the Management Charter Initiative (MCI) standards and their relevance to the Management of Learning.

This provided an opportunity to work with the pilot cohort of students who functioned as a focus group for a more detailed analysis of both the substance and the wording of the standards in the context of Flexible teaching/learning strategies. Primary, Secondary, Further and Nursing Education were represented within the group. A contextualised version of the standards using some revision of wording in language more consistent with an Education environment but retaining the substance of the originals

has been developed (Haldane, 1993). The contextualisation focused on the management of learning processes and work organisation for learning autonomy rather than any contribution participants made to the management and administration of their place
of work.

Further work is in progress to examine the response of
larger numbers of teachers to the model developed. However,
the project outcomes to date appear to support the proposition
that the required competencies of educators and managers of
businesses overlap significantly even though they may exercise
them in different environments.

Many of the practices alluded to in this chapter may not yet
be the norm in either education or industry but they do appear
to represent an emergent pattern. Education and industry appear
to be following the same signposts and moving along the same
route.

References

Baaken, B., Gould, J. and Kim. P. (1992) Experimental learning organisations:
    a management flight simulator approach. *European Journal of Operational
    Research*, **59**(1), May, pp. 167–182.
Ball, Sir C. (1991) *Learning Pays*, London, Royal Society of Arts Manufactures
    and Commerce.
Beard, D. (1993) Learning to change organisations. *Personnel Management*, **25**,
    January, pp. 32–35.
Babbington-Smith and Sharp, A. (1990) *Manager and Team Development*,
    London, Heinemann.
Burdett, J. O. (1992) A template for organisation design. *Business Quality*, **57**,
    Summer, pp. 35–41.
Cascio, W. F. (1993) Downsizing: What do we know? What have we learned?
    Academy of Management Executives, **7**, February, pp. 95–104.
CBI (1989) *Towards a Skills Revolution — report of the Vocational Education
    Training Task*, London, Confederation of British Industry.
Davies, W. K. (1993) Measuring quality in lifelong learning. *Comment (European
    Lifelong Learning Initiative)*, (6), July, pp. 1–2.
Dixon, K. and Haldane, A. B. (eds) (1994) *Towards Lifelong Learning — the Role
    of Further Education*, Stafford, SOLU.
ERT (1991) *Lifelong Learning Developing Europe's Future Capability*, Brussels,
    European Round Table of Industrialists.
Employment Department (1991) *Flexible Learning — A Framework for Education
    and Training*, Sheffield, Employment Department UK.
Flavell, J. H. (1985) *Cognitive Development* (2nd edn), London, Prentice Hall,
    Englewood Cliffs.
Haldane, M. J. (1993) *A Competence-based Approach to the Management of
    Learning*, Project report to Employment Department, Crewe, Manchester
    Metropolitan University.
Handy, C. (1992) The birth of the conceptual college. *The Director*, **46**(3),
    October, p. 23.

Handy, C. (1993) What is a lifelong learning organisation? in Combey and Doherty (eds) *Lifelong Learning for European Business Enterprises — Priorities and Proposals*. Proceedings of 3rd European Lifelong Learning Initiative Conference, Oxford, ELLI.

IRDAC (1990) *Schools and Industry — Report of Industrial Research and Development Committee*, Brussels, European Commission.

IRDAC (1991) *Skills Shortages in Europe — Report of Industrial Research and Development Advisory Committee*, Brussels, European Commission.

Johnson, R. S. (1993) 'Leadership for the quality transformation' Part One, in *Quality Progress*, **26**(1), January, pp. 73–75.

Katz, R. L. (1955) 'Skills of an effective administrator'. *Harvard Business Review*, **33**(1), pp. 33–47.

Knowles, M. (1992) Another view of learning comment. *European Lifelong Learning Initiative*, **1**, January.

Langford, D. P. (1992) The state of quality education. *Journal for Quality and Participation*, **15**(3), June, pp. 92–93.

Lundberg, C. C. (1991) Creating and managing a vanguard organisation. *Human Resource Management*, **30**(1), Spring, pp. 89–112.

Malerba, F. (1993) 'Learning by firms and incremental change'. *Economic Journal*, **102**(413), July, pp. 845–859.

Mills, D. Q. and Friesen, B. (1992) The learning organisation. *European Management Journal*, **10**(2), June, pp. 146–156.

Maul, J. and Gillard, P. (1993) Training today's managers to effectively use TQM. *Industrial Engineering*, **25**(1), January, pp. 49–50.

Meyer-Dohm, P. Lifelong learning for the automotive industry in Combey and Doherty (eds) *Lifelong Learning for European Business Enterprises — Priorities and Proposals*. Proceedings of 3rd European Lifelong Learning Initiative Conference, Oxford, ELLI.

Mouton and Blake (1984) *Synergy*, SF, Jossey-Bass.

National Training Task Force (1991) *Foundation Learning Target No. 4*, National Education and Training Targets, Sheffield, Employment Department, UK.

Otala, L. (1993) *European Approaches to Lifelong Learning*, CRE-ERT — The European University Industry Forum.

Savory, C. (1990) 'SACLA project: co-operative learning in the classroom'. *LINKS*, **16**(3), Autumn, pp. 23–26.

Taylor, S. (1992) Managing a learning environment. *Personnel Management*, **24**(24) and (10), October, pp. 54–57.

Tomlinson, P. and Kilner, S. (1991) *The Flexible Learning Framework and Current Educational Theory*, Sheffield, Employment Department, UK.

Tribus, M. (1992) Creating the competitive organisation. *Journal for Quality and Participation*, **15**(3), June, pp. 6–19.

8 'To see the world in a grain of sand'. . .?

Blake *Auguries of Innocence*

The risk of reductionism in open and distance education

Ian McNay

Introduction

In this chapter I look at three initiatives aimed at making education more open: the articulation of course outcomes particularly those relating to 'competence', the development of modular course structures, and the design and delivery of 'learning packages' used in open and distance education. I applaud the aims and intentions of those promoting such developments; indeed I have shared in work on all three. Much of the rest of this book will have lauded their achievement. In the interests of balance, I develop an argument that severally and collectively they create a *risk* of reductionism — of diminishing learning, of impoverishing the student learning experience. Instead of inciting wonder, excitement, curiosity and a window on the world, as Blake hoped for from even a small fragment of creation, the world is reduced, compacted, simplified, contained — 'closed' — in a constraining structure. Sadly, at times, staff and students collude, if not conspire, in this tendency, often for what appear to be the best of motives in the short-term but with a long-term threat to the ethos of education — its rigour and vigour, its capacity to liberate, to challenge, to inspire the imagination and thirst for more in favour of a 'domestication', a taming of tough issues and a satisfaction with conforming to norms, accepting what you are presented with almost without question.

These three factors — packaged learning with closely defined outcomes within a modular course structure — are likely, in combination, to be prominent in higher education in the future (CSUP, 1992). This early warning is to promote awareness of the dangers involved so that staff and students may consider pre-emptive or preventative measures.

My approach will be to use a number of witnesses to develop this 'case for the prosecution'. You may wish to follow up the references or to use contributions elsewhere in the book to refute, or at least balance their arguments.

Outcomes and competences

Work on learning outcomes in higher education (Otter, 1991) is one of the most significant contributions to openness in recent years, and the pressure on academics from such research has been reinforced by the political pressure of the charter movement. Students have a right to know what they can expect to gain by their investment in study and to know what will be expected of them in assessment. Secrecy here has done the reputation of education no favours. Openness helps break down the ivory tower and move assessment away from the academic bias perceived by, for example, Richard Winter (1993), where those who get top honours do so by being closest to clones of their academic mentors with emphasis on academic discipline skills rather than on those more appropriate to most employment. The spread of transparency in this respect widely through the system will be welcome.

But . . . the swing of the pendulum risks knocking the baby out with the bath water. The competence movement now reverses the previous dynamic of curriculum design and delivery by defining job needs, then how to assess competence in appropriate skills and then how to teach to that assessment. The main manifestations of this approach are in National/Scottish Vocational Qualifications (N/SVQs) and in the Management Charter Initiative (MCI). It is from reviews and commentaries on these schemes that the following list of charges is mainly drawn.

1. Burgoyne (1993) questions the theoretical underpinning of the approach: the behaviourist psychology applied to individuals which confuses external task performance with internal traits of

personality and, in sociology, the narrow positivist determinist approach to functional analysis of organisations. Terms such as 'naïve', 'discredited', 'inadequate', run throughout his critique.

2. There is ideological concern too. Burgoyne, again, raises the issue as to:

> 'whether the competence movement represents an attempt to realign the education system away from one of its traditional functions of producing citizens who can critically question and help to reformulate the existing social and political order, towards one which produces people who are skilled at implementing the current order without questioning it (Burgoyne, 1993).

Richard Pring, in his address to the 1994 North of England Conference knew which side he was on in any debate:

> The ambition of the National Council for Vocational Qualifications to translate all learning outcomes into a list of 'can do's', and of the Council for the Accreditation of Teacher Education to provide lists of easily measurable teacher competences, and of the National Curriculum Council (that was) to spell out in detail the learning outcomes of 15 million young people, starts not from a careful examination of the complexity of learning or of the nature of those problems that young people or trainee teachers have to face. Rather does it start from the administrative and the political urge to control.. . . The concentration of the control of learning in the hands of a few must get things wrong. It is logically impossible for planners to grasp the complexity of learning and indeed its relevance to the diverse aspirations of so many.

As Mintzberg (1990) points out, one way of achieving control is by standardisation of skills. People are what they do in many ways and if pushed to behave in particular ways reconcile their way of being to their way of doing.

3. There are concerns, too, about the domination of the narrow values of vocationalism. The National Education and Training Targets (NETTS) for lifelong learning are all job related (CBI, 1992) implying that life is only about paid employment which abandons many in the adult population. McGivney (1992) suggests that there is discrimination against older students being admitted to certain courses, because vocational commitment is increasingly a criterion for selection in FE (Clarke, 1989). The approaches to teacher development in

the latest in a long record of education legislation which shift much work into schools implies a learning-by-doing, trial and error approach and diminishes any theoretical underpinning — a view which has, regrettably, some support from PGCE students if a letter to *Guardian Education* (18.1.94) is symptomatic. My concern here is that we will produce restricted professionals (Hoyle, 1974) who, lacking the confidence of a sound theoretical base, and having not been exposed to alternative views will fail to transmit the value of diversity and imagination. They act locally but reduce the effect of that action by an inability to think globally. As Roebuck (1993) says about SVQs:

> Workplace learning may be suitable for some individuals in some circumstances, but experience in colleges suggests that periods out of the workplace can be just as valuable. SVQs must, therefore, be flexible enough to encompass a range of learning techniques and situations rather than the prescriptive.

4. The concern about narrowing and de-skilling is voiced by others. Collins (1991) suggests NVQs adopt a model of learning characterised by a myopic perspective on needs in which, though:

> management interests are well served, education and training programmes are trivialized, while occupations are increasingly de-skilled through the deployment of narrowly defined prescriptions.

Callender (1993) offers evidence of this narrowing of skills and curriculum related to the construction industry.

5. Hyland (1993) who uses both Collins and Callender in developing his argument has other criticisms of the competence based curriculum:

> NVQs fragment and atomise learning into assessible chunks; rather than valuing process and experience, competence based education is concerned only with products and outcomes and, most importantly, instead of encouraging critical reflection, NVQs present a one-dimensional view based on the satisfaction of performance criteria directed towards fixed and pre-determined ends.

These problems are not just British. Watson (1993) in a review of developments in Australia noted the fragmentation, the focus on discrete tasks or sets of operations with lack of an holistic approach or of integration. And, despite lip service to the need for understanding and underpinning knowledge, assessment concentrated on the narrow technical aspects of task performance.

6. Higher order skills are ignored. Burgoyne (1993) is concerned about the 'privileging of behaviour over knowledge' and the bad practices of learning by rote or habit when learners:

> will not understand the principles which make the actions effective, and therefore may not be able to adjust their performance to variations in circumstance, or to deal with contingencies.

Stevenson and McKavanagh (1992) believe that the fragmentation of learning into chunks ignores certain cognitive skills required to integrate and apply the knowledge gained. Elliot (1993) believes the MCI approach means managers don't reflect on their personal characteristics. Barrington (1993) believes Kolb's work on experiential learning (Kolb, 1993) is being ignored at the loss of individual integrative learning which allows managers to cope with change. The 'static model of competence . . . is far removed from the reality of today's workplace'. There is a danger that we are training for yesterday, not developing the enterprise skills needed for tomorrow (Burgoyne, 1993).

7. Competence statements and awards were intended to be encyclopaedic, comprehensive and universal. They were to encompass the world, and encapsulate it in simple statements easily assessed. Roebuck (1993) points to problems with this. In estate management there is no provision in the SVQ statements for water-based activities — boat handling, sea fishing, etc. Roebuck heads a college in Stornoway. Field (1993) monitors the penetration of NVQs and finds them being used mainly at low levels with marginal groups outside manufacturing industry so that even within the government's terms of reference their success is doubtful.

8. Assessment is a problem. It involves much more work than other approaches (Haffenden and Brown, 1989) and is still of doubtful reliability and validity. Burgoyne (1993) points out that there is no test of retained learning and sustained enhanced job performance. Wolf (1993) challenges the assumptions on which assessment approaches are based:

> The assumption is that, once you have the specifications right, and generate, on the basis of them, a good ('valid') test, the process of actually making a judgement

about a candidate is unproblematic . . . . Reliability is implicitly treated as guaranteed by the transparency of the specifications.

She demonstrates that:

perfect transparency is not to be had, however detailed one's definition, and searching for it merely produces atomised objectives in a forest of verbiage.

She quotes James Popham, an early advocate of criterion referenced testing and now recanting:

About the only way we can ever attain functioned homogeneity is to keep pruning the nature of the measured behaviour so that we're assessing ever more trifling sorts of behaviour. That would be inane (Popham, 1984).

The *Guide to National Vocational Qualifications* states that 'standards of success are already defined and are available to both the assessor and the candidate. Assessment decisions are thus a matter of judgement as to whether the standards have been met'. That seems simple enough but Wolf shows that there is significant difference among assessors about interpretation, towards compensation or limits of tolerance of marginal performance and at the implementation stage 'an obstinate refusal, on the part of test items and candidates, to behave according to plan' (Wolf, 1993).

The 100 per cent accuracy needed in the work place according to her industrial informants was moderated considerably. If insisted upon, the minimum level defined for competency becomes very low as American experience has shown in both college grade inflation and professional programmes (Lazarus, 1981).

That, then, is the first part of the case. Good motives — openness as to objectives and assessment, the opening of an alternative route to demonstrating learning without formal 'education' — risk being distorted in practice with low attainment thresholds in an undemanding, narrowly focused, prescriptive, curriculum framework. Perhaps we are learning: Hyland (1993), in his damning critique, welcomes *General* NVQs which look at attainments and achievements more broadly and using a variety of assessment techniques.

Modularity

Here, I will be briefer. Modularity is a less recent feature of education than the competence movement. There are established programmes which can demonstrate success and satisfaction: not least in the Open University. What is newer is the emphasis on credit transfer and accumulation which has driven most institutions and their staff to embrace modularity. It may, therefore, be timely to rehearse the risks of reductionism. My witnesses here are colleagues at Anglia Polytechnic University, students from various institutions and the former chairman of the Academic Council of the University of London.

One of the participants in my professional development courses summed up the experience of many on modular courses: 'you never had time to draw breath and were constantly being examined.' Open University students have always complained that in terms of courses one full credit course is less demanding than two half credits. The tendency of academics is not that of Procrustes: if the amount to fit into a teaching space is too great, they do not chop bits off. They behave more like the Japanese students employed to cram people into commuter trains. And the smaller the module size the greater the problem.

This has two consequences. First, it reduces the 'browsing' factor, the time to explore an interesting by-way, so that the curiosity and serendipity factors are reduced. Libraries are underlining this by adjustment to their acquisitions where there is now more emphasis on multiple copies of core texts, with each module being built round a very constrained number of set books. As one of the points behind modularisation was to allow students to make unpredicted connections this directiveness down a narrow, prescribed path seems to defeat that objective.

Students at Nottingham (King, 1993) recorded this overload. They related to loss of extra-curricular activity, a further risk of an impoverished experience, and for *all* students, not just those studying full time on campus: ask OU students about family life! More importantly, they linked it to assessment. If assessment is not to be pitched at a low level it has to be some way into the period of study. With modules this pushed any *course* work assessment close to the end of module *exam* so there was a significant peak of work. Given pressure on library books, students adopted the tactic of doing their assessed course work early to get use of the books and so submitted *before* the teaching was complete. There was also pressure on staff to comment, grade, record and return assignments before the exam, and little time for exam scripts to be processed before the start of the next module, for which a pass in the current one may be a prerequisite.

One argument for modularity is the enhancement of student freedom of choice, making their study profile open to their control. Alderman (1993) records the danger of such freedom, without capping of student numbers by module, and his views are echoed by the Nottingham students. One of the reasons for the module choice may have been the teaching team, or a particular 'expert'. A large class to cope with popularity may mean a change in the teaching approaches they have adopted which led to that popularity in the first place. Where modules are repeated, often those staff are not available and classes are taken by non-experts or casual labour. My colleagues at Anglia see the increased use of part-time staff as an inevitable by-product of modularity and extended choice with a risk of loss of both academic coherence in the course and the sense of an integrated professional and academic community.

Those colleagues echo concerns over fractionalisation and frag-mentation of the learning experience from the competence section as well as the risk of over-assessment and the reality of administrative overload. Their other major concern is over the loss of student *group* identity. Part of this is directly content related: common knowledge cannot be assumed. One person commented that he used to be able to cross-refer to other parts of the course offered by different people and, therefore, help relate his input to theirs and help students make connections. 'Now there is a wall round my work' he said. 'It has to be complete in itself without locating it in a wider body of knowledge and learning'. The second loss is a process issue. People in a group learn from one another if they have time to develop confidence within the group. Modularity means that the continuity essential to such a group ethos risks being lost.

Packages

The tendencies I have already commented upon feature also in learning packages supporting open and distance modes of delivery. My first two witnesses are a lecturer in Wales and a senior academic in Australia. They put, perhaps, an extreme case.

Iphofen (1993) is concerned that the rhetoric is not borne out in practice: 'So far open learning has merely reinforced the trend for education to become training. Despite its promise of flexibility, its hidden curriculum is one of passive assimilation.'

He challenges the idea of students 'owning' knowledge when the packages have been constructed by others for marketing: 'the notion that knowledge can be someone's property must be a cultural and political anathema for an advocate of truly "open learning".' Even with interactive hypertext which may allow some freedom to browse or explore:

the problem is that while it may be interactive and, therefore, allowing a certain degree of creativity, one can only interact with data that has (*sic*) already been stored there by someone

else or by some organisation which has deemed certain data
to be worth storing. It cultivates an encyclopaedist mentality
based on an absolutist or factual knowledge-base derived from
some self-appointed authoritative source and finds it hard to
accommodate 'relative' truths (Iphofen, 1993).

His article is a mix of anger and sadness at the way the utopian,
de-institutionalised learning ideas of Illich have become manifest
in practice.

Bruce Kaye (1993) regrets the loss of disputation and challenge,
and of the organic community of scholars which has been replaced
by:

> an information supermarket in which, for directly usable
> purposes, individuals take what packages attract their
> attention on the shelves . . . . It is difficult to retain some
> sense of inquisitiveness, let alone pass it on to students, if
> you are simply a shelf packer in an information supermarket.

Those are perhaps overstatements but there is a growing body of
concern which echoes them in some form. Marjorie Reeves (1988)
takes the 'tyranny of pre-packaged information' as one element in
her analysis of the crisis in universities and feels we are losing,
in independent distant learning in isolation, Polanyi's concept of
conviviality, the sharing of good things of mind and spirit (Polanyi,
1958), and the concept of personal knowledge: 'the personal skill
of seeing which facts are significant is an integral part of discovery'
(Scott, 1985).

Certainly the discipline involved in preparing texts to budget
in the Open University means that some have the air of edited
highlights of a cricket match with the consequent loss of full
flavour. Given the political pressure for 'balance' as perceived
by government there may be further loss of the spice of certain
excluded viewpoints or of the passionate depth of the pursuit of a
particular school of thought.

Package-based programmes also restrict any support contributions from people. Part-time tutors in the OU, those who
have contact with students, have the most proscribed curriculum
to deliver of any I know. There is little encouragement to go
beyond the texts; indeed some students resist any efforts to do
so — their 'learning contract' says they can achieve high grades
using only the material provided. This must be so to equalise the
potential outcomes for those with no easy access to supplementary
material. In an MBA course offered by another institution there is
positive discouragement from going beyond the text even when it
has become dated. I have a vivid memory, too, of chairing an exam
board where one script marker had failed two students for giving

no evidence of having read the course material. It was eventually acknowledged that they had demonstrated that they satisfied the stipulated course objectives by drawing reflectively on professional experience, as the course encouraged them to do. In a system which offered a chance to learn 'otherwise', the text was holy and there was no acceptance of a different route — another 'otherwise'.

I have other concerns:

— about print based material favouring certain socio-economic groups and (relatively) excluding others (Mealyea, 1985)
— of the prestige status given to print material which endows it with more authority than it might merit
— about the cultural imperialism when packages are used outside their indigenous setting: one case asks students on the Asian Pacific Rim to comment on the English 1988 Education Reform Act
— about its use as a cheap option when it is not fully appropriate. The Open Tech Unit promoted packages in the 1980s as 'a way to cut training costs', not to extend provision or enhance quality
— the encouragement of surface learning only. This is a concern shared by a major report on teaching and learning sponsored by the heads of Scottish Universities (CSUP, 1992). One example will suffice to show that some students will drift to that as a short term efficiency expedient. In one UK university the MBA programme offered to full-time residential students is recorded, with video tapes being sent to 'external' students within forty-eight hours with students in attendance standing as proxy participants for them. A great idea. The tapes were also placed in the university library. Within weeks, attendance at classes fell: students did not wish to contribute actively to collective learning. They simply wanted to borrow the tape, observe and absorb.

Conclusion

Edward Said, in his 1993 Reith lectures, believed that, in safe-guarding values, intellectuals could be 'embarrassing, contrary and even unpleasant'. I hope I have avoided the last. The CSUP Report referred to above echoes many others in commending clear outcome statements with transparent assessment, open to view; modular organisation to allow flexible movement by learners through and between courses; and structured learning packages. So do I, up to a point. All can contribute to openness. There are, though, as with freedom, limits to openness and like recidivist criminals, many want to return to imprisonment and distort or subvert the best intentions of planners.

My basic argument has been that in over-specifying everything, in trying to pin down the elusive butterfly of learning for the benefit of learners, we constrict their choice, their freedom to be different, to challenge prescriptions; we deter them from diverting into discovery of a personal agenda and the delight that it brings. We surrender to external prescriptions of what we should learn. We package 'flexibility' in modules of a size which are too small to allow for flexing of the muscles of curiosity, detached from other related areas because all modules should stand alone. Through being decontextualised, they are devalued. They are offered to students in a system which fragments learner groups as soon as they move to the next module, and fragments and casualises the academic workforce, risking in both an anomie. We encourage in both groups a dependence on a detailed text written elsewhere. Competence-based, criterion referenced assessment can encourage instrumental approaches to learning with a conspiracy, overt or covert, among learners, teachers and assessors to confine experience within defined limits.

The CSUP report acknowledges that OU material is widely used throughout the higher education system. My dystopic vision recognises four factors in the future: pressure on resources for efficiency and economies of scale; the impending peak of retirements in the academic workforce with pressure not to replace them; the continual advances in communications technology; and the continuing explosion of knowledge in some subject areas. Remember that the National Curriculum was introduced at secondary level to make student movement easier. With credit transfer added to my four factors we may face a national core curriculum in higher education with standard packages delivered to all students via print, discs and screens in the corner. The openness of choice is then that offered by Henry Ford and instead of Blake's opening up of the world by the wonder of a grain of sand, state control promoting academic entropy through narrow vocational reductionism may deliver Eliot's 'fear in a handful of dust.'

References

Alderman, G. (1993) 'Boarding the space module'. *Guardian Education*, 2 November.

Barrington, H. (1993) 'Competence and confidence'. *College Management Today*, October.

Burgoyne, J. G. (1993) 'The competence movement: issues, stakeholders and prospects'. *Personnel Review*, 22(6).

Callender, C. (1993) *Will NVQs Work? Evidence from the Construction Industry*, Institute of Manpower Studies, University of Sussex.

Clarke, J. (1989) *Learning is a Lifetime Thing: outcomes for adult basic education students from Hackney Adult Education Institute and the Hackney Reading Centre*, ALFA.

Collins, M. (1991) *Adult Education as Vocation*, London, Routledge.

Confederation of British Industry (1991) *World Class Targets — a Joint Initiative to Achieve Britain's Skills Revolution*, London, CBI.

Conference of Scottish University Principals (CSUP) (1992) *Teaching and Learning in an Expanding Higher Education System*, Edinburgh, CSUP.

Elliot, K. (1993) 'Managerial competences'. *Training and Development*, November.

Field, J. (1993) 'Still waiting for the Spring offensive'. *College Management Today*, October.

Haffenden, I. and Brown, A. (1989) 'Towards the implementation of competence based curricula in colleges of FE' in Burke, J. W. (ed) *Competency-based Education and Training*, London, Falmer.

Hoyle, E. (1974) 'Professionality, professionalism and control in teaching'. *London Educational Review*, 3(2).

Hyland, T. (1993) 'Mismatches, paradoxes and square circles: making NVQs fit adult learning'. *Adults Learning*, 4(10).

Iphofen, R. (1993) 'The hidden costs of open learning'. *Adults Learning*, October.

Kaye, B. (1993) 'University challenge — anchoring timeless identity in a fast turnover world'. *Campus Review*, October 21–27.

King, S. (1993) *Report by the University of Nottingham Union on the Initial Impact of Modularisation and Semesterisation at the University of Nottingham*, Nottingham, UNU.

Kolb, D. (1993) 'The process of experiential learning' in Thorpe, M. et al. (eds) *Culture and Processes of Adult Learning*, London, Routledge.

Lazarus, M. (1981) 'Goodbye to excellence' cited in Wolf, A. (1993) *Assessment Issues and Problems in a Criterion Based System*, London, FEU.

Mealyea, R. (1985) 'Working class students and the TAFE curriculum'. *Victorian TAFE Papers, No. 3.*

McGivney, V. (1992) *Tracking Adult Learning Routes*, Leicester, NIACE.

Mintzberg, J. (1990) *The Structuring of Organizations*, Englewood Cliffs, Prentice Hall.

Otter, S. (1991) *What Can Graduates Do?*, Leicester, NIACE.

Polanyi, M. (1958) *Personal Knowledge, Towards a Post-critical Philosophy*, London, Routledge and Kegan Paul.

Popham, W. J. (1984) 'Specifying the domain of content of behaviours' in Berk, R. A. (ed) *A Guide to Criterion-referenced Test Construction*, Baltimore, John Hopkins University Press.

Reeves, M. (1988) *The Crisis in Higher Education: competence, delight and the common good*, Milton Keynes, SRHE/Open University Press.

Roebuck, M. (1993) 'Views on VQs'. *College Management Today*, October.

Scott, D. (1985) *Everyman Revived. The Common Sense of Michael Polanyi*, Lewes, The Book Guild.

Stevenson, J. C. and McKavanagh, C. W. (1992) 'Skill formation in the workplace' in Poole, M. (ed) *Education and Work*, Hawthorn, Victoria, ACER.

Watson, A. (1993) 'Competency-based vocational education and training in Australia: some unresolved issues'. *Australian and New Zealand Journal of Vocational Education Research*, 1(2).

Winter, R. (1993) 'Education or grading? Arguments for a non-subdivided honours degree'. *Studies in Higher Education*, 18(3).

Wolf, A. (1993) *Assessment Issues and Problems in a Criterion Based System*, London, FEU.

Part II
Course delivery and assessment

9 Opening up learning: credit accumulation in FE — the learning gain

Maureen Hanley

The nature and diversity of Further Education

The current ethos of further education is **demand led, flexible and responsive to change** — in many instances its survival has depended on these characteristics. New qualifications have been introduced into the curriculum in response to the demand for a better skilled workforce, and an alternative funding methodology is currently being implemented which places far greater emphasis on achievement and the process of learning.[1]

Within further education, provision is exceedingly diverse, ranging from adult basic education through vocational/non-vocational awards, to degree level and professional qualifications. A vast number of qualifications and awards exist to accredit this multitude of programmes. Each qualification and award has its own criteria for assessment, its own assessment schedule and a preferred/recommended method for accrediting achievement. There are many awarding/validating and industry-lead bodies whose primary aim is to recognise and record achievement in one form or another.

This diversity is vital if colleges are to offer accessible and relevant learning opportunities to their local communities. However, a diverse curriculum is not in itself enough to create learning which is open in every sense. What is required is a system that enables not only part-time, off-site study but has the following features.

First, it must encourage individuals to become better qualified
and to achieve beyond their previous expectations. Secondly, it
must become accessible to more of the population. Thirdly, it
must make explicit the outcomes of learning.

It must also acknowledge that learners will realise their goals
in a variety of ways, and encourage them to achieve these outcomes
in the way that is best suited to their personal requirements. In
other words, there is a need for a coherent post-16 curriculum,
and the current indications are reassuring. Both the Confederation
of British Industry (CBI) and the Government seem to be
pushing in the direction of an overarching credit accumulation
and transfer framework for the whole sector. As a result, many
colleges are starting to develop and implement their own credit
accumulation and transfer systems, thus attempting to bring a
degree of coherence and structure to their provision. In addition,
many colleges of further education offer a wide range of student
support services in an attempt to become more student led and to
help learners make sense of the variety of options that are available.

Prior to entry, colleges attempt to provide the student with a
range of information and advice/guidance services as a basis for
informed choice. Many colleges will have a centralised admissions/
advisory service whose primary role is to provide quality information to students. In addition, tutor advisers and careers advisers
are specifically trained to offer guidance on progression and career
development prior to enrolment and throughout the learner's time
at college.

Increasingly, facilities are available to help students identify
their individual learning needs. Initial assessment materials that
are specifically related to the core skills areas are frequently used in
many organisations. In addition, learning support materials linked
to the curriculum are being developed in both computer and paper
based formats. These resources are available to students on an
open access basis in study centres and open learning workshops.
At Wirral, such learning resources are available on the computer
network which currently has 750 workstations in 95 different open
access locations throughout the college.

Students are also encouraged to develop their own individualised action plans, and are informed that achievement should be
reviewed on at least a termly basis. (Indeed, the current funding
methodology makes the production of an action plan a necessity
rather than an option.[2]

Moreover, learners are invited to examine their current
knowledge and skills with a view to accreditation of prior achievement, and specialist advice/guidance is available for students who
take this option.

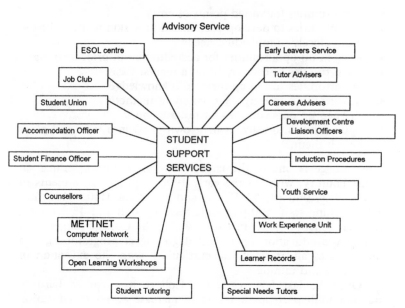

Figure 9.1

Specialist units have been set up in many organisations to support students who have English as their second language, and to support students with special needs. In addition, many colleges have a counselling service, a financial advice unit, an accommodation service, and a student union. Figure 9.1 provides an indication of the services available to students at Wirral.

The Wirral experience

In 1989, with a new internal structure designed to withstand the transition from a course-based structure to a student based one, Wirral Metropolitan College set out on a five year plan to establish and test a framework for credit accumulation and transfer.

At a local level, feedback from learners and course evaluation had long since indicated that significant improvement in the quality of learning depended upon putting a credit accumulation and transfer system into place (i.e. moving from a course based curriculum to a student led one).

Learners want:

• a basis for informed choice

- opportunities for varied points of entry
- opportunities to develop customised provision which is linked more closely to individual needs
- to open up opportunities for accreditation of prior learning
- opportunities to gain credit on a regular basis
- opportunities to top up their skills/knowledge
- opportunities to learn by a variety of methods
- to open up opportunities for progression
- opportunities to learn at their own pace, in a time and place to suit them.

The College is one of the largest colleges of further education in the country, with (in the early 1990s) student enrolments in excess of 37,000 (8,233 FTEs) and a staff of 1,400 (450 full-time teaching staff, 500 part-time teaching staff and 450 support and maintenance staff). Provision within the College ranges from adult basic education up to full degree level programmes, and encompasses all areas of the curriculum with the exception of agriculture and mining.

Over the last few years, the College has worked hard to increase adult participation, and to increase access to education and training for non traditional groups, by developing a student centred approach to learning which includes:

- establishment of community-based neighbourhood colleges
- open access to information technology
- a wide range of learning resources available on METTNET, the computer network which spans the three sites of the College and will also soon be connected to the neighbourhood colleges
- a range of student support services
- basic skills support
- a unitised curriculum providing opportunities for credit accumulation and transfer
- open learning workshops
- an assessment service incorporating accreditation of prior learning (APL) facilities

Although open learning workshops do exist in the traditional sense within the college, the aim is to extend, primarily with the aid of technology, the principles of open learning by developing comprehensive learning resources which can be used by learners however and wherever they may choose to learn. One initiative to take education and training to the learner is the College 'bendy bus'. The College operates a fully staffed technology bus, which travels around the community and is often parked and operated in employers' car parks.

The credit accumulation and transfer model being developed at Wirral is called the Learning Framework. Credit accumulation and transfer is not, however, a new concept. David Robertson, in his paper entitled *Credit Frameworks — An International Comparison* (1993) discusses the American credit system which has been in existence since the early nineteenth century and compares it to the frameworks evolving both in Europe and in New Zealand.

Systems for credit accumulation and transfer have been in existence in Britain also — notably National Vocational Qualifications, the National Open College Network and the HE Credit Accumulation and Transfer model which is emerging in many higher education institutions. None, however, provide the mechanism for encompassing the breadth and diversity of provision in further education, nor for bridging of the academic/vocational divide which the Wirral system can potentially deliver.

The many benefits to learners of implementing a framework for credit accumulation and transfer have been well documented elsewhere (e.g. FEU, 1992) and need not be discussed further in this context. What has not been well documented, however, and what is arguably more pertinent to open learning, is the issue of implementation and how the framework for credit accumulation and transfer can 'open up' opportunities for learning. These issues provide the focus for the description of the work at Wirral.

The Learning Framework provides the mechanism for harmonising the whole FE curriculum through outcomes and credit value, as well as a method for recording the gains that learners make from their experience of being at college i.e. a system for accrediting the **full range of gains** made by the learner. The framework is aptly named — it was devised to facilitate learning and to maximise achievement. Right from its inception, it has always had the learner and their needs very firmly at the centre of its development.

Before describing the work undertaken at Wirral Metropolitan College, it is necessary to clarify a number of issues. First, there is a distinction between a 'modularised' curriculum and a 'unitised' curriculum. The accepted definition of a unit is a 'coherent and explicit set of outcomes' — so units relate to assessment/accreditation of achievement. 'Modules', on the other hand, refer to the delivery of the curriculum. One undesirable consequence of this is that the way in which the curriculum is broken down into units for the credit accumulation and transfer system is not necessarily reflected in its delivery. Modules can often be developed without reference to the needs of the learner, the deliverer, and indeed the programme of learning to which it belongs. Very often, modules of learning have been developed on a somewhat archaic basis and do not contribute to the overall coherence of the curriculum. This does not need to be the case of course. For example, where the structure of modules and units coincide, then the credit framework has the potential not only to promote, but also to provide a basis for overall coherence within a modular curriculum. The issue of curriculum coherence is an important one and will be discussed in more detail later.

Secondly, it is useful to compare a **learning** framework with an **assessment** framework. An assessment framework is one which allows credit to be given for achievement. A learning framework does this, but in addition it addresses issues around curriculum coherence, which encompass quality assurance, and it emphasises the very best of teaching and learning expertise.

Finally, in common with the model for a national credit framework subsequently put forward in February 1992 by the Further Education Unit (FEU, 1992), the Learning Framework subscribes to the model of an 'open system' which is 'open to all users, is potentially comprehensive, and is owned by all its users'.

One of the consequences of adopting an 'open system' is highlighted by Peter Wilson in his paper 'Developing a post-16 credit accumulation and transfer framework: the technical specifications' (FEU, 1993):

> It is important that *A Basis for Credit?* is not seen simply as a useful way of dividing up the FE curriculum nor that credits are conceived simply as a subset of post-16 qualifications (pp. 11–12).

In terms of our work at Wirral this is a very pertinent point. The Learning Framework is not just an audit of the curriculum. It enables tutors to describe achievement in an holistic manner and at the same time provides the vehicle for establishing a coherent structure to the curriculum.

This has had considerable impact on the process of unitising the curriculum; developing the Learning Framework has always been a 'bottom-up' as opposed to a 'top-down' process. In other words, it is the tutors directly responsible for delivering the programmes who decide how the curriculum will be broken down into smaller chunks of learning. There is always a possibility, if the credit accumulation and transfer system is linked to a funding/resourcing methodology, that tutors may break the curriculum down in a manner which attempts to maximise resources rather than the coherence of the curriculum. In order to ensure that this does not happen, it is important that the credit accumulation and transfer system features within the organisation's overall framework for quality assurance.

The rationale for adopting a 'bottom-up' approach stemmed from the need to ensure that the framework reflected an adequate definition of achievement (i.e. the **full range of gains** made by the learner). If achievement is to be defined by externally set standards alone (i.e. a 'top-down' approach) then there is a risk that we may lose the breadth and depth of knowledge and experience which is an integral part of provision, but is all too often neither acknowledged nor credited. Many of these additional outcomes could be described as 'process' skills. They include aspects of study skills, analytical thinking, critical thinking, conceptual thinking as well as broader personal skills such as motivation, self esteem, personal evaluation and perseverance. It is ironic that the very skills which might conceivably provide information about future capability are the skills which do not generally receive formal accreditation.

A research programme on students' approaches to studying which was conducted at the University of Lancaster during the late 1970s also emphasised the importance of examining study processes. Previous research at Lancaster funded by the Joseph Rowntree Memorial Trust had:

> shown clearly the limitations on the input–output model
> in thinking about higher education. Relatively stable
> psychological characteristics of students proved to be only
> weakly related to levels of academic performance. It became
> clear that greater attention would have to be placed on study
> processes and on the context, or academic environment,
> within which students learn (p. 6). (Entwistle N. and
> Ramsden, P., 1983).

The research at Lancaster was based on an earlier series of studies conducted by Ference Marton and colleagues from Gothenburg which investigated students' approaches to reading and under-standing academic articles.

This research highlighted a distinction between 'deep' and 'surface' approaches to studying and provided valuable insights into student learning. The work also revealed that a mismatch between the learners' approach to studying and the teachers' style of teaching can have a detrimental effect on the subsequent level of achievement.

Extrapolating from this research and the experiences of students, I believe there is a real danger that if the full range of outcomes is not acknowledged and developed then the future capability of learners will deteriorate. Moreover if funding/resourcing mechanisms are linked to existing qualifications which do not always recognise these additional outcomes, then a consequent downward spiral of skills will be inevitable.

A report published by the Unit for the Development of Adult Continuing Education (UDACE, 1989) reinforces this point:

> Some of these outcomes, particularly those concerned with knowledge and its application, are described and recognised through formal qualifications. However, there are other outcomes which are not described and recognised in this way but which may be of great value to both the learner and the provider of education and training
>
> Failure to recognise and accredit these outcomes leads to measures of the effectiveness or efficiency of the course being concerned only with the number of students attending or completing the course, or with examination results rather than with reflecting the full range of gains made by the learner (p. 3).

A 'bottom-up' approach is also needed if staff are to understand and implement the credit accumulation and transfer system, and to have a real sense of ownership. Finally, in the absence of a national top down framework, it is simply the best method available.

In an attempt to capture the additional outcomes of the learning experience, individual course tutors have themselves defined the learning outcomes in a manner which reflects the full range of achievement. In addition, core skills units have also been developed at a number of different levels parallel to the subject specific units, and these are identified as associated core units on each unit specification. Furthermore, a number of units are being developed which attempt to enhance the definition of the 'value added' dimension. These are 'effective worker' units and 'effective learner' units. 'Effective worker units' attempt to encompass the all round integration, application and transferability of knowledge, skills and personal qualities which distinguish a capable from a competent worker. 'Effective learner' units encompass those evaluative/analytical skills, and aspects of personal skills such as motivation, perseverance and time management, which differentiate more readily a learner who is likely to progress. Figure 9.2 provides an illustration of aspects of an 'effective learner' unit.

Parallel with this work is the development of a set of advice and guidance units describing certain specific aspects of the learning process. These include action planning, reviewing achievement, opportunity awareness, all of which are an essential part of learners taking responsibility for their own progress and development.

Assessment practices have also changed considerably over the

Wirral Metropolitan College Learning Framework	
Programme Title: *Core Skills Programme*	
Unit Title: *Effective Learner (Draft)*	Unit Key:
Associated Qualification:	
Awarding/Certificate Body: *Wirral Metropolitan College*	
Unit Status: *Stand Alone*	Unit Level *E, 1,2,3*
Learning Outcomes: • reflects on overall learning goal and associated learning programme • appreciates the importance of planning and structuring own learning to meet learning goals • identifies the purpose of individual learning tasks and activities • outlines how individual tasks/activities relate to and are relevant to the overall learning programme and to issues beyond the subject area • • •	

Figure 9.2

last two decades. There is now widespread recognition of the benefits of making assessment practices and procedures visible and explicit to the learner.

The Learning Framework not only provides details of the learning outcomes but also defines the assessment criteria associated with each unit. In addition, the Learning Framework database has the facility to produce an 'assessment toolbox' for each unit which learners can use for assessment on demand. It is also important to recognise that some assessment methods may be more appropriate than others within certain contexts. Continuous assessment has, for example, become an accepted part of college provision in many areas and the introduction of NVQs into the curriculum has promoted the value of work based assessment and assessment on demand.

The discussion so far has focused on the development of a credit accumulation and transfer system and has emphasised the need for both an adequate definition of achievement as well as a coherent structure for the curriculum, in an attempt to 'open up' opportunities for learning.

The emphasis on a coherent curriculum structure has particular relevance in relation to 'opening up'/increasing opportunities for learning. The curriculum mapping process to date has highlighted areas of significant commonality and overlap. In effect, this means that certain units (not only core skills units) are generic to a number of different programmes. As a consequence, learners will not only be credited with partial achievement of one programme of study, but the same will also be true wherever else that unit appears. This may influence learners' perceptions of achievement, and they may then be sufficiently motivated to continue with other programmes of study.

The format of the credit accumulation and transfer system is also an important consideration when trying to make the curriculum more accessible and flexible. A paper driven CAT system lacks the interactive/dynamic qualities which are an essential part of 'opening up' opportunities for learning.

Although the Learning Framework exists in a paper based format, it is also available on METTNET, the College's computer network system. The Learning Framework database contains all the curriculum information about programmes/qualifications in the following fields:

- title
- level
- credit rating
- learning outcomes
- assessment criteria
- awarding body
- associated qualification
- programme/unit outline
- guidance on APL
- unit status
- recommended unit combinations
- recommended entry requirements
- assessment schedule
- category/type of unit
- delivery modes/location
- unit/user information
- administration details

In addition, learners can interact with the database to produce individual action plans, to accredit prior achievement, to review achievement against the learning outcomes, to record achievement (including the opportunity to contextualise the learning outcomes) and to produce a credit transcript. It is the potential for interaction which makes the Learning Framework a dynamic educational tool which can facilitate learning and achievement.

However, it is not only the development and the format of the CAT system which provides opportunities for 'opening up' learning. The way in which the credit accumulation and transfer system is implemented is also important. What then are the aspects of implementation which will make the curriculum more accessible and flexible?

Clearly one of the main advantages of introducing a credit accumulation and transfer system into an organisation is that it provides learners with a real basis for choice and enables them to devise individual programmes of study which meet their own personal needs. However, one of the dangers is also the increased potential for adopting a 'pick'n'mix' approach to programmes of study. There may be a temptation for learners to select a variety of options which although attractive, may lack any coherence and clear progression opportunities. The issue of coherence can be addressed in two ways. First, it is important to have the necessary advice and guidance services available to ensure that learners 'mix'n'match' their options to ensure successful achievement of learning goals and to identify appropriate progression routes. Secondly the issue of coherence can be addressed through 'curriculum maps'. In the past the tendency has been to rely on qualifications to provide coherence and consequently the potential to 'open up' opportunities for learning through individualised programmes has not yet been fully realised. It is important to reconsider our understanding of the issues surrounding the concept of coherence and to define coherence in terms of the learner rather than in terms of existing qualifications.

'Curriculum maps' can help to describe what constitutes a coherent curriculum offer in terms of existing qualifications, student entitlement, enhancement and progression for most learners within particular specialisms.

There has been a significant amount of research over the years in both educational research and psychology which has examined the effects on achievement of different approaches to teaching and learning. The conclusions are not surprising — students learn more effectively when their preferred approach to learning matches the style of teaching (e.g. Pask, 1976). The implications are clear

— learners should have the opportunity to access different modes of delivery. In this context the role of advanced technology is exceedingly important in creating opportunities for introducing alternative modes of delivery.

The capability for developing advanced information technology linked to learning and training is vast, as is its potential for promoting a more flexible and accessible curriculum. Computers can now be enhanced by sound, graphics, photographic-quality pictures and moving images. Multi-media developments can link interactive, computer based packages to the credit accumulation and transfer system, and many programme leaders are beginning to develop computer based learning packs and simulated assessment techniques, through **Smartbooks** or **Metronics**, which can enhance achievement. (**Smartbooks** provide the opportunity to put text and graphics into an electronic format, with a display that is similar to a traditional paper-based book. **Metronics** provides the facility to include text, graphics and assessment in an electronic format that is interactive.) The potential of providing access to the network by way of modem links opens up exciting new opportunities for the learner, and may of these are currently being developed at Wirral Metropolitan College. Students will have the opportunity to control their own learning and will be able to select the method of delivery most appropriate to them at any given time and place. They may, for example, opt for live lectures delivered through videos and computers.

Wirral Metropolitan College has an extensive computer network, METTNET, which connects the three sites of the College by a fibre-optic Megastream link. Staff and students can access the network on any one of over 750 workstations in 94 different locations throughout the College. More than half of the computers are available on an open access basis, and students do not have to book terminals. To gain access to METTNET, students are issued with a Learning Pass which entitles them to unlimited use of the £250,000 worth of software which is available on the network. The purchase and development of new software is demand led and both software and hardware use is carefully monitored by a system 'PCeptor'. The Megastream link has been extended to other organisations also. Currently two other colleges outside Merseyside and a secondary school in the locality have shared access to the network.

Traditionally, information retrieval has always been associated with books and libraries. The advanced technology developments described above, however, open up a wealth of opportunities to access and retrieve information in many different ways that may encourage and motivate learners. Increasingly, there is recognition

Student Led Curriculum		Course-Based Curriculum
Learning Framework with Credit Accumulation and Transfer	**More or Less Open to**	**Course-Based Provision Without Credit Accumulation and Transfer**
• the curriculum is broken down into coherent manageable chunks of learning.	L	• almost all College provision exists in the form of already established courses.
• initial assessment materials for core skills units are available.	E	• initial assessment materials are linked to existing courses and programmes.
• learners can customise programmes of learning to fit their individual needs.	A	• if a learner doesn't have the necessary skills/knowledge to gain entry to the course, they may have to do another course either alongside their chosen one or as an alternative.
• learners can access learning resources linked to the learning Framework units, to 'top up' their skills/ knowledge in areas where they may require additional support.	R	• learning resources are linked to the course.
• learners can be given credit for their achievements at regular intervals.	N	• depending on the nature of the course, learners may or may not be assessed at regular intervals.
• learners can accumulate and transfer credits if appropriate.	E	• depending on the nature of the course, learners may or may not be able to accumulate and transfer units of the course.
• if learners have to leave for some reason, their achievements can be credited and they can carry on from where they left off at a later date.	R	• if a learner has to leave the course, they may not get any credit for what they have done.
• learning can happen on or off campus.	S	• if a learner returns at a later date, they may have to restart the course from the beginning.

Figure 9.3

that encouraging students to access and retrieve information in a variety of innovative ways may promote the development of a range of additional skills which have potential transferability into a number of other contexts. By ensuring that technology is accessible, easy to use and relevant to the needs of the user, learners can be encouraged to access a range of learning resources.

Extending the range of learning resources and introducing new modes of delivery are not the only ways advanced technology can 'open up' opportunities for learning. It can also have a profound impact on the location of learning. 'Colleges without walls' are not only possible but also, in many instances, may well be desirable. Specifically in areas of high unemployment where the patterns of employment are changing, there are tremendous gains to be made from taking learning out into the community.

Through modem links, there can be access to the curriculum, learning resources and tutor support in a variety of different locations which could range from the learner's own home to any base in the community.

In conclusion, readers should judge for themselves the benefits of introducing a learning framework, with credit accumulation and transfer, and open access to learning resources by comparing what happens to a learner in a more traditional system (Figure 9.3). From a learner's perspective, I believe the former creates not only an accessible college, but truly open learning.

References

Entwistle, N. and Ramsden, P. (1983) *Understanding Student Learning*, Beckenham, Croom Helm Ltd.

FEU (1992) *A Basis for Credit? Developing a Post-16 Credit Accumulation and Transfer Framework*, FEU, February.

Marton, F. and Saljo, R. (1976a) 'On qualitative differences in learning. 1 — outcome and process'. *British Journal Educational Psychology*, **46**, (pp. 4–11).

Pask, G. (1976) 'Styles and strategies of learning'. *British Journal Educational Psychology*, **46**, (pp. 128–148).

Robertson, D. (1993) 'Credit Frameworks — an international comparison' in *Discussing Credit. A Collection of Occasional Papers Relating to the FEU Proposal for a Post-16 Credit Accumulation and Transfer Framework*. FEU.

UDACE (1989) *Understanding Learning Outcomes*, A UDACE development paper.

Wilson, P. (1993) 'Developing a post-16 credit accumulation and transfer framework: the technical specifications' in *Discussing Credit. A Collection of Occasional Papers Relating to the FEU Proposal for a Post-16 Credit Accumulation and Transfer Framework*. FEU.

Notes

1. The Further Education Funding Council (FEFC) implements its new funding methodology for the first time from the 1994–1995 academic year. The aim of this new approach is to fund processes and outputs, rather than inputs as before.
2. The Further Education Funding Council's approach allocates funds to three basic elements — entry, on-programme processes and achievements — and evidence of action planning is one of the requirements for the entry phase.

10 Open learning in the FE mainstream — a case study

Rosemary Hawksley and Ron Munroe

Introduction

The first student enrolled on a flexible learning programme at Stockport College in September 1987. The twelve months from January 1987 to January 1988 encompassed the research, planning and implementation phase of what was still a Flexible Learning Project, supported by both the then Manpower Services Commission and the Local Authority (Hawksley and Munroe, 1988). The evolution of the project into what is now Stockport College Flexible Learning Services reflects the influences of both the original plan, with the vision it encompassed, and the modifications made necessary by a changing environment.

The dedicated suite of accommodation in the College known as the Flexible Learning Centre, with direct access from the street to reception and administration offices, tutorial rooms and a study centre, was established almost from the beginning on the main College site. From this Centre a steadily expanding range of Flexible Learning Services has been provided. From 620 enrolments in the first year of operation the annual total increased year by year to 2,936 who enrolled in 1992–3 (Figure 10.1). The ratio of males to females has remained relatively constant at approximately 80 per cent females, 20 per cent males, as has the age profile with approximately 90 per cent of learners aged 19 and over. One figure of considerable significance that has actually declined is the drop out rate, from 10 per cent in 1987–8 to 6 per cent in 1991–2 and 5 per cent in 1992–3.

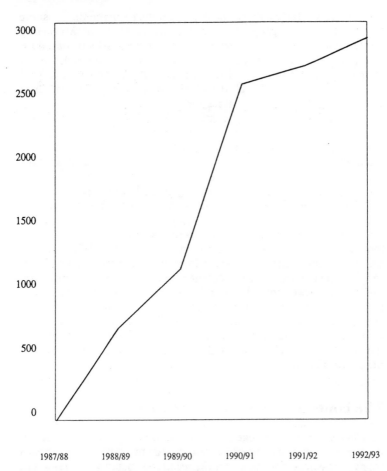

Figure 10.1 Flexible learning annual enrolment totals 1987–1993

The strategy from the beginning was to involve full-time members of the College staff whenever possible. A case loading system is in operation for all tutors, approximately half of whom are full-time members of staff and half are on part-time contracts. There is staff development and briefing packs for new tutors. The number of tutors involved has risen from 41 in 1987 to 96 in 1992–3 with a relatively small turnover each year, perhaps 6 or 7.

A wide range of programmes is on offer, extending beyond the usual GCSEs, 'A' Levels and Office Technology (the staple fare of many open learning centres) to include options on HNC programmes, the delivery of the theoretical elements of some construction craft programmes, and the Institute of Marketing Diploma amongst others. New programmes are added, based on assessment of 'market' need. This may be by an approach from a course manager to Flexible Learning Services, or vice versa if need has been identified through the routine monitoring of enquiries at Flexible Learning Services Reception.

Accessibility of these services to clients and potential clients has always been a priority and the Flexible Learning Centre is open 9.00a.m. – 8.00p.m. during term time and 9.00a.m – 5.00p.m. during vacations. Learners may enrol any month of the year including August, and Figure 10.2, showing the enrolment flows for 1991–2 and 1992–3 are very typical annual patterns with just over 10 per cent of enrolments coming during the 'traditional' enrolment time of September.

However, the interest in any statistics clearly comes not from looking at totals in isolation, but in their context. What are the trends, if any, and what conclusions may be drawn from them? In the next part of this chapter 'The context — pressures for change', we consider the broad framework in which the flexible learning developments at Stockport have taken place; subsequently we highlight the ways the present model differs from the original concept and the key lessons learnt. Finally, we risk a few conclusions and predictions based on the experience of Stockport College.

The context — pressures for change

In 1987 when the College first considered the need for a specific initiative to increase flexibility of provision, there were already many pressures for this, and precedents set by others. The effects of the huge investment in the Open Tech Programme were still working their way through the FE System; the Further Education Unit, in many seminal publications (FEU, 1987a, b and c; 1988), was highlighting the increasing need for more flexible access to learning. TVEI was stressing suggested self-study developments (TVEI, 1987). Overall, however, the effect was of raising awareness rather than revolutionising delivery methods in FE.

However, in recent years the further education sector has steadily moved from the back row of the chorus — or perhaps from the props room — into the political limelight. Admittedly, this happened only after politicians had intervened in primary, secondary and higher education, but when they did turn their

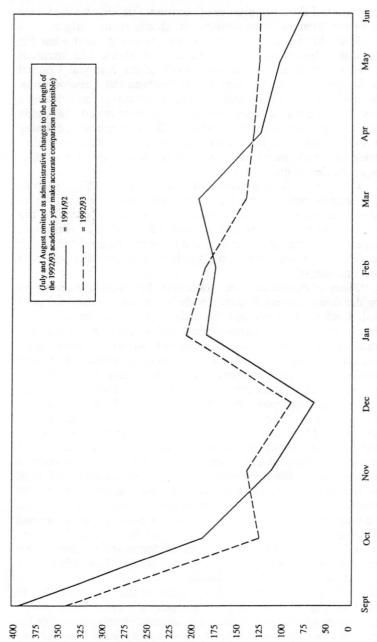

(July and August omitted as administrative changes to the length of
the 1992/93 academic year make accurate comparison impossible)

——— = 1991/92

– – – = 1992/93

Figure 10.2 Monthly totals of enrolments through the Flexible Learning Centre 1991/92 and 1992/3

attention to FE the importance of vocational training for the future economic strength of the country was clearly acknowledged.

With this political attention came questions about what FE was doing, how it was being done and for whom. The attention to skills highlighted by the early work of the National Council for Vocational Qualifications led to fundamental questioning of the traditional structure and content of vocational qualifications as well as the way in which achievements were tested. Alongside this came the increasing demand for skills training and re-training as a consequence of the introduction of new technologies and/or changing employment patterns, with more frequent job changes requiring new skills.

One reason for job-change, of course, was the significant rise in unemployment in the late 1980s and 1990s. In contrast to other recessions, on this occasion the economic difficulties did not lead to a direct decline in demand for further education. Expectations changed, however, and there was an increasing focus on value for money, both from the bodies funding FE and from our 'customers'.

Many of the elements of 'traditional FE' were being assessed for the degree to which they met the needs and circumstances of both funding sponsors and the wide range of customers. There were complementary changes from within vocational education which ensured that those assessments would be both heard and acted upon. In particular, the growing interest in quality standards in education gave a completely new perspective on colleges' relations with their clients. Further Education has always had a customer focus, but this focus often lacked the rigour and consistency inherent in the adoption of quality management principles. The attention of colleges was sharpened also by the growing awareness of competition, actual and potential, from other providers of training and — on the back of NCVQ — assessment services. Faced with the increase in in-house training by employers, by the growth of specialist national training services, private providers and the increasing competitiveness of other colleges, individual institutions looked much more closely at their own offerings.

Colleges needed to respond to change in ways which would maintain their markets — and their survival. If a college had already developed flexible learning systems seriously, on an institutionally integrated model, the response to the new demands and the changing FE environment was obvious. However, although there were well-known examples of successful, innovative flexible learning developments in 1987, the majority were free-standing developments, not administratively integrated into their existing

College management systems for enrolment, resourcing and staffing. Indeed there was plenty of anecdotal evidence at that time that many College senior managers had backed away from the considerable challenge of trying to make their flexible learning/ open learning management and administrative systems compatible with those for mainstream programmes. Many of even the most successful developments at that time were bolt on extras to their colleges.

The response

The original concept of the Flexible Learning Centre at Stockport College took as its starting point the FEU definition of flexible learning as 'The provision of learning opportunities tailored to meet the needs of the learner.' These tailored learning opportunities were to be delivered in three ways:

(i) by drop-in workshops for subjects needing access to practical facilities
(ii) by supported self-study using learning packages where this methodology was appropriate
(iii) by 'brokerage' into existing classes where this provision was already modular or unit based.

The third category was recognised to be the smallest to begin with but likely to grow as modularisation increased. The Flexible Learning Centre was seen as the shop window for information about entry and for enrolment onto the new flexible College programmes.

The Centre was to be (and remains) an integral part of the College, not owning students in resource terms, but funded as a central College service, drawing on full-time College staff as tutors wherever possible and responsible for the administration of all flexible learning programmes. The ultimate objective, seen as necessary even in 1987, was the flexible college. The stages of progression envisaged towards the flexible college, without a fixed timescale and on a voluntary basis, are represented in Figures 10.3a–c showing a gradual extension of growth points established in the Flexible Learning Project phase, into a whole College development.

The actual model achieved by the voluntarist approach to 1993 can be seen at Figure 10.3c. Certain parts of College provision are significantly more flexible and accessible than they were five years before. The range of provision available by a flexible learning

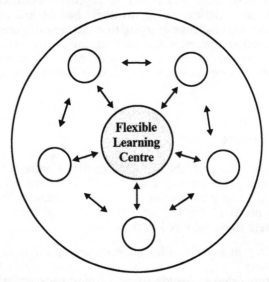

Figure 10.3a The situation in 1987. The Flexible Learning Centre as a pilot development at the centre of a cross College developmental network

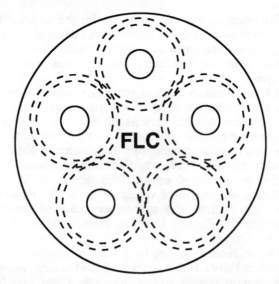

Figure 10.3b Original theoretical model envisaged — gradual expansion of growth points thus creating a flexible college

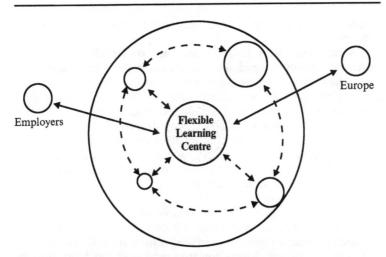

Figure 10.3c Representation of the model in practice after five years. Some growth points expanded and thriving. Others developed strongly and now independent. Some tenuous or defunct. Flexible Learning Services as the focal point of College OL/DL provision and with strong links to employers and European partners

route continues to expand, most successfully where subject staff have developed an interest in, and enthusiasm for flexible learning and have recognised its potential. However, clearly it is easier to give the learner a high degree of control though a flexible learning programme in some areas of the curriculum than it is in others.

Subjects which require access to workshops and laboratories have safety and supervision requirements which considerably restrict the ability of staff to offer freedom of access. At the same time many exam syllabuses are increasing the requirements for assessment of skills in a workshop or laboratory environment.

Other subjects, for example in the broad field of 'caring' include elements of the curriculum in which skills and personal development require extensive group interaction and discussion.

To develop increased flexibility in areas like this requires a radical review of the curriculum and the identification of those elements which can be made available on a flexible basis to give learners improved access and control. Two examples where this has been done successfully at Stockport College are hairdressing, where flexible learning developments have led to a considerable increase in adult enrolment; and in brickwork where theoretical elements of the course were transformed into flexible leaning packages, again very well received by the learners concerned.

A decision taken in 1987 and not so far changed is that potential students aged 16–18 should wherever possible be counselled onto learning programmes where there is a greater amount of learner/tutor contact than on flexible learning programmes. Experience elsewhere suggested to us that few students of this age found it easy to take a high degree of control for their own learning. Where a flexible learning programme is part of a more traditional course, or an adjunct to one, the flexible learning methodology works well for this age group and drop-out rates are no higher than for older students. Only 10 per cent of flexible learning students are aged 16–18.

The key concept is now not 'flexible learning' but the broader one of 'flexibility', encompassing as it does all the processes which together provide a client focused and responsive college. Some of the current *external* drivers towards increased flexibility are the introduction of NVQs and GNVQs; the demands of TECs for year round access to College programmes, particularly for unemployed people; the driver to modular programmes to increase choice and cut costs. Will these now accomplish in the College what voluntarism alone did not?

Flexible learning developments not envisaged in 1987 have been those beyond the College walls. The major moves into Europe via funded projects for training the trainers, and the work with employers, including the contract management of employers' own in-house open learning facilities, have considerably expanded the sphere of operations of Flexible Learning Services already and many more developments are in train in these areas.

The original model of the flexible college may not yet have been reached but factual evidence collected from 1987 to the present allows some conclusions to be drawn. Firstly, the public demand for flexible access to learning continues to grow. Total annual College enrolment 1987 – 1992 rose from 11,800 to 15,000 but flexible learning enrolment as a proportion of this expanded steadily. There is also no doubt that the Flexible Learning Centre has made a significant contribution to the improvement of access to the College. The 80 per cent of women on flexible learning programmes compares with 50 per cent average for the College as a whole and the analysis of college enrolments by postcode shows a significantly higher proportion of students from the most deprived wards of the borough enrolling on flexible learning than on class-based programmes. Interestingly though, the percentage of students on concessionary fees is lower than for the College as a whole. The age profile of flexible learning students compared

	All enrolments %	Flexible learning enrolments %
under 19	33	10
19 – 24	32	19
25 and over	35	71

Figure 10.4

with the whole College profile also emphasises the contribution of the Flexible Learning Centre to second chance education and continuing education and training (see Figure 10.4).

Flexible Learning Services is located administratively in the part of College organisation responsible for marketing, for links with employers and TECs, overseas developments and short courses. A major part of the role of Flexible Learning Services is now recognised to be outward looking, in attracting new clients, and in developing market led provision. Flexible Learning Services has also become a highly saleable part of College services as a resource of expertise on flexible learning systems, methodology and materials.

Key lessons

The Flexible Learning Centre has proved itself as a successful working model able to deliver quality flexible learning programmes cost effectively through five years of radical change.

From this experience the following key lessons seem to emerge for post-16 education and training:

Client focus — The delivery of appropriate training at the right time and in the most suitable place to meet client needs is essential. To meet these needs fundamental questions must be posed and answered accurately about who are the clients for FE in the 1990s. Only then do we know what training they will need, at what time and in which place.

Stockport College is not unusual in having discovered that in the mid 1990s our client group is changing rapidly. A higher proportion of students are older; organisations which previously employed large numbers of people (and sent large numbers of students to college) are disappearing or restructuring before our eyes; there is increasing emphasis on the concept of access for previously under-represented groups, by women, people with special needs or members of ethnic minorities; TECs are recognising the need to tailor training more to the individual needs of both employed and unemployed people of all ages.

A satisfactory response to the diverse needs of all these clients, whether learners or sponsors, can only be a flexible one. Individuals with hearing loss or visual impairment, women who are managing a flexible learning programme along with onerous home and work commitments, employers whose need for training is great but fundamentally different from that of only three or four years ago — all need and will increasingly demand a flexible and client focused response to their requirements. The flexible approach to meeting individual or corporate training needs is through joint work on analysis of the need, preparation of the training programme and delivery and evaluation of the training delivered. The challenge of providing such individually negotiated solutions cost effectively while guaranteeing the high quality outcomes of a systems approach cannot be underestimated (see *Quality systems* below).

Individual learning contracts — The concept of individual learning contracts is based upon the willingness and ability of both parties to engage in the process. Essentially contracts give learners a share of the responsibility for the management of their learning. Therefore, it requires learners to have the maturity, motivation and understanding to engage in the negotiations leading to a contract. It is essential also that the provider has both the willingness and the diagnostic and negotiating skills to engage in a purposive dialogue with the learner.

A successful contract will take account of the learner's objectives and potential as well as their existing attainments so that both learner and provider understand the targets, appreciate that they are attainable and have made a commitment to achieve them together. There can be no doubt that the initial negotiations with prospective clients in the Flexible Learning Centre represent a major contributory factor to both the 95 per cent retention rate and the excellent assessment/examination results. At the very outset this involves a fifteen-minute session, offered free to all, confirming their understanding of the concept of flexible learning and clarifying their objectives before they decide whether to enrol or not. Once enrolled, there then follows a detailed discussion of specific targets with a specialist tutor in the first tutorial or workshop session.

New markets — The evidence from the response to the offer of flexible learning opportunities is that recognition of different client needs can open up new markets by assisting those clients to gain access to the college's services. With enrolment rising from 11,800 to 15,000 the College could not be described as unsuccessful in attracting students. But marketing theory emphasises the importance of discovering which clients are not being attracted as well as those who are. Analysis of enrolments through the Flexible Learning Centre, which shows a much higher proportion of women, of older learners, of people from within the Borough of Stockport and especially from the more deprived wards of the Borough than on class-based College courses, highlights student groups who were not and are not attracted by traditional provision to the same degree. A survey in 1992[1] by The Flexible Learning Centre of 450 learners who had completed a wide range of flexible learning programmes showed that when they were asked to identify which aspects of the Flexible Learning Centre and its facilities mattered most to them when they were choosing and using a Flexible Learning course, the following six ranked highest:

	%
Helpful tutor support	54
Opening hours	49
Easy to find location	38
Comfortable relaxed atmosphere	32
Equipment available	25
Private room for tutorials	25

Of lesser importance was, for example, the provision of a study area, or the availability of learning materials. There would seem to be clear marketing messages here about preferred learning styles, about the facilities and their availability, which have attracted new client groups to the College through the Flexible Learning Centre.

Quality systems — If the administrative systems for recording student activity, progress and achievement are set up to comply with quality standards and measurement of progress to those standards is applied rigorously, it ensures that flexible learning provision meets the requirements of both the institution and the learner. In our experience the importance of administrative support is often underestimated in comparison with the more usual emphasis on tutor support. Flexible Learning programmes are recognised to be 'admin heavy' and this burden should not, for a variety of reasons, be carried by tutorial staff. The clerical and administrative role is not, however, a back room

one in flexible learning and these staff become the key third
partner in the learning relationship, alongside the tutor and
learner. Their support is valued by both learners and tutors
and successful flexible learning provision is critically dependent
on this team approach. Efficient administrative support is also
essential for central college tracking of the relatively fragmented
tutor/learner contact in flexible learning. The extremely low drop
out rate of flexible learning students at Stockport, lower even
than on class-based traditional programmes, is an exception to
the high drop-out rates usually recorded on flexible and open
learning programmes. The financial consequences will be severe
for colleges who introduce the increasingly flexible programmes
now required in further education over a wide range of provision
without reviewing staff roles and recognising and budgeting for the
central part played by administrative staff.

An Admin Assistant is occupied for the whole of her time
in tracking and recording the tutor/student contact of all flexible
learning students in the College. New computerised record keeping
is helping in this task. It is interesting that the individualised
student record used now for six years in the Flexible Learning
Centre is the format required under the FE Funding Council's
new funding methodology.

Curriculum — The extension of flexible learning methods into
new areas now demands very careful thought about the structure
of learning programmes. Successful flexible learning has always
required programmes of study which are organised coherently, with
clear objectives and identified pathways to reach those objectives.
Increasingly, only learning programmes structured this way will
satisfy learners and their sponsors. In flexible learning terms
two conditions must be present in addition to effective tutor
support:

   (i) the ordering of the curriculum so that it is developmental and
        reinforcing for the learner
   (ii) the availability of high quality learning materials to support
        the independent learner.

It is possible that providers will wish to develop learning materials
themselves if they are unable to find any of a suitable quality. If
so, great care must be taken to ensure that quality standards are
applied to their own products. However, before embarking upon
the extremely costly process of producing new learning materials
in any medium, the potential should be recognised for tutors to
use their skills, and knowledge of individual learners, to adapt the
use of existing materials for specific needs. In our experience this

has proved to be generally a most cost-effective approach in many disciplines.

Assessment on demand — There is no point in offering learners flexibility of pace and time if they come to the end of a programme phase only to discover that they have to wait several months to be assessed. Therefore, the client-focus must extend to assessment also. That has significant implications for the nature and costs of assessment and the respective roles of assessment bodies (BTEC, RSA City and Guilds, the GCSE and 'A' Level Boards, etc.) and of their local agents, including colleges. As yet, not all examining/assessing bodies seem to have recognised the needs of the increasing numbers of people who follow a flexible learning route to assessment and qualification.

The examination results of students on flexible learning programmes have always been collated and compared with students who have followed a class based route to the same qualification. A fully validated statistical analysis remains to be done but there is strong evidence that college flexible learning students' results are consistently as good as, and in some subject/ course areas, better than results from class based tuition. It could be speculated that the ability of flexible learning students to pace their own progress towards examinations or assessment and, within the constraints set by examining bodies, to choose the timing of the assessment, could be influential here. There is absolutely no indication that a flexible learning route is a second best route to a qualification.

Where are we going?

The challenge facing colleges in the nineties may be summarised as the need to increase numbers of students, which will take them beyond their existing markets and require them to respond to the increasingly diverse demands of different client groups, whilst simultaneously improving the quality of the learning experience for all clients. This has to be achieved within cost parameters which are acceptable to both the institutions and their clients. It is important, therefore, to assess the contribution, actual and potential, of flexibility of provision to the ability of colleges to address these issues.

Evidence presented above shows that, in the case of Flexible Learning Services at least, new kinds of students have been attracted. Whilst the enrolments on standard programmes continued to rise without significant changes in the characteristics of the student body, the rapid growth in the Flexible Learning Centre was a result of attracting older students with a substantial majority of women. Our evidence suggests that the difference was attributable to the Centre's capacity to meet the different expectations of the various learner-groups, by enabling their learning programmes to be adjusted to the specific needs and personal commitments of individuals. Those commitments change over time, of course, and a flexible learning programme can respond by allowing repeated adjustments whilst maintaining continuity of learning. It is interesting to compare this with the flexibility offered by a modularised taught course, which can offer a choice of entry point, course content and often assessment date, but cannot offer the individual the fine tuning of a flexible learning programme. It is these characteristics of flexible learning which will help to make 'life-long learning' more than just a political slogan. Moreover, as any retail store manager will tell us, it is far cheaper to secure repeat business than constantly to attract new customers.

Accessibility through flexibility has a further important consequence — it puts the learner much more in charge of her/his own learning. This in turn impacts profoundly upon the role of the tutor. The development of systematic, structured learning programmes places a question-mark over those teaching styles which tend to create a dependency of the students on the teacher. This is true equally of the paternal — 'don't worry your heads about it, just do exactly as I say' — as of the charismatic 'follow me and I will show you the frontiers of knowledge!' And since the learner has access to the whole course in the learning materials, it is no longer possible for the tutor to select the moment to reveal the next tasty morsel of 'knowledge' as though from a personal store. The tutor is just as important but the role has changed.

Indeed, flexible learning raises fundamental questions about the volume and nature of human contact required to achieve effective learning. Successive technological developments have made learning more accessible and ODL is the arena in which that is being exploited most fully. But we are still not sure which features of human support for learning are unique and irreplaceable and there is an urgent need to identify the optimum amount and timing of tutor intervention needed to achieve successful learning outcomes from programmes delivered in this way. In a world which measures inputs against outputs the respective costs of new technology and tutor support required for effective learning must also be assessed in terms of cost/benefit. The costs of qualified staff may be high but the volume of support needed from them for effective individualised learning may be much less than is generally supposed. Flexible learning students at Stockport College achieve their results in many subjects with only one face-to-face tutorial each month.

Of course, flexibility of provision is not the exclusive domain of colleges. A visit to any major supermarket, for example, will find a trainee cashier learning on-the-job with in-house support. Therefore, if colleges are to achieve their growth targets, they must ensure not only that they are able to tailor programmes to client-needs, but that the cost/benefit of the total learning experience maintains their competitive edge.

When the Flexible Learning Centre was established at Stockport College it was an interesting initiative which the College, the LEA and the then MSC believed had considerable potential for adding value to the institution's whole curriculum. Developments in the years since then have shown that flexibility is no longer an option; it is fundamental to success into the next century, and any college ignores that at its peril. However, it is not sufficient that this situation is recognised in the design and delivery of learning programmes. It must also be reflected in the way in which colleges are managed and upon the future funding regimes of education and training. The new funding model introduced by the Further Education Funding Council seems to have begun to recognise this. Perhaps in five more years the flexible college will be a reality.

References

Hawksley, R. and Munroe, R. (1989) 'Flexible Learning — A Way Forward' in Paine (ed) *Open Learning in Transition — An Agenda for Action* Kogan Page.

FEU (1988) *Flexible Learning Opportunities*, FEU.

FEU (1987a) *Learning Workshops*, FEU.

FEU (1987b) *Relevance, Flexibility and Competence* FEU.

FEU and the Manpower Services Commission (1987c) *Implementing Open Learning in Local Authority Institutions*, FEU.

TVEI (1987) *Technical Vocational Educational Initiative*.

Notes

1. In the survey of 450 learners referred to earlier the two most popular answers to the question 'What did you like most about your flexible learning course?' were 'I could study at a time that suited me' — 64 per cent and 'It allowed me to work round my commitments' — 62 per cent.

11 Collaboration for open learning in higher education

Steve Ryan

Introduction

In recent years considerable interest has been shown in developing open learning within Higher Education. In part this interest stems from a desire of individual institutions to reach out to a wider and more diverse clientele, who may not be in a position, perhaps for reasons of geography, or work or domestic commitments to attend conventional courses. Changes in funding arrangements may also encourage the recruitment of more part-time students.

But increasingly there is also a recognition that open learning techniques can be used effectively for teaching on a traditional campus. Learning packages, using a variety of media have demonstrated their effectiveness in distance education — notably in the case of the British Open University. Could not these techniques also be used successfully in conventional universities? It would then be possible to combine the best of both worlds, offering opportunities for student support and contact in a campus environment, allied to the flexibility and cost effectiveness of media-based learning packages. Potentially this offers an exciting learning environment, students working at their own pace on high quality materials with opportunities for contact, group work, seminars and laboratory sessions on site. In addition if such methods are shown to be cost effective they may also offer universities the possibility of increasing intake at a time of restricted resources.

The potential of open learning methods is enhanced when the new technology is exploited. Computer-based learning, multimedia, video-conferencing and computer-mediated communication are all seen as offering methods of delivery that are not only novel and exciting but also appropriate to the image of a modern university in a way which, perhaps quite wrongly, more traditional paper-based open learning packages are not. A result of this is that many of the issues relating to collaboration and shared development of open learning materials are becoming linked to issues relating to the appropriate use of the new technology.

A number of potential benefits are claimed for the use of the new technology in education including:

- improved access
- reduction in failure rates
- flexibility of movement between courses
- the shift from passive learning to active learning (Macfarlane Report, 1992, pp. 34–35)

But how is this potential to be realised? The time, effort and cost of producing materials has led to an increasing emphasis on collaborative development between institutions. Encouraging such collaboration is now the explicit policy of some funding agencies. The Teaching and Learning Technology Programme, an initiative from the Higher Education Funding Councils, for example, specifically encouraged bids for funds from consortia of institutions and departments. In other cases individual institutions may receive earmarked funding to develop materials that are then made more widely available throughout the sector.

The scenario outlined so far raises many questions. If these methods are to achieve their full potential, careful examination of some of the assumptions underlying this approach is required. In particular I would argue that while programmes for the collaborative production of materials are necessary, in themselves they are not sufficient. We also need to address key questions of collaboration for implementation and delivery. How are these materials to be used once they have been produced?

It is also important to guard against too great an emphasis on the role of the new technology. An emphasis on questions relating to the technology itself can very easily mask issues relating to its appropriate use for teaching and learning.

'Traditional' paper-based open learning materials (whose development and production is increasingly underpinned by the new technology) have a key role to play. Their development may not attract the funding opportunities offered for example, to the development of computer-based materials, but this should not be taken as a measure of their value.

Finally, although the focus of this chapter is on collaborative development, what of the students? Open learning is student-centred learning, and if we overemphasise materials development but do not devote the time and resources needed to help students make best use of the materials being produced, the benefits claimed for these methods will not be fully realised.

Towards the future? The Macfarlane report

How is this change to be achieved? One way would be through a major initiative to change fundamentally teaching and learning in universities. This would be nationally led and not be based on piecemeal development.

The (1992) Macfarlane report *Teaching and Learning in an Expanding Higher Education System*, examined many of these issues. The report argued for the collaborative development and sharing of resources and materials, particularly using the new technology.

The report advocates a national strategy on an ambitious scale.

A first phase, lasting perhaps five years, could be one in which a national network of discipline-based centres was developed for the production of high quality shareable learning resources, aimed particularly at mass enrolment courses (a course being say 250 study-hours). Staff in these centres would receive training in materials development. Consortia and teams would be the main mode for production. During this phase, existing resources, such as the Open University's course materials, could be made available for wider use, with or without adaptation. For this phase, it would be reasonable to have as a target 100,000 student courses provided by these means.

During a second phase, lasting another five years, one would see the first generation of new learning resources distributed and in general use, while a second generation was being produced. It should also see a substantial reorganisation of space and time for study within institutions, resulting in a mixed economy of teaching means and methods in almost all UK Higher Education. The target should rise to perhaps 500,000 student courses during this period (Committee of Scottish University Principals (Macfarlane Report) 1992, p. 33).

The report offers a fundamental reappraisal of teaching and learning within Higher Education, one which seeks to produce an innovative high quality teaching and learning environment drawing in large measure from collaborative undertakings. In order to achieve this the report advocates new organisational structures, in particular a Teaching and Learning Board. This Board would *generate* and *manage* (my emphasis) a programme to:

- foster the large-scale production of shareable resources; stimulate innovation in teaching and learning support systems
- generate and support a research and development community in the fields of teaching and learning support
- create and oversee arrangements for the quality control of the shareable resources which it endorses
- establish national arrangements for the dissemination of teaching materials; for the maintenance of development and delivery systems; and for the creation and maintenance of the associated support infrastructure required in individual institutions (ibid, p. x).

Collaboration is at the heart of this strategy. But what can be learnt from collaborative undertakings already underway?

Collaborative development using the new technology

Funding bodies are now explicitly encouraging collaboration and sharing between institutions. The recent Joint Information Systems Committee (JISC) New Technologies Initiative for example emphasised that proposals for funding must demonstrate mechanisms for transferring results and benefits to other higher education institutions.

The Teaching and Learning Technology Programme (TLTP), deliberately set out to encourage collaboration between institutions. In this it has been successful: consortia of up to forty-four member institutions can be found developing and evaluating materials. The main thrust has been on courseware development. In phase 1 almost three-quarters of the projects funded were concerned with developing materials. The range of projects funded under the TLTP programme is vast. Consortia are producing materials in disciplines as diverse as archaeology, law, engineering, physics and music (CTISS File, 1993, pp. 27–70).

Considerable sums have been invested in these initiatives. The Computers in Teaching Initiative, by the end of the 1980s had brought together funds of over £20 million and the Teaching and

Learning Technology Programme, in total, over phase 1 and phase 2 is allocating some £10 million.

This has had many positive developments. It is providing some staff with the opportunity to be involved in the collaborative development or evaluation of materials and has led to the establishment of many formal and informal networks. It is also providing the experience of using collaboratively developed resources in individual institutions.

Many university staff are interested in exploiting the new technology. The 'Beyond Lectures' (1992) survey reported that almost 70 per cent of respondents would be interested in using computer-based learning (Information Systems Committee Courseware Development Working Party, p. 16). This positive attitude gives much to build on as large-scale development means that the use of the technology will be extended beyond the committed enthusiasts into mainstream teaching.

But to date the impact of computer-based learning has not been great. One survey suggests that only 27 per cent of academics have at some point used computer-based learning and of academics who have seen computer-based learning in their field half judged it to be of very mixed quality (Information Systems Committee Courseware Development Working Party, pp. 15–17). There are many possible reasons which may account for this lack of impact. In many cases it is too early to assess the courseware being produced under the national initiatives, much is still under development. But some of these difficulties may stem from the emphasis placed on the technology itself rather than seeing the new technology as one possible means to a particular end. This is well summed up by Laurillard (1993):

> It is a sad fact of research and development funding
> in educational technology that the focus is always on
> a particular medium or method. Vast sums are made
> available to investigate the best way of using computers,
> where the subject matter taught is incidental. The more
> rational approach, seldom adopted, is to offer vast sums
> to investigate the best way of teaching a particular topic,
> and through that to fund the use of computers as an
> incidental part of the strategy. As a result of irrational
> funding we have studies that tell us that computers,
> video, etc. can be effective and can also fail utterly,
> but we have very little idea of how they might work in
> combination, or how design relates to the content being
> taught (p. 7).

Collaboration for open learning

So far the emphasis has been on collaborative initiatives using the new technology and I have suggested dangers of this emphasis. But what of other approaches? One important initiative is that of the Open Learning Foundation.

The Open Learning Foundation

The Open Learning Foundation (OLF) was established in 1990 by twenty polytechnics (now universities). The OLF does not enrol students, rather it provides a range of services to its members to achieve the objectives of growth, quality and greater efficiency.

The OLF has, in the main, concentrated on developing open learning using 'traditional' media, print, audio and to some extent video. There are sound reasons for this. By working with media with which institutions and users are relatively familiar, development times can be reduced and a wider range of potential contributors drawn upon.

The OLF's materials are both developed by members or bought in from existing providers. Two points are particularly interesting. First, some 80 per cent of member institutions are involved in the development of OLF materials, this is broadening considerably the base of experience and expertise in the development and production of such materials. It also facilitates the exchange of experience and expertise between member institutions through for example the running of workshops.

Secondly, OLF materials are used by members under a licence agreement which gives the user a right to adapt and 'customise' the materials in ways which are seen as appropriate for local circumstances. In some instances materials are distributed electronically to facilitate this process. This has not been without its difficulties, and it would appear that recently hard copy as opposed to disc versions of materials have been in demand.

The concept appears well worth developing. Providing materials in a form (and with the right) to adapt and to customise offers the possibility of using the same core materials in different ways in different institutions. It has the potential of reducing any reluctance among some academic staff to the importation of externally produced materials into 'their' course.

Universities need to exploit both the advantages of direct face-to-face contact between staff and students in a resource rich campus and the advantages of media-based learning materials developed on a scale beyond the practical reach of most individual institutions. Using collaboratively produced materials, stored electronically for ease of adaptation, appears to provide a rich and effective means of extending open learning.

However, two qualifications need to be made: First, the materials must be suitable for the context in which lecturers plan to use them and secondly lecturers need to be aware of ways in which such materials can be used. This requires staff development programmes geared towards facilitating lecturers in using such methods.

The OLF recognises that materials development in itself will not enable institutions to achieve the goals of growth, quality and efficiency. Increasingly, it is placing greater emphasis on implementation with the objective of helping institutions to make best use of the opportunities offered by open learning.

A range of activities including staff development workshops, the establishment of interest groups and visits to institutions are being offered by the OLF to all members. Recent examples include the establishment of a network of fourteen universities interested in the use of open learning in mathematics and the organisation of a conference on the implications for open learning in business studies (OPUS, 1994). These activities offer the potential of contributing to the major change in culture which is required if open learning is to achieve its potential.

Interest groups within the OLF containing members drawn widely across the country, cover topics such as assessment, learner support and learning technology.

Continuing collaboration

While the Open Learning Foundation provides a national focus, there are many examples of smaller scale developments which are contributing to effective open learning.

The polytechnics and Colleges Funding Council initiative on Teaching More Students[1] for example, enabled institutions across the sector to benefit from materials and workshops dealing with issues relating to independent learning. A series of further workshops and materials on resource-based learning on a subject-specific basis is being produced. This will enable academics across the sector to draw on the experience of others in their discipline who have had the experience of developing materials.

We need to know far more about how best to implement these developments. We need to explore, document and share experiences of 'what works best' and why. This does not require major national initiatives or huge expenditure; rather much more can be done via regional collaborations, publications and workshops and conferences. Publications from organisations such as

SEDA[2], such as the recent publication on science teaching is an excellent example (Exley and Moore, 1993).

The M1/M69 link is a consortium of staff developers in universities in the East Midlands united by a motorway network and a commitment to networking ideas, methods and practice in staff development. The work of the link includes development activities relating to, as well as personal and professional development for, all groups of university staff. They run a series of workshops and other activities on a reciprocal basis (each of the nine participating institutions hosts one event per term) to which staff from all the participating institutions can attend. Members of the link advise and support each other and join together to seek external funding for collaborative activities. This is a good example of the way collaboration and co-operation can be fostered with minimum cost.

Greater use can be made of electronic bulletin boards and conference systems to facilitate collaboration. The NISS[3] System for example contains a wealth of information including subject-specific information from various discipline groups. A conference for staff interested in flexible learning has also been established.

Towards implementation

A cluster of key issues facing universities relates to implementation rather than materials development, to the need for piloting, staff development and evaluation (Laurillard, 1993). An appropriate investment in the delivery infrastructure is also required if we are to see a major impact from media-based open learning utilising the new technology. The Nelson Report (Computer Board, 1983) recommended a ratio of one workstation to five students, and if we are to exploit the possibility of multimedia the workstations need to be modern, relatively well configured machines.[4] In a recent survey only two universities reported meeting this recommendation (Macfarlane Report, 1992: Appendix C).

Infrastructure development needs to be supported by a major emphasis on staff development. New patterns of working, teaching and supporting students will be required and the process of developing new skills and applying existing ones in a changing context is one which staff developers are familiar with. The thrust of this staff development will be towards facilitating collaborative modes of working where the materials developed are the property of the course team rather than that of the individual lecturer.

But this investment in both infrastructure and human resources can be best justified if the new technology is exploited at all stages of course development and delivery. An over emphasis on the production of courseware can lead to other fruitful explorations of the technology being missed. So what might this mean?

Getting the balance right — using the new technology from design to delivery

The new technology has a continuing role to play at all stages of course development. At the course design stage E-mail systems may be used to improve communication, module planning templates and on-line information systems, can help identify existing materials which may be appropriate.

It is important to emphasise that institutions already have a valuable resource in the form of materials and lecture notes currently being produced by staff for 'conventional' teaching. While it would be mistaken to assume that they can be easily converted into open learning materials, 'packaged lectures', inter-active handouts and laboratory and practical guides can all be developed (Gibbs, 1992, p. 33). Using the new technology to pool these resources by providing data bases and text retrieval systems offers many possibilities for development.

At the materials production stage, the use of desk top publishing systems to customise existing resources, linked to flexible print production systems which provide the number of sets of materials as required is now possible. This has many advantages over the stockpiling of resources that become dated.

The application of desk top video digitising systems, and scanners to capture images to disc has moved away from being the concern solely of the computer specialist. Now many academics are using them routinely in the production of materials. The end result may not be computer-based courseware. They may be used in desk top publishing or for presentation purposes in lectures.

At the course delivery stage, there is potential for the use of computer mediated communication to establish electronic support systems for contact between staff and to facilitate collaborative learning. At present, the best examples of this are found within distance learning contexts but they have considerable potential for on-site use (Alexander, 1994).

The role of the new technology in assessment is now being explored. A Teaching and Learning Technology project, project ALTER: Assessment of Learning through Efficiency and Rigour, led from the Committee of Vice Chancellors and Principals Staff Development Unit, is examining technology-driven procedures for the marking of scripts and the processing of results. A major outcome of the project will be to encourage dissemination and implementation across the sector (CTISS File 1993, p. 38). Individual Universities are investing in technologies such as optical mark readers which enable the automatic marking of multiple choice questions and similar materials.

This perspective then raises questions of integration. How will these elements be integrated within conventional teaching programmes? If they are to justify their cost, they cannot be relegated to optional extras bolted on to existing courses; rather they must form a fundamental, integral part of course provision.

The general trend towards modularisation facilitates such integration. Courses are restructured so that they are made up of a number of modules. Individual modules may be shared across a number of courses and offered a number of times. Staff who designed the module may not be involved in its teaching and the module may be specified in terms of student study hours and learning outcomes. Course handbooks may outline in detail assessment strategies, aims and objectives and course content. The entire structure of a course and its various components becomes clearer with the result that planning, collaboration, and the pooling and sharing of materials, across courses and across institutions becomes easier.

However, the major obstacle facing such initiatives in my experience is that of time, time for lecturing staff not only to be involved in the development of open learning materials whilst still maintaining their 'normal' teaching and research loads but also to be involved in the selection, adaptation and integration of materials into their teaching programme. Lessons from the Open University and others, about the time required to produce good open learning materials, have not yet been fully accepted. These time pressures were also identified in the *Beyond Lectures* (1992) survey

> Given poor staff-student ratios and ever increasing numbers of students plus pressure to pursue research, time in an 86 hour week is at a premium (Information Systems Committee Courseware Development Working Party, 1992, p. 12).

Conclusion

Major change in teaching and learning within higher education will require a massive commitment to the development of collaborative modes of production and delivery exploiting the new technology. While such changes are likely to be evolutionary and will build on existing developments, much is already happening. These initiatives require underpinning and support but their potential is considerable.

Some lessons can be learnt from the experiences to date. The advantages of collaborative approaches, both through national initiatives and at the regional and local level are clear. We are all still very much feeling our way and the more experience and expertise can be pooled the better. But while the focus for this collaboration may be based on the application of new technology, the technology should not be overemphasised at the expense of the content. We need to move rapidly beyond 'technology demonstrations'. The recommendations in the *Beyond Lectures* report for discipline based consortia working collaboratively rather than in competition is relevant here; particularly with the emphasis on the involvement of professional institutes and associations and validating bodies.

We must also address the entire course development and delivery process. Concentrating excessively on courseware development will not lead to the conditions in which the effective use of these materials can be made. Ways in which the technology can underpin not only courseware development but also the delivery and support of teaching must be addressed as must the need for appropriate staff development activities.

Finally we must not only focus on national initiatives, much can be done locally with bodies such as the OLF providing co-ordination. Such issues are to an extent within the control of institutions. By drawing on the experience of others and facilitating collaboration, by funding initiatives internally and seeking best use of existing resources, much more can be done.

References

Alexander, G. (1994) *Renewable Energy Technology: An interactive learning course with technology based support.* Report no. 52 Training Enterprise and Education Directorate, Department of Employment.

Beyond Lectures (1992) Report of the Information Systems Committee Courseware Development Working Party. CTISS Publications University of Oxford, July.

Computer Board for Universities and Research Councils (1988) Report of a working party on computer facilities for teaching in universities. London, The Board, (Nelson Report).

CTISS File 15 April 1993. CTISS publications, University of Oxford.

Exley, K. and Moore, I. (eds.) (1993) *Innovations in Science Teaching*, SCED Paper 74. Birmingham.

Gershuny, J. I. and Slater, J. B. (1989) *Computers in Teaching Initiative*, Report. Bath.

Gibbs, G. (1992) Teaching more Students. 5 *Independent Learning with more Students*, PCFC.

HEFCE circular 13/93 Higher Education Funding Council England, Bristol.

Laurillard, D. (1993) *Rethinking University Teaching: a framework for the effective use of educational technology*, London, Routledge, p. 7.

The Macfarlane Report (1992) *Teaching and Learning in an Expanding Higher Education System: Report of a Working Party of the Committee of Scottish University Principals Edinburgh.*

Open Learning Foundation Annual Report 1992–1993.

OPUS (1994) *Newsletter of the Open Learning Foundation* February.

Notes

(1) This project led to a series of workshops in a number of different institutions and the publication of a series of booklets.

(2) SEDA, the Staff and Educational Development Association was formed from the Standing Conference on Educational Development and the Society for Research into Higher Education Staff Development Group. It is active in promoting co-operation and collaboration among all in Higher Education concerned with educational development and teaching and learning.

(3) This can be accessed via JANET from Higher Education institutions in the UK.

(4) For PCs this will mean in today's terms Multimedia PC level 2 or equivalent specifications. Not older DOS-based machines which may be perfectly adequate for word processing and other student uses.

12 The accreditation of prior learning: opening the door to experience?

Christine Butterworth and
Richard Edwards

In his influential article 'What is open learning', Lewis (1986, p. 5) identifies three key features of open learning:

- open learning is learner centred, rather than institution centred
- open learning implies the use of a wide range of teaching/ learning strategies
- open learning is about removing restrictions ('barriers') to learning, particularly those barriers inherent in conventional education/training provision.

Open learning is, therefore, associated with extending the range of opportunities and the forms of teaching/learning available to learners. One aspect of such development has been the increasing recognition given to the accreditation of prior learning (APL) by educational providers. In making provision for APL for people to draw upon their prior learning from experience, it can be argued that providers are extending opportunity by opening the door to experience. APL is learner-centred, it implies the use of a different teaching/learning strategy from the norm, and in providing access or credit within learning programmes, it removes certain of the barriers to education and training. It can, therefore, be argued that APL is a central feature of the development of more open forms of learning; as part of open learning systems and in contributing to the openness of more conventional systems.

However, like open learning itself, APL is not without its difficulties. In this chapter, therefore, we explore two programmes for APL offered by two universities in the UK in an attempt to explore and examine some of the ambiguities in opening the door to experience. We will also suggest that these ambiguities reflect back on the notion of open learning itself and raise questions about simplistic views that an open door is always appropriate or a 'good thing'.

The purposes of APL

All schemes for APL are offered with the intention of widening opportunities for individuals to gain certification. They represent a willingness on the part of qualifying institutions to accept that in mature individuals, work and life experiences can lead to valuable learning. APL can be used for access (in place of formal qualifications) or for advanced standing, where course credits can be given for uncertificated learning acquired before entry.

The intention of any APL process is that it should enable the individual applicant to review their past experience and determine which parts of it may be eligible for credit towards a qualification. The process should then provide support for the applicant while they collect and present evidence of that past learning in a form suitable for assessment and accreditation.

It should be clear from this definition that it is not appropriate to see APL as a course of any kind: there is no established body of content which all candidates must acquire, nor one conception of the end 'product' which they should all submit. The amount of credit awarded may vary between candidates. This scope for individual variation means that by its very nature, APL can be considered as an aspect of open learning, enabling the individual, with whatever advice and support they find necessary, to produce their own unique account of their past learning from experience.

The two variants of programmes to assist learners in preparing APL claims described here are first, one which was offered face-to-face, and second, one offered at a distance. The purpose of both was to make credit available to more students by assessing and accrediting relevant, demonstrated, learning from experience. One APL facility (offered by the School of Post-Compulsory Education and Training at the University of Greenwich), gives the opportunity of advanced standing to in-service students from education and training who are attending professional courses.

The second APL process described was a pilot distance-learning programme offered to a similar group of professionals taking an Open University professional Diploma. In the former, therefore, APL contributes to the openness of a face-to-face system, while in the latter it was introduced as part of an open learning system.

Different types of APL

APL has spawned its own vocabulary and debates. One such controversy has surrounded the form of the learning to be assessed. Notions of 'competence' and 'learning outcomes' are deployed in these debates, but are not always interchangeable (UDACE, 1989). Sometimes their use marks a different philosophy under-lying the APL process (Butterworth, 1992).

APL used to gain National Vocational Qualifications (NVQs), demands evidence of 'competence' from applicants. Competence-based qualifications have been developed under the auspices of the National Council for Vocational Qualifications. The aim is to produce a coherent range of vocational qualifications tied to a common national set of standards at a variety of levels of performance. NVQs emphasise the possession of 'competence', which is defined as effective performance in a work role. This breaks the traditional link between time-serving and qualification: if an individual *comes* to an assessor already competent, then their past learning can be immediately accredited.

The Council's intention is that APL should be offered by employers and by trainers in further education: in 1994, it was still more commonly found in further education and at lower vocational levels. The introduction of NVQs and APL, therefore, contribute to the increased flexibility of further education institutions. A competence-based APL scheme places most importance on the evidence of learning which is presented for assessment. Competent performance has to be evidenced for the award of credit (see Simosko, 1992).

This may be documentary (letters or reports showing word-processing skills, for example), or it may be actual objects made by the individual. An assessor may ask to observe the applicant demonstrating their competences.

APL in higher education is primarily used to offer individuals advanced standing on professional qualifications. Fields where APL is currently most readily found include education, social work, nursing and management. Some of these areas are encompassed by the NCVQ framework. However, for many working in these fields, acquiring an understanding of a body of theory is an important part of professional qualifications. Thus, they tend to express their aims in terms of 'learning outcomes' rather than 'competences' to accommodate this emphasis on the understanding of underlying theory rather than primarily using particular work performances as the main indicators of professional effectiveness.

Early on in the development of APL in higher education, the now disbanded Council for National Academic Awards (CNAA) stressed the principle that the applicant for APL had to be able to make their prior learning explicit (rather than merely describing past achievements) before credit was justified (Evans, 1988). Claimants on these schemes, therefore, were asked to provide, in addition to evidence of their past activities, an account (most commonly written) of how these experiences produced the learning they were claiming. This reflective account is at least as, if not more important than, the items of evidence as an indicator of the level of the individual's professional development. This requirement was the basis of the APL processes at Greenwich and the Open University pilot.

However, we shall also draw where relevant on a parallel development in the Open University's Open Business School, into which a pilot APL scheme to accredit management competence was introduced in 1992 (see Shields, 1993). In this way while wishing to explore the issues raised by APL for different types of institutions, we also wish to highlight how certain issues are endemic to any APL scheme, whether it is based on competence or learning outcomes.

Common elements of the APL process at Greenwich and the OU

Both institutions recognised that many professionals from the field of education often bring with them substantial amounts of learning from experience which can be accredited as professional development. At Greenwich in-service students on several courses are offered the opportunity of gaining course credits by compiling a portfolio of these relevant past experiences. A similar portfolio-based approach to APL was piloted at the Open University for professionals in the post-compulsory field to provide a distance learning route to accreditation.

Within these programmes the basis for an APL claim to secure advanced standing on the course, is that the candidate has already acquired some of the learning which that course offers. To facilitate this the curriculum needs to be expressed in a form which helps the candidate match their past learning with areas of the course i.e. course modules or units need to be expressed in terms of learning outcomes. Course units on awards at Greenwich were already expressed in outcome terms as part of the validation process. On the Open University Diploma modules aims had to be re-written in outcome terms.

Two sorts of claim are possible: the candidate can claim general credit (i.e. that they have already achieved some of the overall course aims, though in a particular field which does not feature as a course unit or module), or they may claim specific credit, i.e. they can match some particular unit or module outcomes, and seek to be credited with having achieved that particular unit. General or overall learning outcomes are needed for candidates whose particular field of achievement is not covered by course content.

The APL process in both institutions was designed to support the continuing professional development of this group of learners. It did this by requiring them to provide a written account and analysis of their past experience. This was consistent with models of experiential learning (see Kolb, 1984 and Boud et al., 1985) which emphasise the importance of a phase of reflection after action, and with theories of professional practice (see Schon, 1991 and Elliott, 1991) in which this period of reflection generates an explanation (called a 'theory-in-use') which the professional uses to analyse and guide their continued practice. For purposes of assessing academic standards, this reflective statement can be used to judge the candidate's level of understanding and stage of professional development.

Each APL claimant is required to produce a portfolio containing a learning claim, a list of learning outcomes, the written reflective account and supporting evidence. We shall go on to consider next the process by which this document is produced, and the contrast between the face-to-face mode (at Greenwich) and the distance mode (at the OU).

APL on in-service professional awards: the University of Greenwich model

APL is offered on all the in-service awards in the School of Post-Compulsory Education and Training: the CertEd/PGCE, the BA(Ed), Professional Diplomas, and the MA(Ed). The facility is offered on an open learning basis, i.e. an initial induction stage, (by individual contact or group workshops) followed by one-to-one tutorials to a timetable negotiated with the candidate.

There are some constraints on the degree of openness underlying this learning programme.

First, the APL claimant must already be registered on a course. Access criteria to all awards are fairly flexible, always allowing a student to substitute appropriate professional experience for academic qualifications. Students engage in an APL process alongside more traditional studies.

Secondly, students are not encouraged to embark on APL without initial academic guidance during the induction stage. The purpose of this is that they should understand the work that will be involved, know the assessment criteria which their portfolio will have to meet, and have had advice as to the potential credit value of their learning from experience. This extended induction tries to ensure an APL claim is a 'no-fail' procedure by ensuring a high level of well-informed motivation in candidates, and by 'cooling out' those whose experience is not relevant to the course or sufficient to generate credit.

If entry to APL on these professional awards was completely open, i.e. with no 'filtering' at the induction stage, the drop-out level would be greater, leading to a wasting of effort on the candidates' part. More destructively still, from the point of view of the candidates' confidence, more portfolios might fail the assessment, and incidentally more tutorial time be wasted supporting such candidates.

Once past the induction stage, applicants begin a series of tutorials with the APL counsellor, who supports them during the preparation of their portfolio. A printed form serves as a tutorial contract, recording tasks completed and goals negotiated for each tutorial. Within certain limits, it is up to the applicant to set their own submission date. There is no fixed amount of tutorial time available and most applicants complete with between four and six tutorials.

Each portfolio is assessed by the programme leader, and all portfolios are moderated internally by a group consisting of pro-gramme leaders and APL counsellors. External assessors see a sample after internal moderation. Candidates receive different amounts of credit, up to a total of 50 per cent of that required for the award.

APL by distance learning: the Open University pilot

In 1990 the School of Education at the Open University developed a pilot APL facility linked to the Professional Diploma in Post-Compulsory Education (for a fuller discussion of this pilot see

Butterworth, Edwards and Raggatt, 1993 and Butterworth and Edwards, 1993). This is an open access, two-credit award for professionals, and APL was offered as a quarter-credit option amongst other quarter-credit postgraduate modules. A common feature of the design of these modules is the emphasis on the reflective practitioner as an example of good practice, and students are encouraged to keep a portfolio in which they reflect on the connection between their own professional experience and the concepts and models they are introduced to in the course. This made the Diploma a suitable vehicle for an APL pilot.

Tutoring for APL candidates was available on the same basis as for study-based modules, i.e. tutoring began once the candidate had registered on the course. Thus, the particular induction questions that all candidates face meant that the distance learning course had to provide for the same needs as the Greenwich APL programme; most importantly, candidates needed help in assessing the credit potential of their claim. Unlike Greenwich's programme, access to the Open University Diploma was completely open: there were no requirements about previous experience. This made attention to these issues of self-assessment particularly important.

Consequently, distance materials were produced to enable students to take themselves through the induction stage. A booklet of activities, with case study examples, helped them to review their past experience, define their own learning outcomes, and find Diploma module learning outcomes against which they could match their learning. Each candidate was then asked to decide for themselves if they had the basis for a claim, and whether to register. Since all these diagnostic needs had to be dealt with *before* the decision to register, these materials were provided free.

Once registered, APL candidates received course materials — detailed guidelines on how to collate the material for their portfolio with case study examples at each stage of the process.

Tutorial support was provided at two key stages. There was an introductory group workshop after registration, to confirm the candidate's outline plans for their portfolio. Unlike the Greenwich APL candidates, the Open University candidates had a deadline for submission of portfolios: seven months after registration. At a mid-point in the course (three months before the deadline) a postal Formative Assessment tutorial was provided for each candidate. Each candidate completed a form listing their learning outcomes, their selected Diploma learning outcomes, and identified the items of evidence they intended to offer in support of these. By written feedback, the APL adviser checked that the outcomes and the evidence were adequate to earn the quarter credit required, and confirmed that the choice of general or specific credit fitted in with the candidate's plans for future study on the Diploma.

Once submitted, each portfolio was double marked. Every marker had a list of specific assessment criteria, each allotted a proportion of the marks. All portfolios were seen by the external examiner. Any portfolio that was believed not to merit the quarter credit was returned to the candidate with a report indicating how it could be brought up to standard.

Evaluation of the Greenwich and Open University APL programmes

The Greenwich APL scheme has been in place for five years and there is no formal external evaluation process: the internal moderation panel is also able to monitor the facility, and changes can be made to accommodate critical feedback from students, staff and external assessors. The Open University scheme, being an externally funded pilot, was formally evaluated by survey questionnaires and interviews with candidates and staff.

The model of APL common to both schemes has been identified as the 'developmental' model of APL (Butterworth, 1992) appropriate to professional training. The developmental effect follows from the structured written reflection each candidate produces on their past experience, reinterpreting it in the light of theories from their professional field, and linking it with a personal evaluation of their own professional development. However, it is important to note that certain developmental effects have also been found to occur in competence-based APL schemes (Simosko, 1992). It may, therefore, be that the very process of portfolio construction has a developmental effect, whether or not it includes a reflective piece of writing.

In both schemes examined here candidates reported that they found this kind of thinking and writing very challenging, but that once it was done, they could appreciate that the process had been of real benefit to their development. Reviewing their portfolio work, one candidate wrote:

> I feel that gaining qualifications and recognition for one's past experiences and subsequent learning outcomes is a stimulus for pursuing further personal development. It makes a refreshing change from the traditional courses and final set examinations.

Stating their own achievements formally had clear benefits for their self-awareness. Another candidate said their own motivation to claim APL had stemmed from realising that 'putting the portfolio together is a reflective process, and should produce further learning'.

This model of learning is demanding, however. By its nature, APL is something candidates do at the start of their course, but the actual activity of putting together this kind of portfolio has more in common with producing a dissertation than writing a course-work essay. It is a self-directed activity, resulting in the compilation of a substantial document. Reflective writing at this level is a sophisticated intellectual task, and assumes a high level of study skills which not all students possess in the early stages of their course.

The second important aspect of APL which both programmes highlight is the crucial role of the APL counsellor. This is a more complex role than the tutoring needed to support traditional study, and staff development is essential. Some skills necessary for other roles (dissertation supervision, tutoring, pastoral counselling, giving academic guidance) can be called on, but many aspects of APL are unfamiliar, and this, combined with the complexity of the role, means staff need to be well prepared. This was also found to be the case in the Open Business School pilot (Shields, 1993) and the competence-based scheme evaluated by Simosko (1993). Interestingly, with regard to the latter, open learning techniques alone were not found to be satisfactory in supporting staff introducing APL processes.

Some clear differences between the two APL processes were the result of the contrasting modes: face-to-face tutoring versus distance learning. The Open University advisers all agreed that the APL route to credit meant students needed more tutorial support than Diploma students on the study-based route, and all advisers had provided, informally (and unpaid) more support than the two-hour group workshop and one twenty-minute individual tutorial which was formally allowed for. Written course materials alone were insufficient to answer all the students' potential questions during the induction stage: the Greenwich process indicates some contact with a counsellor/adviser is essential during induction. This may particularly be the case given the unfamiliarity of APL to potential learners and the complexity of deciding whether or not a claim is appropriate. The Open Business School suggested that five years' prior experience as a manager was a useful guide as to whether or not a claim was viable, but given the focus on individual attainment that APL is meant to provide, this may have been more expedient than desirable.

The other contrast was in the amount of credit available to applicants: the quarter credit limit on the OU course did disadvantage at least one applicant, whose portfolio, all assessors agreed, merited more. The disadvantage was double: not only was the amount of credit limited, but the level at which the claim was being made was tied to the course the applicant was on. At Greenwich, by contrast, a particularly experienced and able student on, for example, the degree course, can use their portfolio to demonstrate that they are in fact operating at Masters level. This example shows how the 'openness' of a scheme can apply to its end result as much as to access and patterns of learning.

APL and openness

The APL schemes outlined above are only two in a diverse field of developing practice. In evaluating these schemes, a number of critical issues arise for both providers of APL and developers of open learning.

First, open access does not necessarily provide people with the opportunity to progress to completion of the course. Providing APL in the field of professional development necessitates that a candidate has the requisite amount and level of learning from experience to be able to make a successful claim. This entails pre-entry guidance to provide potential candidates with some understanding of what is required of them. The lack of availability of such guidance may have led to a significant level of drop-out in the OU pilot, a position avoided at Greenwich by the initial 'cooling out'. However, other face-to-face APL schemes have also attracted significant levels of drop out, so initial guidance may not be the sole issue involved (Simosko, 1993).

This means that APL is not 'open' to all: it is an alternative route to credit for those who prefer to work independently and are certain that they have reasonably substantial experience which they want to evaluate. APL might therefore extend opportunities to the already educationally proficient rather than widen opportunities, a criticism which might also be turned against the notion of open learning.

Secondly, it might be suggested that with greater levels of tutorial and counselling support, APL could be made more open; the problem lies with the educational institutions allocation of resources for such developments. There is certainly something in this, as the additional support offered by the advisers in the OU pilot demonstrates. When the OU second intake of candidates ran with an experienced APL adviser, there was significantly less drop out. This highlights the importance of staff development in enabling tutors to develop their role as APL advisers.

However, if APL demands greater levels of individual support to students, in the developing market in education only two solutions seem possible. Either institutions will provide the support as a 'loss leader' to attract people into their institutions, or individuals will be asked to pay more for APL than conventional courses. This goes against many people's expectations that APL will be a quicker and cheaper route to credit, an expectation also found in competence-based APL systems (Simosko, 1993). In all systems for APL, issues of cost, efficiency and effectiveness have proved major hurdles to development. Usually, solutions are based on 'slimming down' the assessment process and recognising APL is not appropriate for everyone. This, of course, raises issues of quality and access. Similar issues have been raised in relation to many forms of open learning, where assumptions about relative costs have not always been realised in practice.

Thirdly, while recognising the important role APL can play in opening the door to experience, the particular issues surrounding openness in a face-to-face and distance institution need to be addressed. It may well be that the process of APL is more suited to face-to-face institutions as the ongoing support of the counsellor may facilitate the development of the student's portfolio in a way more problematic through distance learning. Distance learning materials may aim to provide such a process, but students unfamiliar with APL may study them for content, failing to engage with the activities necessary for constructing their portfolio. As with other developments, therefore, APL may contribute more readily to the openness of face-to-face institutions than become a part of distance learning institution.

Stepping back even further to reflect on the significance of the development of APL we would also want to suggest that it, like open learning, adds to the individualising and commodification of learning tendencies currently being developed in education and training (Usher, 1992). It therefore sits within a currently central ambiguity of education and training theory and practice; the extent to which learner-centredness 'empowers' individuals or is a necessary prerequisite for the marketisation in education and training. In the many forms that APL is being introduced, is it the power of learners and learning that is being enhanced or the power of consumers or a combination of both? Does it matter?

References

Boud, D., Keogh, R. and Walker, D. (1985) *Reflection: Turning Experience into Learning*, London, Kogan Page.

Butterworth, C. (1992) 'Contrasting models of accrediting prior learning', *Journal of Further and Higher Education* **16**(3).

Butterworth, C. and Edwards, R. (1993) 'APL at a distance', *Open Learning* **8**(3), pp. 36–43.

Butterworth, C., Edwards, R. and Raggatt, P. (1993) *E878 Making Experience Count: Accrediting Your Prior Learning. An Evaluation of the APL Project in the School of Education*, Milton Keynes: Centre for Youth and Adult Studies, The Open University.

Elliott, J. (1991) *Action Research for Educational Change*, Buckingham, Open University Press.

Evans, N. (1988) *The Assessment of Prior Experiential Learning*, London, CNAA.

Kolb, D. A. (1984) *Experiential Learning: Turning Experience into Learning*, Englewood Cliffs, NJ, Prentice-Hall.

Lewis, R. (1986) 'What is open learning?', *Open Learning* **1**(2), pp. 5–10.

Schon, D. (1991) (2nd edn.) *The Reflective Practitioner*, Avebury.

Shields, D. (1993) *Assessment of Prior Learning for the Professional Certificate in Management*, Report to The Open University's Examination and Assessment Committee.

Simosko, S. (1992) *Embedding Accreditation of Prior Learning (APL)*, Sheffield, Employment Department.

UDACE (1989) *Understanding Competence*, Leicester, NIACE.

Usher, R. (1992) 'Experience in adult education: a post-modern critique', *Journal of Philosophy of Education* **26**(2), pp. 201–214.

Notes

(1) The initials APL are used generically in this chapter and include what is referred to as the accreditation of prior experiential learning (APEL). As well as learning from experience, for our purposes it also includes other forms of organised non-certificated prior learning.

13 Competence-based assessment and open and distance learning

Denise Hevey

Introduction

One of the most significant trends in education and training in the United Kingdom in the past ten years has been an increasing focus on the detailed specification and measurement of the outcomes of learning. This can be illustrated in compulsory education by the introduction of the National Curriculum Key Stage specifications and standard assessment tests (see for example, *Science in the National Curriculum*, DFE, 1991). In post-compulsory education the same trend is epitomised by the introduction of General National (and Scottish) Vocational Qualifications which are specified and assessed in terms of vocationally relevant learning outcomes (National Council for Vocational Qualifications 1993a). In Higher Education there has been growing interest and research activity in learning outcomes of relevance to employment. Attempts have been made to identify the generic and transferable skills that are an implicit part of the learning outcomes for graduates in a variety of subjects (Otter, 1991). Projects have been funded in some fifty-six Higher Education institutions under the Enterprise in Higher Education Scheme (Employment Department, 1990) to promote the explicit specification and measurement of employment-related learning outcomes in Higher Education courses. But perhaps the most clear-cut example of the growing focus on outcomes is the implementation of National (and

Scottish) Vocational Qualifications (N/SVQs). Within the N/SVQ system, assessment is entirely competence-based and performance in real work situations is judged against targets set out in nationally agreed standards (NCVQ, 1991).

The logic of the focus on outcomes in N/SVQs precludes specification of the nature of 'inputs' in terms of entry requirements, curriculum content, teaching and learning methods, time serving and so on (Jessup, 1991). Far from denying the importance of knowledge and learning as some have suggested (Smithers, 1993), the N/SVQ system recognises that individuals learn and develop their knowledge and competence in different ways and at different speeds and that experiential learning is at least as valuable as formal education and training courses. Open and flexible routes thus have an important role to play in overcoming barriers to access to qualifications at all levels of the framework, up to and including 'professional formation' (Local Government Management Board, 1993).

Competence-based assessment

Competence-based assessment is about the collection and judgement of evidence to demonstrate that an individual not only has the knowledge and skills that underpin occupational competence, but that he or she can actually carry out specified roles and functions competently in real work settings, with all the additional pressures and constraints that implies. Competence-based assessment is not a new concept nor is it exclusive to the N/SVQ system (Hevey, 1993). It has a long and chequered history dating back to the American behavioural objectives movement of the sixties and competence-based education and training programmes for teachers as advocated by the US Office of Education (Fletcher, 1992). However, if one extends the concept to include supervision and assessment of actual practice, competence-based assessment, in varying forms, has been part of many vocational and professional training courses for a very long time (Eraut and Cole, 1993).

The main features which distinguish the approach to competence-based assessment exemplified in the N/SVQ system are the degree of emphasis placed on assessment in real work settings and the use of criterion referencing against national occupational standards. The latter set out the expectations of performance for different occupational roles as agreed by representatives of the relevant industry. By the end of 1992, agreement had been reached on national occupational standards covering over 80 per cent of the UK workforce (NCVQ, 1993b).

In contrast to the criterion referenced system of N/SVQs, most traditional academic assessment is norm referenced in that each student's performance is compared against his/her peers and graded accordingly within broad guidelines for content, treatment, presentation, etc. Most assessment takes place outside the workplace by methods which are assumed to be highly reliable (but see Newstead and Dennis, 1994) but bear little relationship (low validity) to the activities and functions within the work role which the student will eventually be expected to undertake (Atkins, Beattie and Dockrell, 1993). In addition, assessment of knowledge has been relied on to the exclusion often of the assessment of skills and other learning outcomes.

Within a competence-based system, demonstrating what Eraut and Cole (1993) term 'capability' through the possession of relevant knowledge and understanding is rarely considered sufficient evidence to infer competence. In addition, criterion referencing implies little scope for selectivity reflecting student's preferences for different parts of the course or work role. N/SVQ candidates must meet *all* the specified criteria in order to be deemed competent on each function within the qualification (or element as it is termed in the N/SVQ system). But then one would not want to be flown by a pilot who was very good at 'take-off' but managed to get through the assessment without tackling a single question on 'landing'!

The new orthodoxy of competence-based assessment appears to assume that the best person to carry out assessment is a line manager or supervisor in the workplace who will observe the candidate's competence in the course of the normal work role, judge it against the criteria set out in the national standards and fill in the gaps in observational evidence by oral questioning. This over-simplification of the N/SVQ approach to competence-based assessment has managed to acquire the status of a myth in some quarters (Smithers, 1993). The reality is much more complex. As the NCVQ/SCOTVEC framework has been extended to higher levels, so the model has been adapted and extended. Competence in higher level occupations is characterised by large amounts of cognitive processing (such as analysis and evaluation of problems) which can't be readily observed; by professional and ethical judgements in relation to multiple variables and options; by the ability to recall and apply a large body of underpinning knowledge and understanding; and by the ability to synthesise experience with underlying principles, techniques and theories in ways which create novel solutions to complex problems. Under these circumstances outwardly observed behaviour cannot be interpreted without a rationale and the scope of the knowledge-base underpinning competent performance cannot be covered adequately through oral questioning alone. So a wide variety of alternative sources of evidence of knowledge competence have become accepted within the N/SVQ system, including: reflective accounts of practice; work-based case studies and assignments; log books, diaries and plans; work products such as papers, letters, reports and manufactured objects; peer-appraisal and witness testimony; multiple-choice tests, short answer papers and even traditional written examinations.

Implications for open and distance learning

National Education and Training Targets (NETTs) jointly agreed by the CBI and the TUC set dual targets for 'Foundation Learning' of young people and for 'Lifetime Learning' for those already in employment (NCVQ, 1992). These are based on the premise that Britain's economic survival depends on achieving a highly-qualified, multi-skilled, flexible and self-motivating workforce and on recognition of the implications of demographic trends. By the year 2,000 replacement rates for skilled workers will be running at 12–15 per cent per year while the declining birth rate implies that only 2 per cent of this figure will come from young people entering the labour market for the first time (Hevey and Smith, 1993). Emphasis on 'Lifetime Learning' is thus no longer the isolated plea of adult educators but is becoming an economic necessity. The targets state, for example, that by the year 2000, 50 per cent of the workforce should be qualified to at least NVQ level III or equivalent. Such targets cannot be achieved without a significant culture shift towards workplaces as training and learning environments within which the continuous updating of skills and knowledge are encouraged. This in turn implies a dramatic increase in markets for distance learning materials in the coming years.

On the job training and supervision of developmental work experiences are often best complemented by the use of open and distance learning methods rather than by off-site course attendance. In addition, education and training providers may be in a position to devise collaborative models for competence-based assessment which enable those in the work place to make an effective contribution to evidence collection without carrying the total responsibility for the assessment process. The latter is a particular problem for small and medium sized enterprises which currently provide 75 per cent of jobs (Hevey and Smith, 1993) and which may not be large enough to comprise a viable 'Approved Centre' for assessment of N/SVQs in their own right.

The extent to which open and distance learning can meet these forms of training and assessment challenge will depend on a number of factors. Distance learning materials have traditionally been considered good for providing the knowledge and under-standing which underpins competent performance in the workplace but recent experience has shown that a much wider range of outcomes are possible that relate directly to the development and assessment of competence:

- *skills awareness* — candidates can be made aware of skills and their uses through description in text and case studies.
- *skills observation* — the audio-visual component of multi-media distance learning materials can give candidates the chance to observe skilled practitioners in action. This may be especially useful for demonstrating specialist and confidential techniques like interviewing in child protection.
- *handling emotional responses* — video and audio material can be particularly effective for tackling highly sensitive and emotive issues. Use of audiotape, in particular, can convey a sense of privacy and intimacy.
- *individual skills rehearsal* — exercises associated with video and audio materials can encourage skills rehearsal. For example, using a tape-recorder for feedback can be of particular value in developing counselling, interviewing skills or in learning a foreign language.
- *skills rehearsal in groups* — where supported open learning is an option, skills rehearsal can be extended through role play and simulation in the safety of a structured group.
- *skills practice* — 'home experiment kits' are already used to enable simple experiments and procedures to be practised by distance students. An extension of this idea might enable vocational candidates to practise work related skills in their own homes.
- *IT skills* — the increasing availability of personal computers means that a wide range of information technology skills can be taught at a distance.
- *IT in assessment* — increasing sophistication in telephone facilities and electronic networking is beginning to open up possibilities for on-line assessment in fields such as languages as well as IT skills (see Bull, 1993 for a review).
- *interactive assessment* — the potential of CD-ROM and interactive video-disc is beginning to be explored for devel-oping and assessing some types of competence. For example, those relating to health and safety emergencies which may be impractical to carry out or simulate in the work place.

- *self-assessment* — skills check lists can help candidates identify past experiences and current competences as a basis for drawing up a development and assessment plan or for Accreditation of Prior Learning (APL) purposes.
- *identifying evidence* — exercises and exemplar materials in distance learning text provide a good means of helping candidates identify the sorts of work products etc. that can count as evidence of competence and how to go about authenticating such evidence as their own work.
- *generating evidence* — work-related exercises and activities which help develop relevant skills and generate evidence of competence can be built in to distance learning materials.
- *presenting evidence* — distance learning materials can be extremely useful in guiding students/candidates through the complex process of putting together a portfolio of evidence of competence and cross referencing to the relevant national standards or other target outcomes.

The above list gives a brief summary of the ways in which open and distance learning can contribute to the development and assessment of competence. However, there are outstanding features of competence-based assessment, particularly as set out in the N/SVQ system, that make it difficult to operate at a distance.

First, not only does all the evidence have to be directly relevant to the work role, but a substantial proportion has to come from a real work setting. Although a wide variety of types of evidence (such as reflective accounts of practice, witness testimony, work products, etc.) can be used which do not require the presence of an assessor in the work place, there are some types of competence for which observation is the only valid method. An example would be competences that hinge on the quality of the interactive process between the candidate and a client or a child. Indirect observation (e.g. by video or audio recording) may be a possibility but may prove unacceptably contrived.

Secondly, competence-based assessment within the N/SVQ system ideally should be candidate driven. Each candidate follows a pattern of learning and assessment at his/her own pace and should be able to negotiate a personalised assessment plan with an assessor to suit his/her particular work role and setting. The logistics of providing personalised, context sensitive and locally available assessment opportunities poses another significant challenge to many distance learning providers. Despite the rhetoric of being learner-centred and self-paced, economies of scale are often achieved through centrally devised (hence, usually, context insensitive) assignments and through mass administration of standardised tests.

Thirdly, the fact that competence-based assessment is criterion referenced rather than norm referenced has significant systems implications for the assessment process. Criterion referencing across a number of separate functions (units and elements of competence) effectively requires multiple assessment decisions within a single award rather than the overall averaging typical of traditional academic assessment systems. Each individual assessment decision has to be recorded and the accumulated record, once verified, is used to trigger certification. If all the criteria have not been met, feedback must be given to the candidate in the form of an assessment profile which specifies those elements on which competence has not yet been demonstrated (or for which there was insufficient evidence to make a decision) and credit must be given for unit achievement even when a full award cannot be made. This means that there can be no simple pass/fail distinction and that an unprecedented level of detail is required in assessment judgements and record keeping and in the feedback given to candidates. Furthermore, the absence of comparison or rank ordering of an individual's performance with that of his/her peers creates problems for the sorts of standardisation procedures commonly used within large scale norm-referenced systems.

Fourthly, since candidates within the N/SVQ system who have not satisfied all of the criteria for an award on the first occasion are not deemed to have failed but are judged 'not yet competent', they are entitled to go on submitting additional evidence of their developing competence on outstanding elements for an as yet unspecified period. This implies the need for considerable flexibility in the assessment system since candidates who present themselves for assessment with partial credit for a range of competences will only require assessment for those components which they have not yet achieved.

Developing new models

All of this adds up to a situation in which the sort of open assessment strategy required for competence-based qualifications and characterised as being candidate driven, individualised and highly flexible, is better suited to small scale, local and face-to-face modes of delivery than to large scale, centralised distance learning systems. What large scale distance learning systems are good at and can deliver cost effectively and with rigorous quality control, is precisely the opposite i.e. assessment that is systems driven, standardised, mass administered and relatively inflexible.

For example, they may offer only one or two pre-set assessment opportunities a year which double as chance to confirm the authenticity of the candidate's work. These features are not unique to assessment within distance learning but are also characteristic of traditional forms of academic assessment currently administered through examination boards such as GCSEs and 'A' levels.

Does this mean that, ironically, open assessment is impossible to reconcile with open and distance learning? The answer has to be no, but the problems of reconciling systems with such differing characteristics require innovative solutions. Just as the N/SVQ model breaks the automatic connection between curriculum inputs and competence outputs, so open and distance learning training providers need not automatically assume that they are best placed to provide open assessment opportunities. A variety of factors need to be considered, the most important of which are the scale of the operation, the predominance of distance versus open modes of delivery and, most significantly, the costs involved. Locally organised open and flexible learning centres which make use of distance learning materials but have regular face-to-face contact with relatively small numbers of students/candidates have greater flexibility to tailor learning programmes and assessment opportunities to meet individual needs. It could well be cost effective for such a centre to operate a peripatetic assessor service over a limited geographical area to supplement portfolio-based evidence generated by candidates. Centrally organised and predominantly distance learning providers with only limited contact through tutors/intermediaries and with large numbers of far-flung students (such as the Open University) face a far greater challenge. In the face of this challenge a number of models are emerging which may or may not incorporate competence-based assessment within the overall education and training package:

(a) *The publishing house model* — in which the distance learning provider provides all the materials necessary to support the development of competence in the workplace but plays no part in direct training or assessment. Candidates purchase study modules to match their previous experience and current learning needs and take responsibility for their own development and assessment arrangements.

(b) *The training support model* — in which, in addition to the above, the distance learning provider provides a group work guide for local trainers suggesting how group sessions and supervised practice/coaching can be used in support of the distance learning materials in order to develop competence. This might include a practice curriculum setting out the full

range of work experiences candidates will need to meet the
requirements of a particular N/SVQ.

(c) *The training partnership model* — in which employers,
line managers and/or others in regular contact with the
candidate in their workplace, are encouraged to play a structured and substantive role in assessment as well as in direct
training. Briefing material from the distance learning provider
might include advice on setting up an Approved Assessment
Centre for N/SVQs or participating in local consortia for
assessment and on the requirements for becoming a qualified
assessor.

(d) *The open learning provider model* — in which distance
learning materials are provided to students in the workplace
but most direct training and assessment is in the hands of
tutors/assessors employed by the open learning institution.
Contribution of evidence from the workplace is encouraged
but the role of line managers/supervisors is restricted to
that of authenticating evidence generated by the candidate
and providing witness testimony rather than making actual
assessment judgements. Under this model assessment is largely
based on a portfolio of evidence collected by the candidate,
supplemented as necessary by peripatetic observation visits by
a tutor/assessor and/or by a viva of the candidate.

All these models are currently in use or under development
in some form within the Open University. Many vocationally
relevant courses are already available in pack form to individual
purchasers (model a). Some courses in addition provide a group
work or tutor pack which includes additional audio-visual material
and suggestions for face-to-face training sessions (model b). The
'Pathways Project', centred on the OU's Vocational Qualification's
Centre, is in the process of producing a series of pathways guides
for students to accompany existing Open University courses.
These describe how best to make use of materials to support
the development of competence in relation to a range of N/SVQs
including environmental conservation, management and information technology. The guides also provide suggestions for
exercises or activities which might be used to generate evidence of
competence and advice on assessment. In some cases, for example
particularly in the health and care field, students will be able to
register as candidates for assessment in their own work place; where
this is not possible, students are directed to 'Access to Assessment
Initiatives' operated by their local Training and Enterprise Council
(or lec in Scotland). A variation on model (c) for competence-
based assessment outside the N/SVQ system is provided by the

new distance learning Postgraduate Certificate in Education which requires the involvement of school-based teacher/mentors in the assessment process. While model (d) is in operation through the Open Business School which offers a portfolio-based route to the assessment of N/SVQs in Management.

Developing these new models of support and assessment in relation to a competence-based approach has presented a considerable challenge to the systems operated by the Open University that will have parallels in the operation of other open and distance learning providers. It remains to be seen the extent to which a large scale distance learning institution, like the OU, with a hard won reputation for academic standards and quality control, will be prepared to devolve responsibility for assessment and, come to terms with new procedures for quality assurance (rather than an exclusive hold on quality control) in order to grasp the opportunity for developing true partnerships with the workplace for competence-based vocational and professional training.

References

Atkins, M. J., Beattie, J. and Dockrell, W. B. (1993) *Assessment Issues in Higher Education*, Sheffield, Employment Department.

Bull, J. (1993) *Using Technology to Assess Student Learning*, Sheffield, Universities Staff Development Unit.

DFE (1991) *Science in the National Curriculum*, London, HMSO.

Employment Department (1990) *Higher Education Developments — the Skills Link*, Sheffield, TEED, Moorfoot.

Eraut, M. and Cole, G. (1993) 'Assessment of competence in higher level occupations'. *Competence and Assessment* No. 21, Sheffield, Employment Department.

Fletcher, S. (1992) *Competence-based Assessment Techniques*, London, Kogan Page.

Hevey, D. (1993) *What is Competence* Paper 1 in occasional paper series from the Vocational Qualifications Centre, Open University.

Hevey, D. and Smith, P. (1993) *Towards a European Qualifications Area: the UK Perspective*. Background paper prepared for the European Forum on Vocational Training, Autumn 1993.

Jessup, G. (1991) *Outcomes: NVQs and the Emerging Model of Education and Training*, London, Falmer Press.

Local Government Management Board (1993) *Professional Development: Challenge and Change*, Luton, LGMB.

National Council for Vocational Qualifications (1991) *Criteria and Related Guidance*, London, NCVQ.

National Council for Vocational Qualifications (1992) *World Class Britain Fact File*, London, NCVQ.

National Council for Vocational Qualifications (1993a) *GNVQ Information Note*, London, NCVQ.

National Council for Vocational Qualifications (1993b) Annual Report, London, NCVQ.

National Council for Vocational Qualifications (1993) Skillscan series, London, NCVQ.

Otter, S. (1991) *What Can Graduates Do?*, Leicester, UDACE.

Smithers, A. (1993) *All our Futures — Britain's Education Revolution*, London, Channel 4 Television.

Newstead, S. and Dennis, I. (1994) 'Examiners examined'. *The Psychologist*, 7(5), Leicester, BPS.

14 Creating a learning organisation: the Rover Group and open learning

Barrie Oxtoby

Introduction

The Rover Group is Britain's largest motor manufacturer. In the early to mid 1990s, annual sales of Rover Group amounted to over four billion pounds, including exports of over £1,700 million to 100 markets worldwide. The Group employed 33,000 people in the UK and internationally. However, the purpose of this chapter is to document a dynamic application of open learning ideas which began in 1982 with the establishment of open learning centres, and has culminated in the current status of Rover as one of the leading corporate learning organisations in Europe. The Department of Employment, through a Policy Studies Institute research, identified Rover as one of ten leading Companies in 'releasing employees' potential' through learning (Metcalf, 1992); an organisational survey in 1992 by Price-Waterhouse identified Rover as *the* Case Study Learning Organisation in the UK; the Royal Society of Arts exampled Rover as a best-practice organisation in their 'Profitable Learning' national report (Royal Society of Arts, 1992); Rover was a National Training Award winner in 1992, and has been invited to share what we have learned and the way we have learned at over 100 national and regional conferences in the early 1990s.

This chapter describes how Rover's vision and business objectives are being supported by a corporate learning process which grew out of use of open learning approaches. Rover aspires to be a learning organisation, accepting that this can never be finally achieved or completed. The aspiration to learn more effectively as an organisation will always be in front of us.

Open learning centres

Open Learning Centres were first launched in 1982, as part of a strategy to reduce the unit costs of manufacture. The training function needed to make its contribution by reducing the unit costs of training across the whole business.

A major research project was launched during 1980 on this subject. A total of eighty-two training programmes delivered by traditional methods were the subject of thirty-nine checks from concept through to validation. Conclusions were drawn and recommendations were made to improve quality, reduce time and involve learner capability in a more direct, overt way.

The plan involved a heavy investment in computer-based learning delivery — but whilst enthusiasm, and enough expertise was available, money was not forthcoming for equipment purchase. However, the Manpower Services Commission launched its 'Open Tech' initiative at this time and Rover, (then known as British Leyland) became the first UK Company to agree a contract for the establishment of Open Learning Centres. Such centres were a focal point for new methods of learning delivery. A three year plan (funded partially by MSC) was implemented and secured the foundation of open learning in what has now become the Rover Group.

The first centre to be established was at Haseley Manor, a staff training centre in Warwickshire. It was a pilot centre to act as a development centre for subsequent centres throughout the Group. We created all of our own courseware which, in the initial phase, amounted to about one hundred hours for a suite of approximately twenty programmes.

Teamwork was a fundamental contributor to the success of the pilot centre. A combination of learning strategists, a project manager, a learning designer and a graphic artist were all supported at main board level by a Group-wide champion for success.

Eventually, fourteen centres were opened over three years and used computer-based learning as the main method of delivery. They were all based on the principles of provision for learner-paced delivery, at a convenient time to company and employee, to a quality programme and minimum cost.

Haseley Manor was the supply source, the remaining centres — the 'distribution' centres. With experience, the range of delivery methods within open learning centres has increased dramatically. An extension to computer-based learning has been made through text-based, audio-cassette, audio-visual slide cassettes, video-based to interactive video. During this time, an equally dramatic reduction in the amount of trainer-led, calendarised, in-house training courses on generic subjects has happened. The whole focus of learning has shifted to line-manager led processes aligned to business needs where, in the main, the tutors for the learning process are identified from among the subject experts.

The devolution of control of open learning centres in 1987 from the centre to individual plants was a major move forward in their effectiveness. The leadership for the centres was transferred to a local level. Therefore, they were more easily integrated in shaping attitudes and accelerating the expansion of skills and knowledge with business requirements.

A core of expertise has been retained in the centre, but more in an advisory and support role. As a result of local leadership, the roles of open learning centres have significantly expanded. They have become a focus for all sorts of learning in addition to their original role. Career counselling and advice, registration for learning opportunities and accreditation systems and the recording of learning accomplished and resources available are all part of their new role.

It is interesting that at a time when 'open learning centres' are still being pioneered all around the UK, Rover dropped the title in 1991 because of their role expansion. They are now known as Employee Development Centres but include everything that Open Learning Centres originally offered.

Business growth through learning

In 1989 the company entered a new and more intensive phase in both corporate change and in its development of learning. The vision of becoming internationally renowned for extraordinary customer satisfaction was declared, and the degree of change necessary to realise this vision demanded much faster learning — by the whole organisation as well as by each employee.

The concept and operation of growth in the business and within individuals through learning was approved by the Board of Rover in November 1989. This concept has now become more widely known as that of 'a learning organisation'. This can be defined as incorporating four elements:

- a clear vision and objectives
- aligned and dynamic processes
- a learning process as a primary driver
- management-led learning.

The corporate learning process

The Corporate Learning Process is a framework which captures the main features of organisational learning at Rover. (See Figure 14.1) Many managers refer to the process as 'the Change Management Process', and change and learning are terms often substituted for each other. Learning has become embedded into the way business operates. The importance of this process requires brief description of some of the key elements outlined in Figure 14.1.

Champions/customers for change

The person, at director level who has the accountability and resources for a major change needs to be, and to be seen-to-be, the champion for learning within the change. Traditionally, such a role was rarely thought about or only superficially played.

Many potential champions needed a fair amount of coaching to see this role in a business context. However, once persuaded, their leadership for learning was very visible. It often took some in-depth process questioning to help champions to articulate their requirements for attitude, knowledge and skills in the people to be involved in change through learning. When such requirements were in place, an equally powerful thought process was needed to establish the way it would be decided when people had acquired the appropriate level of competence.

The champion was also usually in a strong position to identify people who were key players and/or experts in contributing to the desired change. Such a 'group' was critical in supporting the champion by virtue of their qualifications, experience and ability to contribute as team players. The champion would often use such a group to help him or her brainstorm the need for the change and keep abreast with 'world best practice' of automotive industry state of the art — an alternative way for injecting learning into the day-to-day business activity.

The champion would often need to be helped in crystallising all of the core requirements into a 'big picture' of change through learning. Finally, agreement always needed to be reached on how

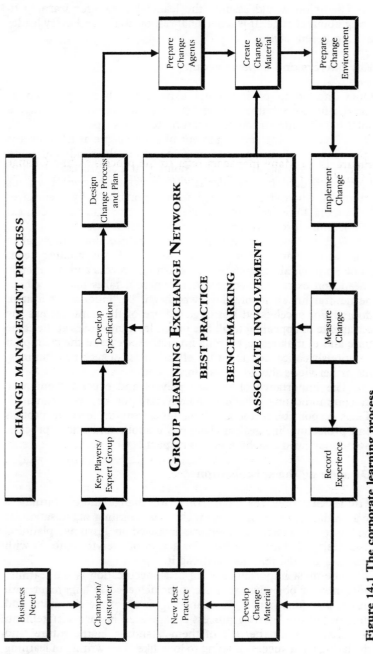

Figure 14.1 The corporate learning process

the champion would assume the leadership role for learning to bring about change. It is a personal responsibility and every leader has a different style.

Key players and experts group

Once the group of individual experts has been identified as significant contributors by virtue of their previous learning, a solid base of infrastructure is starting to take shape.

The enrolment and alignment of such people at the outset is critical if full advantage is to be gained from their individual and collective learning. It is at this point that the process of team-building should be considered. All individuals have enormous strengths. Such strengths need to be appreciated by themselves and others. Often this process takes a long time but, in the context of a learning organisation, needs to be accelerated.

Within Rover, massive amounts of team-building have taken place at the start of major change projects. Team-building needs to be an integral part of the total learning process and not merely an add-on extra. The environment where it takes place needs to be neutral for all involved — whether it be 'indoors' or 'out of doors'. For accelerated learning, the use of the outdoors has the advantage of appealing to all five of our learning senses at the same time and of making very strong impact. However, if the champion is seriously concerned about the effectiveness of such programmes, his or her views should prevail in the end.

The importance of the key players and experts group role in communicating what's going on can not be over-estimated. Their responsibility for enrolling others in the learning process and projecting 'images' of change is a subtle and skilful process. Some may need coaching in this respect.

Developing the specification

The specification (see Figure 14.1) for change and/or learning is a 'foundation piece of paper' within any learning organisation. It needs to be owned by everyone involved in learning, planning and design. It forms the basis for action of everything to do with learning and the reasons for doing it.

The most important feature of a specification is the learning outcomes or objectives that are to be achieved in alignment with business requirements. The clarity of vision of the champion and designer of the learning process is expressed in such a statement. It is really about the pair of them 'standing in the future' and declaring what success is going to look like. The writing of learning objectives/outcomes requires precision and imagination. Every outcome/objective will contain the three elements of performance, conditions and standards. Specifications should also contain learning methods, suppliers, validation and evaluation measures and any information which a champion needs to support and approve as the basis for work to proceed.

Specifications, in draft form, can be used to involve and enrol others into the project by asking for opinions and ideas for comment before final approval. Specifications should enable the champion to come to terms with 'hard and soft' issues, e.g. facts versus feelings, objective versus subjective outcomes so that learning validation instruments can be employed. The champion needs to agree such measurement criteria and they should be noted in the specification.

In a learning organisation, the specification for learning is the most important and powerful piece of direction in bringing about change through learning.

Designing the project plan and learning process

This is part of the process where the leadership and technical skill of the learning designer in a learning organisation comes to the forefront. Once the specification has been approved by the champion, a project plan from concept to completion needs to be designed. The plan should identify the sequence of events and activities which are going to absorb time and resource for the delivery of learning objectives.

The project plan's value extends from that of a self-teach mechanism for a designer to a document that persuades a champion that the designer knows what he or she is doing. Learning organisations are littered with project plans for learning. They enable a learning project manager to keep many 'balls in the air' by dealing professionally with several projects at the same time.

Project plans assist the champion to develop review mechanisms that can be integrated with existing management processes but make visible the learning dimension — so often overlooked. Budgets are more straightforward to establish and supplier contributions more easily proposed, implemented and validated.

Within the project plan are woven the learning processes and methods which allow the learning to be transferred from the source of expertise to the learners in need of growth. The selection of an appropriate combination of learning methods to achieve specific objectives and satisfy established principles of learning — needs imagination and sensitivity to the prevailing culture.

All methods of learning which are selected need to end up with the application of learning to the job of work owned by the learner. It is at the point of application that the added value to business performance can be realised. At first, the added value may be limited. However, repeated and improved application over a sustained period should result in a value that gains competitive advantage. The way that the learner's manager or supervisor is integrated into the learning process is key to the effective application and assessment of learning.

Preparing change (or learning) agents

Change agents in the Rover context are 'how' people as opposed to 'what' people. Their expertise is how to make change happen and not what change is to happen. They need to have been enrolled into the change or learning process by the champion or key players group.

Invariably, they achieve results through personal skill, expertise and commitment with a high level of interpersonal skills. Very often, it is the culture of the learning organisation which empowers them to take risks and cross 'boundaries'. Rarely do they need to resort to formal authority in an overt way to overcome resistance to change or learning. Teaching is a very minor part of their role.

Change or learning agents are competent at using a wide range of tools for analysing issues and situations upon which a prognosis may be developed. They are 'street-wise' in overcoming obstacles to learning and action and include research and survey methods in their tool kit. Interviewing, coaching, counselling and persuading are day-to-day activities. Formulating, recommending, communicating and testing views, opinions and strategies also feature largely in this role.

Rover has invested substantially in this role as a key part of the learning organisation. Up to now, external awarding bodies do not appear to have recognised the competences necessary for effective change agents. They seem to remain within the domain of management consultancies with national and international standing.

Creating change or learning material

All change agents need material to reinforce communications designed to bring about learning and feed-back. The commissioning of such materials, which may include video, audio-text, learning packages and workbooks, is often a major feature of any learning process.

Influences which exert themselves in this context are the preferred or dominant learning style of learners as well as the learning objectives and resources available. The selection of learning material suppliers and thorough briefing of the chosen source is a critical part of the process. A plethora of suppliers on all aspects of learning needs to be screened to establish a new and reliable source for the Learning Organisation. Once satisfied, it is important to hang on to suppliers and to use them as regularly as possible — they should become part of the team.

The development, introduction, use and validation of materials is a skilled job. The capability to produce all of our own learning material is an integral part of Rover's aspiration to be a Learning Organisation. Investments in video, audio-visual material and desk top publishing are adding value to all parts of our work.

Preparing the Learning Environment

It can be rightly said that the learning environment is the Learning Organisation. It is the culture to be created, celebrated and sustained. Such a culture affords learners the opportunity to become vulnerable because they admit they don't know, to take risks in finding out what they need to learn, to be allowed to make mistakes and to feel at all times that they have something to learn and something to give.

In Rover, the vehicle for creating and sustaining a learning environment is the Rover Learning Business (RLB). A business within a business, with its own vision objectives and infrastructure, it was launched on 14 May 1990. Rover Learning Business is the facilitating body for Rover's aspirations as a Learning Organisation. Although all employees are customers of Rover Learning Business, the primary customers are line managers who have the leadership role for creating a learning environment in their own area. RLB was founded upon Total Quality principles, has its own Board of Governors which includes most of the Rover Group Board and Executive Committee and employ staff as change agents.

In 1990, Rover Learning Business initiated the Rover Employee Assisted Learning (REAL) process for all employees. In essence, every employee can spend up to £100 a year to learn anything they like — as long as it is nothing to do with their job. This is a 'return to learn' process for some employees — a stepping stone in self-esteem for others, and an effective lubricant for the learning process.

Learners are encouraged to become involved in business change which often results in an 'over-subscription' of applications from individuals. Learners needs are evaluated through consultations with their managers, identification of learning styles, reference to Personal Development Files as well as the important self-assessment by the learner.

Establishing infrastructure to support the learning is a three-way network involving manager, provider as well as learner to ensure the transfer of learning to the work situation. Regular feedback mechanisms, both formal and informal, from previous and existing learning processes are used to cultivate and improve the quality of the learning environment.

Implement learning

This is the point at which the target population of people for whom the learning process has been designed are formally engaged in the learning. They are the most important people as it is they who will add direct value to the product or process by applying the learning to their job. In the process, they will become a more valuable asset to the business when the learning objectives have been achieved.

The quality of preparation in the build up to the learning is directly proportional to the quality of experience felt by the learner. An example of learning activity introduced by Rover in 1992 has become known as corporate learning events. A subject of major importance to Rover's business performance is identified and all of our existing learning on the subject is woven into a multi-dimensional process and staged within one day.

Associates who have demonstrated their capacity to learn are invited by leaders to share that learning with others who are in a position to improve upon and apply the learning. The event releases the creativity of those who have learned to exhibit their learning on display stands. Such a form of role-modelling has now become a way of life across Rover because follow-up and feed-back are integrated into every corporate learning event.

Measure change

A Learning Organisation, aligned behind a vision and clear business objective, must be a contributing organisation to the growth of that business. The growth comes about through the individual and team contribution through learning and application of learning to work over a sustained period. The indications that this has happened within Rover are many and varied. Such indications are on both a macro and micro scale.

Inclusion of the contribution through learning within parent company annual reports, business reviews, company newspapers and group-wide communications have all been prominent over the last three years. The attention given to learning by the most senior businessmen at Board and Functional Review meetings in measuring and planning contribution has been significant. The Chairman for example, commissioned a group-wide survey, to estimate the financial return from learning investment. The subsequent report was favourably received. The results of successive employee attitude surveys have all been positive. Also on a macro scale, the external 'measurement' of Rover as a learning organisation by institutions, professional bodies and government has yielded some very prestigious recognition.

However, on a micro scale, for every piece of learning process a range of evaluation and validation techniques is used to establish the effectiveness of that learning. Having agreed criteria, processes, methods and resources for measurement at the specification stage — data is collected which is fair and reliable. The aim is to identify 'bottom-line' benefits of learning in financial terms, but it is often more appropriate to measure in organisational or behavioural terms where alternative units of measurement are more relevant.

The process of measurement only yields a useful return if the findings are analysed, conclusions are drawn and actions are initiated to further improve any given situation. Such actions must always be approved by the 'champion' for the work in hand. Measurement of results in a learning organisation always provides opportunities for stimulating the environment. Successes through individuals and teams may be recognised in a way that provides encouragement for others. The sharing of progress and overcoming barriers provides opportunities for learning in a dynamic environment.

Recording experience

The Report and Accounts of any business provide an objective status report on the health of that business. However, if that business aspires to be a Learning Organisation, the quantification of learning is not yet included and ways need to be found to uncover this most precious asset.

Significant improvements in recording learning experience have taken place in Rover over the past three years. On an individual level, every one of our 33,000 employees has been invited to keep their own Personal Development File. Over 20,000 employees have accepted the invitation and keep a File which includes a self-assessment form, an individual development plan and certificates which have been internally and/or externally accredited.

On a far more ambitious scale, a Corporate Learning Database has now been set up. This is a computerised system with Group-wide access for recording and retrieving best learning practises and resources — it is rapidly becoming a major asset for spreading corporate learning in a user-friendly way. Rapid learning means rapid change in an effective way — which means aligned behind business performance. The quality of 'experience records' is a mirror for the learning organisation to learn about itself.

New best practices

Flexibility of working with changed working practices are now a reality in Rover, as opposed to the sacred cows of inflexibility and the demarcation disputes of the 1960s and 1970s. If every job is regarded as a learning opportunity, every leader is responsible for creating an environment where people learn quickly, every person is encouraged to share their learning with others who would benefit — then we have 'World Class' in all that is accomplished.

New best practices are the natural evolution of integrating a learning process inside the range of business processes that add value and eliminate waste in any organisation. They are foundation stones for prosperity, made visible for all to observe, owned by the organisation and people who created and developed them. Most important of all, they set a new standard from which we can learn and then surpass.

Inside Rover, new best practices emerge from rigorous and disciplined application of the Corporate Learning Process to business needs.

Copy plus and benchmarking

Copy Plus means 'adding to' what has been learned elsewhere in Rover and therefore improving it. This concept, although not new, was first articulated in 1992 and is now being embedded into our way of working. The importance of delivering the business performance necessary for investment and growth remains the ultimate goal, and therefore, we need to learn from each other rather than starting each time with a blank sheet of paper.

The culture of the Rover organisation is different at each location — Longbridge, Cowley, Canley, Solihull, Swindon and Bickenhill in the United Kingdom. Nevertheless, the opportunity for transferring learning from areas within the same location, across locations and to and from suppliers and dealers is immense.

Benchmarking is comparing what we do now against the best in the world outside Rover. Benchmarking learning in the UK,

Europe and across the world is now a way of life. Rover was instrumental in establishing a UK Learning Organisation network in November 1992, across sector boundaries and regardless of company size. At the time of writing, an invitation has been received to become a 'case study' at the first meeting of the European Consortium of Learning Organisations held in Brussels in November 1993. It is by Benchmarking that Rover's aspirations to become 'World Best in Class Learning Organisation' can be tested.

Continuous development

The epitaph of a learning organisation might be phrased thus: 'we only do things the way we do before we think of a better way.'

It is not a case of 'if it works, don't fix it', but a striving for radical improvement through systematic processes based upon sound principles.

Rover knows that, to achieve our vision of being internationally renowned for extraordinary customer satisfaction, we must improve every aspect of our business. This means we should add value and eliminate waste from every one of our nine business processes. The common denominator and primary driver of every process is learning. It is at the heart of business performance and quality strategy.

Every time we think we have won, all we have had is a learning experience on which we can improve. Every time we think we have lost, the same is true. After any learning or change project, the opportunity for continuous development is an integral part of the project. Compare our product range of the 1990s with that of the 1970s and conclude the amount of learning that has taken place.

As soon as something has been learned, there is a realisation that the 'journey' is still in front of us. A complacent organisation feels like the opposite of a learning organisation.

References

Ball, C. (1991) *Learning Pays. The Role of Post-Compulsory Education and Training.* London, Royal Society of Arts.

Metcalf, H. (1992) *Releasing Potential: Company Initiatives to Develop People at Work.* Volume Two: the Case Studies. London, Policy Studies Institute.

Price-Waterhouse (1992) *Organisational Trends. Who is Doing What?* London, Price-Waterhouse.

15 Gender and power: a case study from the UKOU

Gill Kirkup and Lee Taylor

Inequality of women in distance education — the issue that won't go away

In 1988 the first collection of articles about women in distance education was published (Faith, 1988). In 1994 this remains the only internationally available collection on gender issues in distance education. During the same period there has been an exponential growth in research and publication in all aspects of gender and women's studies; including education. There is work on every sector from schooling (Whyte, 1985) to adult education (Zukas, 1989) and every aspect from computing (Lovegrove, 1990) to counselling (Bailey, 1993). Yet distance education provides a different mix of 'women friendly' and 'unfriendly' aspects than is the case in conventional higher education. Female participation rates of distance education institutions are highly variable, and in some cases remain very low (Taylor and Kirkup, 1994). Our initial research suggests that figures for women students vary considerably, from around half at the UK Open University (UKOU) and Spain's Universidad Nacional de Educacion a Distancia to 27 per cent at the Fernuniversitat in Germany. Why is it then that distance educators have not considered gender (and other aspects of inequality) to be as worthy of study as our colleagues in other areas of education? This cannot be because we believe that issues of gender inequality do not exist in distance education. Could it be that the apparently late acknowledgement of the importance of gender is a reflection of the relative 'youth' of distance education and open learning? Could it be that as distance educators we feel that we are working in an undervalued area of education and our major activity should be its promotion, rather than its public examination? Could it be that resources in distance education are directed to technical and organisational development rather than critical reflection? Or worse could the gender (and inequality) blindness of distance education reflect the fact that its structures and ethos are inherently conservative, and with respect to women, patriarchal and unfriendly?

This chapter aims to redress some of the imbalance in considering women's issues in distance learning through a case study of two initiatives at the Open University of the UK. These are placed within the context of contemporary feminist debates on equality and difference and their success is discussed in the light of post-structuralist theories of the process of organisational change.

Despite the lack of publicity for women's initiatives, they do exist, in different forms in different distance education institutions. Their focus of concern has moved from identifying the simple under-representation of women in the student body, especially in certain subject areas, to one about whether certain delivery mechanisms and forms of student support are more appropriate to one sex than another (Kirkup and von Prummer, 1990), how men and women study different subjects (von Prummer, C. and Rossie, U., 1987) and have different motivations for studying the same subjects (Dale and Kirkup, 1988), and the participation and status of women staff in distance education (OU, 1990).

Feminist writing argues that women should no longer always be looking for simple equity with men, but that instead the ways in which women are *different* from men can merit privileging that difference in order to validate it (Scott, 1992). Feminist initiatives for women students in distance education reflect this new focus on the particular needs and experiences of women. For example in the Indira Gandhi National Open University, there is an extensive and successful programme for women's education; in Germany there have been experiments with special distance education courses for women who were not in paid employment due to their family responsibilities (von Prummer, 1993), the Open University of the Netherlands is attempting to develop a women's studies programme, and in the past has developed special teaching material for women in areas such as computer science (Crutzen and de Goey, 1993). The UKOU has developed a series of initiatives, such as a women's studies course and access materials in management and technology (Carter and Kirkup, 1991, Kirkup, 1988, and Smith, 1987) However, it is only now that information about these initiatives is being more widely circulated, and the theoretical insights which have been gained debated in the literature.

Theorising gender and power: difference and equality

Feminist writing in the 1980s has been concerned to develop an understanding of the inter-relationships of different aspects of oppression; in particular the dynamics of the interactions of race, gender and disability, which could no longer be seen as simply layered one on another. Policies for gender equality have been adopted into wider institutional Equal Opportunities (EO) policies. This acknowledges that inequality has many dimensions, provides an institutional basis for activity with attached resourcing, legitimates issues and makes initiatives less dependent on the energies of a few active women. Pragmatically, general EO policies have tended to find more favour with educationalists and managers than single issue policies on gender. And yet this incorporation of initiatives for women into an institutional framework of 'liberal' reform has many critics.

It has been argued that liberal equality politics focuses on male activities and does not value the predominantly female activities of caring and servicing that women do in households. Women are only 'equal' in so far as they can be like men. Feminists have asked: Why shouldn't the *world* be made to change rather than *women*? (Phillips, 1992)

The liberal reform notion of equality described (Scott, 1992 p. 257) as being in opposition to a politics of 'difference'. The proponents of the first position argue for the irrelevance of sexual difference, and the proponents of the second argue for recognition of the special qualities and needs of women (or members of other categories of difference).

This seems to us to oversimplify concepts of 'equality', and what has been achieved for women under the banner of equal opportunities. It also ignores the fact that 'equality' initiatives, because they deal with factors other than gender, attempt to deal with differences between women in the way that many 'women-only' initiatives do not. In this chapter we argue that what have been claimed as more radical feminist aims *can* be incorporated into institutional equal opportunities practice.

UK institutions adopting equal opportunities (EO) policies were prompted by the Sex Discrimination Act 1975 and the Race

Relations Act 1976, which in turn arose from the women's and anti-racist movement of the previous decade. Jewson and Mason (1986) argued that there are two bases for conceptualising EO. On the one hand, there is a liberal concept of EO, which starts from the premise that 'equality of opportunity exists when all individuals are enabled freely and equally to compete for social rewards . . . policy makers are required to ensure that the rules of competition are not discriminatory.' This leads to an emphasis on the removal of barriers especially in the recruitment and selection process, and an expectation that a 'level playing ground' will ensure EO. It is this version of equal opportunities which is the rationale underlying most open learning.

In contrast is the 'radical' concept of EO, 'which seeks to intervene directly in workplace (or other institutional) practices in order to achieve a fair distribution of rewards among employees . . . (it is) primarily concerned with the outcome of the contest rather than the rules of the game' (Jewson and Mason 1986, p. 315). This approximates to a more radical notion of a feminist transformation of an institution, or a curriculum in order to incorporate women's values and needs.

Cockburn (1989) argues cogently from research undertaken with a number of UK employers professing themselves to be EO employers, that this dichotomy between radical and equal opportunities approaches to gender in institutions is not an adequate explanation of what is happening. It is more useful to understand organisations as adopting a short or a long agenda for equal opportunities, which relates to scope of vision rather than conflict of values. The short agenda is broadly akin to the liberal approach, and introduces new measures to minimize bias in recruitment and promotion. The long agenda is more similar to the radical position and 'has to be recognised as a project of transformation for organisations . . . it brings into view the nature and purpose of institutions and the processes by which the power of some groups over others in institutions is built and renewed.' It is this more radical, long agenda that many feminists hope to see embedded in particular EO policies.

Equal opportunities at the Open University of the United Kingdom

Many distance learning institutions are based on an educational philosophy of equality of opportunity. The Open University was founded on principles of openness and equality, and this philosophy has been reinforced and extended through an institutional EO policy, agreed in 1990, which applies to both staff and students, employment, access and curriculum, (in a way that the original 'Open' philosophy did not). Institutionally, the UKOU has spent considerable time in re-examining its 'Open' mission and refining what it implies. The clarion statement of the first Chancellor, Lord Crowther that the University is 'open as to people, as to places, as to methods and as to ideas' remains the basis of the UKOU's mission, but the interpretation of what that means in the arenas of its programmes, mix of staff and student body remains an active issue. Does openness imply institutional welcome for all-comers — the liberal 'level playing field' approach — or more radical strategies of targets or other interventions to recognise and legitimate differences for particular groups, such as women, who have hitherto been under-represented in higher education?

To put the UKOU into a gender context, some figures may be useful. In passing, it is interesting that there is no accessible comparative data available on women students or staff in distance learning institutions worldwide; indeed, in some institutions, basic data on women's intake and progress is lacking.

At the UKOU, women are now 51 per cent of new undergraduates (19,682 new students), compared to 27 per cent in 1971. This is higher than the national proportion of women undergraduates (46.5 per cent), but lower than the national proportion of part-time women undergraduates (59.5 per cent) in UK universities before 1993. We know that in the UK, as internationally, there are disparities in women's participation in traditional higher education. Whilst women are increasing their participation in higher education, as in the labour market, they are less likely to opt for qualification bearing courses, and to make different subject choices. There is a strong connection between women's traditional position in the labour market and their choice of educational levels and subjects (McGivney, 1993).

The proportion of women entering the undergraduate programme in different faculties varies substantially, as shown below in the data for the 1992 intake to the BA programme:

	%
Arts	69.6
Social Sciences	66.0
Maths	25.6
Science	39.6
Technology	24.2

In higher level courses, the proportion of women drops off dramatically, for example the 13 per cent at third and fourth level in technology.

The undergraduate programme is the university's largest, but there are also significant differences between the different programmes the university offers. So community education and health and social welfare programmes attract over 80 per cent of women students, compared to the MBA programme which attracts 22 per cent. The heavily technological computing for commerce and industry/manufacturing, manufacturing and technology programme attracts less than 10 per cent women.

Once in the OU, women progress better than men. Although often coming in with lower previous educational qualifications, women do better in the crucial achievement of success in their first year course (in 1992 82 per cent of women passed compared to 78 per cent of men, OU, 1993b). An analysis of the progress made of an early OU student cohort (1975) indicated that 52 per cent of women had gained a BA degree by 1989, compared to 45 per cent of men (OU, 1991b). The 1992 BA graduates were virtually equally split between men and women.

In overall terms, the OKOU has a more equitable staffing pattern than other UK universities, and has certainly offered very considerable numbers of women (including the 55,000 graduates) a route through higher education that they might otherwise not have had. However, the significant imbalance in the proportion of women in certain areas cannot be ignored, and, as the UKOU is historically committed to redressing educational disadvantage, it can be argued that the UKOU should have higher targets than parity with the population. In staffing terms, women still constitute a majority of the UKOU's workforce, and there is still evidence of a 'glass ceiling' and 'glass walls' between categories of staff. However, there has been a steady overall increase in the proportion of women academic and administrative staff at all levels, and there is a striking difference between the national and UKOU figures for academic staff. Women are virtually 50 per cent of administrative staff, although there are only two women at the most senior level (5 per cent). At the second most senior grade, there are 27 per cent women. For central academics, women represent 28 per cent of all staff, including 12 per cent of professorial staff. This compares with national figures of c. 15 per cent for lecturing staff and under 4 per cent for professorial staff. It has been argued that as women 'work their way through' the system, the current imbalances at more senior levels will improve, but there remain concerns about whether issues of difference in career patterns have been addressed sufficiently for the 'glass ceiling' to be broken.

There are 7,000 part-time tutorial and counselling staff in the university and there has been an increase in the proportion of women in these groups, particularly in those faculties, regions and units which have put effort into targetted recruitment. If we look at the executive leaders within the UKOU, then at the time of writing (1994) two of the five Pro-Vice-Chancellors are women, representing two of eight on the Vice Chancellor's key team. Four Regional Directors of thirteen are women, and at present none of the elective Deans are women, although both Arts and Social Sciences have elected women Deans previously.

During the 1970s and 1980s the UKOU was the site for a variety of women-friendly initiatives (see Kirkup in Faith's edited collection, 1988). These include women's studies courses (Leonard, 1984; Kirkup, 1983; 1988), a course for aspiring women managers (Smith, 1987) special initiatives for women students and staff in technology (Carter and Kirkup 1991; Swarbrick, 1986) and computing (Kirkup, et al. 1991), a variety of policies related to flexible working practice and a campus nursery (Open University, 1990). In 1990 the university adopted an Equal Opportunities (EO) policy with a five year plan for its implementation. These events were paralleled in many UK, North American and Australian universities during the same period, and earlier. In the UK, the OU has been seen as a leader in higher education in terms of equal opportunities initiatives.

Codes of practice: an EO case study

Two equal opportunities initiatives at the OU are discussed in order to explore the assumptions about strategic action for institutional change towards women. A crude distinction can be drawn between feminist and equal opportunities activity to suggest that the first is concerned to change the way we think and the latter the way we behave. Guidelines and codes of practice are more usually aspects of EO activity than feminist activity, partly because they also fit well with management strategies to control or influence behaviour in organisations. Several codes of practice have been produced as part of the university's EO initiative. The first we want to discuss deals with sexual and racial harassment and the other with using language that does not embody racism, sexism or other offensive practices. Both grew out of feminist critiques of workplace practice, and were extended to deal with other aspects of oppression; however the reaction to each has been very different.

A guideline for language and imagery

Feminist analysis of English based languages has for many years criticised the unnecessary gendering of words, whereby the generic person is represented unnecessarily by a 'male' term. From the early 1970s, English speaking feminists have campaigned to reform the sexism of the language, and have won the day on many issues, often highly symbolic, such as the right to be entitled 'Ms' which although not gender neutral, enables women not to be identified through their marital state, or the right to be addressed as the 'chair' or 'chairperson' of a committee rather than 'chairman'.

In distance education the appropriate use of language and image can be seen as crucially important since the student learns largely through text and broadcast media. Women in the UKOU have been very vocal in their criticism of some forms of inappropriately gendered language. The first foundation course in technology produced in the 1970s was entitled 'The man-made world'. When it was replaced in 1980 the title was changed to 'Living with technology', and the inappropriate gender bias of the first title is now evident to almost everyone. In the mid 1980s different academic areas were addressing the language issue differently. The university's School of Education developed a short document on sexist language which made some suggestions for change. In other areas course teams were recommended to use the UK National Union of Journalists (NUJ) guidelines, and many used Miller and Swift's *Handbook of Non-sexist Writing* (1981). However prior to the EO policy there was no institutional policy to change language across the university; where it happened, it came about because women (in the main) were committed to changing their own practice and male colleagues were forced to respond to criticism. By early 1990 a range of course teams had become convinced that they needed to change their practice in language use not only with respect to gender but also race and disability. They wanted guidelines so that they could improve their writing at the first draft stage and not wait to respond to criticism.

In 1991, as part of the development of the EO curriculum initiatives, a small group of professional editors in the university offered to produce a short guide which would cover all aspects of unnecessary discrimination in language. As professional editors, they spent a good deal of time 'cleaning up' the writing of academics, often having to argue the case for non-discriminatory language; they felt that if academic authors had short guidelines to start with, it might make their editing job much easier. The university's EO steering group, chaired by the Vice Chancellor, supported the plan, and a short booklet was written: *An Equal Opportunities Guide to Language and Image* (OU, 1993a). It was hoped to make a booklet that would be useful not only to academic authors but to all members of the university who set pen to paper, either to students or to other members of the university community.

The booklet starts out by setting the issues in context, arguing that 'Language reflects and enshrines the values and prejudices of the society in which it has evolved, and is a powerful means of perpetuating them.' (p. 3) It draws attention to the university's EO policy, and makes the simple suggestion that care should be taken to be as inclusive as possible in writing, and aware of the possibilities of excluding, belittling or patronising. The booklet was piloted within the university and received overall a very positive response. Even those people with criticism of various parts supported the aim of the booklet, and most detailed criticism was incorporated into the final draft. The language guidelines were sent with a letter from the Vice Chancellor commending attention to the booklet to all full-time members of staff and to part-time tutorial and counselling staff.

There was immediate, and considerable, strong reaction — positive and negative — to the published booklet both internally and externally. Although designed as an internal document, a copy found its way to the national press. Despite the fact that the booklet offered guidelines and there was no suggestion anywhere that anyone would be penalised for not following them, they were characterised in the press as prescriptive and compulsory with headlines such as 'Outlaw "man" dons told' (Bristol Evening Post, 4.2.93); 'Black is Blacked' (Sunday People, 7.2.93); 'Ouch! Your manhood's for the chopper' (Daily Mirror, 4.2.93); 'University bans the word "man"' (Daily Express, 4.2.93) and so on. Usually it was the gender aspect that was picked up on, followed by race, despite the fact that gender is only one of the issues dealt with in the booklet and not the first or longest; issues such as age, disability, and sexual orientation are also covered, and are potentially more controversial. There was also a lively internal debate, with coverage in the staff and student newspapers. Here, too, there was a sharp focus on ridicule, mainly in gender terms, seizing on terms not covered in the original booklet, and suggesting that the 'thought police' would insist on 'personhole covers' and the like. There was also debate on more academic grounds, for example, raising research on language development and the assertion that the document was naïve — a criticism familiar on other feminist issues. Women as well as men felt strongly enough to take up cudgels against the document. An old argument used against feminism was brought up again — the perceived lack of humour and tolerance on the part of those who supported the code.

It is clear that the production of the guidelines hit a raw nerve. The attempt to change the way we speak, write and think about perceived minorities is still regarded as extremely radical and threatening. Although there was internal debate about all the sections (unlike in the national press), the reaction to the gender part of the document was significant; ridicule was the chief weapon employed, and the proposals derided in a way that would not be tolerated with proposals about other groups, such as disabled people.

On the other hand, the guidelines were welcomed by a range of staff, many of whom reacted in turn strongly to the criticism. The production of the guidelines legitimated the views and working practices of a significant proportion of OU staff, and it is clear that the existence of the guidelines is changing practice. In addition, they have had a powerful external influence — over 150 external institutions and individuals have requested copies, sometimes multiple copies. They are always sent with the advice that they should be tailored to an institution; nevertheless, it is expected that the OU guidelines will provide the basis for a proliferation of like codes in other institutions.

A code of practice on sexual and racial harassment

The reception of the Code of Practice on Dealing with Sexual and Racial Harassment (OU, 1991a), has been quite different, despite the fact that sexuality is usually considered a more sensitive area to deal with than language (Hearn, et al, 1989), and despite the fact that embedded in the Code is a disciplinary procedure which has led to disciplinary action being taken against some members of staff. A code of practice on sexual harassment was developed largely as the result of institutional recognition of the messy way in which a clearcut serious incident of harassment had been handled institutionally. The Code was then subsumed within a revised and wider-ranging code dealing with racial and sexual harassment, which takes as its starting point the view that 'the Open University is committed to a working and learning environment that is free of intimidation or unlawful discrimination'. Both racial and sexual harassment are described, and examples given. The Code also encompasses other forms of harassment such as bullying, persistent teasing, comments about personal characteristics or unfounded criticism of the performance of work. During the drafting, there was some debate about the different forms of harassment, and a clear acknowledgement that sexual harassment is a form of sex discrimination likely to involve unequal power relationships. The OU Code therefore has a firm foundation in the feminist model of identifying sexual motives in harassment.

Other organisations report a high incident of complaints and investigations into harassment after publishing a code; Central Lancashire University has a full-time Sexual Harassment Officer dealing with complaints for example., and US universities report statistics suggesting that up to a third of students and women staff feel that they have been subjected to harassment. Distance learning presents a different scenario in terms of potential harassment as there is less face to face interaction. Harassment can, however, take place over the telephone, in computer interaction and during the intensive periods of face-to-face contact at residential schools, where it can flourish.

There has been little reported activity within the formal procedures for complaint that the code offered, but there has been widespread discussion about what constitutes harassment, and how this can be handled particularly in tutorial and residential school settings. A set of brief case studies illustrating the complexity of potentially harassing situations (that is, those that detract from the optimum study conditions) is circulated to all residential school staff; the reception has been good, indicating that this form of staff development has worked well.

Despite the paucity of formal complaints, it could be argued that the climate of opinion — and behaviour — is slowly shifting. Gross forms of harassment are considered unacceptable, and challenges to other forms of harassment more commonly taken up informally. The debate is now around issues to do with wider challenges to cultural norms, such as the social environment of residential schools, the links between harassment and personal safety and detailed concerns to do with record keeping and communication of information.

Evaluating the codes

It is hard to evaluate the effectiveness of either code, regardless of the different reactions to their publication. A radical feminist analysis would suggest that a code of practice would have little effect on attitude, except perhaps to inflame a male backlash; an EO analysis would suggest that a code is a useful organisational tool to affect behaviour, largely because of the clear expectations it sets out, and the disciplinary and legal 'sticks' behind it.

The two codes aim to change both discourse and behaviour. The focus on language and interpersonal behaviour is important for a distance learning institution; written material is the basic delivery mechanism and the tutorial and residential school experience provides much of the limited but intensive direct interaction with tutors and other students. The codes challenge the gendered nature of these fundamental aspects of distance learning.

A new way of understanding power in the institution

Most equal opportunities policies in higher education have had grassroots involvement of women from the early stages, many of whom now find themselves in more senior and powerful positions. It is not surprising then that embedded in these policies is a more radical gender analysis pushing past the managerial one.

Feminists in open and distance learning are developing the more complex procedural issues of Cockburn's long agenda, such as the examples we describe on changing language use and dealing with sexual harassment, whilst also putting in place basic EO building blocks such as staff and student monitoring and fair selection and assessment procedures. These too are crucial for the 'long agenda'. Perhaps most importantly at the UKOU, equal opportunities policy has provided the legitimation for women (and men) to raise issues of 'difference' and get these routinely on the mainstream agenda. This experience is legitimated by a post-structuralist view of power which reveals the actions of individuals and groups as contesting power relations from within an organisation, at any level.

There has been a tendency, amongst structural feminists to criticise reformers who worked for change within institutions, as either naïve in not appreciating inevitable defeat at the hands of the 'power structure', or as co-opted in some way. Post-structuralist theories of power (Foucault, 1972) argue that relationships at all institutional levels embody and create power in a dynamic way. Power is not only created, it is most importantly contested, through every human interaction, and especially through those involving language. Under these conditions, everyone in any institution has some capacity to contest power.

Post-structuralist theories of power therefore support initiatives for change by individuals (and groups) because these have the potential to contest and create power from within an organisation. Post-structuralism also puts a priority on contesting conventional language and imagery, and thereby challenging the discourses in which power is embedded.

Most work in relating post-structuralist theories of power to feminist work for change (although it applies to other aspects of change too) has been done in Australia on the experience of feminists working in education and public sector industries (Savage and Witz, 1992). Watson (1992) has coined the term 'femocrats' to describe women bureaucrats who have been able to change state, and institutional policy to the benefit of women by deliberately exercising their power as bureaucrats within organisations. Distance learning organisations, more than face-to-face institutions, can be seen as attempting to combine the power structures of hierarchical commercial organisations with the ideology of a participative democracy — of staff if not of students. It is important for any initiator of change to develop a theoretical framework to help us understand how to create and contest power in this complex situation.

We believe that gender issues need to take a more central place on the agenda of distance and open learning. International activity on gender issues is expanding. For a number of years now there has been a Women's International Network (WIN) of women connected with the International Council for Distance Education (ICDE). This has provided a network for women in particular to get together at conferences and exchange information and ideas through a newsletter. One outcome of this network was the 1988 book by Faith which set the scene. Feminists in different distance education institutions are beginning to explore the possibility of international projects addressing gender issues across different national contexts. In 1993 a conference in Umea, Sweden[1] brought together an international group of women who found themselves in agreement both about the issues and about the basics of a theoretical framework for understanding them.

This chapter has discussed in detail two interventions which aimed to make one institution more accessible to all, because we have felt it more important to understand these particular events and relate them to theory than give an overview of a range of activities. We would expect, however, to see similar interventions in different institutions contesting the nature of power, and the assumptions about women and gender. We return to our introductory concern that it is surprising that distance learning organisations have largely ignored these issues so far, and anticipate a welcome growth in debate and activity about women and distance learning.

References

Bailey, D. (1993) 'Gender and educational guidance: questions of feminist practice' in *British Journal of Guidance and Counselling*, 21, (2) May, pp. 161–174.

Carter, R. and Kirkup, G. (1991) 'Redressing the balance: women into science and engineering at the Open University' *Open Learning*, 6, 1 Feb.

Cockburn, Cynthia (1989), 'Equal opportunities: the short and long agenda'. *Industrial Relations Journal*, 20, (3).

Crutzen, Cecile and de Goey, Tania (1993) Women's Studies and 'women-friendly' Curriculum Development at the Open University of the Netherlands. Unpublished paper given at the Feminist pedagogy and Women-friendly perspectives in distance education conference June. Sweden, Umea.

Dale, Eileen and Kirkup, Gill (1988) 'Women who do T101 and Why', Student Research Centre Report No. 18 available from the IET, Open University, Walton Hall, Milton Keynes MK7 6AA.

Faith, Karlene (ed.) (1988) *Toward New Horizons for Women in Distance Education: International Perspectives*. London, Routledge.

Foucault, Michel. (1972) *The Archaeology of Knowledge*, London, Pantheon/Tavistick.

Hearn, Jeff, Sheppard, Deborah L., Tancred-Sherrif, Peta and Burrell, Gibson, (1989) *The Sexuality of Organization*, London, Sage Publications.

Jewson, Nick and Mason, David (1986) 'The theory and practice of equal opportunities policies: liberal and radical approaches' *Sociological Review*, 34.

Kirkup, Gill (1983) 'Women's Studies "at a distance": the new Open University course' *Women's Studies International Forum*, 6, (3).

Kirkup, Gill (1988) 'Sowing seeds: initiatives for improving the representation of women', in Faith, K. (ed.) *Towards New Horizons for Women in Distance Education. International Perspectives*, London, Routledge.

Kirkup, G. and von Prummer C. (1990) 'Support and connectedness. The needs of women distance education students.' *Journal of Distance Education*, 5 (2) pp. 9–31.

Kirkup, Gill, Carter, Ruth, Keller, Laurie, Lewis, Jennie, Saxton, Chris and Sutton, Diane (1991) 'Home based computing for women students' in Lovegrove, G. (ed.) *Women into Computing Selected Papers 1988–90*, Springer-Verlag.

Leonard, Diana (1984) 'The changing experience of women at the Open University' in Hughes, M. and Kennedy, M. (eds.) *Breaking the Mould*, London, Routledge and Kegan Paul.

Lovegrove, G. (ed.) (1990) *Women into Computing. Selected Papers 1988–90*, Springer-Verlag.

McGivney, Veronica (1993) 'Patterns of participation and non-participation' in *Learning through Life: Education and Training Beyond School* (EH266) Milton Keynes, The Open University.

Miller, Casey and Swift, Kate (1981) *The Handbook of Non-sexist Writing for Writers, Editors and Speakers*, London Women's Press.

Open University (1990) *Report of the Equal Opportunities Team*. Milton Keynes, Open University.

Open University (1991a) *An Equal Opportunities Guide to Dealing with Sexual and Racial Harassment. A Code of Practice*, Milton Keynes, Open University.

Open University (1991b) *Review of the Open University*, Milton Keynes, Open University.

Open University (1993a) *Equal Opportunities Guidelines for Language and Image*, Milton Keynes, Open University.

Open University (1993b) *Equal Opportunities Statistical Digest, Vol. 1, Students*, Milton Keynes, Open University.

Phillips, Anne (1992) 'Feminism equality and difference' from Phillips, Anne (1987) *Introduction to Feminism and Equality*, Oxford, Basil Blackwell, reprinted in McDowell, Linda and Pringle, Rosemary (eds.) *Defining Women: Social Institutions and Gender Divisions*, Cambridge, Polity Press.

Savage, Mike and Witz, Anne (1992) *Gender and Bureaucracy* London Blackwell.

Scott, J. W. (1992) 'Deconstructing equality-versus-difference; or, the uses of post-structuralist theory for feminism,' from *Feminist Studies*, (1988) **14** (1) pp. 33–48 reprinted in McDowell, Linda and Pringle, Rosemary (eds.) '*Defining Women: Social Institutions and Gender Divisions*' Cambridge, Polity Press.

Smith, Rosemary (1987) 'Equal opportunities in management education and training' *Open Learning*, **2** (3) Nov.

Swarbrick, A. (1986) 'Women in technology: a feminist model of learner support in the Open University'. *International Council for Distance Education Bulletin*, **12**.

Taylor, L. and Kirkup, G. (1994) 'From the local to the global: wanting to see women's participation and progress at the OUUK in a wider context'. *Open Praxis*, **1**, Spring, pp. 12–15.

von Prummer, C. and Rossie, U. (1987) *Gender-Related Patterns in Student's Major Subjects*, Hagen, FernUniversitats.

von Prummer, C. (1993) 'Women Friendly Perspectives in Distance Education'. Unpublished paper given at the Feminist pedagogy and Women-friendly perspectives in distance education conference June Umea, Sweden.

Watson, S. (1992) 'Femocratic feminisms' in Savage and Witz (1992) *Gender and Bureaucracy*, London, Blackwell.

Whyte, J. (1985) *Girl Friendly Schooling*, London, Methuen.

Zukas, M. (1989) 'Women and adult education: learning the hard way'. *Adults Learning*, **1** (4) December.

Note

1   Feminist Pedagogy and Women Friendly Perspectives in Distance Education, 10–13 June 1993

Part III
Learning development and support

16 Guidance at the heart of open learning

Vivienne Rivis

I want to be an independent learner — but first I need to be
shown *how to learn* (Liz Smith, Adult Learner, 1993)

This chapter presents a critical examination of the development of
guidance in relation to open learning. Guidance and open learning
have not always been viewed as compatible: some exponents of
open learning dislike the perceived directiveness of the term
'guidance', whilst guidance practitioners have sometimes queried
the promotion of open learning to adults, for whom group or
community-based learning may provide a richer, albeit more
costly, experience. This chapter will argue that, in fact, the
development of guidance for learning and the growth of open
learning have been inextricably intertwined, and have some of their
origins in common value systems. However, during the 1980s both
were vulnerable to political interference and both became vehicles
for the introduction of market principles, sometimes without
adequate safeguards for learners and potential learners.

In this chapter, the term 'guidance' is used to denote an
intervention offered to enable people to make decisions about
the course of their own lives, particularly in relation to learning,
education, training and employment. It is impartial, non-directive
and its outcomes are not pre-determined. Guidance also has
the dual function of providing essential feedback about the
requirements of learners to policy makers and providers of education,
training and employment opportunities (UDACE, 1986). This
definition of guidance has been particularly associated with
the field of educational guidance for adults, which has stressed

the interdependence of educational, vocational and personal guidance.

This chapter will focus on the learning and guidance requirements of adult learners, who are defined here as people who have completed initial education and who are seeking to continue learning for personal, developmental or economic reasons, usually after a period away from formal or structured learning. The term 'open learning' is used here to encompass open, distance and flexible forms of resource-based learning.

Guidance and distance education — a symbiotic development

As the Open University (OU) was being established in the late 1960s, Dorothy Eagleson in Belfast and educators in North America and Germany were setting up innovative services to provide educational guidance for adults. These services focused first and foremost on the learning requirements of their users, rather than on short-term employment or career choices and laid emphasis on one-to-one interactions with enquirers (Eagleson, 1978; Ironside, 1981). Guidance was usually free and accessibly located in town centres. Meanwhile, the Open University placed counselling at the heart of its regional structure, reinforcing the idea that tutors were responsible for both the assessment and teaching of their assigned students but also for their guidance and counselling.

Until the early 1970s guidance for those wishing to embark on learning or for those already engaged in learning was not differentiated from teaching. Teachers and lecturers who were interested in the progress of their students' learning would offer informal advice and guidance on study options. Vocational guidance had been available to most young people through the Youth Employment Service and to some young people and adults through government-run occupational guidance units. However, there were few systematic arrangements to provide guidance for learning as a discrete activity.

The development of educational guidance independent of learning provision was further promoted by the Venables Committee of the Open University (Open University, 1976) which recognised that there was a need for a comprehensive system of guidance independent of educational providers (Richardson, 1987). As more small educational advice and guidance services for adults emerged, the OU provided both intellectual and practical support. Some of the key figures in the development and promotion of educational guidance for adults were in fact OU staff (Kennedy and Redmond, 1979; Butler, 1984; Brown, 1987; Bailey, 1987). The support provided by the OU included staff time, administrative support, pump-priming funding, promotion, and, critically, research and development. Three innovative pieces of work were undertaken by the OU and partners in the late 1970s: the Bradford Education Advice Service for Adults computerised information project, the ERIC project in Cardiff (Murgatroyd and Patterson, 1978) and the Education Advisory Services Project undertaken jointly with the British Library and later the Advisory Council for Adult Continuing Education ACACE (Butler, 1984).[1] The latter organisation produced the first report in England and Wales on educational guidance for adults and set out an agenda for guidance which was picked up by its successor body, UDACE (ACACE, 1979).

UDACE drew together a development group of policy makers and practitioners, several of whom had close links with the OU. Through discussions and development projects, an influential policy document, *The Challenge of Change* (UDACE, 1986), was produced which set out the activities of guidance and proposed a multi-agency network approach to development at both local and national level. The report was widely circulated within local authorities, further and adult education and some parts of HE. However, by using the generic term 'guidance' to encompass seven component activities of guidance (informing, advising, counselling, assessing, enabling, advocating, feeding back), UDACE provoked considerable debate about the relationship between guidance, counselling and counselling skills (UDACE, 1986; Woolfe 1987).

The OU had generally used the term 'counselling' to describe this cluster of activities whereas others preferred to use 'guidance' as a generic term (Miller, Taylor and Watts, 1983; UDACE, 1986; Pettit, Crook and Silver, 1990; Kneafsey, 1993). Woolfe, Murgatroyd and Rhys, (1987) argued that guidance was a directive activity fundamentally opposed to counselling which they saw at the heart of their andragogic practice within the Open University and elsewhere. However, UDACE and the organisations which adopted the UDACE model stressed the impartial, client-centred nature of educational guidance and argued that guidance was essentially non-directive.

The National Educational Guidance Initiative was established in 1988 by the DES and MSC (UDACE, 1990). Its remit focused on consultancy and support for local developments, as well as advice to national bodies on policy issues. Its main initial constituency was the network of local authorities, particularly those receiving Educational Support Grant (ESG) development funding from the DES for educational guidance for adults.

The approach to guidance endorsed by government with the establishment of the National Educational Guidance Initiative was in essence continuing the agenda of the 1970s, which linked lifelong learning with the redressing of social and economic disadvantage (Russell, 1973; Open University (Venables), 1976; ACACE, 1979). Both the provision of learning opportunities and of guidance were seen to be the prime responsibility of the public sector, and in particular the local education authorities. High levels of unemployment had reinforced this view and had resulted in initiatives like the REPLAN programme of the DES, which provided educational, rather than training, opportunities for unemployed adults. The development of guidance provision was thus part of a social and political response to unemployment, which stressed the collective nature of the experience, its impact on whole communities and social groups, and was typified by its emphasis on outreach work and targeting of disadvantaged groups (Bradford EASA, 1984, 1985, 1986). However, this community-based, collective approach was accompanied by a more individualistic, person-centred developmental stance which was strongly influenced by humanistic psychology and counselling, and which was also reflected in the OU's tutor counselling system (Grugeon, 1987; Rivis, 1991).

Both approaches acknowledged the importance of information and information technology in supporting both guidance and learning (Butler, 1984; Allred et al., 1988). However, some policy makers persisted in the view that guidance was in effect unnecessary and could be largely replaced by sophisticated information systems (Jessup, 1991). Such suggestions were largely rejected by guidance workers and many open learning practitioners. Nevertheless, the potential for the provision of computerised information had been demonstrated by ECCTIS — the Educational Counselling and Credit Transfer Information Service. In 1986, just as UDACE was presenting its final recommendations on educational guidance, the MSC announced the launch of its Training Access Points pilot programme, which was intended to create local databases of training opportunities. The original concept included the use of credit cards at terminals in high street stores to purchase open learning materials electronically. This idea was quickly dropped, although TAP was eventually linked with databases of open learning materials as well as with ECCTIS. However, for the MSC at least, guidance remained an adjunct of information provision, which was to be chiefly concerned with instrumental, individual learning related to training and employment.

During the mid 1980s the government had also espoused the cause of Open Learning with the establishment of the Open

College. This multi-million pound initiative provoked controversy among guidance practitioners, adult educators and others. Although in some areas, effective Open College centres did get off the ground, the College failed to become the Open College of the Air originally conceived as the further education counterpart of the OU. Unfortunately, this left a legacy of some cynicism in its wake (Scribbins, 1993).

Guidance, open learning and the market

By 1991, the National Educational Guidance Initiative was able to demonstrate that the ESG programme, together with independent investment and development by local education authorities and networks, had led to the existence of educational guidance services in 61 per cent of LEAs, and that these services were dealing with at least a quarter of a million users per year (Rivis, 1992). Detailed monitoring and evaluation systems had been introduced, so laying the foundations for the quality systems demanded by the 1990s.

However, the Initiative and its host organisation, UDACE, did not escape the reconstruction and reform of the education system from 1988 onwards. By 1990, the local agencies charged with guidance development were not the local authorities, but the newly established Training and Enterprise Councils (TECs). The Employment Department had absorbed the MSC and taken on the role of promoting training for adults through a wide-ranging set of measures which the TECs were expected to implement. Open learning was among the priorities highlighted. From the beginning of the 1990s, the Employment Department encouraged the new Training and Enterprise Councils to develop open learning programmes, targeted at unemployed people and other disadvantaged groups. These usually included elements of guidance as part of the programme, sometimes provided by colleges in association with local educational guidance agencies, as in Cornwall (Watkins, 1993). Another initiative used local libraries as the main source of learning resources and support for open learning by unemployed people.

Meanwhile guidance, hitherto perceived as 'soft' and expensive compared to the computerised information provided through Training Access Points, moved rapidly to the forefront of government policy on adult training. By 1993, over £9 million had been allocated to the TECs for guidance developments compared to £1.5 million originally allocated by DES in 1988.

Within three years of the establishment of the National Educational Guidance Initiative and the DES programme to support LEA-run guidance services, government was planning completely new agencies, *Gateways to Learning*, run by the TECs, of which the essential features were the capacity to create local markets in guidance, through the issue of guidance vouchers to certain groups and the introduction of charging policies. These initiatives were launched with little regard to the earlier ESG programme, where free, impartial guidance independent of provision was the model endorsed by DES, and, implicitly, by MSC/Employment Department.

Local providers, actively encouraged by the Initiative and the ESG programme to work collaboratively in networks, are now obliged to compete for clients in areas where *Gateways to Learning* have been introduced. The voucher systems allow targeting of specific groups, but these are no longer identified through the democratic processes of the local authority but by the priorities of the TEC Boards, which have no local accountability. There is anecdotal evidence from guidance staff that the bureaucracy surrounding the schemes may have outweighed benefits to clients: the initial round of Gateway pilots offered individual TECs up to £200,000 to develop the voucher scheme infrastructure, a sum in excess of the annual budgets of many local services dealing with several thousand users per year. In some areas, those not eligible for vouchers have to pay up to £100 (in 1993) for a guidance interview.

The government White Paper, *People, Learning and Jobs*, published just before the 1992 general election, linked new initiatives in guidance and open learning with the market (Employment Department, 1992). The rapid introduction of market principles and mechanisms into a hitherto public service, delivered by a mix of mainly public and voluntary sector providers, had a profound but as yet unquantified and unevaluated impact on existing guidance services. By 1995/96, the local authority Careers Service will have been privatised. Some commentators have questioned the appropriateness of market principles in this field, stressing the role of guidance as a market maker, in relation to education, training and employment opportunities, rather than as an ideal candidate for the introduction of untrammelled market forces (Watts, 1993).

At the CRAC Conference on Open Learning, held in Cambridge in July 1992, Sir Geoffrey Holland, then Permanent Secretary at the Employment Department and soon to move to the same role at the Department for Education, illustrated current government policy on both guidance and open learning, linking both to an explicit focus on the individual. He envisaged the availability of vouchers to purchase information, guidance, assessment (both psychometric and competence-based), and open learning materials (Burton (ed), 1992). However, his main message was that both guidance and open learning were now key tools of government in the achievement of the new National Targets for Education and Training (NTETs).[2]

A flexible learning market?

The government's market-led strategy for achieving NETTs, whilst recognising the central roles of both guidance and open learning, was complemented by the raft of policy changes which began in the mid 1980s onwards, as well as by significant changes led by the providers of education and training themselves. The higher education institutions and, more recently, further education colleges, have undertaken significant expansion of student numbers, within only a few years. Both sectors achieved this with a far greater emphasis on resource-based learning. Learners are currently taught in larger groups for a more limited proportion of their overall learning programme, and are offered more opportunities to use a variety of learning resources within the institution, at home, or in the workplace. Both further and higher education institutions are now competing with private companies in the development and marketing of open learning materials.

Open learning, a feature of work-based learning from the days of correspondence courses for technical and knowledge-based occupations, is now a major enterprise both for in-company training and for the marketing of in-house packages to other employers and users. The open learning 'opportunities market' has thus been boosted by employers seeking to provide appropriate work-based and work-related learning opportunities for their staff, and by individuals seeking to gain skills and qualifications (Duckenfield and Stirner, 1992).

The notion of the learner as customer, choosing between a vast range of learning options has been reinforced by the development of modular and credit-based learning opportunities, both within open learning and in more traditional programmes. The new universities (former polytechnics) have led the drive to modularise and credit rate their courses, mainly using the former Council for National Academic Awards (CNAA) Credit Accumulation and Transfer (CATs) model. The Higher Education Quality Council, whose Division of Credit and Access carried forward the agenda of CNAA in access and CATS, placed the quality assurance of guidance and learner support arrangements among its priorities, as well as undertaking a national development project on CATs. This has in turn been complemented by initiatives of the Employment Department's Further and Higher Education Branch, which has supported development projects in higher education institutions. These include a guidance in higher education project (Herrington and Rivis, et al., 1994) and a series of substantial projects on guidance and learner autonomy, designed to link educational and careers guidance with flexible learning and the recording of achievement.

Recent developments suggest that guidance has, on the one hand, become more integrated into flexible learning programmes of all types but, on the other, is being organised — and charged for — quite separately by some agencies, especially those led by the TECs. There is a possible danger that some learners interested in open and flexible learning will only receive guidance in very specific contexts, that is, once they have enrolled on or purchased a particular programme. Others may seek impartial guidance from a specialist agency but may find that the lack of a guidance voucher, or cash, may restrict their access to the service.

The Employment Department has created a branch dedicated to 'individual commitment'. It was, in 1993, explicit government policy to promote the notion that individuals should take responsibility for their own education, training and guidance and that, as far as possible, they should pay for it. Ironically, both the OU and National Extension College have demonstrated that large numbers of adults, primarily those in employment, have been willing to pay modest amounts for learning programmes leading to qualifications or academic credit. The non-profit-making National Extension College has continued to provide an effective, moderately priced, attractive and expanding range of distance learning programmes. However, neither the OU nor the NEC has deemed it appropriate or necessary to make a charge for the initial guidance which potential students receive every time they enquire about a course or programme, and both organisations pride themselves on offering an objective service. Evidence that even modest fees act as a barrier to would-be learners on low incomes suggests that the availability of free, accessible guidance is a pre-requisite of a 'learning society' (DeBell and Davies, 1991).

The steady expansion of open and flexible learning opportunities, heavily promoted by government, raises fundamental questions about the relationship between open and flexible learning:

- Should learners be encouraged to choose open learning opportunities on the grounds that they are cheaper for the individual, for employers — and for society? What is the evidence that the true cost of open learning for the learner (taking into account all the associated costs of learning —

books, audio visual and information technology resources) is actually cheaper and more convenient than traditional forms of education and training?

- Do market-oriented strategies intended to maximise the learner's 'customer choice' between pre-determined programmes and packages sit well with the notions of autonomy and empowerment underpinning much of open learning?
- Do 'customer-learners' require different guidance support from those within learning structures which are at least notionally democratically accountable? For example, many existing impartial guidance services undertake advocacy on behalf of learners: in a market model will customer choice suffice?
- How should guidance workers and tutors teach learners about making learning choices and decisions, especially where finance for the purchase of programmes and packages is a major factor?
- In a mass system heavily dependent on resource-based learning, can guidance strategies maximise scarce teaching resources? How far will additional guidance support need to be provided by guidance specialists, how far by academic advisers and counsellors and how far by all teachers and tutors?
- In an open learning market, can sellers of learning resources also offer impartial guidance?
- In a guidance market, will voucher holders be steered towards open learning as the most cost effective option for providers — and will this be in the learners' interests?
- How should the costs of enhanced guidance in open and flexible learning be met? Should the cost of guidance be integrated into overall unit costs, or provided as a discrete and separately costed service? If the latter, who should pay — the prospective learner, the provider, the employer or the State?
- What standards of service delivery are needed to assure the quality of guidance in relation to open learning? For example, how will adherence to principles of confidentiality and impartiality be demonstrated? How will staff who are not guidance specialists be trained and developed in their guidance roles?

Guidance at the heart of open learning

As all learning becomes more 'open' and flexible, with the widespread adoption of modular programmes and with the renewed emphasis on work-based learning, comprehensive guidance systems will be needed to ensure that all learners make the best learning

decisions and are adequately and appropriately supported throughout their learning.

For much of the past twenty years the prime guidance
requirements of learners have been deemed to be better information about education and training courses. The proliferation of
computerised databases of opportunities and learning packages,
and the increasing sophistication of computer-assisted guidance
programmes has dramatically enhanced the resources available to
learners, potential learners, their teachers, advisers and employers.
Such information is critical at the point of decision-making about
which programme of learning to follow, offered by which provider,
through which mode and at what cost. However, the range and
complexity of these information sources has not reduced the need
for personal guidance support, both at the decision-making stages
at the beginning and end of a piece of learning, and during
that learning itself. The direct personal support of learners and
potential learners in fact becomes a feature of the roles of
far more people, not all of them deemed to be professionals.
These include receptionists, administrators, tutors, admissions
staff, open learning managers in education and industry, specialists
in educational and careers guidance, counsellors and other advisers.

In order to take account of the changes in both the organisation
of education and training and in patterns of learning, new models
of guidance are being developed in a range of settings:

- Independent educational guidance services for adults continue
  to provide guidance on the full range of post-school learning
  opportunities, including open and flexible learning (Briggs,
  et al., 1993).
- Higher Education providers are reviewing the operation of
  their personal tutor systems and developing new models for
  academic guidance, such as that in operation at the fully
  modular University of Central Lancashire (Plum, 1992).
  Other institutions, such as Anglia Polytechnic University and
  Sheffield Hallam University are implementing organisation-
  wide strategies for guidance and learner support, integrating
  initial guidance and on-programme support structures (Cooper,
  1992; Layer and Booth, 1992). The Higher Education Funding
  Council for England has supported projects developing
  integrated student support systems, linking IT, library and
  guidance services.
- Education and training providers in further education are
  developing guidance and learner support systems which recognise
  the increasing flexibility of learning programmes, encouraged
  by the new funding methodology developed by the Further

Education Funding Council. Much more emphasis is being placed on guidance and assessment at the pre-entry stage, and on learning support systems which facilitate independent learning (Kneafsey/FEU, 1993).

- The Open University now operates a decentralised regional enquiry and admissions service which offers expert advice based on the principles of educational guidance. The OU's practices, processes and procedures for learner support are also being re-examined in the light of the emergence of new programmes of study (Bailey, Brown and Johnson, 1993; Brown, 1993).

- The National Extension College, a leading, non-profit-making distance learning organisation, provides information and advice by telephone, post or fax about its own courses and learning packages. If the college does not consider it can provide an appropriate course for a student it will refer enquirers to other providers such as the Open University or to specialist educational and careers guidance services. Some guidance is also offered through the tutorial system (Rutherford, 1993).

- Employers and Training and Enterprise Councils have recognised the importance of providing guidance in support of open and flexible learning. Local employers and South Derbyshire TEC developed a joint code of practice for guidance in their open learning centres (Barnes, 1991). The ASSET programme run by Essex County Council Social Services Department and Anglia Polytechnic University included academic guidance in its programme of workplace-assessed post-qualifying education for practising social workers (Maisch and Winter, 1993).

Quality in guidance in open learning

Work undertaken by the National Educational Guidance Initiative on quality standards has suggested that there is a series of prerequisites, constituting a 'quality framework' which would ensure that learners are assisted to make appropriate decisions about learning, and, once embarked on a programme, supported adequately until and beyond its conclusion (Rivis and Sadler, 1992).

Guidance practice, wherever undertaken, should be able to demonstrate principles of client-centredness, impartiality, confidentiality, free availability, equity, and accessibility, as well as adherence to codes of good practice. It should be underpinned by explicit policies, specified resources, appropriate organisational

structures, including quality systems and procedures for accountability. Each of these factors can and should be linked to standards
of service delivery, whose achievement can be ascertained through
the use of quantitative and qualitative evidence. For example,
impartiality can be ascertained by the use of monitoring records
to detect possible skewing towards particular outcomes, such as
evidence that disproportionate numbers of enquirers have been
referred to a single provider or programme (Rivis and Sadler,
1992).

For potential learners not yet enrolled or embarked upon
a programme of learning, guidance may best be provided by
impartial guidance agencies not directly linked to providers. Such
impartial guidance enables maximum choice between options and
places the learner firmly in control of the decision making
process. Whatever decision is finally made, the learner should
be made aware of the advantages and disadvantages of open
and flexible learning, compared to more traditional methods.
Wherever possible, potential learners should have opportunities
to discover the most appropriate learning style for them before
making their final decision: this might be achieved by appropriate
use of interactive computer-aided guidance systems and other
diagnostic approaches.

Once a learner is enrolled on a flexible learning programme,
the need for guidance does not of course diminish but may focus
more closely on aspects of the learning process, specific forms of
learning support and on-going decisions about modules, options
and progression routes. Such guidance may be provided by
tutors, academic counsellors or advisers, resource centre managers,
open learning managers, training and staff development officers,
workplace assessors and even other learners in the peer group.
Before completion of a piece of learning, learners may require
further support in making decisions about progression and career
choices. Here access to impartial guidance staff and specialist
careers advisers will be essential, wherever possible supported by
computer-assisted guidance resources if required.

All of the above has considerable implications for staff recruitment, training and continued development. As many education
and training organisations adopt open and flexible learning methods,
and as more learners embark on programmes, so staff in all roles
with contact with the public, with enquirers and current and former
learners will need to demonstrate their ability to offer appropriate
guidance. The development of occupational standards for advice
guidance and counselling by the sector Lead Body by the end of
1994, should provide the stimulus for training, some of which may
itself be offered through open learning.

Occupational standards for staff engaged in offering guidance to learners form an essential part of the wider service standards which need to be in place for guidance within open and flexible learning. The HEQC's National CATs Development Project has suggested a model of good practice for guidance in modular and credit-based systems in higher education (Layer, Booth and Moore 1993; Robertson 1994): HEQC has taken this and the Quality Framework as starting point for the development of quality assurance guidelines for guidance and learner support in all HE institutions, including flexible, open and credit-based systems. The Charter for Higher Education (DFE, 1993) also recognises the importance of guidance at entry to and at each stage of learning:

> You should receive well-informed guidance from your tutors and careers staff and appropriate access to counsellors.
>
> You should know in advance how your course will be taught and assessed. You should receive a high standard of teaching and research supervision. This includes effective management of your learning by teaching and other staff. You should also be given the opportunity to register your views.

The current emphasis on teaching and learning in higher education has also focused attention on guidance and learner support issues, although these have not been built into funding methodologies as is planned in further education (FEFC, 1992). BBC, Broadcasting Support Services and the National Educational Guidance Initiative have proposed the establishment of a National Educational Guidance Helpline which would make information on all types of post-school learning accessible to everyone, irrespective of their place of residence (Sadler and Rivis, 1993). The CBI and RSA have combined to take forward ideas proposed by educational and careers guidance activists to create a National Advisory Council for Educational and Careers Guidance (RSA, 1993).

Conclusion

Both guidance and open learning have come a long way since the pioneering days of the early 1970s. In both cases provision is more extensive and more diverse than could have been foreseen twenty years ago. The close relationship between guidance and all flexible forms of learning is perhaps better understood than ever before. Resources are being made available to support both guidance and open learning initiatives, nationally and locally. There is an emphasis on quality, and a growing realisation that feedback from the guidance process is a valuable source of information on 'customer satisfaction', which can be used to improve provision and to tailor learning programmes and resources to expressed demands.

Yet despite this, the introduction of a market-driven ideology has threatened both the impartiality of guidance and the perceived value of open learning. The guidance market empowers only those learners with the ability to pay, with either cash or vouchers, which are strictly rationed. It is driven by outcomes pre-determined by the agencies responsible for issuing the vouchers. Provision of 'pre-entry guidance' is likely to vary even more widely from area to area than it did under the LEA system. Guidance within learning opportunities may thus have to evolve to compensate for the deficiencies in pre-entry guidance, and may not be sufficiently well-resourced to provide the kind of on-going support that learners engaged in open learning actually need. Where open learning is promoted chiefly as a means of driving down institutional costs, and not as the most appropriate option for the learner, then the quality of learning will undoubtedly suffer. On the other hand, where open learning is made available to enhance the range of opportunities available, to provide more genuine and flexible choices about modes and styles of learning, to widen access, and is subject to rigorous quality assurance, then good guidance practice will, by definition, be found at its heart.

References

ACACE (1979) *Links to Learning: A Report on Educational Information, Advisory and Counselling Services*, Leicester, Advisory Council for Adult and Continuing Education.

Allred, J. et al. (1988) *Managing Information in Educational Guidance*, Leicester, UDACE/NIACE.

Bailey, D. (1987) *Guidance in Open Learning: A Manual of Practice*, National Institute for Careers Education and Counselling and Manpower Services Commission.

Bailey, D., Brown, J. and Johnson, A. (1993) *Guidance in Higher Education: Reflections from the Open University*, Open University, March 1993, mimeo.

Barnes, C. (1991) *Southern Derbyshire TEC Open Learning Network: Project Report*, National Educational Guidance Initiative, mimeo.

BBC Education/Quigley, K. (1992) *Second Chance Evaluation Report*, London, BBC, mimeo.

Bradford Education Advice Service for Adults Annual Report: 1983, 1984, 1985.

Briggs, H., North, K., Rivis, V. and Wilson, R. (1993) *Educational Guidance Services for Adults: UK Directory 1993*, London, FEU.

Brown, J. F. (1987) 'Pre-study counselling and advisory needs' in Thorpe, M. and Grugeon, D. (eds.) *Open Learning For Adults*, Harlow, Longman.

Brown, J. F. (1993) *Personal Communication*, 23 November.

Burton, T. (ed.) (1992) *Open Learning: A Quantum Leap*, Cambridge, National Extension College.

Butler, L. (1984) *Case Studies in Educational Guidance for Adults*, Leicester, NIACE/ACACE.

Collins, T. (1989) 'Where will all the guidance for grown-ups go?' *Newscheck*, **6**, (8), pp. 15–16.

Cooper, C. J. G. (1992) *Guidance and Counselling in Higher Education Project Report*, Anglia Polytechnic, mimeo.

DeBell, D. and Davies, B. (1991) *Paying for Skills: Financial Barriers to Access to Vocational Training for Adults*, Norwich, City College.

Department for Education (1993) *Charter for Higher Education*, London, HMSO.

Duckenfield, M. and Stirner, P. (1992) *Higher Education Developments: Learning Through Work*, Sheffield, Employment Department.

Eagleson, D. (1978) 'Educational counselling of adults'. *British Journal of Guidance and Counselling*, 6 (2), pp. 225–228.

Employment Department (1990) Draft Standards for the Delivery of Open Learning, Sheffield, Employment Department.

Employment Department (1992) *People, Learning and Jobs*, Sheffield, HMSO.

Further Education Funding Council (1992) *Funding Learning*, Coventry, FEFC.

Grugeon, D. (1987) 'Educational counselling and open learning' in Thorpe, M. and Grugeon, D. (eds.) *Open Learning for Adults*, Harlow, Longman.

Herrington, M. and Rivis, V. M. with Brown, J., Jones, P. and McNair, S. (1994) *Guidance and Counselling in Higher Education*, London, Higher Education Quality Council.

Ironside, D. J. (1981) *Models for Counselling Adult Learners*, Department of Adult Education, Ottowa Institute for Studies in Education.

Jessup, G. (1991) *Outcomes: NVQs and the Emerging Model of Education and Training*, London, Falmer.

Kennedy, D. and Redmond, M. (1979) *Education Advice Service for Adults: Newsletter — Issue No 2*, November, Yorkshire Region, Leeds, Open University.

Kneafsey, P. (1993) *Learning Support Services in Further Education*, London, Further Education Unit.

Layer, G. and Booth, J. (1992) *Guidance and Counselling in Higher Education Project*, Sheffield City Polytechnic, mimeo.

Layer, G., Booth, J. and Moore, R. (1993) *Guidance, Support and the Student Experience*, Sheffield Hallam University/Higher Education Quality Council, mimeo.

Maisch, M. and Winter, R. et al. (1992) *The ASSET Programme Final Report*, Anglia Polytechnic University, Essex County Council, Employment Department.

Miller, J., Taylor, B. and Watts, A. G. (1983) *Towards a Personal Guidance Base*, London, Further Education Unit.

Murgatroyd, S. and Patterson, A. (1978) *An Adult Education Counselling Service in Wales*, Cardiff, Educational Resources and Information Centre, Open University in Wales, mimeo.

Open University (Venables Committee) (1976) *Report of the Committee on Continuing Education*, Milton Keynes, Open University.

Pettit, A., Crook, G. and Silver, R. (1990) 'NVQs and the role of guidance in competence-led curricula' in Bees, M. and Swords, M. *National Vocational Qualifications and Further Education*, London, Kogan Page/NCVQ.

Plum, M. (1993) *The Role of the Academic Programmes Advisor*, University of Central Lancashire, mimeo.

Richardson, M. (1987) 'Venables — 10 years on'. *Open Learning*, **2** (2), pp. 37–42.

Rivis, V. M. (1991) *Principles and Pragmatism: An Analysis of the Development of Educational Guidance for Adults in the United Kingdom 1970–1991*, University of Hull, unpublished M Ed thesis.

Rivis, V. M. (1992) *Guidance for Adult Learners: The New Challenges, Towards a National Strategy*, National Educational Guidance Initiative, mimeo.

Rivis, V. M. and Sadler, J. (1992) *The Quest for Quality in Educational Guidance for Adults*, Leicester : UDACE.

Robertson, D. (1994) *Choosing to Change : Extending Access, Choice and Mobility in Higher Education*, London, Higher Education Quality Council.

RSA (1993) *The Case for Establishing a National Advisory Council for Careers and Educational Guidance*, London, Royal Society of Arts, Manufactures and Commerce.

Russell, Lord L. (Chair) (1973) *Adult Education: A Plan for Development, Report of a Committee of Enquiry*, London, HMSO.

Rutherford, N. (1993) *Personal Communication, 23 November*, National Extension College.

Sadler, J. and Rivis, V. M. (1993) *National Educational Guidance Helpline and Referral Network: A Feasibility Study*, National Educational Guidance Initiative/BBC/Broadcasting Support Services, mimeo.

Scribbins, K. (1993) 'One voice, shouting loud', *Times Higher Educational Supplement*, 27 August.

Smith, L. (1993) *Personal Communication*, 20 September.

Toyne, P. (1979) *Educational Credit Transfer : Feasibility Study. Summary of Final Report*, mimeo.

Training Agency (1990?) *Standards of Performance for Open Learning Staff: An Interim Framework*, Sheffield, Training Agency.

UDACE (1986) *The Challenge of Change*, Leicester, Unit for the Development of Adult Continuing Education/NIACE.

UDACE (1990) *Educational Guidance for Adults in England and Wales: Policies and Practice 1988–1989*, Leicester, NIACE.

Watkins, R. (1993) *Personal Communication*, 29 September, Cornwall Education Guidance Service.

Watts, A. G. (1993) 'Promoting careers guidance for learning and work' in *Educational Guidance News and Views*, Autumn, National Association for Educational Guidance for Adults.

Woolfe, R. (1987) 'Counselling: a process or an activity?' *Open Learning*, **3** (1), pp. 51–52.

Woolfe, R., Murgatroyd, S. and Rhys, S. (1987) *Guidance and Counselling in Adult Continuing Education*, Milton Keynes, Open University Press.

Notes

1. ACACE was the government funded Advisory Council for Adult and Continuing Education, established in 1977 in the wake of the Russell Report, and wound up by government in 1983.

2. NETTS, National Education and Training Targets, were originally suggested by the CBI (as National Education and Training Targets) and adapted and promoted by government especially through the TECs and the NVQ System.

17 Making open learning work at access level

Andy Northedge

Introduction

Access courses are not, at first sight, a promising context for open learning methods. The remarkable achievements of the UK access movement in the 1980s were based on face-to-face, 'student-centred' teaching and learning. People from a wide diversity of backgrounds were carefully guided back into education through imaginatively designed discussion-based courses, which eschewed the traditional 'A' Level syllabuses and instead built from everyday adult experience and topical case material, with very selective use made of formal texts. The sympathetic human presence of a tutor and fellow students encouraged apprehensive returners-to-learning to set aside earlier failings and develop the skills and confidence to continue to Higher Education. Within such a personalised, contact-based arena of education, what place could there be for mass-produced, highly structured self-study materials?

Indeed, the Open University, which had been *the* access university in the seventies, found itself little more than an onlooker as the access movement burgeoned a decade later. This was partly because, with its policy of open entry at degree level, its prospective students did not need to acquire access qualifications, but also because of uncertainty as to whether the OU's heavyweight systems for materials-production and teaching support had a role to play in this localised, person-sensitive, confidence building form of education.

On the other hand, there *was* concern that the OU was failing to reach out effectively to all sections of society, and that those entering with few prior qualifications were significantly less successful in their undergraduate studies. As a result, pressure grew to develop some form of pre-degree preparatory study. Several initiatives were undertaken and one of these, *Living in a Changing Society* (LICS), has in effect emerged as a full-blown open-learning access course in the social sciences. This chapter discusses how LICS adapts open-learning methods to meet the challenge of access level study and points to the benefits which open-learning offers in this field.

The 'Living in a Changing Society' project

LICS takes the form of six free-standing modules, each offering between twenty and ninety hours study (depending on a student's choices of options within a module). The modules may be taken singly, or in any combination and any order. As with most access courses, the content is designed to draw out understanding from students' own experience, using activities carefully structured to encourage reflection on their existing ideas, while systematically leading ahead towards more formal frames of analysis. The series is held together by interwoven themes so that, as students study more modules the ideas they develop accumulate to give a more sophisticated analytical grasp of society. Activities and discussion to develop study skills are interspersed throughout and continuity of development is achieved through reference to a specially designed core text *The Good Study Guide* (Northedge 1990).

Modes of delivery

The modules are designed to provide unsupported independent study, if that is what a student chooses. But they also have accompanying essay topics and an *Essay Booklet*, introducing writing skills to those who opt for tuition. Correspondence tuition is currently offered by the National Extension College, some WEA branches and by a co-operative of OU tutors (Open Access Tutors, or OAT). However, it is recognised that for many Access-level students face-to-face support is a vital ingredient, so the materials are designed to work in this context too, (supported by an extensive Tutor Handbook: *Teaching Access*).

Institutional collaboration

The LICS project has enabled constructive links to be forged between different educational structures. At the *intra*-institutional level, the project arose out of a collaboration between the OU Community Education Department and the Social Sciences Faculty, and also involved close links with the OU regional structures. At the *inter*-institutional level, the National Open College Network offered extensive advice on accreditation, enabling the first known instance of a *correspondence* study route to a 'kite-marked' access certificate. (This involves a final *Consolidation Module*, based mainly on an extended essay and project work.) In practice, accreditation for correspondence study involved collaboration between the OU, the Manchester Open College Federation and the National Extension College. Subsequently, a wide range of face-to-face education providers (FE colleges, WEA branches, community projects, etc.) have constructed a variety of courses around the materials and have established accreditation through local Access Validating Agencies.

LICS in practice

The first modules became available in January 1992 and the first full-length accredited courses were completed by students in July 1993, so evaluation is still in its early stages. However, up to the time of writing, signs are positive. A survey of people who studied LICS *unsupported* reported that 93 per cent found the subject matter very or fairly interesting: 74 per cent found the level of difficulty about right; 80 per cent felt the module they studied had helped a great deal, or quite a lot, in understanding British society and how it is changing. Eighty-one per cent felt it had helped a great deal, or quite a lot, in understanding social science ideas and ways of thinking and 69 per cent felt that their reading skills had improved a great deal or quite a lot (n.b. this group had *not* opted for tutor marked essay writing practice). The figures are encouraging because unsupported private study is not the ideal mode for access studies.

When it comes to *supported* schemes of study, reports are even more encouraging. The NEC and OAT schemes offering *distance teaching* have received enthusiastic testimonials from students. Yet there *is* a problem with this form of support. Surprisingly, perhaps, it is the *cost* to students (£25, or more, per module, on top of £15 for the study pack itself). Unlike many face-to-face access courses, distance support is unsubsidised. As a result, this potentially very accessible form of support has had difficulty in attracting some of the students who would most benefit.

Where the materials are supported *face-to-face*, whether in part-time or full-time courses, exceptionally high levels of student motivation and course completion have been reported. Mackworth

College, Derby, for example, offers LICS modules within three
different programmes concurrently: a part-time access course, a
full-time access course, and a full-time Level 0 foundation degree
course. The part-time course, which is based entirely on the LICS
modules, has been particularly popular, producing a sharp rise in
applicants for its second year. In the full-time courses LICS plays
a part alongside other modules so that its specific contribution
is more difficult to isolate. However an interview study found
students impressed with the materials.

> I don't honestly think you could better it . . . It seemed to
> be all there, to flow so well. I didn't feel it was talking down
> to me, but I didn't find it too difficult either. It got the
> terminology in without being difficult. All my academic skills
> have improved dramatically over this year, and especially over
> this module — it makes you feel proud of yourself.

One attraction of a modular, credit-based system is that
students can switch between modes of study as their circumstances
change. (For example, the student quoted above spent time
in hospital, but kept up with the group through independent
study.) Indeed, students can if they choose undertake extra modules
independently to speed up progress towards certification. Thus
modular open learning enables adult students to tailor a course
to their own needs, rather than being constrained by the academic
year and college timetables. South Trafford College Manchester,
for example, offers a roll-on-roll-off, round-the-year presentation of
LICS with new starters joining each term. The tutors report that new
students are able to pick up the pace straight away, discussing with
confidence the links between their own experience and the social
science ideas developed within the materials.

There has been a particularly interesting development recently
in inner-city Liverpool. The Department of the Environment's
Toxteth-Granby Task Force is funding a collaboration between the
Liverpool Institute of Higher Education, and the Parent Support
Programme, a local community network based in schools. This
scheme, titled *REACHout*, offers fifty places a year to community
members selected on the grounds that they have no other means of
entering education. They study the LICS modules over two years,
to acquire an Access Certificate with the Merseyside Open College
Federation. People who would not dream of entering a formal
FE or HE establishment, meet in small groups in local schools
(often those attended by their own children) and are tutored and
counselled by members of the community. Good creche facilities
are also available. The first intake, in autumn 1993, was quickly
over-subscribed, and the reactions of both students and staff to the

first half-year of study have been very enthusiastic. This is a striking example of how the availability of flexible open-learning materials can enable different elements of educational provision within an area to be brought together to create new learning opportunities. People from an exceptionally deprived inner-city area now have available to them up-to-date social science analysis of their own society and a flexible programme of study-skills development, while remaining within and drawing support from their own community.

> *Without LICS I believe that a project like this would not be possible. The quality put into those materials I think would take most HE full-time institutions decades to produce. And I don't say that lightly.* (Dr. Martin Carey, Project Director, *REACHout*, Liverpool Institute of Higher Education).

The advantages of structure

These early indications of success raise questions as to what it is that open learning materials offer in the access context. Why are highly structured materials found attractive in courses where the emphasis is on meeting the needs of very varied individuals? To understand this we must begin by recognising the nature of the experience of re-entering the educational milieu.

Institutionally induced inadequacy

To return to study is to experience excitement and renewal, but also confusion and disorientation. In spite of the best practices of tutors, the first meetings of a study group tend, for the students, to be a melée of unfamiliar people, activities, ideas, language and modes of discussing. It is hard to comprehend either immediate goals, or the general frame-of-reference. As a result, people who are perfectly competent in their daily lives are rendered almost childlike in their dependence on the tutor. They depend on being told 'what to do', both in class and in their studies outside the class. Equally they find themselves intellectually dependent — having to obtain approval for what they say and write. The result tends to be a kind of institutionally induced 'regression' to a *child-like* state on the part of the student. This in turn has the effect of eliciting *parent-like* support from the teaching institution. Students find themselves offered diagnostic assessment to identify their weaknesses, then remedial support, study skills workshops, counselling and so on. Valuable though these supports may be in their own terms, they can have the side-effect of confirming students' perceptions of their own inadequacy and dependency.

As a result there is the danger that first experiences of returning to study are unexpectedly undermining; the fires of intellectual ardour being damped down by an over-intense focus on remedial and support activities.

Empowering through structure

Purposeful action can only be undertaken within a frame of reference of some kind. Thus, situations in which we experience a lack of structure are profoundly dispiriting and debilitating — our actions are drained of purpose, coherent intent eludes us, and even shaky or flawed structures come to seem attractive. Because the aims and structures of the educational milieu are complex and diffuse, adults returning to study have difficulty internalising them. As a result, they experience 'lack of structure' more intensely than in most other walks of life. For them the process of achieving competence and self-sufficiency as a student is generally less a matter of 'remedying weaknesses', than of *imposing sufficient pragmatic and conceptual 'structure' upon study activities to allow established strengths to be brought into play.* Consequently, when a course has a strong and explicit structure built into it, students are able to become *independent* far more rapidly.

This is where open-learning materials can make a significant contribution. A well structured open-learning text helps to inject coherence and purpose into studies. (As LICS tutors have noted, students very quickly start speaking out confidently.) The structured text provides clear short-term goals and at the same time a broader framework within which the goals make sense. It gives contained, defined tasks, which demonstrate to students that they *can* study (as opposed to focusing on what they can't do). And, *because* it is tightly structured and explicit, the text can at the same time set out to *challenge* students without overwhelming them — giving them a sense of being respected (not just cared for). Moreover, with a well laid-out text, it is easy for students to look ahead and check back, to ascertain whether the course is teaching them what they had hoped to learn, thus providing a sense of control over their own learning.

Putting structure into part-time study

The advantages of structure are particularly apparent to adults who are studying part-time. Studying is a diffuse activity at the best of times, sprawling over the time-boundaries we draw. When students also have demanding family and work commitments competing for their attention, study tasks which are weakly defined, or poorly understood, easily slip off the agenda. A text which sets out discrete tasks and time targets makes a dramatic difference to a student's capacity to 'manage' the study process and find ways of fitting it into the flux of life.

Freeing discussion time

But does constructing a course around tightly structured texts limit spontaneity and creativity in teaching and learning? Does it de-skill the tutor and constrain avenues of enquiry for students? The experience with LICS is that the texts are experienced as *enabling* rather than constraining. They release the tutor from the burden of 'covering the field'. Instead of using valuable contact time for 'delivering knowledge', it is freed-up for activities and debates. Together, students and tutor can explore the meaning and relevance of the ideas put in play by the text. In other words, there is *more* time for spontaneity and creativity on the part of both tutors and students. For adult students, this opening up of opportunity for exploring personal experiences and insights makes a significant contribution to the learning process.

Overcoming cultural barriers

There are additional benefits for students entering the educational milieu from culturally remote backgrounds. In a conventional classroom, the more culturally confident students tend to set the agenda, and those culturally less acclimatised can easily lose touch with the focus of discussion. Such students may miss significant nuances of study-group discussions, owing to unfamiliarity with language, or with the assumptions implicit within academic debate. They may be barely aware that this is happening, or they may feel awkward about asking for clarification when other students seem to be coping. And unresolved misunderstandings in one session can mean starting at a disadvantage in the next, so that over the weeks these students drift progressively further away from the collective intellectual focus of the group. However with an open learning text to back up group discussions, such students are in a position to go back over the key issues intensively at home, until they have them clear. They can then arrive at the following session confident of being once again abreast of the group. Thus the open-learning text supplies the means to repair any damage before it becomes serious.

An intellectually coherent study group

From the tutor's point of view, the attraction of working alongside an open learning text is that he or she is dealing with a group of students who have focused their minds on the same issues and the same study activities since the previous session, and have thereby supplied themselves with the same conceptual tools. This provides a grounding for coherent and constructive debates. Each session is able to build on a further stage of private study, so that collective analysis begins each time from a new point and reaches out into fresh territory. At access level this drawing together of intellects nurtured in widely differing settings is particularly helpful.

Open-learning as a pathway into an academic discourse

Having argued the value of structure at access level, questions remain as to the nature and substance of that structure. What, broadly, is one trying to achieve in designing an open learning text? How should one conceptualise the learning that access students have to undertake? The approach adopted by LICS is that an access course should be understood as taking students who think and speak in terms of *everyday* discourses and equipping them to read, think, speak and write within an *academic* discourse. At the end of the access course the student should be able to pick up a first year undergraduate text, read it, discuss it and write about it. To achieve this the student must be provided with opportunities for practice in the following:

- engaging with *ideas* and *concepts* employed within the academic discourse — reading them, hearing them used in the examination of typical issues, and thinking in terms of them
- grasping the underlying *purposes* and *assumptions* of debates within the discourse
- following *the way arguments are constructed* within the discourse
- recognising the status given within the discourse to various kinds of *evidence*
- internalising the norms and values of discourses based on *analysis* and *objectivity*
- *speaking* and *writing* within the terms of the discourse

The social base of discourses

A discourse is understood here as a *social process* through which collective understandings are constructed. Discourses arise out of a *social* base, involving a collectivity of *speakers* (often, nowadays, a loose-knit and dispersed collectivity) and various kinds of *forum* within which the discourse happens. Everyday discourses arise out of such settings as families, workplaces, or communities and involve their inhabitants. Or they are projected through newspapers and TV, being spoken in the first instance by media folk and then recycled within ordinary settings. In the case of academic discourses the relevant forums are published texts, journals, the *Times Higher*, conferences, lectures and so on. And the 'insiders' to the discourses are those who are considered legitimate 'speakers' within these forums — academics, graduates and professionals. From this perspective studenthood is an 'apprenticeship', during which the student is initiated into the practices, values, and ways of thinking of the discourse and a selection of its key ideas and current debates. Having 'mastered' the discourse, the student is personally and socially empowered:

- *personally* by having available a set of powerful analytical tools with which to make sense of the world
- *socially* by being able to speak on (relatively) equal terms to those who hold power and status within a particular sphere (e.g. lawyers, planners, educationists, etc.)

In acknowledging this 'social' aspect of learning, we become aware of the many personal and cultural shifts a student has to make, particularly at access level. (Here an open-learning text can be less oppressive than the direct presence of a tutor and other students.) We recognise teaching as 'communicating' and not just 'telling', requiring imaginative skills in developing compelling intellectual 'narratives'. We also become more sensitive to the many opportunities for misunderstanding and aware of the value of concrete and familiar examples around which both everyday and academic meanings can be constructed, allowing students to move back and forth between the two, instead of feeling stranded in strange territory.

Being able to place ideas in context

Academic discourses are (like any discourse) dynamic and 'political' phenomena. To understand what is going on in the discussions in texts and classrooms, one has to understand the recent history of debates within the discourse. One has to know who is arguing with whom and what is at stake. To understand the nature of the search for academic knowledge within a discipline, one has to understand the position of certain figures and certain ideas, within a long accumulation of debates about certain key issues. One has to have developed a recognition that *answers to questions* depend on *premises* and *assumptions* and the admissibility of certain types of *evidence*. The eventual aim is to *apprehend* the discourse as a complex web of meaning production, within which the meaning of every utterance and idea is constructed against a shifting backdrop of other ideas and debates.

The intangibility of discourses

The dynamic and indeterminate nature of discourses is one of the main sources of difficulty in both learning and teaching. It is difficult, for example, to specify exactly what has to be achieved in the process of becoming a speaker of a particular academic discourse. It is relatively easy for an 'insider' to identify utterances which do *not* work within the terms of the discourse, (hence the temptation to write only negative criticisms on essays.) But it is much more challenging to show how the thought underlying an inappropriate utterance might be *reworked* to give it greater purchase within the academic discourse. Though insightful tutors are able to give glimpses of the thought-shift required, the process of 'apprehending the discourse' nevertheless involves trial and error and takes time. In an open learning text it requires the strategic use of activities, pictures, examples, and case studies, to nudge students towards positioning their thoughts within a different frame.

The problem of frame-of-reference

The meaning of an utterance derives from the framework of assumptions and debates provided by the discourse from which it arises. However, a beginning student does not have available the frames-of-reference of the academic discourse. And it is very difficult to grasp these without listening to some utterances. But, since the student cannot yet make sense of utterances, there appears to be a 'chicken-egg' problem. In a classroom, one way out of this is that the tutor helps with the framing. The tutor can launch a discussion based within familiar discourses, where frames-of-reference *are* understood. Then, while maintaining a strand of meaning, he or she shifts the terms of the discussion to incorporate elements of the academic discourse. Eventually the students find themselves participating in a debate conducted within a frame-of-reference located inside the academic discourse. In this way the students begin to sense the nature of an unfamiliar frame-of-reference and pick up clues as to how utterances work within it.

Establishing 'frame' in an open-learning text

An open-learning text has to find ways of making similar moves, without the advantages of a 'live' discourse. For access level students, the text must launch a discussion based within everyday discourse, so that the reader can accomplish the construction of an initial frame of meaning. This means addressing the student in *ordinary language*, but it also involves establishing a readily accessible *context* and a *purpose*. Without these constructive thinking cannot begin. This suggests the use of *everyday examples* to provide a *concrete* and *specific* focus to the student's conceptual and analytical efforts. Case-studies, for example, presented very briefly as *vignettes* and written in 'humanised' form, encourage empathy, setting in play everyday thinking processes. Alternatively, photographs can be used to bring the student's knowledge of the world into play, without the intervening barrier of language. Such devices get the student's processes of 'constructing meaning' up-and-running.

The use of activities to shift the frame

Having established context, purpose can be sharpened through *activities* which encourage the reader to 'engage' with the issues in play. However, the subtle art of designing such activities is all too easily overlooked. Typically a text writer has the germ of a good idea, but simply presents an activity in the form, 'Here is a problem, what do you think?' Left with an open field, students think so many things they do not know where to begin. Moreover, they sense that only certain lines of thought are going to be relevant to the subsequent discussion. Rather than flail around in the dark, the intelligent option is to skip ahead and find the answer in the text.

To design an effective activity around an issue, or a case-study, the writer must *first* write down in simple propositional terms the conclusions he or she intends to draw from it. In effect this provides the answer to the question. 'What are the significant moves into the academic discourse which this activity is intended to enable?' *Then* the writer is in a position to devise very specific (and where possible concrete) questions which lead students towards the thinking shift desired. For instance, in the LICS module *Changing Communities* students are presented with five photographs of people in settings ranging from peasant fields to London Bridge at rush hour. The students are set nine sharply focused questions. For example — 'How well do you think these people know each other? — If one of them was ill, what do you think the others would do? — Do you think a stranger would find it easy to join the group?' Each of the questions addresses a specific dimension of change in the nature of communities (dimensions which are central to later analysis in the module). Immediately after the exercise, several pages are taken up with discussing each question in the context of each of the photographs, to help the students to crystallise thoughts they are likely to have had themselves as they did the activity. After this the analytic dimensions are briefly sketched and students are asked to apply them to their own experience of community. In this way everyday understanding of the term community is elaborated and gradually replaced by a conception of community which has more purchase within an analytical discourse.

Activities can be much briefer and less elaborate than this, but the tasks set should always be direct, explicit and easy to engage with. Moreover they should never be inserted simply as activity for its own sake (since this encourages the habit of skipping past activities). Activities should always lead the student's thoughts to a new staging post on the journey into the discourse, or else help to consolidate progress just made.

Using 'narrative' and 'plot' to sustain a shifting frame

This notion of carrying the student's thoughts forward is central to success in writing an open-learning text. If the opening move is to set up a functioning 'frame of reference' in the student's mind, the trick after that is to sustain the frame. Thus a teaching text requires a *narrative* which leads the reader on from one page to the next, sustaining active *engagement* with the issues under discussion. The text ought to work like a novel, or a play — the opening scene seizes the reader's attention, and then the *plot* gradually unfolds over several acts. New themes and sub-plots can be introduced, but the overall 'story' keeps moving forward to the denouement. In this way a functioning frame of reference is kept in place throughout, even though it is a steadily shifting one. As a result, students can, at all times, continue to construct meanings instead of getting stuck and losing heart. If the frame of meaning within a text keeps shifting or collapsing, it is like constantly having to get out of a car to crank the engine back to life: progress is slow, exhausting and dispiriting. Writing to a 'plot' inevitably constrains what can be said, but the advantages to the student are immense.

Helping students into the discourse

The LICS modules assume that at the outset students are unable to work within the relevant academic discourse unaided. In fact, the opening sections of each module look extremely easy because they operate within everyday discourses. The narrative then leads the students very gradually into the academic discourse, while regularly supplying links back to everyday discourses, through references to everyday examples and through activities which invite the student to connect their own experience to the discussion in the text. However it is a 'cut-down' and simplified version of the academic discourse (as opposed to throwing them in the deep end, with a standard text which employs the full-blown discourse). This cutting down is achieved by restricting the range of terms in play, by keeping abstractions few and fairly simple (grounding them initially in concrete examples) and by deliberately excluding most of the names and theoretical positions that are normally 'assumed' in social science debates. This version of the discourse is obviously not satisfactory for debates between academics; but it is intended to have much of the *form* and *structure* of the full-fledged discourse, thereby providing a 'staging post' along the way.

The dense thickets of an authentic academic discourse are virtually impenetrable by the inexperienced and ill-equipped lone student. However, with the supports provided by a LICS module, the student can acquire practice at 'making sense' within an increasingly analytical discourse and so gradually make the transition to higher levels. Eventually, the student will acquire the conceptual equipment, and sufficient experience in its use, to enter into a full-fledged discourse, reading its texts and becoming increasingly independent of support. Indeed, even by the end of an access module students find themselves engaged in discussions which are a long way from everyday conversations, and close to first year undergraduate social science discourses. They find themselves reading sentences at a level of abstraction and conceptual sophistication far beyond their capabilities at the outset; thinking about issues which would have seemed irritatingly obscure and irrelevant; and recognising the force of arguments which they would have thought quite unnecessarily complex and circumspect. In other words, they begin to understand and to value the way social science discourses work.

Student-centred and subject-centred

This 'discourse' view of learning helps in positioning one within the long-standing debate over whether teaching should be student-centred or subject-centred. It becomes apparent that good teaching involves *both*. Teaching must *start out* with a discussion centred on the *students*, and the discourses *they* are familiar with. But it should *lead towards* the discourses of the *subject matter*. These are the discourses the students want to be able to operate with. They don't, on the whole, want to construct their own alternative discourse (which would have little social purchase). They want access to prestigious and powerful discourses, which will give them more analytical edge and a stronger voice within society. (This is not to suggest that academic discourses should not be challenged. It is simply to recognise the established power base of these discourses.) The job of Access teacher and text is to construct pathways from everyday discourses into the unfamiliar terrain of an academic discourse.

Conclusion

We have seen that open learning can play an important part, even in Access level study, which has traditionally relied on much face-to-face contact and personal support. Whether open-learning is used to provide distance-learning, or is combined with the benefits of face-to-face support, it offers significant advantages to students who are finding their way into a new field of study. (This is so, whether the Access pathway is intended to lead to a conventional degree course, or to some form of part-time open-learning.) The experience of the LICS project is that the availability of carefully designed open-learning materials enables local providers to construct a wide range of flexible options, bringing education within reach of adults who would otherwise be excluded. The structuring provided by an open-learning text is, in itself, a significant benefit to adults returning to learning. However, to work to proper effect the design of the text should take account of the nature of the process of entering an unfamiliar field of discourse.

References

Northedge, A. (1990) *The Good Study Guide*, Milton Keynes, Open University.

Northedge, A. (1992) *Living in a Changing Society, Essay Booklet*, Milton Keynes, Open University.

Northedge, A. (1992) *Teaching Access: a tutor's handbook for the modular, open-learning course Living in a Changing Society*, Milton Keynes, Open University.

Northedge, A. and Croucher, R. (1994) *Living in a Changing Society, Consolidation Module*.

Sherratt, N., Fletcher, A. and Northedge, A. (1991) *Changing Communities*, Milton Keynes, Open University.

18 Learning through assignments — a genuine dialogue?

Matthew Godsell and Margaret Miers

Open Learning's role in nurse education is expanding in order to provide flexible modes of study and to improve the cost effectiveness of courses. Open learning can make it easier for practitioners to combine work and study, and may thus promote reflective awareness of the interdependence of theory and practice. Staff teaching the pre-registration Diploma in Higher Education in nursing studies in Avon and Gloucestershire College of Health are introducing open learning to respond to individual learning styles of students. With large cohorts of students, staff have already developed methods of working together in face-to-face modes of delivery which share many features of open and distance learning.

Staff work in teams responsible for teaching and assessing key subjects or themes. Up to twelve staff within each team mark assignments, and one or two staff take the role of moderator. To promote standardisation of grades and quality of written feedback, the department uses a feedback grid based on Bloom's taxonomy. (Bloom, 1956) The taxonomy identifies a range of attributes students are expected to demonstrate in written assignments, although the attributes are weighted differently at different stages of the course, and for different assignments (see Figure 18.1).

Our shared experience — Matthew as marker and Margaret as moderator — for sociology assignments has prompted discussion about the role of assignments in promoting student learning, and the factors which may inhibit the independence of both staff and student in any mode of delivery. Tutors' own assumptions about teaching and learning lead them to use the feedback grid

AVON & GLOUCESTERSHIRE COLLEGE OF HEALTH (GLENSIDE)

DIPLOMA IN NURSING STUDIES

STUDENT MARK FORM

PASS

RESULT

Examination Number ....   Cohort .MARCH. 92........

Assessment Title .SOCIOLOGY........   Personal Tutor ....

PRESENTATION	
There should be an imaginative use of ideas	The essay covers a lot of ground by introducing a wide variety of ideas and then relating them to different sociological perspectives
There should be attention to the structure and organisation	The essay has a clear statement of intent, a summary and conclusion.
Accuracy and attention to technical writing skills should be evident	Spelling, grammar and syntax were of a high standard.
KNOWLEDGE	
The referencing should be accurate and support evidence of wide reading	Referencing was accurate and reflected a wide range of reading.
There should be an accurate and appropriate use of a language displayed	Sociological themes were used accurately and in the appropriate context.
The views should be clearly expressed	The writer's views were clearly expressed in his/her own words.
COMPREHENSION	
Any implications should be clearly identified and expressed	The writer made the most of the title. He a she arranged material so that it reflected or undermined the statement regarding shared experiences.
There should be clear evidence of interpretation of knowledge	
There should be expressions in the student's own words	The writer was skilled in producing evidence which supported different points of view as well as providing insight into the limitations of
APPLICATION	accepting them at face value.
There should be clear evidence of application of theories and principles	The writer demonstrated a sound knowledge of the perspectives and issues that were examined.
The reasoning should be sound and well expressed	Reasoning was sound and well expressed.
There should be clear evidence of the ability to explain "Why"	The writer was skilled in providing a variety of explanations and theories rather than accepting

any single notion of cause and effect.

Figure 18.1

<table>
<tr><td colspan="2"><u>ANALYSIS</u></td></tr>
<tr>
<td>The components of the study should be clearly and logically identified

A variety of views should be discussed</td>
<td>You have been successful in selecting material which demonstrates that you are aware of the factors which shape the lives of adolescents eg race, gender identity, peer groups etc.</td>
</tr>
<tr>
<td>There should be clear evidence of the ability to compare and contrast</td>
<td>The essay contains "breadth" of material as well as analytical depth.</td>
</tr>
</table>

<table>
<tr><td colspan="2"><u>SYNTHESIS</u></td></tr>
<tr>
<td>The selection and organisation of ideas and experiences should be clear and show originality

The arguments should be well reasoned and any hypothesis formulated clearly

There should be clear evidence of good writing skills and construction</td>
<td>You seem to have come to the conclusion that divisions based on the life experiences of men and women, ethnic groupings, class and peer groups say more about the lives of adolescents than some of the more generalised statements that appear to be part of a perspectives-led approach.</td>
</tr>
</table>

<table>
<tr><td colspan="2"><u>EVALUATION</u></td></tr>
<tr>
<td>There should be clear evidence of the ability to make reasoned judgements using appropriate criteria

Identification of strengths and weaknesses should be accurate

The conclusions drawn should be sound</td>
<td>You seem to be producing material which has lead you to some conclusions which sound contradictory or awkward. I don't think this is because you have handled the material badly. On the contrary, this is a good piece of work. — continued below.</td>
</tr>
</table>

NB   Please put result in box on front of form

<u>GENERAL SUMMARY</u>

It may be that the conflicts and contradictions that you have seen are the result of a particular method of analysis. Analysing something in terms of issues such as race or gender may create a very different picture of events. You seem to favour this approach rather than one which is dominated by Marxism, feminism etc. You could turn this to your advantage by turning some of the statements around so that they appear to be more critical of sociological methodology. If you think that perspectives are too clumsy or cumbersome and they prevent you from engaging with important issues then why not say so?

Signed ... *Matthew Gabell* ....   Date ... 21/5/93 ....

Figure 18.1   cont.

in different ways, emphasising different attributes and responding
to students in more or less impersonal ways. Tutors' own approach
may inhibit student autonomy. However practices developed to
promote standardisation (the feedback grid, the moderator role),
can in themselves constrain staff and student independence.
Moderators can inhibit or encourage openness.

As moderator and marker, we discussed the role of assignments in our students' learning. Our experience, in face-to-face,
and in open learning, suggests that assignments can be a vital form
of communication between staff and students. Written exchanges
between tutors and students can be used to encourage reflection
and independent thought. When assignments are focused on the
assessment of knowledge, however, the exchange of ideas can be
restricted. When this happens all of the writers: students, tutors
and moderators, lose the opportunity to develop their ideas using
a narrative 'voice' of their own.

We wondered whether writing in dialogue would help students keep their own voices

MARGARET: I see assignments as a crucial mechanism for student
learning, in open learning as in any other mode of delivery.
Assignments can form the basis of a dialogue between tutor
and student. Marking assignments always has the potential to
be a one-to-one conversation.

MATTHEW: But you are not acknowledging some of the constraints in open learning. Writing is a slow and difficult way
of communicating. It is harder to clarify misunderstandings, or
maintain relationships in print. Some open learning packages try
to work around the problems by presenting and assessing material
in a very prescriptive way. I'm thinking about multiple choice and
short answer questions here.

MARGARET: I suspect you are thinking about more than that. You
are unhappy with our own assignments, and our own methods of
assessment. You are worried that we are spending too much time
checking knowledge retention rather than promoting learning, or
even thinking, and that if we make more use of open learning
we'll end up telling the students that we're giving them more
responsibility for managing their own learning when all that we are
doing is pushing them along pre-set paths towards a prescriptive
educational product.

MATTHEW: I'm also worried that students are quite unprepared
to take that responsibility. Alternatively if they are already independent learners, they'll find little room for manoeuvre. Open

learning can seem a quick and efficient method for passing on information, with the purpose of assignments seen as checking how much 'knowledge' was received. What was lost on the way?

MARGARET: It doesn't have to be like that. Open learning can encourage tutors and students to develop a relationship of reflective reciprocity, a relationship that enables both parties to develop their own voices and hence a genuine dialogue that lets us listen, and debate. I believe this relationship is more conducive to learning than the 'tutor as expert' model, (Miers, 1987) and more liberating than some student-centred models. It encourages the students to bring more of their own thoughts, feelings and reactions into their written work, and at the same time it gives tutors an opportunity to address students as equal partners. This relationship is vital in nurse education where students are encouraged to develop through reflective practice. Writing can be a slow method of communicating, but it may be effective. There's *time* for reflection and time to think about a response.

MATTHEW: I can see the benefits of reflective reciprocity but I don't think it's compatible with our method of assessment. We have a set grid for feedback, a shared taxonomy for use in evaluation. The grid leads us to think of a piece of work as a set of tasks which demonstrate defined attributes — knowledge, comprehension, application . . . It is possible for students to gain respectable marks for exercising their précis writing skills rather than using a voice of their own. They master all the techniques for writing their own voices out of the work and presenting the reader with abridged versions of the theories as they are laid out in the course text books. They receive favourable treatment from some markers because the information meets expectations regarding knowledge and comprehension. A student who attempts to describe what happens when he or she applies sociological theories to the world that he or she knows using anything that resembles conversational speech is likely to receive lower grades. If we have a genuine interest in reflection as a way of teaching or communicating ideas then this student has taken the first steps along that road whilst the précis-writers lack any sense of direction because they have not even started to develop a voice of their own.

MARGARET: I can't disagree, and still advocate reflection. But I have to struggle to identify my own role in this, as moderator, and I need to reflect on my view of the grid. I cannot agree that it necessarily restricts independent thought. Knowledge, comprehension and application are starting points, not outcomes. As learners move the ideas through analysis, synthesis and evaluation they transform them. At this stage they are in charge because they are using their own initiative to create something that is completely new. You reward, and encourage this, as a marker (Figure 18.1). I don't want you to feel constrained in the way you use the grid for feedback. If *you* feel you can't use your initiative, your students will feel similarly hemmed in, and out of control.

MATTHEW: But there is too much emphasis placed on knowledge and comprehension, and you allow this as a moderator. We should redirect some of our effort so that we can comment on the ways in which learners use the ideas they have collected. We spend too much time telling learners 'You can have a mark or two for putting this in, but no more. Look you've forgotten to include this and that.' I know you feel obliged to wag a disapproving finger and you like to tell me that learners can not play around with ideas unless they understand them, but I feel obliged to say that exploring ideas rather than simply regurgitating them is a crucial part of understanding. Perhaps we could start to move away from the didactic approach by changing the vocabulary of marking so that it sounds enabling rather than censorial.

MARGARET: My disapproving finger isn't directed at your criticisms of the censorial tone. I entirely agree about that. I see learning as having cognitive, affective and behavioural components, i.e. involving thinking, feeling and doing. If we simply give students negative feedback I don't think they *feel* motivated to learn, and if they aren't motivated, they'll stop listening, stop thinking. My worries are about your interpretation of the exploring, or your recognition of understanding. We have disagreed because you have seen *learning* shown in a script, where I have seen muddled thinking. That raises problems I, and I'm sure others, have with the grid attributes. It isn't easy to identify analysis, synthesis and evaluation except through presentation skills, the way the student has written the ideas down. You have seen skills of synthesis showing behind an inadequate description of knowledge. Others would have denied it. I wasn't sure. It is hardly surprising that tutors emphasize the importance of skills of comprehension and knowledge, simply because it is easier to check if they have been demonstrated. I can't encourage tutors to devalue these skills.

MATTHEW: But that's why some tutors see the learning outcomes of an assignment mainly in terms of knowledge and comprehension, and their feedback emphasizes content not thought. It must be confusing for learners to find other staff are emphasizing the 'right' to express yourself and are looking for evidence of synthesis and evaluation, evidence of individual thought. On the one hand learners are encouraged to use their own voice and on the other hand they are asked to adopt a formal, academic style of writing, a style that obliterates the self. It not only removes the personal pronoun 'I', it can lead people to believe that the author must be some kind of god-like, impartial creature. It seems contradictory to talk about avoiding personal statements in one breath and then plead for reflection and self-awareness with the next. Reflection, and making written statements about first-hand experiences both involve pushing the first person up front. When I mark assignments I feel that I have to drop the impersonal, impartial, omniscient marker's style and 'talk' to the writer using a straightforward 'I' and 'you' style. It feels right in that it offers the opportunity to advise without sounding censorial. The voice of an omniscient marker does not give me the same scope. I suspect that some markers shun the upper levels of the taxonomy and any form of written expression that brings the writer into the material because the allocation of marks or grades is difficult. It involves leaving the stable and safe structures which knowledge, comprehension and application can provide and entering the process of creative writing. If I am going to encourage learners to write in a way which involves their own voices then I would have to encourage markers to reciprocate by addressing the students in a more personal way when they provide feedback.

MARGARET: I entirely agree with you about the importance of giving an individual response and about the absurdity of eliminating the person from formal academic style. It is unnecessary, it is in some senses dishonest. But you are being unwittingly derogatory to our colleagues in not acknowledging the importance of writing in a style that is both clear and widely accepted. Nurses have always needed writing skills, but they have been allowed to get away with the poverty of their record-keeping for far too long. 'Slept well' said little, and often little of the truth. We need to foster writing skills.

But more importantly, I think you are downgrading both the students' struggle to acquire knowledge, and a teacher's role in promoting students' ability to understand new ideas. The understanding comes before using them. *No perhaps it doesn't!* Understanding can come through using them. But that is where the tutor can help, by discussing the way the student is using the ideas and that means talking to the student about all aspects of their work. Why do you address the student directly only in, as you say, the upper levels of the taxonomy? Surely you discuss knowledge, presentation, understanding, with students face-to-face — in which case why not in written feedback?

MATTHEW: I do. But what is the 'knowledge' for, indeed what are you counting as knowledge? You advocate a model of reflective reciprocity, not a 'teacher as expert' model, so why are you worried about students demonstrating a knowledge base. Staff anxieties all too often focus on knowledge, our own, and the students. We don't focus on what students learn in terms of thinking skills or what they can do with the knowledge.

MARGARET: I thought we agreed about 'knowledge'. I have promoted the view that we teach knowledge about sociological perspectives to *encourage* critical thinking, and not for its own sake, although I do think that some basic knowledge of sociological traditions is knowledge worth gaining.

MATTHEW: Can learners become independent, autonomous and capable of reflection *unless* they move away from the security of basic knowledge and principles? How have you arrived at a point where you can describe some aspects of sociology as basic? Because you moved on. I think notions of safety and security are misplaced in this context. We both think that sociology needs to be relevant to the needs of student nurses. I don't believe they will realize that they can make the subject respond to their own ideas until they move away from the established belief that the theories say it all.

MARGARET: Is that the established belief? I both value the knowledge *and* believe the theories we teach do not say it all. I can see we have to be careful about notions of safety and security. Such notions are misplaced when discussing knowledge. My security as a teacher of sociology would be fragile if I thought it were related to what I know rather than how I think, or my ability to learn. Sociology's knowledge base isn't secure. That's the challenge of it. That's why students don't feel safe when learning sociological theories. Nor do staff. I want to test knowledge of sociological perspectives because it is a challenge to think about the world in different ways. Yes I want to trust students to think for themselves and to encourage them to do so, but I also want to trust them to listen to other peoples' thoughts. That means to read ideas, to struggle with them. Not dismiss them without trying.

My security seems to lie in knowing that my knowledge base isn't secure, and accepting this. That means I'm secure in valuing the skills of enquiry you want to value. Perhaps we have to force ourselves to ground our security in warranted uncertainty rather than unwarranted certainty through deliberately taking on a role where we can't be certain all the time, as I have done in teaching interdisciplinary courses for the Open University, and you have done in teaching student nurses psychology and sociology.

MATTHEW: I'm sure that the acceptance of uncertainty and insecurity is a feature of learning. Joy Davis, writing to tutors who teach mathematics by correspondence commented:

> the nature of your relationship with students has its roots in your perception of mathematics. If you see mathematics as primarily about reproducing standard techniques on standard types of questions, then this attitude will be picked up by your students. They will be reinforced in the belief that getting correct answers is all that counts . . . If you see mathematics as an activity which involves conjecturing and modifying conjectures, with struggling to see and to express, then assignments encourage students to further their understanding, rather than hide their ignorance. (Davis, 1987, p. 259)

MARGARET: Joy has also suggested that an aim of assignment marking is:

> to engender a relationship with students in which the student is willing to expose uncertainty and confusion, knowing that this honesty will be respected, and that positively helpful suggestions will be offered. (ibid., p. 258)

MATTHEW: You are suggesting students should be willing to expose their own uncertainties to tutors who do not necessarily know much themselves. Why should students feel their honesty would be respected by tutors they rarely see, and who, from my experience, respond negatively to students' attempts to express their own ideas?

MARGARET: I agree there may be special problems here in open learning. In face to face modes of delivery, we usually have time to generate an atmosphere of mutual trust, but in many open learning courses, we do not have time to earn trust. *Professional Judgment*, an Open University third level course which advocates 'reflective reciprocity' adopts ethical codes for tutors, students and managers of the course, in order to promote trust. I don't think open learning necessarily limits the tutor student relationship, provided methods of encouraging individuality and independence (and trust) are built in to the course philosophy, materials and assessment. Part of my job as a moderator is to promote trust, (in, for example, the parity of marks) and independence.

MATTHEW: So are you saying the course model of tutor/student should be one of reflective reciprocity, the materials based on a view of knowledge as uncertain, and the assessment criteria weighted in favour of individual thought rather than comprehension? And if that is what you are saying, how can you find the grid we use adequate?

MARGARET: I haven't said I am happy with the grid, but as a moderator, I can see that tutors can do almost what they like with it. The tutor/student *relationship* isn't constrained by the grid. There is still the freedom to write to the student, as you do.

In an open learning system, where the mode of delivery may be relatively anonymous, offering an individual response to assignments seems imperative. To do this, I agree, markers have to lose some of their censorial, evaluative emphasis, and as a moderator I have to do likewise. Writers on correspondence marking have begun to develop a language for describing how to develop skills of distance tuition.

Joy Davis, for example, has distinguished between *seeing, saying* and *recording*, and has identified the importance of teachers being able to identify these differences. She gave us a technical vocabulary about learning to 'draw attention to distinctions which may otherwise be overlooked'. *Seeing, saying* and *recording* can become part of the vocabulary of helping students to learn.

> Getting a sense of' is the first, pre-articulate stage in the
> learning process, culminating in the feeling that we can
> see what the concept is all about. We can confirm the
> seeing, and make it firmer by giving it expression, that is
> by saying what it is we have seen. Finally we capture our
> understanding by recording it. (ibid., p. 254).

MATTHEW: I think the vocabulary of seeing, saying and recording is useful. But it is the clear precis *recorders* who gain the high grades.

MARGARET: But tutors' written comments can help students through the saying stage. Helping them through *saying* to a more conventional form of recording doesn't mean resorting to precis-style prose. Students' own voices do emerge in the way they organise comments and ideas. I agree, however, that tutors need to be able to look through the recording, at the seeing, expressed through struggles with the saying stage.

MATTHEW: I don't want it all my own way. I can see that without a structure that learners and markers can follow, essays, and the process of assessment can become shapeless and subjective. I'm not advocating removing or reducing tension by going over to one style of essay writing or marking. We need to maintain it by recognizing different ways of working. That makes my job interesting and yours miserable.

MARGARET: What is difficult about the moderator's job is dealing with the tensions of wanting to treat students equitably, and wanting to give tutors the (necessary) freedom to explore their own teaching styles. What is interesting about the moderator's job is being able to see the range of approaches to marking assignments, and reflecting on the range of underlying assumptions about the tutor's role. What is worrying is that these different assumptions may lead staff to give different weightings to different cognitive skills and hence arrive at variations in grading.

MATTHEW: I'd suggest that the different assumptions about teaching lead to different weightings for knowledge, and individual thought (e.g. synthesis and evaluation). Tutors who want to work as reflective practitioners will value the importance of individual analysis. Reflective teachers probably aren't as interested in seeing, saying or recording, but in *using* the knowledge. They want students to make that knowledge their own, and transform it through its use.

MARGARET: But in practice I would suggest that reflective teachers need to be able to facilitate comprehension and knowledge too. Teachers and learners have to reach a shared understanding of what learning is taking place. If we place a great deal of emphasis on the importance of factors such as *comprehension*, or *understanding*, our problem is how can we 'see' understanding? You have claimed to recognise understanding in a script where I have not seen it. Other markers will only recognise it when it is *recorded* with a high level of literary skill. Perhaps we need to record in a different way if we want students to develop their own voices and enter into a dialogue with tutors. *Professional Judgment* has acknowledged that the conventional academic essay may not be the best way for students to struggle with their own uncertainties. To encourage students and tutors to work together in a spirit of 'reflective reciprocity' students are asked to write some of the assignments as 'teaching conversations'. Writing assignments as conversations could help tutors and students develop an 'emancipated dialogue — emancipated in the sense that neither party is seeking to mystify or exploit the other on the basis of either superior technical knowledge or social/language skills' (Dowie, 1993). More mundanely, writing conversations may at least encourage students to find their own voices. (Have we found ours?)

MATTHEW: Writing assignments as conversations may also develop students' willingness to talk back to a tutor. We cannot know whether we, as teachers, are giving an appropriate individual response, unless we find out how our response is received. (Miers, 1987) In open learning, where face-to-face contact is reduced, the opportunities to do this are limited. Assignments become the main vehicle for tutor student contact. Tutors have discretion to use written feedback to promote discussion, develop dialogue. Assignments (and even feedback grids) may be opportunities for students and tutors to write in their own voice.

MARGARET AND MATTHEW: In conclusion, we would argue that if assignments are to promote and test individual thinking skills then tutors and students need encouragement to develop their own voice. A personalised dialogue style may encourage this. We have discussed a number of issues. One of them was the concern that in most assignments the stress on the importance of recording knowledge leads to pushing students along pre-set paths towards a prescriptive product. We have reviewed our own ways of avoiding this practice and we agreed on the value of reflections on attributes, changes in weighting and experiments in *form*.

Using dialogue as the chosen form is not without its disadvantages. It is not succinct, it remains contrived. As a means of demonstrating analysis and synthesis it may not be efficient. Variability in readers' (markers) response to the *form* may increase concern about equity. The tension between ensuring parity and promoting independence doesn't go away but it may be more easily explored and exposed, no longer hidden in apparent consensus.

References

Bloom, B. S. (1956) *Taxonomy of Educational Objectives Vol. 1: Cognitive Domain*, New York, McKay.
Davis, J. (1987) 'Teaching by correspondence in Mathematics' in Thorpe, M. and Grugeon, D. *Open Learning for Adults*, Harlow, Longman.
Dowie, J. A. (1993) *Professional Judgment Study Guide* Third Level Course D300, Milton Keynes, The Open University.
Miers, M. (1987) 'Reflections on the role of correspondence teaching' in Thorpe, M. and Grugeon, D. *Open Learning for Adults*, Harlow, Longman.

19 Adapting multimedia technologies for academic learning[1]

Diana Laurillard

Introduction

The task of planning and designing educational materials is becoming very complex as the types of media available not only increase in number but also intermarry to produce exotic off-spring, such as multimedia work-stations, interactive satellite teaching, audio-graphics, and others. Evolutionary metaphors are inappropriate, however. The evolution of technology is not at all adaptive to the contexts in which people learn. Education is attempting to adapt itself radically to the promise of the new technologies, but the new technologies were created for entirely other purposes than to save education. Because of this, we must take care, in the educational design process, not to be swept along by the promises of the new technologies, but to use them in a controlled and selective way. Whether they 'open up' learning in the sense of increasing learner control and independence is not something which can be taken for granted.

New media in HE

Higher education in the UK has been well-served by government investment in new technology, in comparison with other European countries. Beginning with the National Development Programme in Computer Assisted Learning (CTI) in 1973, and later the Computers in Teaching Initiative, both programmes were set up to assist the development of computer-based courseware materials, suitable for HE. These programs exploited the computer in various ways, for example:

(i)   its computational properties could provide simulations of systems so that students could interact with them and explore their behaviour — economic models, biological models, engineering systems, etc.

(ii) its interactive properties could provide tutorials in which students' replies to questions could be checked against model answers, making feedback dependent on their input, and without necessitating supervision by a tutor.

(iii) its presentational properties could be used to show animated graphics to illustrate dynamic changes, or to provide visual analogies of abstract concepts or procedures, e.g. manipulation of equations, the sequence of events in a clinical treatment, etc.

(iv) its adaptive properties could allow students to go at their own pace, in their own sequence through the material, thus achieving some of the goals of open learning.

These were valuable explorations of how computers might enhance teaching at HE level, but the developments tended to remain in-house, with little cross-fertilisation of ideas, or transfer of materials. In recognition of this the second phase of the CTI programme, begun in 1989, set up information centres in twenty different universities, each one focusing on the computer-based materials available in a particular subject-area. This meant that users could find out what was available, and developers had some means of disseminating their products. These centres remain an important cornerstone in the implementation of a successful computers-in-teaching programme.

The development of suitable courseware is a continual problem, however. As technological platforms change, old programs either look old-fashioned, or fail to run at all on new machines. Each program requires intensive staff time, and each course needs several programs for computer usage to be worthwhile, so the economic feasibility of computers-in-teaching is quite untenable, if it is treated as though programs can be developed in the same way as lecture notes, by individual lecturers, for their own courses. In recognition of this, the 'Teaching and Learning Technologies Programme' (TLTP) was set up in 1992 by the Higher Education Funding Council for England (HEFCE) with the explicit intention of encouraging development and usage across institutions, through subject-based consortia. These now involve most universities in some capacity — as joint developer, or evaluation site for materials being developed elsewhere. The technologies being covered by the Programme cover computer-based tutorials and simulations (sometimes enhanced by sound and video), multimedia workstations providing hypertext access to encyclopaedic material, Super-JANET-based telecommunications allowing computer and video-conferencing interactions between tutors and students in different universities.

Similar developments are taking place elsewhere in the education system, as the National Council for Educational Technology investigates the use of conferencing, multimedia workstations and lap-tops in schools and further education. The technology infrastructure is gradually being put in place that will make it possible for lecturers to build their course provision around technology-based materials.

All these developments are technology-led. Computers will be used increasingly in education simply because, increasingly, they are there. The key question for educationists is 'will they be used well?'. There is no doubt about their potential — all the points listed above still serve as good reasons to suppose they will enhance teaching, and there are many good computer-based teaching programs to be found. We are still allowing the technology to lead, however — the evidence being the range of new technologies to be found within the TLTP — and this will not guarantee effective educational designs, or more open learning. The educationist has to control the use of technology if it is to be used well.

This chapter attempts to reverse the current direction and consider how education might lead the use of technology. As HE increases access by admitting more students on the basis of scarcely increased resources, there is a general expectation that new technologies will provide a solution. They should enable students to learn and to get access to teaching independently of the direct involvement of a tutor. But first we have to understand what the new technologies can offer, how far they can provide a genuine enhancement, and what their limitations are. We also need an analysis of the extent to which older and cheaper technologies are still valuable, and how all these should be integrated with existing teaching methods. Therefore this chapter begins with a framework defining our pedagogical requirements of educational technologies; then we can compare them on this basis, and establish what each can best contribute to the learning process and use them accordingly.

The learning process as a conversational framework

The learning process operating within academic institutions is importantly different from the procedural learning, or experiential learning that takes place in training or in on-the-job experience. Although it may be oriented towards vocational requirements, it focuses on what students must know and understand in order to be able to do the job, rather than simply on how to do it; an academic education requires theory as well as practice, the advantage being that the theory empowers the individual to cope with new situations or changes in the detail of the practice. Theory, in any subject area, is fundamental to an academic education.

The development of a framework for describing the learning process begins with the assumption that academic knowledge consists in theoretical descriptions of the world. Such descriptions take different forms in different fields — they may be equations of motion in physics, organisational structures in management science, critical theories in literature studies — but common to all of them is that they cannot be acquired through direct experience of the world because they are specialist ways of describing the world. Academic knowledge can only come to be known through a discursive interaction between teacher and student because it cannot be known through experience alone, only through reflection on experience.

Because of its descriptive and reflective nature, academic knowledge certainly requires also direct experience of the world, and much of the pedagogic task of the teacher is to provide the student with the kind of access to the world that enables them to have the experiences they need to make sense of the academic's descriptions — experimental work, fieldwork, practical work, project work, are all adapted to enhancing and extending the student's experiences of the world. If it were to stop there, then students would be competent to perform within the particular context of their experience, but without the reflective process that they engage in when they discuss that experience, and try to represent it in language or symbols, or whatever the academic argot happens to be, their competence remains confined. The point of an academic education is to take students beyond the specific to the generalisable, the comparative, the rule-governed descriptions that empower them to use their immediate experience more effectively, and by reflecting on it, govern it, and control their future actions, and so make progress, whatever the context.

The academic learning process, therefore, consists in four

essential component processes. It must be discursive, adaptive, interactive and reflective, defined as follows:

discursive — allowing discussion between student and teacher, where each expresses their conception of how some aspect of the world is to be described, and reacts to the other's description

adaptive — where, assuming a didactic intention, the teacher adapts the student's interaction with the world to enable them to experience it from the teacher's perspective

interactive — allowing the student to interact with the world in a way that extends or enhances their experience

reflective — where the student reflects upon their experience and its relation to the teacher's description and thereby adapts their own conception and their description of it.

These are all essential aspects of the academic learning process in the sense that if anyone of them is missing then a full understanding of academic concepts is not achieved (a full discussion of this can be found in Laurillard, 1993). They do not have to be contemporaneous, and teaching will often rely on past experience to do the job of the interactive component, hence the frequent appeal in teaching situations to helpful analogies and illustrative examples. The following dialogue is an example of how the conversational framework might be instantiated:

T: . . . the Earth goes round the Sun.   *Discursive*
S: But it *looks* as if the Sun goes round the Earth.
T: How would it look if the Earth went round
     the Sun?
S: Different.
T: No — imagine yourself on a stationary
     roundabout watching a train going round and
     round, what would you see?   *Adaptive*
S: The train whizzing past.   *Interactive*
T: Now imagine the train is stationary and the
     roundabout is going round, what would you see?
S: The train whizzing past.
T: Exactly.
S: Oh yes. So it would look the same to me,   *Reflective*
     standing on the Earth, whether the Earth was   *Discursive*
     going round the Sun or the Sun was going
     round it.
T: Exactly.

At the discursive level, teacher and student exchange views, and their reasons for them, and that may be sufficient. But if a discrepancy arises, as in the student's supposition that you can tell by looking, the teacher adapts the discussion, to lead it towards discussion of a common experience that will allow consensus between them. The interactive phase does not require, in this case, direct interaction with the world — where the teacher, in adaptive mode, might set up the experiment with the roundabout — their past experience is sufficient to allow agreement about the interpretation of that event. The student's reflection on that event then allows them to express their description of it as a new conception of an aspect of the issue under discussion.

Every stage in the framework is necessary. If the student does not express their conception in the first place, the teacher will remain ignorant of it and the rest of their conceptual argument will be building on sand. If they do not adapt the direction of the discussion to extending the student's experience, the same follows. If the student does not perform the thought experiment with the roundabout to extend their, albeit imagined, experience, then they will not see why the teacher does not accept the argument that the two situations are different. If the student does not reflect on the thought experiment, their awareness of it will remain bounded in the particular context of the roundabout, rather than being generalised for application to at least one other situation. If they do not express their redescription of the idea, the teacher cannot know if they have achieved the agreement at the discursive level that will allow the conceptual argument to proceed. Figure 19.1 shows a diagrammatic version of the framework, clarifying the two levels of experience (being interactive with the teacher's world) and description (being discursive between the two participants), and showing both teacher and student as being both adaptive and reflective.

The stages characterised in Figure 19.1 as a 'conversational framework' embody a series of distinct activities on the part of the two interlocutors. The 'discursive' level in the example above contains several different types of contribution: description by teacher of their conception, similar for student, and later a redescription by the student, followed by confirmation of agreement by the teacher. In adaptive mode, the teacher sets up a more familiar example. This allows the student to 'interact with the world', though in terms of the thought experiment with the train and the roundabout. Reflecting on that 'experience', the student can then make the connection with the more abstract topic of the motion of the planets, and offer their own, more accurate, description. The discursive and interactive levels require more than one exchange to do their job, therefore.

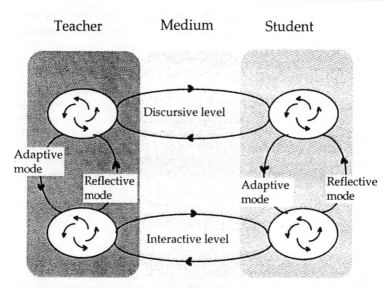

Figure 19.1 The academic learning process: essential component relationships

Similarly, in the course of a continuing dialogue between teacher and student, the teacher, in reflective mode, will be using their observations on the way the student interacts with the world to inform the way they explain and redescribe their own conception to the student at the discursive level. And the student, in adaptive mode, will benefit from adapting their actions in the world given the discussion.

The conversational framework above defines the essential components of the academic learning process, so that we can now express our pedagogical requirements of the educational technologies on offer.

Comparing the media

The conversational framework is a convenient description of the learning process, which encapsulates the essential aspects of learning academic knowledge, and provides us with some criteria against which to judge the educational media. And we immediately encounter the inescapable and inconvenient fact that they do not fit the framework very well. The essence of the academic teaching process is a conversation, but almost all the educational media are incapable of handling a conversation with a student. It is very apparent that the technology has not evolved to fit the academic learning context.

If the individual media do not easily support all the aspects of the learning process, then we need a representation of what each one can contribute, and thereby of the kind of supplementary teaching-learning interaction it presupposes. Consider the canonical forms of the principal educational media: print, including text pictures and graphics; video, including audio and animation; computer-based tutorial, including tutorial dialogue and simulation model; and the teacher-student discussion, for comparison. For each of these we can identify how well they support the learning process, using the framework as guide.

Print

The teacher can offer a description in language and pictures.

The student can only express their conception as written annotations, or responses to in-text activities set, but there is no reaction to them by the teacher (for discussion see Lockwood 1989).

The teacher can offer 'pre-emptive redescription', assuming the student may have some particular misconception, which can be addressed directly in the text.

The teacher cannot adapt the activities set to the student's needs, as there is no opportunity for the student to communicate their conception.

The student cannot adapt their actions as there is no direct interaction with the world.

The teacher may refer to the student's experience as a way of handling the interactive stage.

There is no interaction with the world for the student to reflect upon, though they may reflect upon the experience referred to by the teacher, as well as on the teacher's description.

Video

The teacher can offer a description in language, graphics, and dynamic pictures.

The student can only express their conception as responses to activities set, but there is no reaction to them by the teacher (for discussion see Durbridge, 1984).

The teacher can offer 'pre-emptive redescription', assuming the student may have some particular misconception, which can be addressed directly in the video presentation.

The teacher cannot adapt the activities set to the student's needs as there is no opportunity for the student to communicate their conception.

The student cannot adapt their actions as there is no direct interaction with the world.

The teacher can extend or enhance the student's vicarious experience of the world by showing an interaction with it. The actions are not the student's own, but they can observe the feedback on someone else's actions.

The student may reflect upon this vicarious experience of the world, as well as on the teacher's description.

Computer-based tutorial

The teacher can offer a description in language, graphics, and dynamic graphics, though the use of language must be limited, given the difficulty of reading text from a screen.

The student can only express their conception in a highly constrained form in response to activities set. This often means 'multiple-choice questions' (mcq), which can interfere with learning. A better form is the concealed mcq, which uses keywords to interpret student input (Laurillard, 1993).

If the computer can be programmed to interpret student input reliably, then it can be programmed to react to the particular category of response they make, and on that basis can offer a redescription designed to cope with that response. The redescription is still 'pre-emptive', however, as the form of reply is decided in advance by the programmer.

The program can adapt the activities set for the student both on the basis of their past performance on set activities, and on the basis of the categorised input above.

The student can adapt their actions in the world of the simulated model, on the basis of the feedback they received on previous actions, and in the light of the program's descriptions.

The teacher can extend or enhance the student's direct experience of a simulated world by offering interaction with a computer model of it. The actions are controlled by the student, and they receive feedback on those actions in the form of changes to the output of the model, either numerical, graphical or pictorial.

The student may reflect upon this simulated experience of the world, as well as on the program's description, and moreover the program can support this reflection as it can keep a record of both the student's actions, and the descriptions offered.

Teacher-student discussion

Both teacher and student can express their conception as a description, and can offer a redescription in the light of their reaction to the other's description. It is fully discursive.

The teacher can adapt the activity set for the student only in the sense of referring to a particular illustrative experience.

As there is no action directly on the world, the student cannot make adaptive changes to actions.

There is no interaction with the world for the student to reflect upon, though they may reflect upon the experience referred to by the teacher, as well as on the teacher's description, and moreover the teacher can support this reflection as they know the experience referred to and the descriptions offered.

	Discursive	*Adaptive*	*Interactive*	*Reflective*
Print	T's view as description Pre-emptive redescription redescription	By Student	Refers to experience	By Student
Video	T's view as description	By Student	via Teacher's action	By Student
Comp-based tutorial	T's view as description Pre-emptive redescription S's view in constrained form	By S and T	Using model	By S and T
Teacher/ Student discussion	T's view as re/description S's view as re/description	By Teacher	refers to experience	By S and T

Figure 19.2 Comparison of media coverage in the four component aspects of the academic learning process

From this comparison it should be apparent that the media are complementary to each other, that none supports the whole learning process, but that the computer-based tutorial-simulation program comes closest. The comparison is summarised in Figure 19.2.

It should also be clear that there are a number of design

devices for each medium that are used by designers to enable it to approximate to better coverage of the learning process, for example, the use of 'pre-emptive redescriptions' in presentation of a concept, the use of 'in-text activities' for print, or 'interactive video-cassette activities' for video, the use of a simulated model to allow interaction with a 'world' in computer-based tutorials, the use of reference to experience in discussion. All these devices help the student, but still leave some of the essential component activities unsupported. Students can supply these for themselves, especially if they are experienced or sophisticated learners. But they need support at least some of the time. If it is correct that the teaching-learning process is essentially a conversation, then especially at the advanced level of university study students will need frequent support at the 'discursive' level, and this is precisely the activity that is least well-supported by the media on offer, and also the one that is most consuming of staff time and likely to be reduced as student numbers increase. The most important reason for academics to resist the expansion of student numbers without some increase in staff time is the consequent loss of this essential contribution to the learning process. The analysis above clarifies the importance of the one-to-one conversation between teacher and student, but lectures to large numbers are now the norm. We pin our hopes on the new technologies to fill the gap, but it is a forlorn hope.

The promise of multimedia

At the Open University in the UK multimedia courses have been in operation for over 20 years. In this context, 'multimedia' has always meant using several media — print, audio, tutorial, video and computer materials — in the integrated delivery of a course. The term has now been hijacked by the advent of 'multi-media workstations' that combine all these media in a single workstation delivering text, digitised audio and digitised video as well as computer output via a computer monitor. Open University course materials that deliver these forms of communication via the separate media of print, audio-cassette or radio, and video-cassette or television, must now be referred to as 'multiple media' to distinguish the two.

In a distance-learning university, academics have to be very inventive to overcome the absence, at least for much of the time, of what I have argued is the most crucially important teaching device, the one-to-one tutorial. Using the strengths of each medium for persuasive presentation of the rhetorical argument, together with the interactive devices referred to above, and supporting these with asynchronous text-based tutorials in the form of tutor-marked assignments, and occasional face-to-face teaching at study centres and summer schools, the Open University has been able to achieve a high standard of degree-level study at a distance. But there are still students who drop-out, and the standard of student attainment can always be improved, so there is a continual programme to further exploit the educational media in the enhancement of student learning. As the media and delivery systems proliferate, new combinations are continually explored:

audio-vision	— audio-cassette talking through text-based materials
interactive video-cassette	— video-cassette material plus related activities set for students to do
interactive audio	— computer program with random access to CD-ROM-based audio material
interactive video	— computer program with random access to video-disc-based material
hypermedia	— hypertext program providing associative links within structured text, audio and video material
audio-graphics	— telephone tutoring on one telephone line plus computer-based data link on another giving tutor and student interactive access to the same computer screen
computer conferencing	— modem or cable data link between computers installed with conferencing software giving tutor and students access to the same text messages
interactive satellite tv	— television broadcast using audio-conferencing between studio-based tutor and home-based students.

All these may have their place in the provision of open and distance learning, for either pedagogical or logistical reasons or both. From the conversational framework developed earlier we could deduce that the ideal media combination would be a 'computer-mediated-audio-graphic-tutorial-hypermedia-simulation-conference', which offers experiential learning with 'pre-emptively adapted discussion' of it through the computer based tutorial-simulation, plus access to a database library via the hypermedia, plus synchronous discussion of some experiential interaction via the audio-graphics, plus asynchronous discussion through the computer conference. Such a work-station does not exist. Similar prototypes are being explored from within education, but unless industry and commerce develop a need for such a technology it is unlikely to develop very far.

As hypermedia systems become more widespread, offering computer-based access to large volumes of text, audio and video material, stored on hard disc or CD-ROM, there is an increasing expectation that this will act as the multimedia workstation that supplies all a student could need. It is important to critically assess the wisdom of this expectation. It is debatable whether students would accept screen-based text instead of print-based text to work from — screens are not equal to the 'desk-top' metaphor they aspire to, either in quality or in size, and that degradation will have pedagogical consequences we can only guess at, because the issue has not attracted much research. Secondly, the logistics of using computer-based materials are considerably more complex than those for using print. These two issues alone are enough for us to question the value of the single-workstation approach to delivering study materials. The third issue, in line with the focus of this chapter, is the pedagogical value of hypermedia, one form of the new 'multimedia workstation'.

Two important features of personal computer systems come together in hypermedia — their now large information storage capacity, and the new software formats referred to as hypertext. Both CD-ROM and hard disc systems offer such large storage capacity that it is possible to store whole books, to digitise audio and store, for example, long passages of speech, and to digitise video which, being more information-hungry than audio, can be stored as short chunks of, for example, key dynamic sequences. So the multimedia workstation can offer access to a small library of information using several media.

The type of access it offers determines the aspects of the learning it supports. If it is simply an indexed database of information, then it works in exactly the same way as a library of print materials, offering a description of the teacher's viewpoint on the subject, but is neither adaptive to student needs (except pre-emptively), nor interactive nor reflective. The addition of a hypertext system changes the nature of the access. The database may be indexed, but also makes extensive use of cross-reference between items, or chunks within the stucture, and also allows the user to make their own cross-references and to add annotations as they wish. The latter feature gives rise to some interesting claims for hypertext/hypermedia systems:

> hypertext enables learners to construct, organise and convey personal knowledge . . . learners help to construct the knowledge base [which] is therefore adapted by the learner to make it more meaningful   (Jonassen, 1991).

But cross-referencing and annotating are activities that have always been available to the student studying from text. Does hypermedia really offer anything more than a very small library, a piece of paper and a pencil? These educational provisions, while being recognised as important throughout the history of education, are seldom dignified with the rhetoric of constructivist theories of learning, for the very good reason that while they *allow* learners to 'construct, organise and convey personal knowledge', they certainly do not *ensure* that this happens. That is why the traditional methods of library, paper and pencil have been supplemented with complementary teaching activities, such as assignments with feedback in the form of marks or assessment grades, or tutorials, each of which *require* the student to construct, organise and convey their personal knowledge. A hypertext system offers no such motivation, nor does it offer any pedagogical support for the student trying to make the intellectual leap that links one idea to another, nor can it monitor the validity of the link they make.

The freedom to browse the intellectual territories created by these systems sounds delightful to the subject expert, who already possesses a detailed conceptual map of the subject, but to the novice struggling to understand what kind of territory it is, and what counts as a link between ideas, it could be a nightmare of confusion. When offered an indexed sequential discourse in a new subject, students typically take the default option provided by the author, and fail to rearrange that order, whether it be print or computer-based material (Laurillard, 1984). Insofar as a small library plus pencil and paper might be sufficient educational support for a student, as it often can be, and assuming that the particular selection made to stock its very small library is well-targeted for the task in hand, and assuming that the user has access to the necessary technology, then hypermedia is a convenient option. But the support it offers the learner is confined to controlled access to a description of the teacher's conception.

Summary

Using multiple media for the delivery of media-based course materials allows us to target each medium on the aspect of the learning process it best supports. In combination, these media are certainly an improvement on lectures, at least. Each one has its strengths, as the comparative analysis showed, and none can adequately support every learning activity the student needs to undertake to be sure of attaining a good understanding. Students contribute a great deal themselves to the learning process, making their own links between theoretical description and experiential examples, reflecting on the underlying structure of the teacher's discourse, practising the representation of their description of the world in the relevant academic language. But because students do not always manage to do all this for themselves, they need support, and not just in the aspect of the learning process that one particular medium happens to address, but in all the component activities all the time. That is why each medium has to be used in the context of its integration with any of the others that can complement the support it provides.

As all universities are beginning to require their students to access a range of media, independently of the close support of a lecturer, it is important that an understanding of the limitations as well as the potential of each medium guides their use. If this is not so, we are more likely to find 'closed' than 'open' versions of academic learning offered to students. Technology can be used to foster independent learning, but only if we create the conditions in which all four components of the academic learning process — discursive, adaptive, interactive and reflective — are stimulated and adequately supported.

References

Durbridge, N. (1984) 'Developing the use of video cassettes in the Open University' in Henderson, E. and Nathenson, M. (eds.) *Independent Learning in Higher Education*, Inglewood Cliffs, New Jersey, USA, Educational Technology Publications.

Jonassen, D. (1991) 'Hypertext as instructional design'. *Educational Technology Research and Development*, **39**, (1) pp. 83–92.

Laurillard, D. M. (1984) 'Interactive video and the control of learning', *Educational Technology*, **24**, (6) pp. 7–15.

Laurillard, Diana (1993) *Rethinking University Teaching: A Framework for the Effective Use of Educational Technology*, London, Routledge.

Lockwood, F. G. (1989) 'A course developer in action — a reassessment of activities in texts' in Parer, M. (ed.) *Development, Design and Distance Education*, Churchill, Victoria, Australia, Centre for Distance Learning, Gippsland Institute of Advanced Education.

Note

1   An earlier version of this paper was published as 'Balancing the Media' in the *Journal of Educational Television*, 1993.

20 Drop-out — understandable, predictable or merely inevitable?

Alan Woodley

Introduction

Open learning is being taken up with increasing enthusiasm by governments and employers alike. This is understandable because it appears to offer an inexpensive solution to the need for more education and training. However, for this enthusiasm to be justified, the proponents of open learning need to demonstrate that effective learning is taking place. In part this means showing that learners from the appropriate target groups have acquired the desired skills and knowledge. However, if open learning is to be shown to be cost-effective rather than merely inexpensive, then much more attention must be paid to success rates.

In the heyday of private correspondence colleges, little was known about drop-out rates because few statistics were published. A popular story in educational circles was that most colleges only remained solvent because of high student drop-out. If all the students who paid their registration fee sent in their assignments for marking, the profit margin would disappear. Which, if any, colleges, actually displayed such a callous indifference to the fortunes of their students is open to question, but what is apparent is that today's 'open' and 'distance learning' schemes are obliged to take the matter of student progress very seriously. Employers who run their own schemes want to ensure that it is a sound investment, and where the programme relies upon subsidies from public funds there is also a need to justify continued funding. Also, on strictly humanitarian grounds, any programme which is based on the philosophy of 'open-ness' should be concerned about its drop-out rate.

To the extent that open learning involves adults studying over significant periods of time, then a certain level of drop-out is to be expected. Adult students are generally volunteers and, no matter how well the course is designed, some will decide that it is not for them and will leave. Others will bow to competing demands in the home or workplace, while others will experience sudden crises that make study impossible. In cases where open learning is combined with open entry, it is probable that some will find the material too challenging. However, while some drop-out seems to be inevitable, the variations in rates between open learning programmes, and between courses within programmes, indicate that the actual drop-out rate is not fixed and encourage us to believe that it can be influenced.

In our experience an institution's concern with drop-out is sporadic rather than continuous. The invisibility of the phenomenon means that relatively high levels of drop-out can be tolerated but panics occur when a particular course is seen to have a drop-out rate well above the average, or when drop-out rates in general are greater than in the previous year. During these panics it is common for the wrong questions to be asked and for simplistic solutions to be put forward. Drop-out is actually a very complex phenomenon and can be looked at in a number of ways. In this chapter we attempt to illuminate the problem by isolating what appear to be the key questions and by suggesting certain explanatory frameworks.

Defining drop-out

'Drop-out' is a term frequently used in a variety of educational contexts and, by and large, people share a general conception of what it means. Roughly speaking it concerns students who start a course but do not complete it. However, there is wide variation in how the term is applied in practice and especially in the area of open and distance learning. Which students are considered to have started the course? Those who accept the offer of a place? Those who make the first fee payment? Those who turn up to the first class? Those who send in the first assignment? Withdrawal during the first stages of a distance course can be quite high and choice of a baseline will crucially affect drop-out rate calculations.

Again non-completion of a course can take many forms. As well as students who formally withdraw there are those who effectively 'choose' to withdraw by not attending classes, not submitting assignments, not attending exams, not paying fees, etc. Withdrawal can also be made compulsory by the institution if the student breaches certain regulations or fails to make the required academic progress.

How you choose to define 'drop-out' will depend upon the nature of the course and the definitions used by courses elsewhere with which you wish to make comparisons. It is then up to you to state the definition, to explain its underlying rationale and to apply it consistently. For illustration we outline below an attempt to do this in the context of the OU undergraduate programme.

Example: Defining drop-out in the Open University undergraduate programme

'Drop-out' relates to performance in a given year rather than to 'graduation rates' or 'continuation' from one academic year to the next. Even within a given year there are various ways of defining and measuring student performance. Four measures of performance are commonly used in the OU context, where the study year is from February to October, and students initially register in the year preceding their first year.

(i) *Non-completion of final registration*
This only concerns new undergraduates. The number not completing final registration is expressed as a percentage of those who were initially registered on 1 January of the study year.

(ii) *Withdrawal rate*
Students are considered to have withdrawn if they finally registered but did not sit the end-of-year exam.

(iii) *Failure rate*
Students are considered to have failed if they sat the end-of-year exam but did not gain a course credit.

(iv) *Overall wastage rate*
This is the percentage of students who finally registered but who did not gain a course credit. In other words it includes both 'withdrawal' and 'failure'.

A further complication is that each of these four rates can be 'student-based' or 'course-based'. In the former case, students are generally considered to be unsuccessful if they do not gain any course credit in a given year. Therefore, a student who has withdrawn from three courses but has passed one is still classified as 'successful'. However, in the case of the Open University where the great majority only register for one course, the student-based and course-based analyses actually produce very similar results.

Table 20.1 summarises the performance of Open University undergraduates in 1992.

On the face of it this table presents reasonable and objective measures of student performance. However, even these need interpretation and critical assessment. First, the distinction between 'failure' and 'withdrawal' is not a clear-cut one. Are those students who do not sit the exam because they think they will fail very different from those who actually fail? Secondly, the decision to allow new students a trial period of initial registration, while justifiable on education and moral grounds has profound effects on the statistics. If the percentages in Table 20.1 were based on all new initially registered students then the overall wastage rate for this group would be 45 per cent rather than 22 per cent. Finally, these are performance rates as measured for administrative purposes and do not necessarily reflect the subjective perceptions of the students themselves. For example those who were not studying with the intention of gaining a course credit or who left to transfer to another course would probably not consider themselves to be 'drop-outs'.

As a result of inconsistent definitions in the research literature and variations in regulations between course and institutions, it is impossible to use precise terminology when discussing this topic. For the remainder of this chapter we will use 'drop-out' in a very loose sense to describe all those who do not successfully complete a course for whatever reason.

Table 20.1 OU undergraduate performance in 1992 (course-based)

		Total %	New students %	Continuing students %
(i)	Non-completion of final registration (Base = all initially registered)	NA	28	NA
(ii)	Withdrawal rate (Base = all finally registered)	22	15	24
(iii)	Failure rate (Base = all who sat exam)	6	5	6
(iv)	Overall wastage rate (Base = all finally registered)	27	20	29

Is drop-out a problem?

Glatter and Wedell (1971) concluded from their review of research around the world that drop-out on correspondence courses is much higher than would be expected in full-time courses and that it is particularly heavy in the early stages of a course. Drop-out rates varied with the length and type of course involved but sometimes ran as high as 70 per cent.

Student performance for OU undergraduates in a given year has been shown in Table 20.1. Wastage rates in terms of failure to graduate can never be calculated exactly because students are allowed to accumulate credits at their own pace. However, it can be said that 57 per cent of those who finally registered as new students in 1971 have been awarded an Ordinary degree, and that the final figure is unlikely to be much higher. It seems that figures for later intakes are likely to be closer to 40 per cent. Graduation rates at other distance teaching universities in Canada, the Netherlands, South Africa and Germany appear to be around 10 per cent.

The Open University provides a wide variety of courses. While we have concentrated on undergraduates, there are actually more students studying on other programmes. In 1992 the wastage rates on its taught Masters level courses and on the School of Management Certificate and Diploma short courses were somewhat lower than for the undergraduate programme, being around 20 per cent. Wastage on short post-graduate level Associate courses in the area of computers in commerce and industry, were slightly higher at around 28 per cent. When we consider those students taking single undergraduate courses as Associate students then the wastage rates were higher still at 57 per cent, but it must be remembered that many of the students will have enrolled on these courses with no intention of completing the assessment component.

Clearly an institution will have problems finding and interpreting published statistics on drop-out rates for courses like its own, with similar student populations. In the absence of directly comparable courses elsewhere, much can be learned by looking at patterns and variations in performance on courses within your own institution. For example, Table 20.2 shows that in 1981 the wastage rates for OU maths and technology courses were above average at each of the three course levels, whereas for arts and social science courses they were consistently below average. (Wastage rates also appear to increase with course level, but it must be remembered that the Foundation rates are artificially low due to the 'initial registration' procedure for new students

Table 20.2　OU overall wastage rates in 1992, analysed by faculty and course level (course-based)

	Foundation %	Second level %	Third and fourth level %
Arts	18	27	25
Social Science	21	25	26
Education	NA	29	36
Maths	25	30	37
Science	23	27	36
Technology	27	32	33
Average	22	28	31

that was mentioned earlier.) One response to these figures would be to concentrate on improving higher level courses, especially in maths, science and technology. However, there is actually greater scope for reducing the volume of student wastage on Foundation and second level courses because that is what the great majority of students are taking.

Changes over time are also of interest. Figure 20.1 shows that there have been important trends within the OU undergraduate programme. On third and fourth level courses, for example, wastage rates increased consistently for seven years, and then fell in each of the next four years. If drop-out on your own course is increasing each year, it is clearly important to know whether this is a departure from or part of the prevailing trend within your institution. It is also vital, of course, that the institution should attempt to understand the causes of such trends.

Explaining drop-out

'Explaining' drop-out can take a number of forms. One approach is to attempt to identify which types of student are more likely to drop-out. For example, the performance of OU undergraduates has been shown to be related to previous educational qualifications, age, occupation, sex, region, credits held, length of study and workload (Woodley and Parlett, 1983).

Another approach is to examine the courses themselves and to look for those features which are associated with high or low wastage rates. In the case of the OU we have already looked at variations by course level and by faculty, but it has also been shown that courses tend to have high wastage rates if they have no summer school, are half rather than full credits, have been

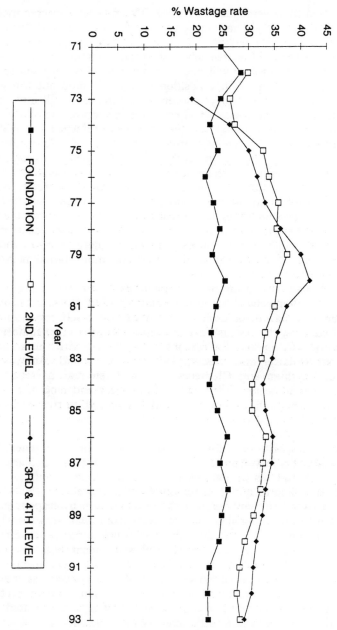

Figure 20.1 Overall wastage rates at the OU over time, analysed by level of course

presented for several years, have few TV and radio programmes, have few students, or have few set textbooks (Woodley and Parlett, 1983).

These approaches are likely to shed some light on the drop-out phenomenon but they will not be conclusive. It is most unlikely that you will ever be in a position to say that drop-out will be lower on all courses displaying a certain feature, or that all students displaying characteristic 'x' will complete the course and all those not displaying it will drop out. Furthermore, even when a variable is strongly related to student progress, there are often difficulties in interpretation. For example, the relationship between previous qualifications and OU performance suggests that academic ability or at least educational experience is a determining factor, but there are other possibilities. Those with low qualifications tend to be in jobs where they are less likely to receive encouragement and financial support from their employer. As they receive no advanced standing they will also face many more years of study before gaining a degree, so there may be motivational factors involved.

We can also attempt to explain drop-out by asking the students themselves for the reasons behind their decision. When this has been done in the past using self-completion mail surveys, the results have suggested that the great majority of students drop out for reasons unconnected with the actual courses (Glatter and Wedell, 1971; Woodley and McIntosh, 1980; Phythian and Clements, 1982). Their reasons tend to centre on domestic and work circumstances and lack of time. However, we believe that such findings should be treated with a great deal of caution.

1. The response rates for drop-out questionnaires are generally low. This leaves great scope for response bias, particularly if those students who are experiencing academic difficulties are less willing to give their reasons for withdrawal.
2. Many researchers feel that the reasons given by respondents tend to be rationalisations. It seems likely that students who find the courses too difficult or who fail to put much effort into them will seek to protect their self-esteem by attributing their withdrawal to external pressures such as lack of time.
3. Even a 'genuine' response of lack of time conceals as much as it reveals. In the sense that it means that students prefer to spend their time on other activities, it is clearly related to the perceived value and interest of the course itself.
4. When main reasons are 'unpacked', features of the courses themselves are often revealed as contributory factors. For

instance, 'increased work pressures' might be expanded as follows: 'Work pressures meant that I had less time for study — but I guess that I would still have stuck with the course if I had found it more interesting.'

Changes in goals or intentions may also arise from the course itself: 'I decided not to become an accountant because I realised from the course that I wouldn't cope with the maths.'

5. Certain factors can be attributed to the institution or to the students themselves. For instance, if students cannot cope with the level of the course, they may blame either themselves or their teachers. It seems likely that mature students returning to education with some trepidation would adopt the former position.

Addressing complexity

The researchers who have approached the problem by asking people who have dropped out for their reasons could be said to have adopted a straight forward 'medical' approach, where you identify the cause and then the cure. In part this has been relatively unproductive because of the methodological problems outlined above. But even if these methodological problems can be overcome, there are unlikely to be any simple solutions, as when medical researchers find a cure for a particular disease. This is because the 'causes' of adult student drop-out are many and various, spreading across personal, social, domestic, academic and institutional areas. As an introduction, we list below some of the factors which can underlie drop-out from the students' perspective.

1. **Course factors**
   — Course found to be too difficult or not sufficiently advanced.
   — Course required too many hours study each week, i.e. 'overloaded'.
   — Course badly designed and/or taught.
   — Content found uninteresting.
   — Content not as expected from the course description.
2. **Institutional factors**
   — Inadequate classrooms, equipment, parking, accommodation, etc.
   — Administrative errors, e.g. not sent the teaching material.
   — Required to leave by the institution

3. **Study environment factors**
   (a) *Unforeseen/unplanned changes*
   — Personal/domestic changes such as illness of student or relative, change in marital status, having a baby, having to care for ageing relatives, moving house.
   — Work changes such as increase in working hours or responsibilities, more travel, e.g. sent abroad, became unemployed, changed job, started work.
   — Other changes such as withdrawal of financial support, loss of a quiet place to study, clash with other leisure activity.
   (b) *Chronic factors*
   — Little time or energy given to other domestic, work and leisure commitments.
   — Lack of money.
   — Lack of encouragement by spouse or employer.
   — Transport problems.

4. **Personal blame**
   — I was too disorganised.
   — I was not clever enough.
   — I lacked the necessary study skills/background knowledge.
   — I was too lazy.
   — I lacked self-confidence.
   — I had unreal expectations of the course.
   — I couldn't face the assessment/exam.
   — I took on too much along with any other commitments.

5. **Motivational factors**
   — Student no longer needs to complete the course as original goal has been achieved, e.g. gained promotion, learned something about painting.
   — Original goal has changed, e.g. enrolled on course in order to become a teacher but now has decided to remain in present job.
   — Goal met better elsewhere, e.g. student transfers to a course elsewhere which better meets his/her needs and circumstances.
   — Realised goal would not be achieved, e.g. enrolled on class in order to meet people but did not get on with other students.
   — Other goal has taken priority, e.g student decides to spend more time on another hobby, trade union activities, voluntary work, etc.

Nor is it simply a case of determining how many students dropped out due to each of the factors on the list. For any given student there will generally be several interacting factors at work. Furthermore, the factors themselves are often ambiguous and contradictory

— Some will drop-out because the course is too difficult, others because it is too easy.
— Some will give the same reason for dropping out that others give for persisting with their studies.
— High previous qualifications indicate that a student can cope academically but this may also mean that they do not need to complete the course.
— Unpredictable life events can affect any student.

If we are to arrive at a more complete understanding of why an individual drops out, it seems that we must move beyond the usual 'check list' approach. We must take into account what participation means to an individual and the total context in which he or she is studying. We must treat dropping out as a complex process in that it generally involves numerous inter-connected causal factors and often builds up over time. Finally, we must have a greater awareness of how people explain their behaviour, both to themselves and to other people. We outline below a model which begins to deal with some of these complexities.

To the extent that they have consciously thought through their decision to enrol, mature students have said to themselves:

— This course appears to offer me what I want, or at least it is the best one available for my purposes.
— I can cope with the level of the course.
— I can afford the cost of the course.
— The course fits in with my personal/social/domestic/work commitments.
— I am prepared to put in the time and effort required by the course.

Essentially they have performed an individual cost-benefit analysis and decided that it is worth their while to enrol. However, this is a continuing analysis and, as the course begins, they learn more about what the course actually offers and what the real 'costs' of attending are in terms of money, time, domestic rearrangements, curtailment of other activities, etc. Also new factors may enter into the analysis such as changes in their personal or work situations.

Although we are not suggesting that students are constantly engaged in a rational, mechanistic weighing-up of the costs and benefits involved in continuing with a course, it is certainly the case that all students are subject to a complex interplay of positive factors which encourage them to continue and negative factors which push them towards withdrawal. What the relevant factors are will depend upon the individuals concerned and the courses that they are taking, but by way of example we present in Figure 20.2 the 'positive' and 'negative' factors acting on an imaginary individual studying with the Open University.

Each student will have a different array of factors which is relevant to his or her situation, and each factor will be weighted in importance by the individual. Drop-out will occur when, in some sense, the sum of the negative factors outweighs the sum of the positive ones. Some students will begin their course with the positive factors barely outweighing the negative, and these 'marginal' students will be particularly vulnerable. Any small new negative factor such as a cold classroom or missing one tutorial may tip the balance. In other cases, the positive factors greatly exceed the negative ones and it will take a dramatic new negative factor, such as a death in the family or being sent abroad to work, to cause withdrawal.

When students are asked why they dropped out, they typically give the most important or most recent negative factor as the reason. In many cases this is a valid and sufficient response. For instance, if a person says that he has moved to a town 100 miles away, he is unlikely to return each week to attend his evening class. However, many of the reasons, while valid in themselves, do not provide a complete explanation. For example, while moving house, changing jobs, pregnancy, etc. may be given as reasons for dropping out, there will also be students who underwent similar experiences but still persisted with their course. To understand these different outcomes, one needs a deeper awareness of the various positive and negative forces operating within a given individual, and the weight which that individual assigns to them.

Negative factors	Positive factors
— Wants to spend more time with family	— Wants degree to get promotion
— Course is very difficult	— Likes to finish something once started
— Fees are high	— Very interested in the subject once started
— Doesn't like course tutor	— Spouse is very encouraging
— A part-time degree is available in a nearby town	— Employer allows time off for studying and summer school

Figure 20.2

Having acknowledged the complexity of the problem, one can attempt to devise more appropriate research methodologies. For example, if one wants to understand dropping out from the point of view of the student, it is most unlikely that the complexities of the processes suggested above can be unravelled via self-completion questionnaires mailed out several months after the student actually dropped out. What is required is a longitudinal study where students are contacted early on then spoken to at intervals throughout the course. In this way one can build up contact with the students so they will reflect upon their own experience and will feel able to relate it in an open fashion to the researcher.

Another approach is to start with a theory of student drop-out, to collect data on variables related to this theory, and then to construct complex multivariate statistical models of the process itself. This has been attempted by distance education researchers such as Kember (1989), building on the work of Tinto (1975). In the final section of this chapter I am going to outline another possible approach that could be described as 'actuarial'. Here the aim is not to understand the causes of drop-out, nor the drop-out process, but to identify 'at risk' students as they enter the system. This is done using information concerning the known characteristics of the students and how, historically, these characteristics related to student progress.

Identifying 'at risk' students

A computer file was constructed that contained records of a random sample of ten thousand Open University student courses. These were Foundation Courses taken by new undergraduates who entered the University in 1990 and 1991, approximately 56 per cent of which resulted in the award of a course credit. Each record contained variables denoting the course subject, the course result and various characteristics of the student taking that course. The data was analysed using 'Logistic Regression'. This is a form of multivariate statistical modelling which deals with dichotomous dependent variables, in this case 'pass/fail', and aims to produce an equation which combines the possible explanatory variables in such a way as to predict which of the two categories a given case will fall into.

The 'Forward Stepwise' option was selected for the logistic regression which means that variables were added to the equation one at a time on the basis of level of statistical significance at each 'step'. The first variable included in the equation was a person's previous educational qualifications. As one might expect, the higher a person's qualifications were, the more likely the person was to gain a credit. Given that a person's educational qualifications were known, the best variable to add next to the equation in order to improve predictions would be their occupation. In this case the implication was that if an unemployed person and a member of the armed forces had the same educational qualifications, the unemployed person would be less likely to gain a course credit. Members of other occupational groups fell within these two extremes.

A further four variables were added to the equation on the same basis. In order, these were the course (arts, social science, maths, science or technology), ethnic origin, age and 'workload' (the number of course credits being attempted). The later a variable was added to the equation, the less it added to the accuracy of the prediction. Thus although the model suggests that those with a heavier workload were less likely to gain a credit, the fact that 'workload' was entered into the equation at the sixth step indicates that it was a relatively unimportant factor compared to those entered earlier. Gender appeared to have no predictive power and was not entered into the equation at all.

As an illustration, let us take a 45-year-old white student with an Higher National Diploma and in a technical occupation, who is taking the social science foundation course and that course alone. On the basis of the equation derived from our model we would predict that this student would have an 82% chance of gaining a course credit. Of course, the key question is how accurate are such predictions.

The equation can be used to assign a chance of success to each student which will range from 0% to 100%. If we classify all those with a 50% or greater chance of success as 'likely to succeed' and those below 50% as 'likely to fail', how accurate would we be when we compare students' actual performance with their predicted performance? In fact, using our model we would have allocated 63% of the students correctly. Of the remainder, some students failed whereas the model predicted success (26%), and 11% passed despite a prediction of failure.

In our study, 56% of the students gained a course credit. On this basis one could say that the best prediction for any single student would be that they would pass. Overall one would predict that all students would pass and one would be correct in 56% of cases. Judged by these harsh standards, our model's 63% accuracy does not appear to be much better than what could be achieved by guess work. However, in the real world when one is trying to decided which students might need special help or which students to admit, such an overall assessment of accuracy might be inappropriate. The figures in Table 20.3 show that when one divides the students into bands according to their predicted chances of success and looks at their actual performance, then a higher degree of accuracy is gained at the extremes. Only two out of ten of those with an extremely low predicted chance of success actually gained a course credit. At the other end of the scale, some eight out of ten of those deemed most likely to succeed actually did so.

If a reasonably robust statistical model can be built, and if the information it depends upon is available at the the pre-admission stage, then this technique can be used to determine which prospective students have only a slight chance of succeeding. These might be offered preparatory courses or other forms of support, or they might be advised to take some other course. While the model might not be accurate enough to be used as the sole means of determining who is admitted, it can be demonstrably superior to assessments based on single variables such as previous educational qualifications. For example, take our hypothetical student who had an 82% chance of success. Now take another student who had similar educational qualifications, but who was black, unemployed, aged 21 and was taking technology along with another foundation course. According to our model that person would have only an 8% chance of success!

A statistical model of drop-out can also be used for broader institutional research purposes. For example, an institution may discover that drop-out rates are increasing over time, but wonders how much of this could be attributed to changes in the student population. A certain course has a high drop-out rate, but is this because it attracts large numbers of 'high risk' students? If courses which use TV seem to have lower drop-out rates, how much of this result is due to the fact that TV is used more in different subject

Table 20.3 Comparing predicted and actual student progress

Predicted chance of success %	% Gaining a course credit
0–29	17.4
30–39	25.5
40–49	36.8
50–59	44.1
60–69	54.3
70–79	67.4
80–89	72.6
90–100	77.6

areas? With multi-variate models the effects of other causal factors can be controlled for in a systematic way, to predict an expected drop-out rate in a given situation and then to compare this with the actual rate. The model presented in this chapter was actually used to investigate why the drop-out rate in one Open University region was markedly higher than in others. It was discovered that the model could explain approximately one half of the difference. The implication one could draw from this finding was that a significant portion of that region's higher drop-out rate was due to the types of students it attracted and the courses they chose. However, other factors were clearly at work in that region — factors that might concern student characteristics not included in the model, or the provision of teaching and support in that region.

Discussion

In answer to the questions posed by the chapter title, I would say that a certain level of drop-out is inevitable, but we can attempt to understand it and minimise it. At the very least we should be monitoring it carefully and looking for patterns, trends and 'blips'. When unacceptable levels of drop-out are discovered, it may indeed have been caused by a single identifiable factor such as a badly designed assignment or an incorrect course description in the prospectus. However, experience at the Open University suggests that it is more usually a multi-causal problem that requires multiple, partial solutions. The corollary of this is that researchers must acknowledge the complexity of the phenomenon being examined and draw upon an array of research techniques which can make a contribution in this area.

   In this chapter we have outlined a statistical procedure that might be worth considering as an additional tool in our struggle to deal with the problem of student drop-out. It is not offered as a panacea. Such models are extremely unlikely to be accurate enough to offer any degree of certainty in terms of the progress made by a given individual. They rely upon the collection of background information and progress data on thousands of students over a long period of time. They offer little in the way of causal explanations of the process of student drop-out.

   The best way to decide whether a prospective student should be admitted, guided to a preparatory course or a course in another institution, or offered extra support, is almost certainly through a face-to-face meeting with an experienced admissions tutor. However, this may not always be possible for reasons of geography or sheer numbers, and a statistical model might be useful for selecting which people require admissions counselling.

Experienced admissions tutors will hold subjective models of their own concerning drop-out. For example, they may have observed that young students seem more likely to drop-out, as are those with low educational qualifications and unemployed people. However, it is extremely unlikely that they can have an accurate perception of how and to what extent these factors are cumulative. A statistical model can go beyond the limits of personal feelings and experience.

Finally, as we have demonstrated in the text, models can be used at broader policy levels. If an institution is trying to assess the likely impact of changes in its course or student profiles on drop-out rates, or if it is trying to assess the performance of certain courses or of its various subunits, then multi-variate modelling is to be preferred to crude 'league tables'.

References

Glatter, R. and Wedell, E. (1971) *Study by Correspondence*, London, Longman.

Kember, D. (1989) 'A longitudinal-process-model of drop-out from distance education'. *Journal of Distance Education*, **60** (3) pp. 280–301.

Phythian, T. and Clements, M. (1982) 'Drop-out from third level maths courses'. *Teaching at a Distance*, **21**, pp. 35–44.

Tinto, V. (1975) 'Drop-out from higher education: a theoretical synthesis of recent research'. *Review of Educational Research*, **45** (1) pp. 89–125.

Woodley, A. and McIntosh, N. (1980) *The Door Stood Open — an Evaluation of the Open University Younger Students Pilot Scheme*', Lewes, Falmer Press.

Woodley, A. and Parlett, M. (1983) 'Student drop-out'. *Teaching at a Distance*, **24**, pp. 2–23, Autumn.

Part IV
International issues and developments

21 Distance education across national borders

Robin Mason

The need for international courses

A number of factors account for the steady growth in institutions offering courses to distant students in other countries, whether to one other institution half way around the world, or to dispersed students in many distant countries, or to their own nationals resident in other countries. Many of these factors are financial: the need to find new markets because of the dwindling number of traditional students, the need for a larger market base to defray the cost of developing software, and the fact that it is cheaper to buy in courses than to develop them in-house. Other factors are technological: the development of a global communications infrastructure which permits affordable textual interaction and even videoconferencing via satellite. The amount of rhetoric about the need to share educational resources, to provide life-long learning and continuing professional updating for both the employed and the unemployed, and finally, to be aware that the whole world is our neighbour in the global economy, has also contributed to the general sense that educating beyond national boundaries is no longer a specialist activity. Indeed, institutions without international connections are the exception rather than the rule in some countries.

From the learner's point of view, there is the cachet of a degree from a foreign institution; there is increased choice of courses offered by more flexible and open distance teaching methods; there may also be a need to broaden the international profile of one's curriculum vitae.

Anyone wanting to take advantage of the large European
job market will in future require further qualifications
over and above his [sic] professional ones. These will
have more to do with the private side, with so called 'key
qualifications' which make him 'fit for Europe' (Hernaut,
1993, p.96).

These 'key qualifications' include the ability to work in other
languages, but equally, the ability to work in other cultures. Multi-
cultural understanding is a significant factor for the 'new age'
curriculum vitae.

In some respects, therefore, international distance education is
meeting the needs of both the providers and the receivers.

The range of provision

At the primary and secondary school level, group email schemes
linking many countries are very common. Children work on
joint projects in such fields as environmental studies, history
and science. Many of the schemes are specifically designed to
introduce children to other cultures, by preparing material on
their own culture to exchange with other schools.

At the tertiary level, international video-conferencing courses
are becoming commonplace. Their popularity is partly due to
the fact that this medium does not challenge the traditional
teaching mode: lecturing with pre-prepared drawings or writing
on a blackboard/whiteboard during the session. Student numbers
can easily be doubled by adding a distant lecture room.

The area of greatest activity, however, is undoubtedly that
of continuing and professional education. Niche and specialist
markets — such as telecommunications — need a wide catchment
area to provide a continuing intake of students. MBAs are also very
popular as a distance education course rather than a campus-based
facility, and many institutions which offer MBAs have students
abroad, usually supported by computer conferencing, but a few
by video-conferencing.

Language teaching is, of course, an obvious subject for
intercultural teaching (see, for example, Baumgratz, 1993). Interactive technologies are frequently used so that students can practice
with native speakers. Specialist language learning, e.g. for bankers
or for business studies, combine subject specific material with
the second language in order to increase motivation and provide
authentic learning situations.

Cross-cultural communication

The truism about travel broadening the mind reflects the fact that we normally tend to communicate with those who share a common outlook, language, belief structure and value system. Most of this commonality actually passes unnoticed, until we find ourselves communicating with people who have a different culture. Then, lack of understanding, or more significantly, misunderstanding, frequently arises.

However, people from different cultures are not necessarily from different countries. Multi-cultural, multi-ethnic communities exist in all countries and large cities. Some would even say that cultural differences within societies are increasing. Differences in life-style and in outlook between any two European cities have definitely decreased, but they may have been replaced by other cultural differences between groups of people *within* any of these cities (e.g. the old and the young, professionals and the unemployed). (Verma and Entzinger, 1992).

Learning is well accepted as a dynamic process in which all of one's life experiences are brought to bear. Inevitably, cultural differences will influence this learning process. As the current multi-cultural mix of many societies continues to grow, so will the need to produce courses of a global perspective even for the national market.

Cultural imperialism

> Universities should not be involved in cultural imperialism. Knowledge should not be monopolized by one country or one institution. The search for global solutions requires universities to co-operate and to share information. International education should receive the support of national governments (Alladin, 1992, pp. 11–2).

The accusation of cultural imperialism has long been levelled at attempts to export courses outside national boundaries, particularly as most of the examples involved Western institutions providing courses for Third World countries. Recently, with extensive funding and pressure from the European Commission, there have been many more programmes for developing courses for a European market. Although the accusation still lingers — for example, in the dominance of the English language as the lingua franca in many instances, the amount of development work and the range of partners involved in the preparation, have brought intercultural distance education out of the closet and into the limelight. For example, The European Association of Distance Teaching Universities (EADTU) has promoted the development of joint courses in three areas: European law, business administration and the humanities. (For an account of the first such course in this area, see Wilson in this volume.) Through its DELTA programme (Developing European Learning through Technological Advance), the European Commission is sponsoring the Multimedia TeleSchools project (described later) and a wide variety of other technology-based courses with pan-European coverage.

A number of such courses have tried to tackle directly the problems of addressing a multi-cultural audience. One of the primary ways of preventing cultural bias is to use joint course teams from the participating countries to produce the courses. Another way is to translate courses, not just into another language, but also into another culture, by using national case studies, idioms and examples. Courses which rely on computer based technologies have sometimes been devised with a neutral interface — icons, colours, images with no strong cultural associations.

Some practitioners have come full turn on cultural neutrality after much negative experience searching for such a Holy Grail.

> We have only to look to the experience of satellite television to become aware of the diminution of quality that arises from trying to serve a mass audience of different cultural origins. In trying to devise generic courseware to try to please all of the people, we may end up with courseware which doesn't really satisfy any of the people (Dixon and Blin, 1992, p.732).

The alternative is to argue that the 'cultural flavour' of one country simply enhances the course, and encourages students to develop an independent attitude to knowledge acquisition. Anyone who has experience of intercultural course provision, however, has a raft of stories about misunderstandings arising from material with different connotations in another culture. Undoubtedly, the 'flavour' of one country can leave a bad taste in another.

Yet another alternative is to allow the learner (or the receiving institution) to 'version' the material to suit their own needs. For example, with computer-based courseware, students could choose the language, icons and keyboard configuration they required. With new developments in software, students could even indicate their cultural preferences and the courseware would present appropriate examples and illustrations.

Interactive technologies provide perhaps the best way out of the cultural imperialist taint. When students from several countries communicate — by text, voice or full motion video — it is possible to promote inter-cultural understanding along with subject understanding. Mason (1994) gives an account of these communication technologies and describes a number of applications.

Scenarios of intercultural courses

As outlined above, co-operative activities across national boundaries take a number of different forms. Many of these do not involve actual courses, such as the schools-based email projects, and various other research level interactions amongst peer groups. The range of course-based intercultural activities can be roughly categorised into the following types:

- *Franchise Type*: in which one partner designs, develops, examines and makes awards, while the other provides students and support mechanisms.
- *Marketplace Type*: in which one institution purchases course materials from the other, adapts and delivers them and examines learners and awards credits.
- *Collaborative Type*: in which several institutions jointly design and develop courses which they use in their respective institutions independently of each other.
- *Technology-Based Type*: in which students from other countries access the host institution via electronic communication (possibly enhanced by print materials, occasional videoconferences or even face-to-face meetings).

Although there are some clear distinctions between these types, in practice there are many overlaps. The 'franchise type' may appear to be a hang-over from the imperialist tradition, but in fact, any of the categories may have elements of inequality. Collaboration does not guarantee equality between the partners and their cultures, and can involve the dominance of one or two partners. The benefits and difficulties of these kinds of courses will be illuminated by specific examples.

The Open University in Eastern Europe — the franchise type

The UK Open University has begun a programme of offering a number of its Open Business School (OBS) courses to students in various Eastern European countries. The OBS received Know

How Fund support with the aim of passing on know how about western management to post-communist economies. Distance teaching of the sort pioneered by the OU was considered to be an appropriate means for reaching large numbers of students in Eastern Europe and Russia. (Farnes and Woodley, 1993).

The basis of the programme is that courses are translated into the national language, and that national case studies are exchanged for the UK examples. Although tutors are selected by the national institution to mark assignments and meet with students, some scripts and exam papers are translated into English for monitoring by the Open University.

As the main purpose of the programme is that Eastern Europeans have access to western management procedures, the situation is inevitably one of a dominant culture transfering its view of the world to a culture which seeks to emulate, at least its economic advantages. How successful has this transfer been?

Farnes and Woodley (1992; 1993) have carried out a number of evaluations, through student and tutor surveys, interviews and on-site visits. In Hungary, for example, they found that the courses work well for students in both small and large companies which are undergoing changes, but less well in organisations with fewer changes. One student said:

> In a centrally controlled company the boss would tell everybody what to do — one direction communication. The bosses are not consultation minded in spite of the fact that they sent us on the courses.

However, another was enthusiastic:

> I have to survive the recession; the knowledge from the courses is very useful in a small enterprise. It has helped me survive and given me ideas for surviving (Farnes and Woodley, 1992).

On the whole, students have rated the courses as being very relevant, and a high proportion have used the information to change aspects of their jobs, or to find more satisfying jobs (Farnes, Woodley and Ashby, 1993).

The Open Learning Institute of Hong Kong — the marketplace type

Great value is placed on educational qualifications in Hong Kong, for employment, promotion and possibly emigration. Consequently, Hong Kong boasts a great number of overseas educational programmes (Ngok and Lam, 1993), many of the 'franchise type' described above.

The Open Learning Institute, however, has developed the 'marketplace type', buying course materials from all over the world to meet some of its curricular needs. The producer of the materials is no more than a supplier, while the Open Learning Institute (OLI) takes complete responsibility for curriculum, delivery and assessment. Dhanarajan and Timmers (1993) have analysed a whole range of difficulties faced by institutions purchasing materials on the open market:

- Courses need a detailed listing of aims, major topics and headings, additional readings or other media.
- Poorly structured courses are much more costly to adapt.
- Digitised versions of the original material are much more desirable for purchasing in the 'marketplace type'.

Although the OLI predominantly buys courses written in English, this is an English for native speakers, not for those with English as a second language. The OLI must pay considerable attention to the readability of adapted courseware and to the reading skills of their expected students. Dhanarajan and Timmers (op. cit.) point out that there are many different readability scoring systems: counting the length of words and number of words used in a sentence are not sufficient to assess the way a piece of writing is comprehended by non-native speakers. Syntax, the use of passive constructions and complex prepositional phrases also affect the degree of complexity and consequent understanding by second language readers.

Dixon and Blin (1992) also found, in preparing software for non-native English speakers, that they needed to 'translate' English into the simplest prose possible:

> We used very short sentences and avoided complicated constructions as well as using 'small' words rather than 'big' words as much as we could. We stripped the material of all slang and we explained all abbreviations, and we provided an online glossary to give simple explanations of key terms. This process was quite complex since we had to be careful not to lose the sense of the material itself (op. cit. p.729).

Humour can be quite difficult to handle in cross-cultural courses. On the one hand, it provides interest and motivation for learners, but on the other, it can easily be misunderstood by non-native speakers.

Adapting courses which contain significant non-print material depends largely on the availability of equipment (e.g. computers, video recorders) amongst the student population. While distance educators are keen to develop multi-media course materials, they are often not saleable abroad.

While the 'marketplace type' scenario has many difficulties, especially cultural ones, the benefits for both producers and purchases are real — financial savings on course development, and the sense of sharing resources rather than continually re-creating the same material.

Multimedia teleschools — the collaborative type

In October 1992, a series of interactive television broadcasts for language learning in Europe was launched. These broadcasts were part of the Multimedia Teleschool Project (MTS), funded by the European Community DELTA Research programme. The MTS project addresses the current market for realistic distance learning systems, based on an optimal mix of telecommunications-based learning and tutoring.

The project has sixteen partners from five European countries; it also has the support of major European enterprises. The prime contractor is Berlitz International, the largest private language training institution worldwide, which has recently developed a new range of foreign language distance learning courses.

Sixteen one-hour live broadcasts — focusing on the range of topics contained in the two Berlitz distance learning courses, *English for Telecommunications* and *English for Banking* are being broadcast throughout Europe over a period of nine months by ARTE, Europe's new cultural channel as well as on EUROSTEP. ARTE transmits the programmes via satellite from its studio in Strasbourg, France.

A large number of employees of European enterprises are taking part in these courses. Using PCs at their workplaces, they make contributions during the live broadcasts, putting questions to the experts being interviewed, and answering questions asked by the tutors in the studio. A computer conferencing system links the participants in their European branches with each other and with the experts in the television studio. All participants receive their study letters and assignments from the Berlitz Distance Learning Centre in Eschborn, Germany via the computer conferencing system. They also use the system to return their completed assignments to their tutors. The system enables participants to communicate with their fellow students throughout Europe, allowing them to work in groups to complete study-based tasks.

A typical television broadcast might consist of a fifteen-minute presentation of the topic by a subject expert in the studio, fifteen minutes of filmed material on the same topic and about fifteen minutes of participants' contributions and questions which are sent to the studio via the conferencing system during the live broadcast.

This project is collaborative on a large scale, as the group includes the course providers, software developers, television programme designers and broadcasters, as well as the companies seeking training for their employees. Collaborative course development is well known to be fraught with inter-institutional rivalries (Kaye, 1991). The funding policy of the DELTA programme, nevertheless, supports only transnational collaborations. It remains to be seen whether the practice will continue after the extensive funding period for collaborative work comes to an end.

Online education and training — the technology-based type

As part of a COMMET project in training-the-trainers, a course delivered almost entirely via computer conferencing was developed by the London University Institute of Education and the Open University Institute of Educational Technology. The course is designed for teachers and trainers who want to develop their online skills and learn how to apply the medium of computer conferencing in their own context. The course is open to anyone with a first degree and access to a computer and telecommunications. The Institute of Education awards a graduate level certificate on completion.

To date, the course has attracted international participation primarily through notices passing on electronic bulletin boards. The 'multiplier' effect of this course has been significant in that many of the students have used it as a launching pad from which to design and run their own computer conferencing courses.

Interaction between student and tutor and amongst students is the hallmark of computer conferencing. This course has, on both occasions it has been run, been a remarkable example of this principle. The fifty students on each course have been divided into small groups to work together on set projects, to discuss readings and to prepare material for the whole group. The quality of discussion during various modules of the course, has been so outstanding that some students have found it very daunting to participate.

I had no idea I was going to find it so hard to join in — I enjoy the medium and have been using it for about eighteen

months and I have composed numerous messages off-line
only to chicken out after reading other comments, better
written, more concise etc. than my own.

Those students working in their second language were undoubtedly more reticent in their messages — in all but a few cases, these
students made fewer and shorter inputs. One of them commented:

It can be quite frustrating in [computer conferencing] that
some people always is very fast with their responses, specially
when you need more time yourself. . . . I have been very
quiet myself, due to problems with reading/writing English; I
therefore need a lot of time preparing before commenting on
anything.

Computer conferencing is usually considered to be a teaching
medium which favours reflective thinkers and non-native speakers,
because responses can be made at any time. Nevertheless, the pace
at which comments were input on this course made some students
feel that they couldn't keep up with the flow of this asynchronous
conversation. Feedback from the majority of students has been
very positive:

I think it has been one of the most worthwhile learning
experiences I have undertaken for a long time. It requires
you to develop all sorts of skills — technical, writing,
communicating, discovering. Many thanks again for
opening new doors for me and giving me the opportunity to
participate in a very innovative course.

This type of course, in which students world-wide can take part
through electronic communication, will continue to grow as
the technology becomes more widely available. Although this
particular course is not open in terms of entry qualifications
or equipment provision, it is very flexible in terms of time and
location of access. The kind of learning community which easily
develops in such a multi-cultural environment is a very positive
educational feature of this medium.

Conclusions

We have seen that there are no simple solutions to multi-cultural
distance education, and there are no short-cuts to providing
trans-national education. For a more detailed analysis of the
difficulties, see Hawkridge (1993). Nevertheless there are financial
and educational benefits. Certainly many forms of provision are
being developed and are spreading to most countries world-wide.

Competition amongst the growing number of providers will allow the student to choose, at least to some extent, and one type of course provision may prove to be the most satisfactory in the long run. Yet, just as there is no archetypal student, so there is no one best way of learning. Multiplicity and innovation are to be welcomed in international education.

The proliferation of computer networking and the growth of various forms of teleconferencing will increasingly influence the nature of distance education across national boundaries. Telecommunications can reduce the long timescales of print-based distance education. The immediacy of human-to-human interaction may make cross-cultural dialogues more effective and timely than print-based course material. However, technology itself will not change educational provision, whether national or international.

Economic forces are also influencing the nature and growth of international education projects. As we have seen, both providers and receivers of courses can find substantial benefits in collaborating. While futurists talk about the emergence of a global civil society, the economics of distance education may play a significant role in bringing it about.

References

Alladin, I. (1992) 'International co-operation in higher education: the globalization of universities. *Higher Education in Europe*, XVII (4) pp. 4–13.

Baumgratz, G. (1993) 'Mobility in higher education: cross-cultural communication issues'. *European Journal of Education*, **28** (3) pp. 327–338.

Dhanarajan, G. and Timmers, S. (1992) 'Transfer and adaptation of self-instructional materials'. *Open Learning*, 7 (1) pp. 3–11.

Dixon, M. and Blin, F. (1992) 'Issues in instructional design for CAL: problems and possible solutions. in Cerri, S. and Whiting, J. (eds.) *Learning Technology in the European Communities*. Proceedings of the DELTA Conference on Research and Development — The Hague 18–9 October 1990. Dordrecht, Kluwer Academic Publisher.

Farnes, N. and Woodley, A. (1992) *Evaluation of OBS Courses in Hungary*. Milton Keynes, Student Research Centre, Institute of Educational Technology, The Open University.

Farnes, N. and Woodley, A. (1993) *Evaluation of OBS Courses in Eastern Europe and Russia*. Milton Keynes, Student Research Centre, Institute of Educational Technology, The Open University.

Farnes, N., Woodley, A. and Ashby, A. (1993) *Report on a Workshop held at Eurocontact, June 17–18*. Milton Keynes, Student Research Centre, Institute of Educational Technology, The Open University.

Hawkridge, D. (1993) 'International co-production of distance-teaching courses'. *British Journal of Educational Technology*, **24** (1) pp. 4–11.

Hernaut, K. A. (1993) 'Europe after 1992: Education and Training Issues from Point of View of Industry' in Ramalhoto, M. F. (ed.) *Proceedings of the*

Second European Forum for Continuing Engineering Education. International Cooperation Between Industry and Academia. Lisbon, Portugal, Instituto Superior Técnico.

Kaye, A. R. (1991) *Computer Networking for Development of Distance Education Courses.* CITE Report No 146. Milton Keynes, Institute of Educational Technology, The Open University.

Mason, R. (1994) *Using Communications Media in Open and Flexible Learning,* London, Kogan Page.

Ngok, L. and Lam, A. (1993) 'Overseas educational programmes in Hong Kong: competition or consortia'. *Open Learning,* **8** (2) pp. 12–17.

Reif, L. (1992) *Interactive Television. An Advanced Training Project for European Human Resources Development.* Frankfurt, Berlitz European Projects.

Verma, G. K. and Entzinger, H. B. (1992) 'Transfering knowledge in a cross-cultural perspective'. in Cerri, S. and Whiting, J. (eds.). *Learning Technology in the European Communities.* Proceedings of the DELTA Conference on Research and Development — The Hague 18–9 October 1990. Dordrecht, Kluwer Academic Publisher.

22 Joint course and curriculum development: the EADTU experience[1]

Kevin Wilson

In the space of a generation open and distance learning in Europe has come of age. The Open University, which pioneered distance education methods at the end of the 1960s, had 120,000 students studying undergraduate courses in 1993 and is, by far, the largest single provider of part-time degree level courses in Great Britain. In Spain UNED's student enrolment tops the 120,000 mark. From Scandinavia to Portugal open and distance teaching institutions are playing a significant role in the provision of higher education. It comes as no surprise to note that in Central and Eastern Europe open and distance learning is increasingly seen as an effective way of widening educational and training opportunities.

Accessibility, flexibility, cost-effectiveness and quality are factors which suggest that open and distance learning will continue to play a leading role in the transition to mass higher education in Europe over the next decade. Such characteristics also provide a framework within which to consider joint course and curriculum development matters amongst providers of open and distance learning, particularly with reference to the creation of a European dimension in national study programmes.

The European Association of Distance Teaching Universities (EADTU) was established in 1987, as a mechanism for fostering co-operation between higher education institutions dedicated to open and distance learning in Europe. EADTU membership comprised the national open universities and consortia of institutions of higher education which included distance teaching among their activities. From its inception the EADTU sought to promote co-operation between members in order to make high quality open and distance learning courses available across Europe. It encouraged arrangements for credit transfer and course exchange, promoted the application of media and technology to course design and pioneered the concept of a European Open University, not by the creation of a European leviathan, but by means of networking between member institutions. In a very practical way it stressed the importance of joint curriculum development by creating, in late 1988, programme committees in the fields of business administration, European law and humanities. It is the work of the programme committees in the area of joint course activity and in particular the experience of developing 'What is Europe?' the first EADTU joint course, that forms the substance of this paper.

Given the scepticism of some commentators about inter-national course collaboration[2] perhaps the first point to make in respect of 'What is Europe?' is to register the fact that the course exists. In 1993 over 500 students in the United Kingdom and a scattering of students in mainland Europe took the English language version of the course. A comparable number of students has enrolled for the second year of presentation in 1994. During 1994 both a German language version of the course and a version for Danish students will be on offer. French and Dutch versions of the course are planned for 1995. There are five partners in this project: the Dutch Open University; the Jutland Open University; the German Institute for Distance Education at the University of Tubingen; the University of Human Sciences at Strasbourg on behalf of the French Federation of Distance Education; and the British Open University. This is the first time that the institutions concerned have joined forces to put together a common course. 'What is Europe?' has four objectives:

1. To provide a context for the understanding of contemporary European developments through a consideration of the history of the idea of Europe.
2. To consider aspects of European cultural diversity through investigations into language, education, mass-media and everyday culture.
3. To examine the theory, function and practice of democracy as fundamental components of European culture.
4. To locate Europe as a political and economic entity in a context of global change.

The course is modular in structure with each module focusing in turn on one of the objectives specified above. These objectives —

and the European nature of the course — are reflected in the titles and provenance of the four course books:

1. *The History of the Idea of Europe* is a Dutch-Danish collaboration.
2. *Aspects of European Cultural Diversity* emanates from Germany, though one of the authors is British.
3. *European Democratic Culture* is a French product, though there are Italian, German and British, as well as French, contributors to the book.
4. *Europe and the Wider World* comes from the UK.

Trans-national co-operation makes for new possibilities in course design but it also raises difficulties not encountered at the level of operations of a single institution. Let's begin with the pluses.

Working as a European, rather than a national, team serves to generate a richer course product. The academic core of the 'What is Europe?' course consists of four books of essays. These essays have been written by specialists from fifteen different universities in six different European countries. Taken together they explore the question of European identity in its various historical, cultural, social, political and economic aspects and they do so from the standpoint of different academic traditions and different national perspectives. Authors have worked to an over-all brief approved by the EADTU Humanities Programme Committee and the end-product is a set of materials with a distinctively European flavour that is unlikely to have emerged from a single institution acting alone.

As a result students are offered a genuinely European dimension to their course profile. In this respect it is worth stressing that students taking the 'What is Europe?' course are mainly adults studying part-time and as such have work and/or home commitments. Unlike conventional students they are not in a position to benefit from schemes such as the ERASMUS student mobility programme; but if they cannot easily travel, the materials, at least, can. By following a course whose agenda has been set by a European team, students can be offered a fitting European perspective in their studies even though they themselves remain in their own country.

One of the standard justifications for institutional collaboration is cost-effectiveness. By pooling resources and sharing in the costs of a project the net outlay per institution can be reduced. This certainly seems to be the case in bi-lateral arrangements between partners of similar size, systems and structures.[3] In more complex situations — and the 'What is Europe?' project falls into this category — the calculation is less straightforward. For those partner institutions producing English language, German language and French language versions of the course there has been no saving in resource since the reduced cost of developing the materials has largely been off-set by extra translation costs. Over the next five years, as the course is licensed to other users and the texts become available on the commercial market, it may be possible to re-coup some of the initial development and production costs. While such a bonus would not be unwelcome it is clear to those involved in the project that the justification for this kind of joint course development activity rests not so much on cost-effectiveness but more in obtaining a distinctive product which is unlikely to have been generated by an institution operating solo.

Nevertheless working as a project team at a trans-national level presents problems and difficulties. Although all five institutions involved in the project are engaged in open and distance education there are significant differences in the institutional cultures of the respective organisations. It is worth stressing some of these differences since they are potential barriers to co-operation. They include: differences in the standard length of courses offered; differences in academic staffing structures; differences in methods of course production; differences in the technical standards required for printed course materials; differences in the modes of student assessment; and differences in the type of localised support arrangements for students. Awareness of these and other differences had a strong bearing on the course design and course delivery arrangements drawn up by the Humanities Programme Committee for the Europe course. Without a flexible approach to planning and implementation the project would have come to grief on the rocks of institutional difference.

Flexibility is manifest in several ways. Although the course is a 200 study hour course (or half-credit/30 points in UK terms) it is organised in four free-standing modules each of fifty study hours. This modular structure allows the materials to be used, in whole or in part, not only by the partners in the project but by other institutions belonging to the EADTU as well as by outside organisations. The fact that each module is capable of being used on its own or in various combinations makes for an adaptable and versatile product. There is also the flexibility to tailor the course to a particular target population by adding appropriate additional material. For example the Danish presentation will contain extra case studies which will provide a Danish/Scandinavian perspective on issues in the course.

Appreciation of the differences in the organisational structures of the partner institutions also conditioned the mode of collaboration. Recognising that different approaches to course production and presentation rendered the prospect of a universal product something of a chimera, the project team drew a crucial distinction between the planning of the course and the presentation of the course; between the design of the materials on the one hand and the way the materials are to be used on the other. Outlines of the course texts were agreed by the Humanities Programme Committee acting in concert and this gave the project an over-all coherence. But an institution presenting the course is able to do so according to its own teaching system and educational procedures. Thus around the core texts different institutions can prepare their own customised teaching materials — for example study guides, audio-teaching cassettes, sources and commentaries booklets and so on — according to the needs and requirements of their own students. Each institution will be responsible for its own tutorial, assessment, examination and accreditation arrangements. So, the project team, in order to accommodate institutional differences, drew a fundamental distinction between the development of common, core academic material at a European/international level and the teaching and presentation of this material at a national/institutional level.

Once the over-all content outlines had been agreed, responsibilities for the initiation of the material were sub-divided between the partners, on a modular basis. Each partner appointed their own authors and met the commissioning costs of the book of essays associated with their module. In this way decentralisation in the course creation phase served to shorten the lines of communication and reinforce joint ownership in the venture without compromising the general European character of the project.

While such a method of working helped in the preparation of draft materials it raised a number of problems and difficulties in the production phase. First of all in order to achieve a single language version of the course, the essays commissioned by the respective partners had to be translated. Translation is a costly business, adds to the complexity of a project and extends the time required to produce a course. It is however a necessary component. To have commissioned a course on European identity by specifying materials in a single language would have placed an undesirable restriction on available expertise and would have run counter to the European character of the course itself.

Secondly, a multi-language approach posed some logistical difficulties in the critical assessment of contributions at first draft stage. Essays for the course books materialised in English, French, German, Dutch and Italian and in many instances required translation before comments could be fed back to authors. This could be a lengthy process and authors, under the impression that they have satisfied their contract, do not always take kindly to requests for revision generated by third parties. Inevitably, in safeguarding academic standards, heavy reliance had to be placed on the quality control mechanisms of the respective partners, though taken together, these arrangements covering course team discussion, peer group evaluation and external assessment ensured that the course materials were thoroughly reviewed prior to presentation. Thirdly, the lead producer — in this case the Open University producing the English language version and committed to a publicly announced starting date for the course — in order to meet its own institutional deadlines, had, in some instances to liaise directly with authors recruited by the other partners. This added a further layer of complexity to the enterprise and made the management of the project much more complicated than a standard in-house production.

There is a further issue worth mentioning, though it is a problem relating not to institutional difference but to the subject matter of the course itself. The course was conceived in the heady year of 1989 and initial drafting began before the revolutions in Eastern and Central Europe, before the coming down of the Berlin Wall, before the break up of the Soviet Union. With Europe in a state of flux how could the risk of obsolescence in a course about contemporary Europe by reduced? Part of the answer lay in emphasising ideas, values, ways of doing things rather than the historical narrative. It also meant being prepared to make substantial revisions between first and final drafts despite the fact that this put pressure on authors, academic editors and the project manager at late stages in the production process. Even so any course on contemporary Europe runs the risk of being overtaken by events. In the case of the English language version of 'What is Europe?' presented by the UK Open University, there is a facility for annual updating by means of supplementary materials and, furthermore, the course has only been approved for four years — less than half the course-life of a standard OU course. Further presentations beyond 1996 will only take place after a thorough re-assessment of the viability of the course.

A single course does not constitute a programme of study. The EADTU Humanities Programme Committee is conscious of the fact that member institutions have a plentiful number of courses in the field of arts, human sciences and cultural sciences and have evolved criteria for identifying those most suitable for a European Humanities strand. Through credit transfer arrangements, students, provided they have got the language competence, can enrich their studies by selecting courses from more than one European institution and in this way can add a European character to course profiles. Currently such credit transfer arrangements are more the exception than the rule though the signs are that numbers of students involved will increase substantially over the next few years.

Yet the EADTU Humanities Programme Committee is even more enthusiastic about the prospect of a select corps of common courses conceived at a European level, written by specialists from different European countries and made available to students across Europe. 'What is Europe?' is an appetizing *hors d'oeuvres*. Other offerings — for example courses on the remote regions of Europe; the declining industrial areas of Europe; mass media and communications in Europe; popular culture in Europe; European integration; paradigms of humanities — could together provide a rich menu. Such is the goal of the Humanities Programme Committee, though resource constraints have so far confined such proposals to the drawing board.

Within the EADTU framework, joint course and curriculum development activity has not just been confined to the humanities. In the field of European law course collaboration has proceeded on the basis of Programme Committee approval for course proposals (thereby ensuring the European character of each proposal) allied to the subcontracting of one of the partner institutions for the development of the course on agreed lines. International course teams have been avoided. Indeed the responsibilities for developing a complete course may rest with a single author. The agreed programme consists of a number of core and optional courses on aspects of European union law in the areas of economics, labour relations, transport and the environment, and on relevant topics outside European law *per se* such as international criminal law. These courses will be made available in English and their level is postgraduate. Two such courses — one on International Criminal Law and the other on European Environmental Law — will be ready for presentation in 1994 and others, though written, require translation and adaptation into English. In developing its profile of courses, the Programme Committee on European law has focused its attention primarily on European/international legal considerations, and only when these have been fully addressed, has it turned its attention to questions of implementation within the different national legal systems. By sponsoring courses written for a European rather than a national student population, and by demanding a European rather than a national perspective, the Programme Committee is making a positive contribution to the development of law teaching in Europe.

Business administration is the other academic area that has benefitted from collaborative curriculum arrangements within the

EADTU context. Under the guidance of an EADTU working group, the core of an EMBA postgraduate programme has been developed as follows:

— 'Human Resources Management and Industrial Labour Relations in Europe' — Study length: 150 hours. Originating institution: Fenuniversität, Germany
— 'Financial Management and Accounting in Europe' — Study length: 150 hours. Originating institution: NCDE, Ireland
— 'Strategic Management in an Integrated European Context' — Study length: 150 hours. Originating institution: The Dutch Open University
— 'International Management Game' — Study length: 50 hours. Originating institution: UNED, Spain

Course providers have undertaken to produce material in English or to ensure its translation into English.

As with European law the Business Administration working group has avoided international or joint course teams. The working group and its associate members have agreed the design, structure and content of course proposals, considered matters of coherence and balance and addressed the question of a European perspective in course content, but each university or sub-contractor has been accorded responsibility for the development of a course according to its own internal procedures. By this process master sets of courses have been produced for use as they stand, or further adaptation, to suit the needs of partner institutions. The exchange of master sets took place in 1993 and from 1994 it is expected that several of the partner institutions will begin to implement the business administration programme. This course model of developing and exchanging master sets of courses at draft stage for utilisation/adjustment/adaptation by the respective partners, avoids the pitfalls of international course teams and serves to simplify the problems of generating a trans-national programme.[4] For providers of open and distance learning joint course development and curriculum development is not an easy option. The inter-play of different institutional cultures, extended lines of communication and the problems of translation add layers of complexity to a process which is already complicated. Nonetheless, the EADTU Programme Committees in Humanities, European Law and European Business Administration have wrestled with the problems of curriculum collaboration and are beginning to see the fruits of their labour. Course gestation has been long and difficult but the emergence of 'What is Europe?', the first EADTU course, shows that trans-national collaboration can work and that the end-product can be innovative, flexible, rigorous and, above all, possessed of an inherent European dimension which gives it, and the programme of which it forms a part, a distinctive cachet.

Notes

1. This is an expanded version of a paper for the European Conference *Flexible Responses in Higher Education*, December 1993.
2. Hawkridge David (1993) 'International co-production of distance teaching courses'. *British Journal of Educational Technology*, 24 (1).
3. Calvert, Jocelyn, Evans, Terry and King, Bruce (1991) 'Course development through inter-institutional collaboration: the Australian master of distance education *ASPESA*'. *Forum*, pp. 102–110.
4. For a discussion of the issue of collaboration see Ross, H. Paul (1990) *Open Learning and Open Management*, London, Kogan Page, pp. 143–151. See also Moran, Louise and Mugridge, Ian (eds.) (1993). *Collaboration in Distance Education: International Case Studies*, London, Routledge, pp. 1–12.

23 Distance learning for pre-tertiary education in Africa

Tony Dodds

A personal safari

I am writing this chapter on a trip to three countries in Africa — Tanzania (including Zanzibar), Namibia and South Africa. In Zanzibar I am meeting with education officials to discuss the introduction of distance learning methods for in-service teacher education. In Namibia I am participating in a seminar where I have been asked to introduce the concept of distance learning in nonformal education. In South Africa I hope to hear news of an experimental out-of-school secondary programme using open learning methods. As I drove in from Dar es Salaam airport I was asked 'have you been here before?'

In the 1960s I worked with some experimental radio adult education programmes in Tanzania which, after I left, turned into a series of mass radio learning group campaigns which at their biggest reached two million adults and left lasting changes of attitudes and practices. In 1975 I revisited Tanzania on a consultancy, related to plans to use distance education to crash-train 40,000 primary school teachers in-service to cope with the popular demand for universal primary education in that country. Large numbers of teachers were trained economically, and, at least initially, seem to have proved to be better teachers than their college-trained counterparts. In the years between I began to work with the International Extension College which in that period helped to set up distance learning programmes (we didn't call it that then) in Mauritius, Botswana and Lesotho for out-of-school secondary education. So I had to answer — with a very strong sense of *déjà vu* — 'Yes, I have been here before!'

This chapter is an attempt to sketch out a map of the development of these kinds of distance education in Africa up until today, with a look to the future. Like all maps it reflects the standpoint and the knowledge of the compiler. It is, therefore, predominantly a map of Anglophone and Swahiliphone Africa — with brief glimpses into the non-Anglophone Horn of Africa, and at Francophone West Africa.

The historical perspective

The early history of distance education in that part of Africa where British colonialism held sway as elsewhere, has two main elements — correspondence education and educational broadcasting. As independence from colonial rule became overtly inevitable, and in the immediate post-colonial period, many of the future leaders furthered their own educational status and qualifications by taking correspondence courses from private commercial correspondence colleges based in Europe (especially the UK) and the USA. They obtained senior secondary qualifications, and a small but important elite gained university degrees, from such studies, which equipped them for promotion or further education. This experience led many future education leaders to recognise the potential of such courses but also their faults and constraints.

As soon as radio began to be widely available in Africa, after the transistor revolution, governments began to use their radio stations both for schools broadcasting and for adult education and community development, especially for agricultural and health extension work. In many countries the introduction and expansion of radio, and later TV, was largely justified on the basis of its ability to extend access to education to both children and adults.

Between 1964 and 1975 there was a quite phenomenal expansion of programmes in Africa which we would now classify as distance education. This was one response by the governments of the newly independent countries to the demand to expand their educational coverage rapidly and to provide opportunities to the young adult section of their population to obtain educational qualifications of which they had previously been deprived. Many such programmes, starting with those in Zambia and Malawi, were set up by Ministries of Education and offered senior secondary school courses. Others were established by University Adult Education Departments, for example in Kenya, Uganda, Tanzania and Ghana, aimed initially mainly at offering academic upgrading to underqualified primary school teachers. The University of Zambia, set up in 1965, pioneered the use in Anglophone Africa of correspondence education for university degrees, a model followed some years later in the University of Lagos, Nigeria and the University of Nairobi, Kenya. In the same period some university degree programmes were offered by universities in Francophone West Africa often in direct collaboration with metropolitan universities of France. The University of South Africa became, in 1946, the first university in the world to offer its courses exclusively by distance education, courses which were taken, often reluctantly, and in the absence of alternatives, by students from all over central and southern Africa. The 1960s and 1970s also saw initial experimentation and eventually some massive national programmes using radio and organised learning groups for mass education campaigns (for example, Tanzania and Botswana), as also a special pattern of agricultural and rural development correspondence education in several countries of Francophone Africa developed by the Institut Africain pour le developpement economique et social (INADES) whose headquarters are in the Ivory Coast.

The spread of distance education programmes at all these levels continued through the late 1970s and 1980s but, as with most other forms of development, it began to slow down and many existing programmes declined in effectiveness as the worldwide economic recession began to bite, in the late 1980s. Ministries of Education found that their budgets could not be increased, and under the pressure of declining resources they tended to concentrate what they had on conventional schools and colleges.

A new determination to expand the provision of basic education in developing countries was given focus in 1990 at the Jomtien Conference on 'Education for All by the year 2000'. This was declared to apply both to today's and tomorrow's children who will not otherwise find places in schools and will be the illiterate adults of the 21st century and yesterday's children who are the uneducated adults of today. The Jomtien Conference led to pledges to provide basic education for all by the year 2000. Basic education is increasingly seen in many countries as including primary and junior secondary (or ten years of schooling) and adult basic education. National and international committees have been set up to try to achieve this. Governments and donor agencies are pledging funds and facilities to resulting proposals. This is the educational development agenda for at least the next six years. The search for economic alternatives to normal and formal schools is on again — and distance education is back in fashion. New programmes, especially for untrained and underqualified teachers, for out-of-school secondary age youth, and for adult illiterates, are being launched, sometimes in countries which have not tried distance education before, sometimes where earlier experiments first flourished and then faded. It is of vital importance to the potential students of this new wave of distance education that the earlier experiences are recognised, studied and analysed so that the lessons of the past can be learned, successes built on and failures not repeated.

Distance education for out-of-school secondary qualifications

When governments in Africa began to become interested in correspondence education the target audience for the programmes they set up was the same people as had previously used commercial correspondence colleges — teachers, civil servants, other adults who needed secondary qualifications for job promotion. The programmes they designed assumed that such people would study largely independently, that printed correspondence courses sent out and tutored by post and occasionally supported by radio programmes would suffice. Initially this proved to be the case. Early achievements in the Zambia National Correspondence College, the Malawi Correspondence College, the University of Nairobi Correspondence Course Unit and the Makerere University Correspondence Unit all pointed to the potential for public distance education programmes to offer satisfactory opportunities for working adults to upgrade their academic qualifications and thereby to improve their career prospects. As formal education structures also expanded at secondary and tertiary level, however, the job-market requirements were increasingly met by the products of the formal system. A new pressure began to develop for distance education: the huge expansion of primary education was not matched by the expansion of secondary school places; the unemployed — and increasingly unemployable — primary school leavers began to demand (or their parents demanded for them) access to secondary education. If adults could be satisfied by correspondence courses, why not answer the demand from out-of-school youth in the same way?

Distance education institutions, first in Malawi and Zambia and later in Botswana, Swaziland, Tanzania, Ghana and Zimbabwe, were enlisted to provide for this much younger audience. It rapidly became clear, however, that the individual home-study pattern, adequate for adults, was less suitable for adolescents who needed and expected more face-to-face support from teachers or tutors. Supervised study groups were born. In Zambia and Malawi the government correspondence colleges took responsibility for establishing and running such groups, usually on a daily basis, where students met together to study their correspondence courses, and listen to radio programmes under the supervision of tutors or supervisors who were redeployed part-time teachers, usually primary rather than secondary teachers whose role was seen (by the institution, though not by the students or their parents) as advisers and helpers rather than teachers. In Zimbabwe a mentor-system was supported by government in study groups using correspondence courses from commercial institutions. In Botswana the study groups met less regularly, more often in the evenings and weekends, with tutors who were themselves often secondary school teachers employed part-time as tutors.

While the pressure for such facilities grew in the late eighties the resources for education generally in Africa began to decline. The distance education colleges, usually departments of ministries of education, suffered similar or often more stringent cuts as those suffered by their formal secondary school cousins. But they were not allowed to restrict their enrolments: they had been set up because distance education was cheap and could cater for very large numbers. They became, in many cases, political safety valves for the growing pressure to provide ever more secondary school opportunities for primary school leavers without sufficient resources. The standard of their services declined: they were unable to keep up with the course production demand to meet dramatically increasing enrolments; they could not pay part-time postal tutor-markers or course writers fees which were attractive enough to encourage them to meet deadlines; administrative and pedagogic supervision and support of local tutors working with study groups could not be maintained; tutors inevitably (and rightly in view of the lack of materials) reverted to face-to-face teaching — or cramming where study time was limited; exam success rates became depressingly low. In at least one country the phrase 'education for failure' has been used to describe the distance education system. And the content on offer, for students whose chances, though not their hopes, of continuing to Higher Education are very low, is identical to that offered in formal secondary schools, i.e. mainly academic but without science or technical subjects because of the cost and perceived difficulty of offering such subjects at a distance and with few or no attempts to orient the curriculum to vocational preparation or development of job-related skills.

Papers and statements arising from Jomtien regularly stress the need to harness modern technology including distance education to the provision of education up to junior secondary level, to out-of-school youth. This has clearly led to a renewal of interest by governments in distance education to provide such opportunities. For this renewed interest to produce programmes which are more successful than their predecessors with such an audience lessons from the past must be learned. Some of these lessons apply to all levels of distance education and are elaborated in the last section of the chapter. There are three crucial conclusions, however, which must inform any future expansion of substitute secondary schooling for out-of-school youth by distance education:

— traditional distance education/self-study methods are less appropriate for young students than for working adults: a larger component of face-to-face support and tutoring, though costly, is almost certainly necessary; the balance between such support and the use of distance learning materials may well need to be systematically changed, making perhaps for a more flexible or open learning rather than a distance learning system

— it is highly likely that considerable saving could be achieved by sharing course development costs between countries or by utilising course materials already in existence

— an appropriate curriculum for such an audience can and should include vocational and technical subjects: this again may well lead to special arrangements for practical face-to-face learning and supervision.

Teacher education at-a-distance

As already stated, much of the early use of private correspondence courses and of the pioneer government-backed distance education programmes was by teachers seeking to upgrade their academic qualifications for purposes of career advancement. Primary school teachers, in fact, became the primary target audience of several such programmes, for example in Kenya and Uganda. Initially such programmes tended to see their main purpose as upgrading the subject knowledge base of existing teachers — through courses leading to formal secondary school qualifications. Very early, however, as Kinyanjui (1992) has pointed out in relation to the Kenyan programme, the discussion began about the appropriate balance between academic content and pedagogy and teaching methodology both in terms of their respective importance in making better teachers and in terms of distance education's ability to provide effective learning. But, though the debate continues, the reality has been that academic content has heavily predominated in such programmes, as it has in the curricula of most primary pre-service teacher training colleges in Africa. Such primary teacher education programmes are, in Africa, predominantly pre-tertiary training programmes, providing secondary-level content upgrading at the same time as professional training — and are likely to remain so in many countries, for at least the next decade.

Two special trends marked the 1970s and 1980s in distance-based teacher training programmes in Africa. First was a series of limited-time programmes in which, with UNESCO support, governments set up programmes to train a finite number of untrained teachers in their schools by a combination of distance education/correspondence courses and vacation in-college courses. These projects drew inspiration from the UNWRA/UNESCO Institute of Education's programmes for Palestinian refugee teachers in the Middle East (Clark and Erdos, 1970). They are best exemplified by the Botswana Francistown College programme which upgraded approximately 600 teachers in Botswana in the late 1960s and early 1970s and the William Pitcher College training programme in Swaziland.

The second trend to a large extent grew out of the successful experience of the first: a series of initial training programmes by in-service methods using distance education where suddenly there was a need for huge numbers of new teachers to meet crisis situations created by political events. Tanzania decided in 1975 to move rapidly to universal primary education which created a demand for approximately 50,000 new primary school teachers in six years; Zimbabwe made a similar commitment immediately after independence in 1980 and its primary school population nearly tripled in ten years (Chivore, 1993); in Somalia a huge refugee influx in the early 1980s of approximately one million Ogadeni Somali's from Ethiopia created a demand for large numbers of primary schools in the refugee camps where they were settled — a demand which could only be met on an in-service basis. All three drew on the UNWRA-UNESCO and the Swaziland and Botswana experiences to create large-scale crash training programmes, again combining residential training courses (varying in length from three weeks to one academic term) with correspondence courses. All three recognised the need for some form of continuing tutorial support during the periods while students studied their correspondence courses and taught in schools, and created different patterns of field tutorial networks where students met tutors in or close to their schools on a regular basis and received advice both on the subject matter of their courses and on problems they encountered as teachers.

By the middle of the 1980s, according to Nielsen, eighteen African countries had distance education programmes to train teachers (Nielsen, 1990 quoted in Murphy and Zhiri, 1992). There is a general consensus that these programmes compare favourably in effectiveness and cost with their college-based counterparts (Perraton, 1993). There now appears to be a new wave of programmes for teacher upgrading sweeping through Africa, sometimes building on, sometimes complementing, sometimes replacing previous programmes.

In many of them, however, there is a new emphasis on local support for the teachers-in-training and on pedagogical training rather than purely on academic and theoretical knowledge. This is partly in recognition that some of the previous programmes have suffered, or even broken down in the face of limited resources to print and distribute course materials leading teachers to rely on self-help tutorial and study groups (Wort et al., 1993) and partly in recognition that teachers need continuous access to local resources and advice if they are to put into practice new methods and new attitudes learned in their courses. In several new experiments, therefore, the combination of distance education courses, on both content and methodology, with tutorial support through local teacher resource centres is being tried.

Distance education for adult basic and nonformal education

Adult and nonformal education have in almost every country at all times been the Cinderella of education provision. Unhappily this is equally true for distance education in Africa. As already stated, radio was used very early in its life as a mass medium in Africa for community development education as a supplement to agricultural or health extension services. To begin with this largely consisted of open broadcasting to farmers, or to families, with information and messages about better health or agricultural practices. As it became clear that information on its own did not change attitudes or practices radio began to be used as part of multi-media programmes, supported by print materials and used as the basis for group discussion. The Canadian and Indian farm or rural radio forum model was introduced to Africa by UNESCO in Ghana in the early 1960s and rapidly spread to many other countries in Africa. But it never caught on or grew to the size and significance it had had in India or Canada, possibly because it never attracted the wholehearted support of government departments and was left to the radio stations to run and coordinate. The rural forums, however, inspired the much larger use of radio study groups in national adult education campaigns in Tanzania, Botswana, Zambia and Northern Ghana in the 1970s and 1980s. In these campaigns limited series of messages (on health and nutrition, civics, reafforestation, land usage, co-operative organisation, water and hygiene) were made into radio series lasting between two and three months, supported by printed study guides, and were distributed to networks of study groups, meeting under briefly trained group leaders organised and supported usually by consortia of ministries and adult education institutions. The most successful campaigns clearly reached very large numbers and appear to have made significant impacts on the knowledge and attitudes of many participants. They tended, however, to be one-off, isolated learning events, with little or no localised follow-up and it proved difficult or impossible to sustain the momentum they created.

Two other programmes of nonformal distance education programmes developed in the late 1960s and early 1970s and have survived, with significant though smallscale success. In Francophone West Africa, from a base in the Ivory Coast, INADES has run a programme of agricultural education by simple correspondence materials, mainly aimed at groups of peasant farmers through local extension officers. The programme spread through many of the countries of Francophone West Africa in the 1970s and set up branches in Kenya and Ethiopia in the 1980s. In Tanzania, Kenya and Zambia programmes of correspondence education for members, committee personnel and staff of local cooperative societies, run by the local cooperative colleges, were set up in the 1960s, 1970s and 1980s respectively and have continued to offer education and training. Their impact and profile has varied with the differing political emphases put on cooperative development. A similar pattern of training for rural health workers has been developed by the African Medical and Research Foundation (AMREF), a Kenya-based medical NGO working also in neighbouring East African countries.

Most of these programmes have achieved successful results — but usually either on a small scale, or for a limited period of time. They have failed to catch the sustained imagination of politicians or administrators or educators and so have failed to establish for themselves an institutional niche from which they could expand and prosper.

At this level also, as at secondary level and in teacher training there are signs of renewal. Large scale adult literacy drives are in fashion again (Namibia, Ghana, South Africa, Sudan) as 'education for all by the year 2000' is seen to include adults, and as the World Bank remains convinced that a literate farmer is more productive than an illiterate. But what is the role of distance education in such adult literacy or adult basic education drives? Because the experience has been spasmodic and often isolated there is very little evidence from carefully conducted research nor even a pattern of received wisdom. Four tentative conclusions can however, be drawn:

— it can be used successfully to spread the impact of nonformal education much more widely than can be achieved by traditional face-to-face methods
— it can be used successfully to train and support adult education and extension workers, teachers and facilitators
— it can boost the interest in the practical or functional themes which make mass adult literacy into functional literacy and emphasise the links between them and with literacy and numeracy, and provide opportunities for real learning around these themes which the literacy facilitors usually cannot provide themselves
— it can provide opportunities (perhaps the only realistic opportunities) for continuing learning at post-literacy level without which newly mastered literacy and numeracy skills can rapidly disappear.

A ray of hope from the new South Africa

Even as the dramatic political changes in South Africa began to dawn educationists of the ANC and of the internal political opposition began to explore and promote distance education as crucial to the radical restructuring of education in that country for a democratic future. The old regime had created and lavishly financed the University of South Africa (UNISA), a distance education Technikon and a distance education technical college, so distance education was not new on any side. The new regime, however, has declared open learning as a major philosophical plank of its educational manifesto, and distance learning as a major means of achieving the redress of educational opportunity.

Policy discussions have taken place and will continue, and detailed policy documents have been prepared on how to implement such an approach at all levels — at tertiary level as well as at the three levels discussed above. What will emerge in terms of institutions and programmes is still unclear. Experience from other continents and from elsewhere in Africa is being drawn on as plans are made. What is clear is that distance and open learning will be at the centre of educational change in South Africa in the next few years.

South Africa has the resources, the personnel and the political will to bring about such changes. The rest of Africa can, perhaps draw encouragement from these initiatives, and, as well as sharing its own previous experiences with its newly liberated member state, it may well be able to benefit directly from the materials and systems which are developed there, and, mutually, benefit from resources made available for those developments.

Issues, prospects and problems

The story of distance education in Africa however has been a long story of high hopes, successful experiments, inadequate resourcing and often disappointing long-term impact. It is essentially a story of hope deferred. Africa in general has been through economic and political Hell in the last decade — and its education systems have suffered seriously from that torment. There are some signs that many of the countries of Africa are generally, and not without struggle, emerging from that Hell and are seriously seeking ways to relaunch their educational development. Distance education is clearly seen to have important roles to play in that relaunch.

Politicians and educational planners, in many African countries, have been forced to learn some bitter lessons in the last two decades, some imposed on them by the impact of economic restructuring policies accepted under pressure from the World Bank and the IMF. Educational expansion at any of the three levels examined in this chapter will not be possible through dramatically increased building of new schools or colleges or farmers or womens training centres. Educational budgets will not expand. The only hope is the economic use of new methods and increased use of existing institutions and educational infrastructure. Yet ways must be found of providing for continuous upgrading and retraining of professional educators in-service and on-the-job if quality is to be regained and retained. Effective out-of-school parallel opportunities for children — certainly for post-primary-school-age adolescents — must be created if political demand is to be met and if the spectre of growing numbers of unemployed primary school leavers flocking to towns for nonexistent jobs is to be avoided or at least postponed. Such parallel opportunities must be oriented towards employable, or income-generating skills. Mass adult literacy campaigns, now back in favour because of the supposed link between literacy and increased production, can only succeed if flexible, nonformal (almost self-sustaining) post-literacy learning networks related to self-help development can be established. And such expanded in-service training and out-of-school continuing education must somehow, at least in part, be resourced and financed by the recipients and their communities. Distance education approaches are being turned to, by government after government, in the desperate hope that in that direction some solutions to growing educational problems can be found.

I started this chapter by stressing the need to learn from past experiences both successes and, however depressing, failures and disappointments. Some of these experiences can be drawn from other parts of the world, particularly in the field of technical and vocational education at-a-distance or through open and flexible learning networks. But the major problem in Africa is lack of resources, a problem of wholly different proportions in, for example, Europe or Australasia. My opening paragraphs belied a sense of cynicism and pessimism about distance education in Africa — yet the previous paragraph suggested hope. All three emotions are present and justified, yet I wish to end on a note of realistic optimism. There is evidence from the limited study of past experience in Africa that distance education can contribute to educational expansion and the maintenance or improvement of quality at all three levels discussed. It must: there is no alternative. But it will only achieve more impact in the next decade than in the last if certain key lessons from that past are learned. I would like to emphasise five such lessons as pointers to the way ahead.

First, distance education at these three levels must concentrate on developing more flexible combinations of print, radio or audio support, telephone tutorial networks (as old and inefficient telephone networks are replaced by modern systems with tele-conferencing capacity, as is beginning to happen) and face-to-face support systems based on existing institutions and personnel. The 'distance' media may come to play equally vital but less dominant roles, especially in parallel secondary and adult basic education. Multi-purpose community study-centres, in some cases based on teachers centres, in others on church-community centres or farmers co-operatives or women's clubs, need to be supported with modest but shared resources (libraries, audio-cassettes, study group meeting rooms) and modestly but crucially-trained super-visors and tutors most of them employed on a part-time basis. Significant increases in part-time fees, which nevertheless had minimum overall budgetary implications (given existing teachers' salaries) could make huge differences to reliability and quality. More flexible approaches to assessment and certification, allowing distance and open learners to accumulate qualifications incrementally, through regular and frequent recognition of credits, could help to maintain learners' motivation. These variations, modes though each might seem, represent my interpretation of open learning for Africa.

Secondly, such improvements in quality, effectiveness and coverage can only be achieved if distance education and open learning are allowed to develop more effective self-managing and soundly structured institutional bases. This has something to do with critical mass: many small units in different sections of different ministries all struggling to create their own materials development infrastructures and student-support and outreach networks will usually fail, as they have in the past; multi-purpose institutions of distance education, able to capitalise on the required infrastructures and to develop adequate professional expertise and career paths are more likely to be able to exercise quality control over their products, to achieve public recognition for their results and thereby achieve status for their courses.

Thirdly, both these conditions can only be realised if such distance education institutions are realistically resourced and financed. For this to happen they need to be able to achieve the economies of scale on which so much of distance education's political popularity depends. To achieve this, as Perraton has pointed out, minimum resources are needed 'starvation [of minimum resources] may be an uneconomic use of resources when, with comparatively modest improvement in funding, considerable improvements in effectiveness could be achieved' (Perraton, 1992). Such extra resources, however modest, must be found from somewhere. Some can realistically be raised by distance education institutions being allowed to sell their services and their products to their own ministries as well as their students at realistic but affordable prices, and to use that income for their own development. Some must come from persuading Ministries of Education and Finance that this is a more effective use of resources than some of their expenditure on traditional and conventional provision.

Fourthly, there is much greater opportunity than has yet been exploited for distance education institutions in neighbouring countries, working on similar programmes, to share resources, especially materials and expertise. Surely, for example, junior secondary and senior secondary English, or French, or Arabic language courses, or science and maths courses follow broadly parallel curricula in many different African countries; could the same course materials not be shared, thereby avoiding expensive materials development duplication? Similarly at least five countries in East, Central and Southern Africa are currently developing or testing primary education pedagogy, or child psychology or principles of education courses. Are primary children so different from country to country that the same course materials could not be used — or adapted for use — in all those five countries?

Fifthly, and finally, adequate resourcing and status and recognition depend on the political will to make it succeed. I have no easy recipe for creating such political will. But it relates to the title of this book. If education for all is to be achieved by the year 2000, or even by 2050, distance education can no longer remain at the periphery of national educational provision, with peripheral resources and marginal status. It must be brought to the centre and must be used in harness with traditional and conventional institutions and structures. But it must remain flexible and innovatory in its approach so that it infects the traditional with its new methods of provision and new attitudes to learning.

References

Chivore, B. R. S. (1993) 'Pre-service teacher education at a distance in Zimbabwe' in Perraton, H. (ed.) *Distance Education for Teacher Training*, London, Routledge.

Clark, J. H. and Erdos, R. (1970) *Correspondence Courses for Inservice Teacher Training at Primary Level in Developing Countries*, Hamburg, UNESCO Institute of Education.

Kinyanjui, P. (1992) 'The organization of teacher training at a distance with particular reference to Kenya' in Murphy, P. and Zhiri, A. (eds.) *Distance Education in Anglophone Africa*, Economic Development Institute of the World Bank.

Nielsen, H. D. (1992) 'Using distance education to extend and improve teaching in developing countries, Jomtien (1990)' quoted in Murphy, P. and Zhiri, A. (eds.) *Distance Education in Anglophone Africa*, Economic Development Institute of the World Bank.

Perraton, H. (1992) 'A review of distance education' in Murphy, P. and Zhiri, A. (eds.) *Distance Education in Anglophone Africa*, Economic Development Institute of the World Bank.

Perraton, H. D. (ed.) (1993) *Distance Education for Teacher Training*, London, Routledge.

Wort, M., Mrutu, J. and Kisi, F. (1993) 'Draft report for the strengthening of inservice correspondence education for primary school teachers in Tanzania'. Sweden, SIDA; Tanzania, MEC.

Afterword
The prospects for open learning

Michael Young

This chapter became the basis of a speech given by Michael Young at Churchill College, Cambridge University in April 1994, in honour of the twenty-fifth anniversary of the Open University.

To anyone like me old enough to have been around in the pre-history of the Open University, as one of the pre-historic creatures of the movement, what has happened in the twenty-five years since it was established seems a bit like a miracle, especially in a country which by and large has not in modern times won the kind of reputation for innovation it had in the Victorian era. The OU represents the most striking and far-reaching development of the second half of the century in Higher Education, world-wide, and perhaps even in education generally. One has only to think of the steady expansion in the numbers of its students — accelerating and up since 1990 by 25 per cent — to over 200,000 now; its 3,000 full-time and 7,000 teaching and consultancy staff; its 310 study centres in the UK and the rest of Europe; its extraordinary Business School and Health and Social Welfare programme; the thirty or so other Open Universities which have been inspired by the British example elsewhere in the world, from Germany to China, from Japan to Israel, from Holland to India; and then there is the widening use in higher education of modules and transferability of credits, and the multiple influence on other levels and kinds of education and other universities. There is, apparently, an OU text in the Cambridge University Library, a few yards away from here, so thumbed over and dog-eared from hard use by ordinary Cambridge students that it is almost falling to bits.

Only the most valued of modern books fall to pieces. The proof of success lies in their extinction.

It is all a remarkable story, with the success being due to a dedicated staff and dedicated students, or perhaps it would be more to the point to put the students first. The OU is quite outstanding for the high morale of its staff, even now when they are being squeezed by the expansion in student numbers without a commensurate expansion in resources. The OU confidence level is all the more striking because it stands in such sharp contrast to that in the country's schools — teacher morale has never been so low in my lifetime, or perhaps ever — and Britain's ordinary universities have been suffering too. I think the sense of confidence which is around in the OU is due more than anything else to something — the enthusiasm of adult students — which I first spotted in the early 1960s when I was beginning to propose an open university (very small 'a', small 'u' then), and Churchill College played a part. It is just chance that Roger Mills chose Churchill for this lecture tonight although it seems a little like serendipity. It certainly feels strange for me to be back here after a gap of over thirty years. I was at that time, my memory tells me, a lecturer in Cambridge University and a Fellow of this College.

In 1960 from my base in Churchill and with the support of only one person in the College, a classics don and Senior Tutor, and I think only one other person in the university, Peter Laslett of Trinity, I tried to persuade people in the university to open a second campus at Cambridge, operating in Cambridge vacations, for the teaching of external part-time students. My use of the word, campus, was a bad mistake. It made Cambridge seem like a mere Michigan State University. This City of Cambridge not a Paradise but a campus? What foolish talk was this? But at least I did not make matters worse, in terminological terms, by urging that Cambridge should become the first dual-mode campus university in Britain teaching at a distance as well as face-to-face, although that is what I had in mind.

It was obvious that not many of the ordinary academic staff at Cambridge would be willing to teach in the vacations, instead of doing their research and whatever else they did. So I once again showed my greenness (before it was a good thing to be green) by proposing not only that most of the external students would be taught at a distance but that this second Cambridge would be staffed by teachers from the Battersea Poly who assured me they at least were prepared to teach in vacations. Oh for the innocence of youth! Battersea Poly taking over King's Parade and the Cavendish! Even later on, when the OU was started, Walter Perry recorded the 'profound scepticism garnished with ridicule and hostility' which surrounded it.

Anyway, acknowledging defeat but not total defeat, I fell back on running single vacation courses at Churchill for London University External Degree students.

The College Archivist at Churchill has checked the story for me. The chain of correspondence between me and the Bursar starts with me, in January 1961, asking for permission to go ahead. I suppose I could consider myself fortunate that in Cambridge the OK for the course came through quite quickly: it only took two years for the permission, although I was rather taken aback by the price — 2s 6d for a breakfast and £3.10d for a double room for a week. But in conjunction with the Cambridge Board of Extra-Mural Studies it eventually happened, for 120 adult students, and since I was teaching sociology in the Faculty of Economics I dutifully chose economics as the subject for the course.

On this occasion the professional economists at Cambridge did not mind teaching residential adults for a week. As it turned out, the economists were overwhelmed, I was overwhelmed, by the quite amazing keenness of these 30-year-old and 40-year-old students. Presented with the first opportunity they had ever had to hear and question real economists and talk with other students like themselves, they started work at 8a.m. and kept at it until midnight for six glorious days. This is now a familiar story at OU summer schools. But at that time some of the dons said they had never, amongst young undergraduates, had such motivated students.

What struck me was the strength of the potential need and opportunity amongst adults who had missed out on university at the ordinary ages, and I determined to redouble my efforts to propagate the idea of an open university for such part-time students as these, and since Cambridge would not take them on and London would not teach them, a new kind of university it had to be. Whatever the weeks at Churchill did, along with much else, to prepare the way for the OU, the Churchill experiment led directly to the London University Degree Service of the National Extension College which is still running well over thirty years later, with over 800 London students studying with the NEC in 1994. London external degrees have been revitalised too and are expanding rapidly. The latest development is that NEC has been asked by Coca Cola/Schweppes to run a degree service for 18-year-olds joining the firm straight from school. They will work and study at the same time.

The danger of being inward-looking

The enthusiasm of those adult students at Churchill and the millions of other adult students of the OU since then have generated and maintained the morale of the OU staff, and as long as morale remains high, the OU will be set fair to continue its progress. But there is a reverse side to it. A well-deserved assurance can easily become a rather smug over-assurance. The shared achievement, the solidarity, the team-spirit of the staff, can become self-congratulatory and inward looking. Outsiders talking to OU staff have noticed how dynamic the staff are when talking to themselves or about themselves and how when a general educational issue is raised, nothing to do with open learning, OU eyes can become glazed over. In so far as this is true, it represents a great danger. Nothing fails like success if it makes anyone think that any right formula has been, or ever will be, found for open learning. The danger could be especially great if the OU thinks of itself as being part of the mainstream instead of being a different and essentially innovatory body. The OU has always sought to be open as to ideas. Is it? Is it really as vibrant with ideas as it likes to claim, and does claim in the University's official document on its 1993–97 *Plans for Change*?

I will answer my own question by saying that, whatever view one adopts about it, at least it is surely worthwhile taking great trouble to ensure that this great institution does not follow the way of so many others and fossilise, go dead from within, get stifled by its own bureaucracy and ingrained habits of mind; to ensure that minds remain open; and to ensure that no possibilities are ever closed off just because they do not fit well with any of the conventional notions of what the OU is about. There are many ways of marrying counter-institution to institution, and I am only going to talk about one of them. The main point I want to make in the lecture is that if the next twenty-five years are to be as brilliant as the previous twenty-five, or more, so, research and reflection on open learning will need to be encouraged in a large way. I don't mean research in the academic disciplines represented in the Open University, but about open learning as a means of education. It is not just a question of being self-critical but of allowing a revolving core of people to have time to think, study and experiment in new practices. Discourse, dialogue, discussion, research are essential to all academic progress but with open learning a very special effort needs to be made to foster research into open learning itself.

My proposal is that a Research Foundation for Open Learning — a look-out tower for open learning — should be set up for the systematic study of crucial issues by scholars given time off on secondment and drawn from within the OU central staff, the regional staff, other Open Universities and open learning institutions in other countries, like Deakin and Southern Queensland in Australia, Athabasca and Laurentian in Canada, UNISA in South Africa and Indira Gandhi in India, and also drawn from people who are quite outside open learning. The Foundation would probably need to be started on the strength of grants from ESRC, from the great charitable trusts like Ford and Rockefeller, Nuffield and Rowntree, Sainsbury and Esme Fairbairn, the Volkswagen and Agnelli Foundations, and there should be enough resources for pilot projects as well as straight research and, perhaps most important of all, for calm reflection. The field would be the whole of open learning and not just that bit of it which operates in higher education.

Perhaps I can best make the case by raising a few of the issues which could command attention, at least for the team projects (as distinct from more individual work) which the new Foundation could support. The issues are about schools, the internationalisation of open learning, the increasing competition the OU will face, the under-privileged, and the encouragement given to individualism. Big questions, I know, for a short space of time.

Schools One does not have to be a very sharp observer to notice that schools, especially secondary schools, are in trouble, and seem to get deeper into it every year. It is partly that schools have been so much embroiled in politics. There have been nine Education Reform Acts in the last ten years, without including this year's new reform of teacher training. It is difficult (to say the least) for teachers who are reformed so repeatedly to keep going at all. They have not assimilated one reform before they are overtaken by another, and another. But teachers also have to cope with a most significant change in the structure of their population, which is that children are in certain important respects growing up more quickly than they did. It is happening sexually. The age of menarche for girls has gone down from 17 to 13 in a century and the age of puberty for boys fallen too but not to as low a level. It is happening socially. With the help of the affluent society children behave like little adults much earlier than they did — with their own music and clothes and paraphernalia — and the authority of parents has weakened, which means that there is less authority for teachers to borrow from parents, and it is more difficult for them to keep order in the classroom. But while childhood has been shortening, education has been lengthening, both the legally compulsory period of education and the conventionally acceptable length of it, after 16 and on into higher education. The result is that teachers are having to struggle with ever less biddable pupils who feel like conscripts even if they are not.

This is where the OU is in such sharp contrast and those economics dons of 1963 got it right too. The adult students of

1963 and the adults of 1994 were, and are, volunteers. They want to learn, often passionately, in a way that is unusual amongst teenagers. The contrast raises the question whether we, or any other industrial country, has got the balance right between school and adult education. Would it not be better to reduce the school-leaving age, find work for them which has a supervised educational content to it, set up a Civilian Conservation Corps like Roosevelt's great organisation in the 1930s, preferably an all-European Corps including Russia, and vastly expand continuing education for volunteers at all stages of life. The entitlement to funded education could be much extended but people could take their ten years of post-primary education at any time in their lives; it would not be confined, as it is for many people, to the years from 11 to 21. Conscription would give way to volunteering; the benefits to education and to society could be very large, as long as special steps were taken to stop exploitation of child labour and provide special support for people who are not going to be able to compete in the labour market.

Myself, I expect this will happen in the next century — it really will be a major reform — but it all needs a great deal of analysis and thought and research of the kind that the new Foundation could take on board. The first step along that road could be for the OU to lower its age of entry to 16 and work with organisations like the National Extension College and the Open School to prepare for the new intake. The Open School has an important role in expanding choice of subjects in the sixth-form, in supporting children with learning difficulties, in helping invalid and excluded children whose education is interrupted. It seems to me odd that a body like OU which prides itself (rightly) on having no entry qualifications should still have one overriding entry bar about age. Why should the age of consent for OU purposes be 18 when for ever more vital purposes it is already accepted that the age should be 16? Given that adulthood comes earlier, should there not be equality centred on the age of 16? As a start.

Internationalisation of open learning   The Research Foundation would fail of its purpose if its brief was confined to the UK. I care particularly about this because my own work in open learning since 1970 has been mainly with the International Extension College in Africa. The same fundamental dilemma which underlies so many OU decisions — the economies of scale tell in favour of largeness while individual educational needs often tell in favour of smallness — arises acutely on the international scene. It would make a lot of sense from a purely economic point of view for the OU to take in more and more students by means of satellite in Eastern and Western Europe, and go on to do the same on the Pacific Rim and elsewhere in the world wherever there is a demand, becoming an educational counterpart of the BBC World Service with its daily audience of over 100 millions. But would it make educational sense? I think not, or at least not in the long run. It would be a kind of educational colonialism

I am sure there are instances of courses which could be globalised, for example in teaching English and for various specialised purposes, but they would be exceptional. Generally speaking, a primary purpose of education is to foster autonomy, for individuals and corporate bodies; so educators in one country and another need to be helped to become autonomous themselves so that they can devise their own indigenous open learning courses suitable for the particular needs of their own countries. But this approach does not in the least rule out co-operation of an intensive kind between open learning institutions in different countries, not just for training and information exchange but in the production of courses with some modules in them which are common and some specific to the country where the students live. This is indeed very much the concept behind the European Association of Distance Teaching Universities and its first joint course, 'What is Europe?'. But there will always be a need for monitoring what is done and considering new co-operative projects, and in this the new Foundation could certainly play its part.

Increasing competition for OU As the OU has helped to spread open learning around the world, so it has increased the number and effectiveness of its competitors. Greville Rumble, in a stimulating article in 1992 in the journal *Open Learning*, argued that Campus-Based Universities (CBUs) could have certain competitive cost advantages over Distance Teaching Universities (DTUs), for instance by developing distance teaching versions of their on-campus courses. The dual-mode university (DMUs in Rumble language) — campus and distance — may be as much the university of the future as DTUs. The OU could, for instance, open its own campus for residential teaching.

The competition in Britain is more evident than ever since the polytechnics became universities. As almost everyone here will know, there is hardly one of them which has not made a feature of open learning for their growing numbers of part-time students and many of the old civic universities are moving in the same direction.

This diaspora inside the country is an advantage in one sense: there are now more and more institutions interested in gaining proper financial support for part-timers and so ready to join what could be called the 'Birkbeck crusade'. On the other hand, there is going to be increasing competition for adult students, and this is very likely to show itself in all sorts of student statistics. The retention rates will be put on a comparative basis and become more sensitive than ever. There will be competition, and the OU can help itself by broadening its range, as it did when it accepted the Open College of the Arts into affiliation. OCA is small now but within ten years could be growing as fast as the OU Business School. But, just as on the international scene, there will also be plenty of scope for collaboration. Many different kinds of alliance between the OU and other universities should be possible. That thumb-marked copy of an OU text in the Cambridge University Library could be a portent. At all events, there is much scope for research and reflection on what kind of shape open learning will take in the future when almost everyone is going to be getting in on the act, or trying to.

The under-privileged I gather that of the entrants to the OU undergraduate programme roughly one third already have qualifications to a degree level or its equivalent, one third have qualifications which would get them into another university, and one third are not qualified to enter other universities. It is that final third which is crucial to the name of the OU and its basic principle of open access, that is lack of formal entrance qualifications; and this being so it is an embarrassment that the proportion is as low as one third. Even that proportion may decline further as there is an increase in the financial pressure to take more students who sail through, and don't drop out. It is also surely an embarrassment that amongst the crucial third there are (despite all that has been done so far to push the numbers up) not more unemployed in the student body, more people from inner cities, more people from ethnic minorities. We are living in hard times which put to the test anyone's allegiance to the goal of equality of opportunity. But the goal matters most vitally to the OU which has all along striven to remain true to ethical principle.

A good deal is known already about this crucial third but more needs to be found out by means of research, building on the good work which has been done at the OU's Student Research Centre. When people of this kind drop out because they just cannot manage the work, what effect does it have on their morale? Are they worse off, more dispirited, than if they had not entered the OU at all? Could they, when they give up, get more useful advice from the OU about what to do instead so that they do not turn their backs on education completely? Then there are the even more difficult questions about the reasons why more people from these under-privileged groups do not join the OU. Of course, it's partly the fees. The OU spends over £2 million a year on financial assistance to poor students. But it's far too little and would be even more so if the far-sighted LEAs who are still able to give Disrectionary Awards were cut back still further. Then how many would-be students, if they know of it at all, think that, by reason of its name of university, the OU cannot possibly be for them. Universities are for toffs or WASPS. If altogether more were known about attitudes, the OU could make its appeal to them more attractive.

There is also room for further pilot projects in the Regions, and the new Foundation could be their sponsor. My own belief is that it could make a great difference — this is the sort of ambitious project that I and my colleagues from the International Extension College have been helping to plan in South Africa in the last three years — if, as courses unfolded, there were at various stages pay-offs for people in terms of earnings and job prospects. Unemployed and other people would exert themselves more if they really thought it might improve their job prospects. All this would require a programme with the same sort of vocational bias as the Open Business School but for quite different sections of the population — the Open Non-Business School, or the Open School for Work, but not, certainly not, the Open College or the Open Tech. The OU would need to learn from the false starts there have been.

Individualisation   I came, lastly, to the part open learning has played, and could play, in the increasing individualisation of society. In this it belongs with a much more sweeping trend which has caught up the whole modern world, largely due to the onward march of technology, and for a moment I am going to have to go a bit wider than I have so far in order to explain what I mean. Technology has, for example, individualised the activities of the home. This is a rather new development. For quite a long period technology was the buttress of the family. In the days when there was a marked division of labour and of power between the sexes many of people's activities were outside the home because the prevailing products of technology were on the scale of the community. But as the scale of industry has enlarged, industry has produced smaller and smaller machines with which to automate the home. The new miniature machines have been home-sized: and at first they brought people back into the home — public laundries gave way to the washing machine; public baths to individual baths; ice-making in factories was replaced by small refrigerators in the kitchen; heated homes became as warm and comfortable as the pub, or more so; the bus and the train were challenged by the car; the cinema was largely replaced by the television; and to watch sports people did not any longer have to go in such numbers to giant stadia when their own sitting room was a tiny stadium for all the family.

Inside the home technology is changing again — even the family is giving way to the individual within it. The whole family no longer need to ensconce themselves in a circle around the telly promptly at 7.30p.m.; if they don't yet have TV sets in different rooms, along with high Hi-Fi and God or Japan knows what else, they can use the video to detach themselves from the collective just as they can use their own, very personal computer to play games about monsters all by themselves. The fairy stories do not customarily come from the parents any more.

Technology, by enlarging choices, has made hurry sickness the modern curse of Midas, and perhaps the major disease of the Western world. If the cost of doing anything is what you give up in alternatives, then it follows that anything which you contemplate as an alternative adds to the prospective cost, or, as one can put it, the pressure on time. People are more and more jumpy, more and more aware of other places in the world where they might be, with other men, or other women, at other meetings, at other conferences, in other beds, on other moonlit nights. They are made continuously aware of what they haven't the time for, and the major tactic used to deal with the time-famine — doing more than one thing at once — like making love and simultaneously listening to a Bartok quartet on the hi-fi are liable to be self-defeating, as all members of the Senate of the OU will of course know for themselves from their everynight experience. They are always missing out on the cadenzas in the scherzo.

I have digressed a bit for a moment only because I want to stress the point that the development of open learning, though not dependent on technology to the same extent as entertainment, belongs to a more general trend towards greater and greater individualisation, and could powerfully augment it. Most of the time of students, at any rate after the Foundation Year, is spent on their own, in the times that suit them and at the pace that suits them — the great virtue of open learning. A common vision of our future is that this will go much further: that as video-tapes replace much of broadcasting, and open learning replaces ordinary schools and universities, people will be sitting at their solo stations online on a network of computer conferencing systems, able at will to join one of the digital superhighways which will span the world, members of a series of subcultural communities trying to keep abreast of the ever increasing obsolescence of skills as people get older, a high-tech concourse in which no-one ever actually sees anyone unless it be on a videophone. Since the birth of the Industrial Revolution, thousands of millions of people have laboured to produce a world populated by strangers, and not all of them are as benign as the absent teacher who is trying to empower the individual rather than dominate him or her for political or commercial reasons. The central problem of modern politics — that of the small man in a big world — is going to get a sharper edge in the next century with the big world getting bigger in one sense and yet also bearing down more harshly on us when miniaturised down to the size of a computer programme.

The implications not just in terms of Can-Do but in terms of Should-We-Do could be spelt out by the work done in the new Foundation. I would hope too that the work might highlight what can be done, quite deliberately, of an opposite kind, leaning and learning against the worldwide trend, encouraging students to work together as well as separately, not just in some schools and tutorial groups but as a necessary part of their courses as well as in other ways. The new OU course on family and community history could point the way.

To this end I would like to see tutorial centres becoming drop-in centres for drop-outs or people who had not yet dropped in, that is places where people could go before they become OU students, or if they didn't ever become students, to meet with tutors and each other to talk about their needs quite informally and about the possible value of education to them. This could be somewhat on the lines of the self-help Universities of the Third Age which have grown so strongly. There are now some 240 local U3As in Britain. The model for the new OU centres could be an illustrious one, classical Athens, where a tiny community without any technology in it shone with an intellectual brilliance which has never been matched in the modern technological world. The great philosophers — Socrates, Plato, Aristotle, Zeno The Stoic, Epicurus — were all open to the community. Socrates was to be found on almost any day in or near the Agora, the market place, available for anyone to talk to. Plato's methods were a little different when he founded the Academy, as the forerunner of all Western universities, in the olive grove of Academus. Aristotle taught in covered arcades by the temple of Apollo Lykaeus — hence the word 'lyceum'. Zeno taught in a Stoa, a painted porch. Education was both august and homely. One of the greatest of modern philosophers, who would by no means have been dwarfed in the Agora, was the Scottish philosopher, David Hume. For him fellow feeling was what kept humanity together and fellow feeling which always needs to be encouraged.

‘So far from thinking’, said Hume, ‘that men have no affection for anything beyond themselves, I am of opinion that tho’ it be rare to meet with one who loves any single person better than himself; yet ’tis as rare to meet with one, in whom all the kind affections, taken together, do not over-balance all the selfish’. Hosannah to that.

Index